LUCHINO VISCONTI
the flames of passion

LUCHINO VISCONTI

the flames of passion

LAURENCE SCHIFANO

translated from the french by
WILLIAM S. BYRON

COLLINS · LONDON · 1990

William Collins Sons & Co. Ltd
London · Glasgow · Sydney · Auckland
Toronto · Johannesburg

British Library Cataloguing in Publication Data

Schifano, Laurence
Luchino Visconti: the flames of passion.
1. Italian cinema films. Directing. Visconti, Luchino,
1906–1976
I. Title II. Luchino Visconti. *English*
791.430233092

ISBN 0-00-215478-1

First published in French 1987
First published in English 1990

© Librairie Académique Perrin, 1987

Typeset in Linotron Bembo by
Wyvern Typesetting Limited, Bristol
Printed and bound in Great Britain by
Hartnolls Ltd., Bodmin, Cornwall

TO MY DAUGHTER ELSA

CONTENTS

ILLUSTRATIONS

ix

Romy coming to life: left, Visconti directing her in *'Tis Pity She's a Whore*; right, in *Le Travail* (*courtesy Roger-Viollet*).

The German photographer Horst (*courtesy Horst Galleries*).

The landing stage on the Erba estate at Cernobbio.

The storm-troopers' orgy on Lake Attersee in *The Damned*.

Ludwig (1972).

Visconti with Claudia Cardinale and Alain Delon during the filming of *The Leopard*.

Making *Ludwig* with Helmut Berger and Romy Schneider.

Silvana Mangano and Bjørn Andresen in *Death in Venice*.

Grazzano, 1911.

Helmut Berger and Ingrid Thulin in *The Damned*.

Visconti shortly before his death.

ACKNOWLEDGEMENTS

The author wishes to thank the following persons for the many interviews they granted her and the personal documentation they supplied: Uberta Visconti Mannino and Nicoletta Mannino, Suso Cecchi d'Amico and Caterina d'Amico de Carvalho, Michelangelo Antonioni, Fabrizio Clerici, Costanzo Constantini, Jean Marais, Enrico Medioli and Michele Rago.

She is especially grateful to Donna Uberta Visconti and to Jean-Noël Schifano, without whom this book would never have been written.

*I found myself between two centuries,
as at the junction of two rivers; I
plunged into their turbid waters,
regretfully leaving the old bank
where I was born, swimming hopefully
towards an unknown shore.*

FRANÇOIS-RENÉ DE CHATEAUBRIAND
Mémoires d'outre-tombe

VISCONTI THE MILANESE

Did I know, lovely stars of the Bear,
that one day I would see you again
glittering above my father's garden,
talk to you again from the windows
of the house where I lived as a child,
and contemplate the end of all my joys?

GIACOMO LEOPARDI

In the heart of Milan, only steps away from the cathedral and La Scala, a serpent still writhes across an undulant escutcheon on the austere façade of an old palace. The building at 44 Via Cerva, now Via Cino del Duca, was long ago sold off and broken up into apartments, but in its more than two centuries as the home of the Visconti di Modrone family, it was a scene of splendour. It was a spacious mansion with three rows of windows, so many windows, said Luchino Visconti's younger sister, that there were servants especially assigned to open and close them.

Like most Milanese palaces, this one had a square inner court-yard where a tree was raised at Christmas and where, on spring evenings, the children careened wildly around the massive arcade on bicycles and roller skates. Benignly surveying these scenes with her escort of dolphins was a smiling Amphitrite rising half-naked from a brown stone shell that stood out darkly against the yellow ochre of the walls. Up the vast marble stairs leading to the long suite of family rooms – salons large and small, bedrooms, gilt and panelled studies – history sent not only the cream of Milanese, Roman and even Parisian society, but all the celebrated painters, playwrights, composers, set designers and singers Milan could recruit: the soprano Maria Garcia, known as La Malibran, and, later, Giulio and Tito Ricordi, the Boïto brothers, Pietro Mascagni, Giacomo Puccini, Arturo Toscanini and many others.

When Luchino Visconti was born there in 1906, the garden side of the house still overlooked the green waters of the Naviglio canal, which was lined with convents, orchards, public wash-houses for the city's laundresses, and water wheels that powered small factories. André Suarès, in his book *Voyage du condottière*, told of suddenly sighting the 'pretty façade' of the 'charming little Visconti di Modrone palace' rising from the mossy banks of the canal like an Oriental mirage in the 'hell' of Milan's slums. It was only moments away from the teeming Herb Market and the 'verminous streets' of the colourfully disreputable Verziere district that 'reeked of rotten vegetables and cabbage stumps'.

The palace, Suarès wrote, was 'just visible through the acacia branches, like a face behind a spray of hair and the spread fingers of a hand. That sadly smiling house! The only house in Milan where one wished to read, to sleep and to love. It seems made to harbour secret and perhaps guilty loves. A steep-faced terrace planted with old trees, jasmine and roses is mirrored in the stagnant water. Edging it is a sculptured stone balustrade, pompous and a bit heavy, yet elegant. Through the openings in the railing, the greenery and flowers enliven the silence, and their gaiety is like a patch of carnival in this wretched district of the city. Cupids support a coat of arms; horns of plenty pour forth their delicately fashioned peaches and grapes; Virginia creeper and branches caress each scroll and swirl in this balustrade. Through the leaves one glimpses a six-arched loggia connecting two wings; roses bloom along a double row of columns. Sweet veiled garden, charming retreat! Water spurts from a fountain to glitter, evanescent, in the sunlight. The canal reflects the branches of the trees and captures their leaves on its gloomy surface. In Milan there is no other haven of dreams, of love and of melancholy.'

To Luchino Visconti, home was a 'haven of dreams, of love and of melancholy', a luxurious setting for reunions and parties, a warm and natural enclave of trees and flowers and pets to come back to. His homes were always lively, always full of friends, houses like the one on Ischia, La Colombaia, a Moorish tower atop a hill engulfed in pines, eucalyptus and lemon trees overlooking the sea. The writer

Giuseppe Patroni Griffi remembers that when the windows were opened in the morning he was dazzled by the two blue seas that met his eyes: the Mediterranean, of course, but also the banks of blue hydrangeas that Luchino had planted along the shaded paths, and to which, as with his rose garden, he liked to attend personally. Everything there, the setting, the art nouveau furnishings, the parlour games, the mealtime ritual, the omnipresence of music even in the names he gave to dishes – fillet steak Visconti à la Beethoven, the 'Pathétique', the 'Appassionata' – was aimed at re-creating the atmosphere of his happy childhood.

The pseudo-Renaissance villa that Luchino inherited from his father in Rome was a place of vital, reassuring disorder, of a multitude of things tossed down carelessly. But 'this house doesn't interest me', he said. 'Do I like it? Yes, a little, but not so much that I wouldn't consider getting rid of it should the occasion arise. At heart, and by birth, I'm Milanese; in Rome I'm just passing through.'

The Milan he loved was gone, and he would never go back there to live. Yet it remained as luminous a memory to him as Combray was to the narrator of *Remembrance of Things Past*, as the lilacs of Méséglise and the river at the Guermantes'. For Visconti, Milan's Naviglio canal and the wisteria at Via Cerva were key fixtures in his personal landscape, archetypes of the settings in which he liked to live because they stirred the 'deep deposits' of memory in what Proust called 'the mental soil' that put him 'in instant communication with his heart'. This landscape that, he said, 'no one can restore' to him was essentially that of Stendhal's Milan: 'The gardens on the canal, the carriages, the aromas wafting out of shops and bakeries, the strident cries of swallows flying around our house at dusk, Via Cerva, the bells of San Carlos, the smell of the horses' sweat when my mother took us to the Bastions [the old fortifications]'.

At the beginning of this century, the writer Alberto Savinio could still see the city Stendhal had adopted as his own; like the Frenchman he could stand in the gardens of the Bastions and gaze at the jagged, snow-capped mountains the Lombards call the Resegone, 'the big saw', and smell woodsmoke on the fog. He could examine Raphael's 'youthful and Peruginesque' painting *The Marriage of the Virgin*, with its clean lines and clear sky, and see in it 'a metaphysical portrait of this cultivated and meditative city, the most romantic of Italian cities'. In his book *I Hear the City's Heart*, Savinio spoke of Milan as 'seemingly hard, a city of stone, but really soft with inner gardens that a coalition of builders, city planners and the twentieth century decided to exterminate'.

Its canals were the city's soul, for until 1929 Milan was a cousin of Venice and Saint Petersburg and all the other cities reflected in the flowing waters of their canals. The Visconti children saw the dark mirror of the old Naviglio every day through the tracery in the stone balustrade at the bottom of their garden, under their centuries-old trees. Every day on his way to school, Luchino crossed the Bridge of Sirens over the winding canal. Its four cast-iron sirens, nicknamed the Iron Sisters, had watched benevolently over the scene since 1842; later they were forced to emigrate to the grounds of the Sforza Castle, where Luchino rediscovered them and filmed them shrouded in February fog for the family chronicle he was then directing, *Rocco and His Brothers* (*Rocco e i Suoi Fratelli*).

This was an emotional, sentimental touch, but what it highlighted was secret and intimate, its reverberations private and muted. Even in *Rocco*, which was entirely filmed in Milan, Visconti avoided re-creating the life and colour of the city he knew as a boy. These we must seek in other cityscapes that haunted him – from the snowy little bridges in *White Nights* to the dilapidated bridges, stagnant water and labyrinthine sets of *Senso* and *Death in Venice* (*Morte a Venezia*). For between the Leghorn of *Senso* and Visconti's Venice there is a sort of family resemblance that distantly recalls Milan's Naviglio, that outer circle of hell where prostitutes roamed. But the twisting Venetian *calle* and the ghostly, fantastic fogs in *White Nights* (*Le Notti Bianche*) transfigured the Milanese Naviglio, endowing it with a whole system of symbols of disorientation and disarray.

The draining of the canals and rice paddies in the Lombard plain finally dispelled these mysterious veils that had made Milan poetic in Visconti's childhood and gave it its special Nordic *Gemütlichkeit*. We are advised, for example, by both Stendhal and Suarès not to view the Duomo – the cathedral – in sunlight. Stendhal thought that moonlight and 'the deep blue of a southern sky hung with glittering stars' bring out better the exuberant whimsy of the cathedral's 'white marble pyramids – so Gothic, but without the idea of death' – rearing exultantly in the air like 'mad illusions of love'.

Suarès felt that gleaming sunlight highlights the flaws in this fragile 'monument of sugar', which he saw as a monstrous effusion of lavish bad taste from which, amid the lacework and scrolls and spires and marble frills, rises 'a Northern Virgin costumed as a Neapolitan bride'. And he went on: 'I accept Northern art's assumption of this pompous form and the grandiloquent showiness of all this marble . . . But such art is a triumph of matter and therefore of lies. The Milan Duomo is what I would call a marvel for the Germans and the Swiss. They have nothing better at home; it is white bread compared to their black bread. Who knows, perhaps the carving of all this marble was subtly guided by memories of Alpine snows and icicles. So many peaks and pinnacles, and a miserable spire. So much space and no grandeur.'

Unless grandeur here derives not from the obsession of one man, like the castles of the megalomaniac architect king, Louis II of Bavaria, but from some madness in the supposedly prudent and calculating Milanese. Perhaps they invested their dreams in the vast, wildly visionary project they called *La Fabbrica* (The Factory) – a seemingly endless task that dragged on from the late fourteenth century to the late nineteenth. Like Ludwig II's fairy-tale castle at Neuschwanstein, the Milan Duomo 'is at its most beautiful in mist or in the rain; all the details are blurred, and it becomes a magical apparition, like a castle of fog in the mountains'.

On foggy days the whole city congregated around the Duomo, which the writer Guido Piovene called 'this grand, heart-stirring edifice', testimony in marble to 'an abiding municipal passion' transmitted down through the centuries. The Duomo became a magic mountain crowned since the reign of Empress Maria-Theresa of Austria by the golden, maternal statue of *La Madonnina* watching over her child-city.

The Milanese like – or used to like – to see their city muffled in fog, mysterious and intimate. When they spoke of the great fogs, their voices vibrated with pride; they affirmed that Milan's fogs were denser, thicker than London smog. In deep winter, Savinio wrote, the city turned into 'a huge candy box and its inhabitants into so many pieces of candied fruit'. The passers-by, the hooded women had the charm of masked revellers hurrying to a Mardi Gras ball. Ah, to 'follow one of these masqueraders into a warm home, to catch a distant glimpse of oneself in a salon mirror among soft carpets and sober, solid family furniture, to exchange kisses of greeting that still smell deliciously of fog while the fog presses against the window and – discreetly, silently, protectively – renders it opaque . . .'.

As a good Milanese, Visconti could not conceive of a winter without the thick mists he'd known in his city as a boy. He needed them to film *White Nights*. Lacking real fog, he swathed his sets in miles of tulle. While filming *Rocco and His Brothers* he waited vainly for the miracle to happen, for the fog to descend, but he finally had to fake it again. When he began a story in the 1930s, or sketched in a landscape, he needed those great fogs of the past, those November fogs that hid things, that made them more distant yet brought them closer together, carrying odours from afar, altering sounds, blurring outlines and smudging the boundaries between earth and sky, between the proud city and the humble Po valley.

In the Po valley, he wrote, 'the roads are channels of fog you can cut with a knife, and you can be ingloriously knocked over by a mere bicyclist. Blind trains feel their way along, whistles blaring. The space between sky and earth is clogged by a leaden fog that looks as if it will never lift. We forget about looking at the sky; we are land animals living our lives on the land. That's when free-ranging pigs sniff out truffles in the rich, moist earth along river banks and in still woods, and when the wind always smells of rain.'

Fog is an element in the aesthetics of concentration, for it forces us to take a proper perspective on our earthly, animal lives. It hides the sky and dissuades us from seeking any but earthly paths. It weakens and humbles our arrogance as rebellious titans, blunts our intemperate attack on heaven. Note Visconti's remarks on a visit to New York in the late 1930s: 'New York covered its face with a shawl of fog and I lost sight of it from its waist up. All I could see of it were its bases planted on the earth like the ankles of titans . . . The city is like an immense organ: the wind howls and whistles in the jagged forest of its monumental pipes. The austere grey stone has the majesty of a Gothic cathedral . . .' As soon as the fog disappears the skyscrapers, the 'giants', resume their assault on heaven, their tops rending the sky, which falls to earth like 'shredded fabric'.

The big city's aggressive vertical images contrast with those of the cities Visconti always preferred: horizontal cities gorged and heavy with the water in which they stand, bathed at night in moonlight and fog, immersed in it like foetuses in amniotic fluid. Before Milan was drained he saw it as a great maternal presence, mysterious, unsettling, yet prosaically, joyously middle class, magical yet familiar.

The first eight years of his life went by in this double-walled cocoon: the sheltering, snug, protective palace on Via Cerva, inside the rich, serene city of Milan, so self-contained, so conformist in its rituals, pleasures, sorrows, food, even its dialect. The differences among its classes and clans may have been sharper than they were elsewhere, but while interests diverged, feelings converged. The result was like Vienna, a city that is distinctly stratified even in its appearance. In Milan the old aristocratic palaces were clustered in the centre, monitored by the Duomo; around them spread the new districts of the industrial middle class, and beyond these ran the concentric circles of the Navigli and the Spanish-built city walls, where the working class lived.

Again like Vienna, this was a city where all the classes conjoined to worship, both at the Duomo and at La Scala, that temple to grand opera, a shrine of Milanese civilization. 'Facing La Scala,' Piovene remarked years later in his *Travels in Italy*, 'are the City Hall and a bank. Here I see the soul of this often misunderstood metropolis: practical and sentimental, businesslike and melodramatic, never intellectual, never dry, but terribly critical, where business always seems to be carried on against a background of lush dairyland and Verdi's music.'

For Piovene, a Venetian who, like Visconti, belonged to an old aristocratic family, Milan more than any other city 'invites the sort of aimless exploration that is guided only by the heart'. He saw the fundamentally middle-class capital of Lombardy not as a marquetry of contrasting clans and classes, of disparate and incongruous architectural styles, but as a smooth expanse, its differences fused in the heat of tradition and the Milanese way of life. 'Closed families and fashionable society, traders and manufacturers, futurists and lovers of the nineteenth century, speculators gutting neighbourhoods and people weeping over the death of old Milan – all these intermingle in an enormous Babel . . . in a common aroma of saffron-flavoured risotto, that rich, succulent, maternal dish that is also saturated with emotion and tastes of the misty, fertile plains.'

Visconti's childhood in Milan left him with a fondness for ritual. And for the dialect his mother taught him to savour, a patois the liberal aristocracy shared with the city's commoners. It was rough speech larded with Germanisms; children learned it through fairy tales and proverbs and mysterious counting rhymes like the sybilline *Enchete, penchete, puff tiné; Abeli, paboli, domine; Ench, pench, puff, gnuff, strauss e rauss*, a more robust version of our meagre 'One, two button my shoe . . .'. Visconti would later delight in speaking Milanese with playwright Giorgio Prosperi and actress Adriana Asti, who would recite bawdy poems by the dialect poet Carlo Porta. Indeed, the director demonstrated his love of vernacular language long before that: he filmed *The Earth Trembles* (*La Terra Trema*) entirely in a dialect spoken around Catania that was incomprehensible even to other Sicilians.

Milan, the 'creamy' city, was dubbed 'Paneropoli' by a poet because of its lavish consumption of rich, sweet milk, the base of what Savinio termed 'the nutritional civilization of Milan' and the mark of 'its great age and its nature'. In Visconti it nurtured a childish, lifelong appetite for cakes, strawberries and cream, and the saffron-spiced risotto that has been ritual in Milan at least since the fifteenth century, when, legend says, a master glassmaker using saffron to warm the colours in the Duomo's stained-glass windows accidentally dripped some of it into a dish of rice on his wedding day.

'Luchino used to ask me to come and make Milanese-style risotto,' his sister Uberta says, 'because he particularly loved Milanese cooking and I was the only one who could do it for him, which put me in rather awkward competition with the cook, who was from the Abruzzi.' In celebrating this domestic rite, Uberta was emulating their mother, Donna Carla, and, beyond her, their maternal grandmother, a commoner. Count Luchino Visconti liked to boast that he had her middle-class blood in his veins as well as his aristocratic father's.

'My mother's name was Erba,' he said proudly, 'and she was

middle class. Her family came from the Porta Garibaldi district and they started out selling medicinal plants through the streets from a pushcart. They rose in the world by sheer hard work. I think my sense of tangible reality came from them, from my mother's side. It seems that my great-grandmother cooked her risotto in the same copper pot used in the laboratory to make castor oil.' The Erba fortune that regilded the Visconti escutcheon had, as we can see, a very work-aday, very plebeian source. Practicality, energy and tenacity, the cardinal Milanese virtues, explain the resounding success of that maternal great-uncle to whom Luchino was later to owe his fortune and the leisure to concentrate on the art of making movies.

Carlo Erba was born in Vigevano, in the province of Pavia, in 1811. His father kept a small apothecary's shop in the San Eustorgio district of Milan that presumably earned enough money to allow Carlo to study pharmacy in Pavia, where he received his degree in 1835. From then on the young man climbed the social ladder rung by rung, first as a mere clerk, then as manager of a Milanese shop with high cupboards behind gilded grates on fashionable Via Brera. The location assured him a select, mainly aristocratic, clientèle.

Year after year he saved his money, built his own laboratory and, in 1853, bought the shop he managed. His firm turned out products that sent tremors of horror through the children of the nobility and the moneyed middle class, who were forced to swallow the stuff – castor oil, salts of iron and bismuth, tamarind extract, valerian acid and magnesium oxide – once a week 'to clean out the system'. Equally ubiquitous were the small phials of Carlo Erba's saffron that the Milanese writer Carlo Emilio Gadda insisted was indispensable to a perfect risotto.

With the aid of city officials, Erba so increased his fame and fortune that within ten years he was named a municipal councillor, taking his place in the political machine supported by the conserva-tive newspaper La Perseveranza. As head of the house of Erba from 1862 onwards, he also became a member of the Chamber of Com-merce and of the influential Society for the Encouragement of Engineering Trades. His name appeared on the roll of the Italian Industrial Association's executive committee, and he became a shareholder in the Industrial Bank, consolidating his fortune at a time when financial failures and scandals were rife in the emerging

Italian nation. He founded the Society for the Commercial Exploration of Africa, sat on the boards of the Edison and Ricordi Corpora-
tions and the Barthe munitions firm – in short, he had a finger in
every branch of industry. In 1886, with an investment of 400,000
lire, he became the first patron of the School of Electrical Engineering; when the government failed to help out in any practical way, he
appealed to private individuals and local organizations to follow his
example in fostering the development of applied research.

This stern Milanese, whose fellow citizens honoured his
industriousness by naming a public square after him, had no other
known enthusiasm except for opera (in Milan, the realism that
makes for success in business is not incompatible with lyricism) and
the scissors collection that he displayed in his shop window. When
this confirmed bachelor died in 1888, his sole heir was his younger
brother Luigi, a musician who thenceforth devoted part of his life to
the thriving family chemical and pharmaceutical company. Among
his achievements: commissioning the commercial artist Marcello
Dudovich to design his splendid posters extolling the purgative
brews and powders and delicious tamarind-flavoured drinks concocted by the House of Carlo Erba.

The person Luchino knew best in that generation was Luigi's
wife, Anna Brivio, herself an heiress to a great silk-weaving fortune
and allied, through her sister Giuditta, with the Ricordi music-
publishing dynasty. He remembered that his grandmother 'resembled the Empress Eugénie a bit, lively, very nice, and strong willed.
Everyone feared her, including her two daughters, Carla and
Ercolina, the first tall and lovely, the second short and much less
attractive – in the family they said Ercolina was "Carla seen through
the wrong end of the lorgnette". '

In that family the mother was the boss, as mothers so often
would be in the motion pictures Luchino later made. Like so many
women in high society then, especially in the wealthy bourgeoisie,
Anna exercised a firm hand not only over her children's upbringing
and the management of a horde of servants, but also over the family
business. She lived grandly in Milan, where her musical salon was
famous, dividing her life, as her daughter Carla would do later on,
among business management, travel for pleasure – especially to
Paris – and her social and family responsibilities.

Much of Visconti's childhood was spent in two houses, his father's palace on Via Cerva, deeply immersed in the past, and his maternal grandmother's huge modern house on Via Marsala, symbolic of the triumph of the forward-looking business class. In the Via Marsala mansion there was a grand wooden stairway, thick carpets, reception rooms and a hydraulically operated lift. Its most distinctive feature, however, was that the family apartments communicated directly with the drug firm. 'The reek of pharmaceuticals was so strong,' Uberta recalls, 'that my grandmother couldn't stand it. And her husband kept telling her, "Go on, breathe it in, it's good for you." There was a dispensary, too, and we had great fun peeking through the keyhole at the workmen who came to get injections.'

Her brother Luchino, whose memories go farther back, fondly remembers those potent fumes: 'We'd enter those corridors that stank of carbolic acid and it was exciting, adventurous, to follow them to a small door opening into the factory.'

A film of Visconti's life might open, not in a fine patrician home like the one in *The Leopard* (*Il Gattopardo*), but in the commotion and red glow of the modern steel mills in *The Damned* (*La Caduta degli Dei*). For factory smoke gradually changed Milan's provincial pace. Luchino's family on his mother's side confirmed the proudly asserted local proverb, '*Milan dis e Milan fà*' (Milan says and Milan does). Despite its respect for tradition, no city in Italy has surrendered less than Milan to a paralysing fascination with the past.

In 1906, the year of Luchino's birth, the Simplon tunnel through the Alps was inaugurated with great pomp. This was an architectural miracle achieved after eight years of work. Artists competed in drawing grandiloquent posters celebrating the titanic power that pierced the mountain; they depicted locomotives driven through the fearsome tunnel into the bowels of the earth by naked men whose muscular bodies shone in the hellish glow from the boilers. Passengers emerging from the tunnel saw in the distance the cathedral spire of the city of the future on the pale line of the horizon. This was Milan, the capital of the North, towards which everything converged.

A month later, in June, the city opened its World Fair to visitors from all over the peninsula, all over the world, who gaped in astonishment at the modern technical wonders invented by Lombardian genius.

It had taken only four decades to convert an already prosperous city, enriched by fertile plains planted with mulberry trees and chequered with rice paddies, into an unchallenged centre of trade, high-technology industry and the nation's most powerful banks. No other city profited so much from the Risorgimento [the nineteenth-century struggle for Italian unity] and the formation of the new kingdom of Italy, which freed it from the Austrians' bureaucratic yoke and from the prohibitive taxes they had imposed for so long.

In this framework of national unification, the new men like Carlo Erba managed to raise small family businesses to the level of great European combines. Those were times of dazzling success stories: of Giovanni Pirelli, the son of a Varenna baker and a staunch early Garibaldian, who by the end of the century ruled over the rubber industry; of Ercole Marelli, an unskilled labourer who used his savings to found a company that would become one of the country's most dynamic electronics enterprises. Vincenzo Breda revived a dying mechanical equipment firm and soon headed the Terni Corporation which, with government help, built Italy's first major steel mill. Industrial empires were created, dynasties founded. What the Krupp family (the model for the Essenbecks in Visconti's *The Damned*) represented for Essen and the boom in German capitalism, the Falck steelmaking family, the Pirellis, the Candianis and the Erbas were for the growth of Northern Italian capitalism, led by Milan.

To promote the city's industrial development and to provide for its increasing population, city planners, businessmen, bankers and municipal councillors were assigned to work out a new urban plan. With scarcely any hesitation they proposed a step that would later be denounced as a shameful defacement of historic Milan: demolishing the old Spanish ramparts from which Stendhal once contemplated the Resegone. They also envisaged destroying gardens and covering over the canals, thus gradually depriving Milan, for purely utilitarian reasons, of its identity as a fortified city in which, everywhere within its rings of walls and canals, all the social classes mingled. The old pattern was doomed to crumble. Demolition went on for more than a century, with rebuilding dictated by the needs of the moment. Milan no longer had the time to grow old.

The first priority was to make abundantly clear the city's supremacy as the economic capital of Italy, on which converged not only the new nation's captains of trade and industry, but the peninsula's 'moral capital' as well. This explains the vast square in front of the Duomo – once defined as a 'choreographic monument to bankers' taste' – that took shape at the end of the nineteenth century.

The Piazza del Duomo was linked to the city's second great historical hub, La Scala, by the Galleria Vittorio Emanuele, which moved envious Rome and Naples to want one just like it and which, in the 1930s, would impress Suarès with its 'conspicuous ugliness'. He damned it as 'an outsized shed useful only as a passageway . . . the tube where Jonah wanders . . . a mouth that sucks in and spits out streams of passers-by' and, above all, the triumph of the Milanese bourgeoisie's ridiculous and naïve hubris. 'The glass vault, on which rain patters and light shatters, the windows that let in the heat, cosset the bourgeois flora inside,' he wrote. 'The Galleria is a monument to a society that is only camping, but pretends to be solidly established. It lacks both scale and taste. And the noise made amid that vulgar luxury reverberates through the empty interior.'

In the *dazio*, the heart of the city, where property taxes soared, big new bank buildings jostled the old aristocratic palaces, and the neo-Gothic, neo-Renaissance and Liberty [art nouveau] mansions of the newly rich rose on the ruins of demolished Old Milan. From the city's centre radiated a series of broad avenues. In keeping with what city planners then called Baron Haussmann's 'grandiose reform of the streets of Paris', a vast programme was launched to 'sanitize' the urban fabric: whole blocks of working–class housing were expropriated and razed and their tenants pushed back towards the city's outer rim.

Thirty years of intensive urbanization and property speculation, along with population growth fed by a steady influx of immigrants, gave the city the form of a constantly widening, increasingly dense web; long before the period of *Rocco and His Brothers*, working-class families were trapped in tenements without gardens and without light that, Suarès said, resembled 'beehives cut down the middle'.

'In the façades, which are painted in vile colours, all the windows are open on cells stuffed with people, like flytraps. Dust, whipped by the wind, powders the honeycombs . . .' From the top of the Duomo Suarès looked down on the 'weighty, compact, dense' city, 'a human cheese veined with streets and squares'. Old Milan, he noted, 'buckles its inner belt of narrow canals at the [Sforza] Castle. Another cheese, concentric with the first and almost twice as long, is crusted with boulevards and bastions. This human blob will probably keep on spreading. Milan is a typical ant-hill. That is why it resembles the cities of China; for good reason . . . it is a storehouse of cocoons, and a silk market.'

Like Paris slightly earlier, Milan exercised a power of attraction over the rest of the country. Piovene remembered that at the turn of the century Venetians went to Milan just as French provincials 'went up' to the French capital, and he recalls his grandfather proudly showing him what he thought was the most magnificent example of modern architecture: the big, white marble Banca Commerciale Italiana, set on a black marble base in the purest late-nineteenth-century style.

The Sicilian author Giovanni Verga also described his trip across the interminable Lombardian plain with its grey, dusty, dry-stone walls, its endless rows of mulberry trees and elms, its straight roads and canals. And he recounted how moved he was when he finally saw the Duomo's spire, the *guglia*, appear on the horizon. He could hardly wait to enter 'Italy's city of cities', to join in 'the merry life of the great city, mingling with the crowds thronging the pavements'. He wanted to ogle the elegant Milanese women whom people called the Parisiennes of Italy and who strolled in the Galleria and shopped at the Bocconi brothers' department store. His mind's eye could already see 'the shops gleaming in the gaslight, the echoing glass vault of the Galleria, the electric light in the Caffè Gnocchi and the magic of an evening at La Scala, a phantasmagoria of light, colour and beautiful women blooming as in a hothouse . . .'.

But Verga's picture of Milan mirrors late-nineteenth-century sensibility and social reality: activity was defined in terms of 'gaiety', of vitality and pleasure. The Milanese wheel, 'with a dome for an axle in its hub of a square', as Suarès wrote, had not yet begun to spin 'night and day, in every direction', like 'a wretched compass, in a clash of steel and torment'. Noise, bustle, hurrying crowds, violence were the price of modernism. Futurist artists anxious to bury the past could find no more appropriate place to issue their manifestos and their challenges than this "city on its way up'. Umberto Boccioni painted it in 1911: in a blood-red dawn light, against a background of apartment houses and building sites, swirls a vortex of strident colour into which men plunge like wisps of straw blown about by irresistible forces.

From what other vantage point could the author Filippo Marinetti pronounce a racing car more beautiful than the *Winged Victory of Samothrace*? It was Marinetti who declared, in the first city lit by electricity, that Futurism was going to 'kill moonlight', meaning that it would wring the necks of pale, anaemic, dying sentimentality and romanticism. Nowhere better than Milan could Futurists 'paint what is new, the future of our industrial era' – not just the speed of trains, cars, planes, but all the forms of human dynamism: 'the great crowds galvanized by their labour', factories with smoking chimneys, tumult in the streets, riots, shouting masses surging through the city. The futurist movement certainly stated its revolutionary aims when it set up its headquarters in a red brick building called, symbolically, 'The Red House', where the walls were covered with frescoes commemorating the glorious events of the Risorgimento.

Futurism and avant-gardism were words that always stirred Visconti even though Marinetti, an apologist for violence and dynamism, would later appear at turbulent fascist meetings in Milan. In hindsight, Futurism was far more decadent than the 'little world of the past' whose most typical and picturesque denizens gathered daily to sit peacefully in the cafés in the Galleria, Milan's great public drawing-room. By the turn of the century, the Caffè Cova, once a den of liberals plotting against Austria, had become a tea-room where the intellectual heart of Milan beat softly. The editor of the newspaper *Pungolo*, Leone Fortis, as self-assured and ostentatious as a Spanish grandee, took up his station in the café's back room in an aroma of hot chocolate and cigars; there, between noon and one in the afternoon, he was joined by the other three F's of local journalism: Paolo Ferrari, Franco Faccio and Filippi.

According to Savinio, the most Milanese of the big daily

newspapers was already *Il Corriere della Sera*, where 'everyone, editors as well as writers, thought and wrote in the same way', reflecting a concordant and harmonious literary tone; no one 'left the beaten track' or tried to grab the limelight or drown out anyone else's voice. When novelist Edmondo de Amicis died in 1908, the *Corriere* bordered its front page in black and ran a six-column headline saying, 'The Chronicler of Goodness Is Dead'. Giuseppe Giacosa was given equal honours. In those days, the death of a writer, no matter how minor, took up the whole front page of Italy's leading newspaper. Minds were not yet troubled by the poison of criticism, the toxin of doubt, the gall of 'informed' gossip.

Giacosa, a tireless talker, was one of those taking part at the Cova in friendly literary discussions that were lively, but more frivolous than controversial. Around four o'clock in the afternoon the Boïto brothers arrived, Camillo, an architect and author of the novel *Senso*, and Arrigo, the composer and librettist who wrote the books for Verdi's operas *Otello* and *Falstaff*. Arrigo would often leave with a box of pastries while Savinio gazed at him in wonder: 'Where did he take those cakes, and to whom? I thought Boïto had ripe, juicy and very beautiful mistresses. Big blonde cats swathed in silk and ostrich feathers . . . He himself looked like the cat in *Pinocchio*, big and pompous, hiding his little paws in low patent-leather boots as shiny and pointed as steam irons.' The last to arrive, between five and seven in the evening, was Giacomo Puccini, who sat comfortably on the red velvet sofas and dunked butter cookies in his creamy coffee.

The Galleria was an odd and theatrical passageway for all the eccentrics, grandstanders and local celebrities with which this rational and disciplined city teemed. Everyone knew the music critic Romeo Carugati, the dirtiest man in Milan, who kept a varied menagerie at home and who went to the Caffè Savini or the Martini with his monkey Tina on his shoulder.

Also in the Galleria were the chic women in their furs and veils, their hats strewn with flowers or bristling with imperious plumes. We see them as little Luchino Visconti drew them in his sketchbook in 1913 as he watched them stroll through the streets. And there were the divas, muffled in their fantastic feather wrappings – Lina Cavalieri and La Pantaleoni, the golden-voiced soprano famous for her portrayal of Desdemona and her intimacy with Arrigo Boïto. Much later in the evening, after the elegant, aristocratic regulars at the Cova had gone home to their mansions and palaces, 'a blond giant wrapped in a cape and wearing a soft hat with an immensely wide brim came out of the door of a bar in the Galleria,' Savinio wrote, 'like a ship on a petrified sea, all sails bellying out in his inner storm. Feodor Chaliapin went to this bar to intoxicate himself with liquor, to get meticulously drunk. Then, when he reached his ideal state, he left the bar, traversed the Galleria on a path that zigzagged like a fissure in a giant earthquake, and disappeared through the stage door of La Scala on Via Filodrammatici to get ready to sing *Boris Godunov.*' In due time, his step firm and steady, he would make his imperious entrance on stage, bestowing blessings right and left and 'unreeling miles and miles of that deep, warm, powerful voice, as vast and serene as the rivers in his native country . . .'.

La Scala, the Duomo – 'my brother's favourite church', Uberta says – and the palace on Via Cerva were the points of the small triangle bounding Luchino's life in Milan. But it is in this sector that the poetry of the city is concentrated, the tenuous, delicate harmony of a society that, like the people in Chekhov's plays, failed to perceive the warning signs of an upheaval that would shatter what Savinio called 'Milan's closed civilization'. This, he wrote, was a 'very mature civilization, complete in itself, that looked for nothing more from the outside, treasuring what it possessed . . . Even in its physical contours, Milan's was a closed civilization. It was a wheel, destined for self-absorption and centralization . . . I remember the closed civilization of Milan as one remembers a dream. It was between 1907 and 1910. For Milan, this was a period of absolute stasis, of supreme splendour. Its closed civilization burst in 1914. The war hastened but did not decree its end. Wars do not act upon civilizations, but they do ensue from their crises. Even without a war, this hermetic civilization would have ended.

'New ideas, sources of turmoil and corruption, began to gather like clouds over the city. Until then Milan had been calm and secure, indifferent to everything it did not possess in its own right. What did it care if Cubism was being born elsewhere, if ideas were changing and poetic values were being upset, if inquisitive and anxious men were once more breaking through the polished but

17

now sterile surface of civilization to search again for the roots of things?'

Visconti lived out his gilded childhood in this golden age, this Belle Époque to which he would keep coming back, not for refuge, but to strip it bare, to show its splendour and highlight the signs of its decay. He would try to understand the forces that 'broke through the polished surface' of a civilization that was more Central European than specifically Milanese. Because of his origins, his training, his own inner conflicts, Visconti was meant to analyse this 'crisis' and mirror his own life in it.

THE LORDS OF MILAN

In the days of Milan's closed civilization, the
archangel of mediocrity, armoured with golden
scales and glittering in the sunlight, swam in
broad strokes around the Madonnina *watching*
innocently and sternly over the roofs of its
darling city.

ALBERTO SAVINIO

1900. The century opened on a lavish wedding: Carla Erba, every bit as beautiful, as much a commoner, and rich, even richer than the radiant Angelica in *The Leopard*, was married to Count Giuseppe Visconti di Modrone, whose suavity, elegance and refined worldliness had conquered many a heart. Don Giuseppe – Don Zizi to his friends – had the very black hair, velvety eyes and sharply drawn handlebar moustache of an Aubrey Beardsley figure.

Everyone agreed they made a stunning couple. Carla Erba had turned down a proposal from King Peter of Serbia to marry Giuseppe Visconti. 'It was a love marriage,' Uberta told us, 'a great love.' They became engaged at nineteen and were married the following year. When they began appearing in public soon afterwards, at the Paris Opera during their wedding trip, and then at La Scala, all eyes were upon them. The first time the couple attended the opera in Milan, in the Visconti box hung with red damask, every pair of mother-of-pearl opera glasses in the house swung to focus on them. The doorknob to the box bobbed up and down throughout the evening, but Don Giuseppe ignored it; he had no wish to gratify the rubberneckers or be distracted from the performance on stage – as, rather more than usually, the fashionable audience was distracted that evening.

In Milan, success, beauty and wealth did not go hidden. The Viscontis' social position made them public figures. Newspapers reported their attendance at balls and parties. Donna Carla's wardrobe was described in detail; her pearls were as famous as the Princess Molfetta's diamonds and the emeralds adorning the Marchioness Luisa Casati, Gabriele D'Annunzio's 'Kore' with the 'antique smile'. Luisa was the perverse and sensual 'anti-ioconda', the hellish bird of paradise whom Giovanni Boldini painted haloed with bizarre peacock feathers. D'Annunzio depicted her in 'very long Oriental veils that the alchemist dyer Mariano Fortuny dips into mysterious drugs and retrieves dyed with strange dreams and marked with new generations of plants, animals and stars'.

Yet not even Luisa, 'the divine marchesa', ranked with Countess Visconti in the fashion magazines; they vaunted Carla's 'good taste', the sober refinement of her clothes, the stunning luxury of her long chinchilla coat and her sable capes. On 20 June 1907, the magazine *La Donna* described her in that aristocratic preserve, the paddock at the San Siro racetrack: vast hat bedecked with flowers, parasol of fine black lace, coat open over a form-fitting dress with a nipped-in waist, gloves marked, as fashion then demanded, with three dark stripes along the back. The whole image, from the cut of the clothes to the accessories, irresistibly recalls the Countess Giuliana Hermil in the last film that Carla's son made, *The Innocents*. Over forty years after that day at the races, the director would reproduce the style in *La Traviata* and *The Three Sisters*, using pastel veils and furs and even the modish boas of the period to soften the rather severe lines of the clothes.

Few women in Milan could compete with Donna Carla for elegance – Countess Orietta Borromeo Doria, perhaps, and Baroness Leonino Alatri. Her children's beauty made her even more admired. The first five were born between 1901 and 1908, and passers-by would stop and stare at their photographs in the shop-window of Sommariva, the aristocrats' photographer. One day, so a story goes, the owner of a toy shop pretended to retain little Luchino. 'I'll put him in my window,' the man said, 'he'll be the prettiest of my dolls.'

The most fascinating of the Visconti family photos was taken in

1911, and shows five dream children in a ring around their mother. Imposing and solemn in a long, dark, elegant gown, Donna Carla is holding three-year-old Edoardo, in a lace dress, on her lap. Luigi, with his arm thrown around his mother's neck, seems a little Lord Fauntleroy in a jacket worn over a shirt with a large collar and ruffled lace jabot and cuffs. Beside him is a dark-haired girl of nine, Anna. She is a miniature of her mother, with the same countenance, the same sad smile and determined chin. Anna is wearing a delicately embroidered white dress, a pale blue silk sash and the pearl necklace her father gave her. Her cheek rests on the shoulder of her younger brother, her favourite, Luigi, while her hand brushes the shoulder of the eldest boy, Guido, then ten years old and already dressed like a little man, in a dark suit and a broad starched collar with a white peony foaming in his buttonhole. He has his father's big, dark eyes and arched eyebrows, and he is pouting – still childishly, or is he already haughty?

Standing in the centre and staring into the camera is the boy his grandmother called 'Prince Jewel', Luchino, wearing a blue dress trimmed with lace. He is tightly, imperiously gripping the plump little hand of Didi – Edoardo, the youngest. His mother's hand rests on Luchino's shoulder. The grouping is exquisitely composed; everything in it, even the finely worked gold detail in an antique wooden cabinet, seems to have been arranged by the photographer to point up the princely magnificence of Milan's most illustrious family.

Milan has always loved a show, including the spectacle of its worldly princes. Just as Stendhal once haunted the famous promenade on the Spanish Bastions, crowds at the start of this century flocked to the paths along what was called the Sunshine Promenade to gape at the handsomest horses and carriages. These were as stately as ever, even if noticeably fewer of them now bore nobiliary coats of arms on their doors. On fine spring and autumn days, beginning on the first Sunday of Lent, when the Alps were still snow-covered but the sun glistened warmly on the horses' rumps and the flunkeys' spotless livery, the Visconti children also rode on the ramparts with their mother, proud to sense that in the eyes of those peering at her she was Milan's first lady, its uncontested queen.

Even to the city's highest society, the Visconti di Modrone family was in a class by itself. The painter Fabrizio Clerici, whose name was a distinguished one in the Milanese nobility, told us of the day he first saw Donna Carla's children: 'It was Mardi Gras, well before the first world war. I'd been asked to a masquerade ball organized by a very select aristocratic circle, the Società del Giardino. At one point there was a sort of stir among the children and, as if the Lords of Milan were about to enter, everyone started whispering "The Viscontis are here! The Viscontis are here!" Then all five of them appeared, in similar black-and-white Pierrot costumes, scattering rose petals as they came into the room . . . There was always an added mark of refinement about them, of fantasy, elegance, of something extra.'

What they personified was fidelity to age-old Visconti traditions combined with the Erbas' brilliant and very modern success in business. Moreover, the Erbas distinguished themselves even from other rich bourgeois families by their lavish life style and their contacts with musicians and with the aristocracy. Few barons of industry had time to devote to receptions and balls and Carnival revelry. They did not feel they had to be seen at the San Siro track, at musical afternoons or in a box at La Scala. The daughter of the steel magnate Enrico Falck remarked that her family stuck to relatively simple ways and did not try to mimic the princely customs of the aristocracy: 'The great balls, with orchestras that played waltzes until dawn, were held exclusively in aristocratic houses.'

The Erbas felt no such restraint, preferring to follow Stendhal's dictum that 'building a fine house confers true nobility in Milan'. They not only entertained Milanese society in their home on Via Marsala, but they built a grand neo-classical mansion in Cernobbio, on Lake Como. This was a summer playground of the nobility, where the Viscontis also had a house; Count Giuseppe and Carla had been friends there since childhood.

Carla's upbringing in no way differed from the strict regime imposed on daughters of the aristocracy. She was taught everything she had to know to preside at her own salon, to entertain guests and run a great house. She spoke fluent French, English and German, took lessons in deportment and attended the dancing schools reserved for the best families in Milan, where she learned to maintain a gap of at least eight inches between herself and her dancing partner and to hold herself straight with or without a corset; hands at her school were shaken, British-style, not kissed.

She also knew music thoroughly and played the piano like a recitalist. As the niece of Giulio Ricordi and Giuditta Brivio, whose musical salon was as famous as that of the soprano Teresa Stolz, the well-known interpreter of *Aïda*, Carla met Giuseppe Verdi and became a close friend of Arrigo Boïto and Puccini, who was then working on the libretto of *Manon Lescaut* at the Ricordis' house in Cernobbio. Carla's life must be seen in this musical setting – one her son later re-created in *The Innocents* – where, to the strains of an aria by Gluck or a Chopin sonata, meaningful looks were exchanged, dreams and romances were born and died.

Money and beauty, of course, but especially worldliness and music opened the tightly closed doors of the aristocracy to Carla and her sister Lina, who was to marry Count Emanuele Casteibarco. Like the marriage of 'Peppe Merda's' granddaughter, Angelica Sedara, to Prince Salina's nephew, Tancredi Falconieri, in *The Leopard*, matrimonial alliances between wealthy commoners and aristocrats reflected the changes in society in the late nineteenth and early twentieth centuries. We can say of the Viscontis di Modrone, as of many great Milanese families – the Melzis d'Eril, the Crivellis, the Belgiojosos, the Casatis – what Proust wrote about the Guermantes at the end of *Remembrance of Things Past*: 'A certain body of aristocratic prejudices, of snobbery that once automatically separated their names from whatever failed to harmonize with them, had ceased to function. The springs in the machinery of repression no longer worked, a multitude of foreign bodies entered and removed all its homogeneousness, all its consistency, all its colour.' Except that instead of effacing the aristocracy's 'consistency and colour', alliances with the bourgeoisie reinforced and invigorated it because of the peculiarly Milanese characteristics of both social classes.

The eccentricities of lordlings like Boni de Castellane and Robert de Montesquiou set the tone for Parisian high society in Proust's day. In Milan, while the elegance of such dandies as Giannino Traversi and Giorgio Trivulzio was esteemed and emulated, no one could or wished to rival the excesses of Montesquiou, who thought nothing of appearing in a white velvet suit or wearing a bouquet of violets in place of a cravat. No one there dreamed, either, of aping the caprices of D'Annunzio who, as a passionate admirer of mad Ludwig II of Baviaria, had his bedroom lined with bearskins and decorated as a snow scene, complete with frost and a sled.

Upper-class Milanese saw distinction in simplicity. Thus they preferred to leave their silver unpolished, to paint only the most inconspicuous coats of arms on their carriage doors and to have their clothes made at home. The gowns, love affairs and shocking behaviour of the volcanic, Austrian-born Marchioness Casati seemed too loony for sober, provincial Milan before the first world war.

Not that Milanese parties lacked extravagance. There was, for example, the Dantesque 1903 New Year's Eve celebration in the Eden Theatre, where each floor represented a circle in *The Divine Comedy*, with hell in the basement, purgatory in the auditorium and paradise reserved in the upstairs rooms for a select few, members of an aristocratic club who gathered around a Pantagruelian table. There were, too, the masked balls given by such highly exclusive groups as the Artistic Family, the Society of Artists and Patriots, the Garden Club: an Empire ball in 1908, for example, and a Japanese ball in 1912 in a setting of flowering cherry trees inspired by *Madame Butterfly*.

For in this frenzy of parties, the fad for 'masked risottos' (as the Milanese called masquerades) that had fallen out of fashion came back stronger than ever. They were announced by posters in D'Annunzian or futurist style, and the rooms of the Society of Artists and Patriots, which organized them, were transformed in accordance with the night's theme into a beach resort, an inn from the opera *Carmen*, a hothouse for tropical flowers, or a Tyrolean village lost in snowy wastes. Artists by the dozens worked feverishly on these confections of plaster and canvas and on panels covered with caricatures that were grabbed off at premium prices the following day.

Prodigality, then, but redeemed by what was called *el gran' coeur* – the great heart – of the rich Milanese, who viewed good works as the quintessence of worldliness and who contributed the income from their festivities to the Red Cross and countless other charities, including the Committee for Abandoned Children headed by Countess Carla Visconti. Milan was a movable feast, but a charity feast that brought members of the noblest families – the Borromeos, who number a pope among their ancestors, and the Viscontis, descendants of the medieval rulers of Milan – to make spectacles of themselves in an equestrian display at the Dal Verme Theatre. In the spring of 1913, for the closing of the old Carcano Theatre, Count Visconti and his brother-in-law, Count Castelbarco, fed cues to the fantastic diva Lyda Borelli and the great comic actor Antonio Gandusio.

The tradition was still alive in the 1950s. Piovene noted then that one of the most popular hobbies among what was known as the *capuccio* – the cream – of Milanese high society was still to hold charity rallies to which they often invited the most fashionable preacher of the day. Doing good works was the most efficient way to gatecrash Milan's high society, the writer noted, because the city's aristocracy and wealthy bourgeoisie are primarily 'open to two arguments, of which one alone is not enough, but which together win everyone's vote: working for charity and feeding excellent meals to other benefactors. In Milan, as in New York, legions of ladies bountiful, young and old, avid for tramps, orphans and handicapped children, swarm through slum districts, grouped in associations such as the Busy Bee, a name that speaks volumes of Milan.' The benevolence of the Viscontis, who took an ambulance to Messina after the 1908 earthquake in Sicily, who visited hospitals and donated to the poor, illustrate this aristocratic and typically Milanese tradition.

At the turn of the century the aristocracy as a whole was weaker and decidedly poorer for having let the period's great movement of renovation pass it by. But there were plenty of exceptions, especially among the lay aristocracy, richer and more dynamic than the conservative Roman Catholic 'black' nobility, historically close to the Vatican and Austria. The Viscontis di Modrone no longer craved glory on the battlefield, as they had in Napoleon's time; now, unlike Prince Belgiojoso, the Counts Borromeo, and the Solas, Gallarati-Scottis and Casatis, they were fascinated by modernism. In many ways they resembled the eighteenth-century British patricians applauded by Voltaire for their dynamism and open-mindedness. Duke Tommaso Gallarati-Scotti founded a review called *Rinnovamento* that was open to debate on all the new social, political and cultural problems. Duke Guido Visconti became a senator and patron of the arts, joined the board at La Scala and saved the theatre from closing down, headed the Lombard Bank and founded three prosperous cotton-textile plants.

The most enterprising member of the family, however, was his third son, Count Giuseppe Visconti, who not only managed the Erba pharmaceutical company, but also plunged into a whole series of challenging activities. As a theatre-lover, he encouraged and financed young players' companies; he also set up a factory to make perfumes and cosmetics, then spread into home furnishings and decoration, selling wallpaper, fabrics and furniture decorated with varnished *papiers collés* designs. The lengthening list of his ventures even included management of the Pinocchio jam factory.

'The Visconti di Modrone family,' Piovene wrote in the 1950s:

constitutes the most remarkable example of those great Lombard families that allied themselves with middle-class families and launched into industry several decades before the other regions of Italy. And the Visconti palace, with its velvets, brocades, gilt and mirrors, its dark rooms and family retainers, is one of those old mansions full of echoes of Parini and Porta floating over the accretions of the new architecture.

There I met Edoardo Visconti, who was heading the Erba company; standing by while we talked were an affectionate dog and a few Chinese statuettes. My host was severely critical of Italian businessmen. Exporting is difficult. To counter nationalistic protectionism, he recommends establishing independent branches abroad and tying local groups in with them. This is what has made Erba successful in all the major Latin American countries, in Spain and, today, in Turkey, Egypt and Japan. But the policy requires self-denial, a willingness to forgo short-term profit, and confidence in the future – a true industrial mentality, which is rare in Italy. Our industrialists are too often speculators looking for a quick killing. The political situation in a way breeds and justifies this vice. Our government, a bureaucracy without skilled technicians, cannot even understand economic problems. Labour peace is impossible because [the trade unions] are controlled by the [political] parties. Industries invaded by incompetents become charities. If the vast sums squandered nationally on welfare remained in Lombardy, the workers' demands here would be met. And then we could think about the people in the South.

Clearly there is a gulf between the Viscontis' vigour and the symptoms of degeneration that Proust spotted in the Paris aristocracy of the Guiches, the Montesquious, the Rochefoucaulds and the Castellanes, the nobility he compared to a 'senile duchess' sinking into degradation. A gap also separates the decadence of the Roman nobility as D'Annunzio depicted it in *Il Piacere* (*The Child of Pleasure*) from the moral prestige of the great Lombard families who still escaped what in the 1880s the writer called 'the grey flood of democratic mud that is vilely submerging so many rare and beautiful things'. Gradually, he said, the tide was extinguishing 'that whole small class of the old Italian nobility that, from father to son, kept alive a family tradition of high culture, elegance and art'. He called this class 'Arcadian' because it shone most brilliantly in the pleasant eighteenth century, and he listed its qualities as 'urbanity, wit, aesthetic curiosity, a passion for archaeology and refined gallantry'. These, in fact, remained very much alive in Lombardy, and especially in Giuseppe Visconti.

'My father!' Luchino later said. 'A nobleman, yes, but certainly not a frivolous man, still less a fool. He was a cultured, sensitive man who loved music and theatre. A man who helped us all to understand and appreciate art.' From their parents the Visconti children inherited style and culture, but also a love of enterprise, a sense of duty stronger than any consciousness of their rights, any pride in their privileges. 'My father,' the moviemaker said, 'taught me that I could not claim rights or privileges through birth. I have never made a thing of my nobility . . . I was not brought up to be an idiot aristocrat growing fat and soft on the family inheritance.'

That his mother was an Erba only reinforced that ethical attitude towards life that Thomas Mann characterized in *The Artist and Society* as middle class: 'Ethics, unlike simple aesthetics, or the delights of beauty and pleasure . . . of nihilism and of mortal idle-

ness, is the true bourgeois attitude towards life, a sense of duty . . .
without which there is no will to work, to make and develop a vital,
fertile contribution.'

'My mother had a very busy social life,' Visconti said. 'All those
grand balls and dinners and receptions now lost in the past . . . The
cream of Milan society frequented our salons. My mother looked
after everything, and especially the children . . . I remember it as
though I were there now: each of us with his musical instrument and
she coming to our rooms in the evening and personally posting a
notice on the walls on which she'd written, "6 o'clock, Luchino's
cello lesson, 6:30, Luigi's piano lesson . . ." They were probably
difficult days, because after that there was school. But this is what
drove us to viable self-development, to avoid becoming dreary little
aristocrats like some of the Roman princes who never wanted to do
anything . . . This is where I learned to be exacting – with myself
and others. Because it's obvious: if you demand the most of yourself, then you'll demand it of others, too.'

Iron discipline was maintained in the household: precise times
for each lesson, for play, for meals, for sleep. 'Thinking back over
my childhood gives me a feeling again of carefree, happy freedom,
yet I realize that our time was terribly filled up, rigidly subdivided,
programmed, controlled. And that we had a time for everything,
and something for every hour of the day.' This was military discipline softened and 'illuminated by my mother's vigilant presence at
every moment of our lives'.

An Anglo-Italian tutor named Bozelli was responsible mainly
for the education of the eldest son, Guido, but he also taught the
other children gymnastics every afternoon. The French nurse, Mlle
Hélène, says: 'The children loved him; he breathed willpower into
them all, and energy.' But Uberta Visconti has horrible memories
of getting up at dawn, of windows wide open even in midwinter,
and gym lessons when she curled up in a ball and refused to move.

Said her brother Luchino: 'We owe our physical education to an
English tutor whose memory will haunt me as long as I live. He was
determined to teach us to despise danger, live uncomfortably and
develop quick reflexes. Maybe he was a great teacher, maybe just a
crank. We'd go out with him and he'd wait until we were distracted
and suddenly race like a hare after a tram. Before we could even

recover from our surprise we had to figure out what was happening, follow him, catch up with him and leap on to the footboard. It wasn't easy, and once you were aboard it was even harder to bear well-behaved people's astonished and disapproving stares. He spoiled the pleasure of our outings that way; when we were with him, we saw trams everywhere.

'To top it all off, our dear tutor was radically opposed to our using the stairs to go up to our rooms. Whether it was freezing or torrid out, we had to climb a rope hanging down into the courtyard and go in through a window. Like firemen or troopers in their barracks.' This finally alarmed Donna Carla, who banned such domestic mountaineering, but away from the Visconti palace, Bozelli had a free hand. '*In i Mudron!*' – 'Here come the Modrones!' – Milanese tram conductors would yelp when half a dozen Visconti bicycles suddenly came into view, ignoring the trolleys' clanging bells and the bleating of outraged horns to race like a piratical boarding party in their tutor's twisting wake.

The children were not to be softened by luxury – that was the point of all these spartan exercises. Training in stagecraft and the cult and study of art were equally strict. The resultant culture was triumphantly artistic, reflecting the humanistic ideals of the Florentine Renaissance.

But by then, the reveries of Lorenzo de' Medici and the other princes of the Italian Renaissance were things of the distant past.

The closing years of the nineteenth century were among the most turbulent in the history of newly united Italy. Financial scandals discredited bankers, industrialists and politicians. A policy of colonial expansion failed disastrously; the absurd sacrifice of six thousand heroic Italian soldiers in Ethiopia – a handful of 'brutes', D'Annunzio commented – brought about the downfall of dictator Francesco Crispi. Anarchists plotted, political leaders fought duels; Felice Cavallotti, a journalist for the Milanese newspaper *Secolo* and the eloquent idol of Italian radicalism, was killed in a duel by a rightist member of Parliament.

Revolutionary and pseudo-revolutionary movements were drowned in blood. In May 1898, twenty-four people were killed when General Bava Beccaris obeyed a government order to turn his cannons on a mob protesting against an increase in the price of bread; the king rewarded him with the Grand Cross of the Military Order of Savoy.

Two years later, a regicide ended the century on a note of confusion and violence. On the evening of 29 July 1900, the church bells of Italy tolled the knell: Umberto I, King of Italy and of the Third Rome, son of that Victor-Emmanuel whom Cavour and Garibaldi had placed on the throne, had just been assassinated in Monza. He'd been about to enter his carriage when four shots cracked out; the king put on his hat, and collapsed. When his wife, Queen Margaret, heard the news she exclaimed, 'This is the worst crime of the century!'

Panic swept the peninsula. It even penetrated into deepest Sicily, if we are to believe Giuseppe Tomasi di Lampedusa, who, although a child then with no clear notion of what was happening, was nevertheless struck by his father's unusual pallor and agitation as he burst into his wife's bathroom to announce the horrendous news. People feared that the regicide, committed by a young anarchist named Gaetano Bresci to avenge the suppression of riots in Milan, would light a fuse that would touch off a revolution. Crowds at the king's funeral stampeded at rumours of another assassination attempt. The crown prince, a small man, was almost swept away by the mob; his father-in-law, the Prince of Montenegro, along with his cousins, the Count of Turin and the Duke of Aosta, and his aides de camp rescued him in the nick of time, valiantly drawing their swords to protect him.

But no anarchists or socialists were lurking to perpetrate fresh crimes that day or in the days and years that followed. Soon it was being said that while Bresci's pistol shots shortened Umberto's life by a decade, they prolonged the monarchy's by a century. The prediction was over-generous, but the writer Giuseppe Antonio Borgese summed up the general feeling: 'It was as if the regicide had been a sacrificial offering that delivered the country. Soon the nation grew peaceful. Those troubled times gave way to years of rapid material progress, of growing prosperity . . . The first decade of the twentieth century was, after all, the happiest the Italian people had ever known.'

When Victor-Emmanuel III mounted the throne at the age of

thirty, D'Annunzio, in his usual incandescent style, warned him in a peremptory ode: 'If you do not give the Italian nation grandeur and glory, you can count me among your enemies.' But the new king dreamed of neither glory nor grandeur. He was in all ways unlike the image of an ideal king drawn up some years earlier by a Neapolitan monarchist writer: 'He must be tall, handsome, as strong as possible, magnificent, lavish, a bit sensual, but, above all, religious.' Victor-Emmanuel was short – in *Golia: Marcia del Fascismo* (*Goliath: The March of Fascism*), Borgese said he was 'abnormally tiny' – and this affected his character. 'From adolescence on he had been bitter and unsatisfied; though he was neither foolish nor wicked, his stunted size, always in this thoughts as, indeed, it was in others' eyes, had taught him an unforgettable lesson in mistrustfulness and timidity.'

He hated ostentation. The ceremonial pomp adopted by the House of Savoy in imitation of the great foreign courts, especially that of the Habsburgs, weighed on him. People said he was greedy. His only known passion was for collecting coins. Borgese saw him as a bourgeois who endured rather than controlled a situation he had somehow wandered into: 'He did not like being king, he only submitted to it. Whenever he could, he withdrew into the Piedmontese woods or the pine forests of Tuscany to savour the simple pleasures of family life. Even when he could not leave Rome, he lingered as little as possible in the palace, preferring a modest suburban residence', the Villa Ada, also known as Villa Savoia, on Via Salaria. 'A good husband, an affectionate and attentive father, he embodied the ideals of his middle-class contemporaries: order most of all, then thriftiness and simplicity. Unfortunately, he was on a throne, one that was too high for his short legs . . .'

Queen Helen (Visconti's father was reputed to have built his house alongside the royal home on Via Salaria so that he could be near her) was said by Borgese to be as dull as her husband, and equally awkward and uneasy in her role as queen: 'Her father was a minor Balkan prince, half robber baron and half poet, who was raised to royal rank . . . in time to see his whole kingdom, a mountain village, swallowed up by the earthquake of war and peace. The queen was certainly the worst-dressed woman in all Italy. She had no contacts with any group, and no good friends, for she could communicate no better in Italian than in any of the other languages this little country girl had been taught at the court of Saint Petersburg. She entered zealously, however, into her social work – a mandatory chore for all crowned heads in an age of democracy – and when she visited a hospital she never forgot to slip a gold coin or two into the hands of children dying of meningitis. Otherwise, her mind, like her husband's, was taken up with household problems.'

For over ten years, Italian politics were in fact dominated by Giovanni Giolitti, who was made prime minister in November 1903 and occupied that office for most of the period until 1909. He, too, was moderate and conciliatory, seeming less a man of action than a bookkeeper, happily spending his Saturday afternoons lawn bowling with his constituents in a small town in Piedmont. Giolitti tried to foster political cooperation between big business, by then entrenched in a stable economy, and the few forces gravitating around the Italian Socialist Party, founded in 1895 at the prompting of the Lombard attorney Filippo Turati. The prime minister understood that the 'upward movement of the working classes' was fast, strong and irreversible, and he dreamed of persuading businessmen and socialist workers to exchange concessions.

True, the proletariat was still downtrodden, and in the opening years of the century the number of strikes rose, especially in Milan, a traditional stronghold of both socialism and laissez-faire capitalism. Nevertheless, Giolitti's moderate policy prevailed, probably under the pressure exerted by the economic situation. The movement was also encouraged by the still humane and paternalistic mask Lombard capitalism wore at first. This temporarily hid the ferocious face that industrial development would reveal in all the big cities after the first world war, when failures and losers were mercilessly eliminated.

In the 1960s, despite the euphoria of the current business boom, the heir to the House of Erba would denounce this marketplace morality by translating Arthur Miller's plays into Italian and by filming *Rocco and His Brothers*.

'The wind whips and stirs the flame,' Savinio wrote, 'but the flame glows brightest in the eye of the storm.' Giolitti's Italy, the bourgeois Italy called 'Italiette' for its lack of intellectual breadth and passion, enjoyed such a calm throughout the first ten years of the century. And the flame glowed brightest in the nicely balanced, highly closed civilization in Milan, where the lives of the rich and titled drifted by on a stream of social rituals.

The great families had their 'days': the Gallarati–Scottis received on Mondays, the Viscontis on Wednesdays, the Borromeos on Thursdays, and on Fridays one visited the Ricordis. Five o'clock tea was served with increasing refinement in Louis XV or Liberty drawing-rooms. Champagne at seven, whist after dinner. Although people in the early twentieth century were already travelling in cars and even planes and enjoying the conveniences of modern life, they nevertheless preserved the nineteenth century in countless ways of thinking and feeling, in a thousand little habits. Certain clubs and cafés had served in the great days of the Risorgimento as forums for the fieriest champions of liberalism, had welcomed Garibaldi and Mazzini and had rightly been eyed with suspicion by the Austrian police; now they were the places where, with equal fervour, the reputations of singers and dancers at La Scala were made and destroyed. In the salons, people didn't plot any more, they gossiped.

'Were they less serious,' Savinio wondered, 'less busy than men are today?' The men then wore sideburns and hairline moustaches, dressed in the English style, wore detachable collars and brought great gravity to choosing their gloves, their bamboo or ivory canes, opal or amethyst cufflinks and the flowers they slipped into their buttonholes. Part of their afternoons was spent dropping cards – giving their visiting cards, with the upper left-hand corner duly folded over, to the servants posted at the doors of fashionable homes to announce callers.

'Flourishing young men of twenty and men of forty weathered by maturity, prepossessing men of thirty and wasted, tottering septuagenarians, all went on their rounds of visits between five o'clock and eight. They filled the salons, their behinds protected by the tails of their dress coats, necks imprisoned in high, starched collars, left hands gloved in yellow with three big, black stripes at the wrist. Holding cups of tea, they perched on the edges of hassocks, their bowler hats beside them on the carpet like black chamber pots.'

In these 'aviaries' described by Savinio, 'a few crows and a few blackbirds, a few robins and a few pipits' stood out darkly 'against a background of chirping, cooing, whistling and cackling by all the hens and chicks, the guinea fowl and turkey hens, pheasant hens and ducks, geese and hen partridges'. Conversations sounded more like concerts than exchanges of serious ideas. And when one wondered afterwards – 'which no one ever felt the need to do – what had been said in the course of the conversation, one realized that during that terribly rich, sparkling, brilliant conversation, *nobody had said anything*'.

The age of great deeds had passed; that of the war, the unrest and turmoil that would usher in Fascism, were as yet barely conceivable. The Risorgimento no longer fascinated the major artists of the early twentieth century as it had Manzoni and Verdi. Rather than revive the glories of the past and tell tales of heroism, the new artists, such as the novelist Giovanni Verga, depicted the tragedies and violence of real life as they actually saw it. These they treated with a turn-of-the-century form of Italian realism called Verism, influenced by Emile Zola. And *crepuscolarismo*, the 'twilight school', imprinted its slightly faded melancholy on poetry that turned away from heroism, bombast and great exploits. This, said the critic Renato Serra, was poetry that lent itself to half-tones – 'childish and provincial stories, slightly naughty girls, crinolines, embroidery and the colour of tea roses; the ambiguity of love without passion, sentimentality without sentiment, and odourless perfumes . . .' In Milan, Amicis, 'the chronicler of goodness', wrote a tear-jerking novel called *Cuore* (*Heart*) that expressed the sentimental, middle-class climate of his period.

One after another, the great Milanese figures who had helped to create the New Italy passed away. Alessandro Manzoni, whom Verdi called 'our saint', died 22 May 1873. The poet Temistocle Solera, a friend of Verdi's, librettist for his opera *Nabucco*, a political agitator for Cavour and General Lamarmora and once a favourite of Queen Isabel II of Spain, who had covered him in wealth and honours, died in poverty. Dead, too, were the patriots Carlo Tenca, lover of Countess Clara Maffei, and Giulio Carcano, who had moved Verdi to tears by offering him the first-edition copy of Manzoni's *The Betrothed* that the author had given him as a present. Two years later, in 1886, another link to a past of struggle and dreams snapped when Clara Maffei died; to her salon at 21 Via Bigli had come Balzac, Liszt, Verdi and Manzoni to talk about and sometimes prepare the milestone events of the Risorgimento, from the Five Days* to Austria's expulsion from the peninsula.

Finally, at the dawn of the century, Verdi passed away. On the threshold of the year 1901, at the Milan hotel where he usually stayed and where he had come to spend the Christmas holidays, he received season's greetings from the Archbishop of Milan. Three weeks later, on the morning of 21 January, he was so weak that he could dress only with the help of his old and faithful maidservant. Suddenly he blacked out and fell over backwards, his right side paralysed.

The news spread like wildfire. Telegrams flooded in from all over Italy; La Scala closed its doors. The street in front of the hotel, where a crowd had gathered, was covered with straw and traffic was re-routed to shield the composer from noise. Don Adalberto Catena, the priest of San Fedele parish who had been in attendance at Manzoni's death, now came to administer extreme unction and recite the prayers for the dying. Six days later, at 2:50 on the morning of 27 January, Verdi died. Present were the singer Teresa Stolz, Giulio and Giuditta Ricordi (she was Luchino Visconti's aunt), Arrigo Boïto and Giuseppe Giacosa.

'I want a perfectly simple funeral,' the composer had specified in his will, 'to be held early in the morning or in the evening, at Ave Maria time, with no songs or noise. Two priests will be enough, two candles and one Cross . . .' At 6:30 on the morning of 30 January, only his closest friends, his lifelong companions, followed the larchwood and zinc coffin aboard the small hearse to the Monumental Cemetery. Along the way, through Via Manzoni, Via Manin and as far as the Volta gate, under balconies hung in black, thousands of Milanese stood silently in the rain to watch the procession go by. There were no speeches; the coffin was lowered into the grave and by 8:30 a.m. the ceremony was over.

But Milan wanted to pay tribute to the man who D'Annunzio had said 'wept and loved for us all . . .' On 27 February, at eight

*The popular uprising from 18–23 March 1848, that liberated Milan and marked the first victory against the Austrians in the Italian war of independence.

o'clock in the morning, Verdi's coffin was placed alongside that of his wife, Giuseppina Strepponi, on an ornate hearse and borne to a crypt in the Musicians' Rest Home that he had helped build in Milan; 300,000 people attended the ceremony, during which Arturo Toscanini led 900 musicians in the chorus from *Nabucco: Va pensiero sull'ali dorate* . . .

As a boy, Luchino never tired of hearing his mother tell of the solemn funeral she had attended. The cult of Verdi and his music remained alive in Milan, from the silken boxes in La Scala to the grey streets in working-class districts where barrel organs ground out the throbbing melodies of *La Traviata*. But the rousing, tumultuous age that had bred that music was over. The public still venerated the survivors of those heroic days; it still loved the mythology of the Risorgimento, when modern Italy had been liberated and built. But sensibilities had changed; the Verdi era had given way to the period of Puccini and D'Annunzio.

Milan was no more immune than the rest of Italy to 'D'Annunzification'. Comparing the poet to Verdi, Savinio remarked that D'Annunzio lived and loved for all Italians. 'Life then was not ruled merely by this star's most recent books, but also by his way of using scent, of dressing, talking, seducing, loving. No actress, not even Cécile Sorel or Sarah Bernhardt, lived as publicly as this writer did.'

Said Borgese: 'It was as if his house were floodlit . . . Today [we hear of] the plot and title of a book that will never be written, tomorrow a duel or a political speech, a formula for a new scent or dismissal of a mistress . . . Like it or not, you have to know by heart how Italy's greatest contemporary poet sleeps and awakens, at what time of the morning he washes, why he chooses to abstain from cigarettes and wine, how passionately he makes love, where he buys his ties and how many greyhounds he keeps . . .'

His books were snatched up as soon as they appeared. Savinio recalls having seen the window of the Treves bookshop in Milan emptied of its copies of D'Annunzio's play *Phedra* within half an hour; customers of the Caffè Cova had swept down on this grove of books 'like locusts on wheat' so that they could read the play two hours before it opened.

D'Annunzio had scored hits with previous plays, *The Dead City* and *The Daughter of Jorio*, both starring the heart-rending Eleonora

Duse, but in 1908 Milan was prodigiously bored by *Phedra*. Its pompous, overwrought lyricism could never have conquered the Milanese, who tended to be ironic and sceptical and who, perhaps for lack of verve and imagination, spoke of the things they loved in euphemism and understatement. They called their Duomo, a thing of marble and spires, 'the bunch of asparagus', and nicknamed the thirteen-foot-tall Virgin at the cathedral's summit *La Madonnina*, the little Madonna; love was expressed as mere fondness, *volersi bene*, and such inflated adjectives as 'superb' and 'colossal' were only used ironically. To indicate that two people were having an affair, a Milanese simply said 'They are talking'. How, then, could this measured, middle-class city have acclaimed D'Annunzio's morbidly deliquescent poetry of ashes and gloom, of voluptuous and fatal idleness, of sterile inertia? Could a city that idolized Verdi have unreservedly admired the murky Wagnerian magic celebrated in so many of D'Annunzio's novels? D'Annunzio would never have been received by the Viscontis.

Puccini, born in Lucca but Milanese by choice, was equally – and unashamedly – bourgeois, equally typical of a new century weary of ideology and struggle. He had briefly toyed with the idea of setting a D'Annunzio libretto to music. But in 1894 he admitted that he had expected 'something original and tender' from him that suited Puccini's style: 'poetry and more poetry, intertwined tenderness and pain, sensuality, a drama full of surprises, full of fire, with a deeply moving finale'. The composer later said a gulf separated him from D'Annunzio, who 'always lacked a true, simple and pure sense of humanity. He is interested only in paroxysm, tension, exaggeration'.

True, Puccini himself unabashedly played on his audiences' nerves and emotions, and many of his operas, up to and including *Turandot*, are saturated with eroticism and sadism, although he never went so far in showing the forms and corruption of sexual perversion as Richard Strauss did in *Salome*, an opera Puccini hated. The Italian's favourite characters were shopgirls and Parisian seamstresses, 'poor, humble, good-for-nothing girls' with hearts of gold, like Minnie in *Girl of the Golden West*. His heroines, remarked Puccini's biographer, Mosco Carner, were sisters to the Viennese novelist Arthur Schnitzler's 'obscure Viennese girls', any one of whom 'might have escaped from the pages of Henri Murger's *Les Scènes de la vie de bohème*. Whether she is a seamstress, stenographer or shopgirl, she lives in a tiny room dreaming of romantic love until she meets the man to whom she surrenders her heart.'

This admirably describes the female characters in verist melodrama, and draws a clear line between the sentimentality of Puccini, who admitted he had 'more heart than mind', and Verdi's epic genius. Verdi had been profoundly virile, the tempestuous chorister of heroism, struggle and sacrifice on the altars of Justice, Freedom and Fatherland. Puccini was complex, neurotic, feminine in many ways. And the ferment of the Risorgimento had subsided. That man, at that time, could not have followed in Verdi's footsteps.

When Puccini spoke to Arrigo Boïto about adapting *la vie de bohème*, Verdi's librettist protested that the subject was trite; he pedantically reminded the young composer that 'music is written to bring to life episodes worthy of commemoration'. Music, he went on, 'is the essence distilled by history, legend, the human heart and the mysteries of nature'.

But Puccini was sixteen years younger than Boïto and had been trained in a different social and spiritual atmosphere. Epic heroes didn't interest him, nor did the great events of history, nor the crashing chords of ambition and power. His characters were 'people with hearts like ours, who are made of hopes and illusions, who have flights of joy and hours of sadness, who weep without wailing and suffer with wholly inner bitterness'. They are fragile, fallen creatures like Manon, Mimi, Tosca, Cio-Cio San, but they can die for love. The central theme of Puccini's work is summed up by the street singer in his opera *Tabarro: 'Chi a vissuto per amore, per amore si mori!'* – Who lives for love, dies for love.

Verdi called for 'virility, powerful drama, character'. Puccini sought 'sensuality, sentimentality, pathos' in the librettos he commissioned from Milanese writers Luigi Illica and, especially, Giacosa, whose plays and whose books for *La Bohème, Tosca* and *Madame Butterfly* reveal his fascinated insight into feminine psychology. He wanted 'great suffering in small hearts, mixed with delicate, luminous, exquisite episodes with a hint of young and joyful laughter'. To harmonize completely with the period's middle-class sensitivity, Puccini's librettists were also asked to insert what amounted to a leitmotif in his work: a nostalgic reminder of the joys of home, of the *casa piccola*, the little dream house.

As the biographer Carner said, the transition from Verdi to Puccini coincided with a shift from a time of struggle to one of prosperity and ease. 'Whereas Verdi's art cried out its creator's peasant origins, Puccini's gushed from the spring of an established bourgeoisie,' especially the 'most advanced Italian bourgeoisie, then represented by the Milanese'.

As sentimental and feminine as the bourgeois Puccini, yet as realistic and virile as that robust 'peasant' Verdi, Luchino Visconti drew the vital substance of his own work from both sources: he began his career as a director with *Tosca* and ended it with *Manon Lescaut*, but throughout his life he was guided by Verdi's vigorous example.

III

FAMILY THEATRICS

Dark red, fringed with gold tinted a dense,
opaque yellow by years of dust, operated by
two functionaries wearing white gloves: the
curtain in La Scala.

CAMILLA CEDERNA

'I came into the world on All Souls' Day by what will always remain a shocking coincidence. Twenty-four hours late . . . for All Saints' Day. Impossible to start living without antecedents. Don't, in any case, accuse me of bad grace. All my life that date has stuck to me like an evil omen.' Visconti wrote this in 1939, at a turning point in his life. He was thirty-three, had achieved nothing so far, created nothing, and he imagined he'd been born under a mysterious curse, a jinx. But in 1963, after twenty-four years devoted to the theatre, motion pictures and opera, he altered the lighting on his past: 'I was born 2 November 1906, at eight o'clock in the evening. Years later I was told that an hour later the curtain went up at La Scala on the umpteenth première of *La Traviata*.' He had chosen a shining star: the world's most illustrious opera house, at least to the Milanese, who silence potential rivals with a fervently peremptory *Ma nun sem nun Milanes el prim teater del mond!* – The world's first theatre can only be Milanese!

He chose his star arbitrarily. The curtain at La Scala could not have risen on 2 November 1906, on the drama of Violetta's sacrifice for love because by tradition the theatre's season doesn't open until Saint Ambrose's day, 7 December. Visconti also knew that the brilliant 1906–7 season began not with *La Traviata* but with *Carmen*, under the direction of the fiery Arturo Toscanini. But by tampering slightly with historical fact he used Verdi's radiant influence to illuminate his own life, made it a part of his personal mythology.

His family's mythology, too: at dinner, when the overhead light was lowered in the dining-room at Via Cerva, his father would say, 'The lights have gone up at La Scala.' After all, the Visconti family had figured in the theatre's history from the beginning. After fire destroyed its predecessor, the Regio Ducale Teatro, the Austrian Empress Maria Theresa offered to build an even finer one on the site of the ducal chapel, Santa Maria della Scala. Architect G. Piermarini's new theatre, which Stendhal later called 'the world's leading theatre', was completed in 1778 on the very spot where, at the end of the fourteenth century, Bernabò Visconti's wife, Beatrice della Scala, had built her chapel. The huge cost was shared by the Austrian court and the nobles of Milan, the ninety families thereafter known as the *palchettisti* because each owned a hereditary box, or *palco*. These potentates hired the musical directors who programmed operas and ballets, and they financed the theatre's lavish productions.

It was ironic that in Austrian-dominated Italy, where 'to think', Stendhal remarked, 'is perilous, to write is the height of indiscretion', only in the temples to opera – La Scala, or the Fenice in Venice, subsidized by the Habsburgs until 1860 – could the political passions of the Risorgimento be given free rein. Audiences rose during Act II of *Norma* and joined in singing the rebellious Gauls' chorus against the invading Romans, shouting '*Guerra! Guerra!*' – War! War! In *Nabucco*, when the enslaved and persecuted Hebrews sang their doleful song of exile, listeners riotously acclaimed the composer, for Verdi's name was used as an acronym for a free Italy; to shout 'Viva Verdi' meant 'Viva Victor-Emmanuel Re [King] d'Italia'. And the show on stage was overshadowed by the scene in the auditorium when, for a gala evening in honour of Emperor Franz-Josef and Empress Elizabeth of Austria, Milan's aristocrats defiantly stayed home and sent their servants instead.

Throughout the nineteenth century, La Scala was first of all a glittering salon, an aristocratic gathering place for fashionable Milanese. 'There alone is where society is,' Stendhal remarked, meaning the only society that mattered to him: the Littas, the Mellerios, the Melzis d'Eril. 'See you at La Scala,' people said for any kind of transaction. They came at the beginning or the end of an act, listened for ten minutes or so and spent the rest of the evening in friendly conversation in those 'two hundred small salons called boxes, with curtained windows giving on the auditorium', that were decorated, furnished, upholstered to their owners' tastes. A communal kitchen called 'the oven room' enabled the *palchettisti* to dine in their boxes. People drifted from box to box, ice-creams were brought, big money gambled.

At the end of the century, balls and festivals were still being organized in the theatre; there was even an equestrian parade in tribute to the king of Italy. Provided they paid the freight, aristocrats could use La Scala to celebrate holidays they felt were somehow connected with the city's life and prestige. For example, the Viscontis were hosts at a brilliant reception to honour Paolo Andreani, who made the first balloon flight over Lombardy.

The name Visconti is not attached exclusively to frivolous social events. Luchino's father outdid his three brothers in carrying on his forebears' 'enlightened' patronage. The first of his role models was Duke Carlo Visconti di Modrone (1770–1836); as adjudicator for La Scala, he invited La Malibran to the palace on Via Cerva, and the opera house orchestra gathered in his garden to serenade her. Most important, in 1828 he founded the Pio Istituto Teatrale to aid Scala artists or employees whose careers were cut short by accident or illness.

Luchino's grandfather, Duke Guido, best exemplified the Viscontis' tradition of patronage, however, and he remained in people's memories as the theatre's tutelary angel, 'the saviour of La Scala'. At the end of 1897, the city of Milan could no longer afford to subsidize the theatre, and performances were suspended. On the day after Christmas, instead of the usual posters announcing forthcoming performances of *Il Trovatore* or *La Traviata*, a black-bordered suspension notice went up on the hoardings at La Scala bearing the doleful announcement: 'Closed because of the death of artistic feeling, civic pride and good sense.'

To supply fresh funds, box-holders' fees were increased and the theatre was given a limited-liability structure that brought it 300,000 lire of the period in share sales. At that point, old Duke Guido, then among Milan's most respected and influential aristocrats, contributed the sum of 78,000 lire, equivalent to some 250 million of today's lire. Thanks to him, La Scala reopened its doors in 1898, at the beginning of Lent, only weeks before the ferociously repressed May riots, sparked by an increase in grain prices, burst upon the city.

The theatre's administration was radically revised and turned over to a 'Scala Management Company' – referred to in the family simply as the 'Management Group' – under the Duke's chairmanship. Arrigo Boïto, then aged fifty-six, was named vice-chairman. He in turn hired a new orchestra conductor, a volcanic young man of only thirty-one, whose direction of *Götterdämmerung* and *Falstaff* had impressed him three years earlier in Turin. With much battling and turbulence, the newcomer proceeded to revolutionize the Temple of Opera. His name was Arturo Toscanini.

Two years earlier, in 1896, at the première of *Tristan* in Turin's Regio Theatre, he had caused a scandal by blacking out the house. The audience, accustomed to strolling, chatting and playing cards, uproariously showed its displeasure, but Toscanini was not to be cowed; during his first season at La Scala, he again darkened the theatre. And he banned hats in the stalls. In preparing his version of *Die Meistersinger* he insisted on a full month of rehearsals. The performance was a triumph that was effaced by the scandal surrounding *Norma* a few days later: at the dress rehearsal, Toscanini decreed that the lead soprano was hopeless in the title role and, despite the combined entreaties of Duke Guido, Boïto and Giulio Ricordi, he cancelled the opera's run on the eve of its première.

Accusations of incompetence, irresponsibility, despotism rained on him. People said he could only conduct unknown operas, like the *Meistersinger*, that he failed in the repertory works, such as *Norma*. Toscanini was most frequently castigated as 'Wagnerist' by an audience split into Verdians and Wagnerians in aesthetic battles that reflected a lingering Milanese hatred of the Germans, the accursed *tedeskh*.

At the end of 1899, the maestro directed the Italian première of *Siegfried*. *Lohengrin* followed a month later. 'The choir and orchestra,' wrote Carlo d'Ormeville in the *Gazzetta dei Teatri*, 'manoeuvred like German regiments drilling in Potsdam. Obviously a military parade. Duke Visconti, who attended the review with his chief of staff, General Boïto, approved highly. Milord's hacks recorded His Majesty's satisfaction in the orders of the day.'

Toscanini's most formidable adversary was La Scala's grey eminence, Giulio Ricordi, owner of the powerful music-publishing company named after him. An impeccably dressed man, with a short, neatly trimmed beard, Ricordi had inherited his business sense and his ambition from his grandfather Giovanni, who had given up his trades as music copyist and violinist (he accompanied puppet shows in the Gerolamo Theatre) to set up a music-publishing firm in ground-floor quarters on a cramped, dark courtyard. Giovanni was a stubborn, determined Milanese who embellished his signature with a sharp, the character that raises a note a half-step above the tone named; this symbolized his intention to rise in the world. And so he did, building his company into one of the world's biggest in its field.

Giulio, under the pseudonym J. Burgmein, had published a number of piano pieces, orchestral works, a ballet and an opera. 'Had he been a writer and not a musician,' Savinio remarked, 'he would have assumed a French-sounding name: Rastignac.' This Machiavelli of music held the exclusive publishing rights to Verdi's works and used his inexhaustible talent for diplomacy to strengthen his links to the composer and increase his influence over him. To stimulate Verdi to write more operas, for example, Ricordi promised to obtain the finest singers of the period to appear in them; he sent Boïto's librettos to the composer and wrote letter after letter to Verdi's wife, Giuseppina Strepponi, who he thought could do more than anyone else to persuade her husband to work. Every Christmas for five years he sent Verdi a traditional Milanese spice cake with a little chocolate Moor set in the icing; this was to remind him of the long-awaited brainchild that was not born until 1887: *Otello*. An elaborate celebration of Verdi's jubilee as a composer inaugurated an equally determined campaign by the publisher to convince him to write his final masterpiece, *Falstaff*.

Being Verdi's publisher gave Ricordi an absolute monopoly of major opera publication, especially of Puccini's works, but also including those of fashionable composers whose music he frankly detested. Although he considered Wagner a retarded Attila, he bought the publishing rights to the German's music from a rival company, Lucca. As the publisher of a magazine, *La Gazzetta Musicale*, Ricordi created triumphs and decreed fiascos. In short, his power was immense.

Moreover, as president of La Scala's orchestral company he could block any opera production he considered unsuitable for the theatre. When, in 1902, he learned that Toscanini was planning to stage the uncut version of Verdi's *Il Trovatore* at La Scala, he set out to sink what he was sure could only be a Wagnerian rendering of the work. After all, Toscanini had just scored a success with *Tristan* in the presence of Siegfried Wagner, the composer's son, and the new Scala season was to open with *Die Walküre*.

Only Boïto's intervention and a general protest forced Ricordi to surrender and allow the work to be programmed. By way of consolation, he listed all of the conductor's heresies in his magazine; Toscanini, he wrote, 'has, for many people, become as infallible as the pope, surpassing even Verdi himself. The composer never prepared or conducted his *Trovatore:* this way.' In fact, other reasons, less admissible than his hatred of Wagner and his adoration of Verdi, fed Ricordi's animosity towards Toscanini: during festivities in Turin in 1898, the conductor had flatly refused to perform a composition by J. Burgmein – alias Giulio Ricordi.

No one but Toscanini would have dared to challenge the power of the publisher who directed a musical empire from his famous headquarters on Via degli Omenomi. There throngs of singers, composers, conductors and librettists waited to be ushered ceremoniously into one of the fateful offices, that of Tito Ricordi, the publisher's son, or of the father, Giulio, in his stiff collar and black cravat.

At first, Duke Guido had smoothed over the quarrels between the conductor and the publisher. After the duke's death in 1902, relations between Toscanini and La Scala's management rapidly deteriorated. The Management Group by then consisted of the duke's four sons: Uberto, the eldest, who considered La Scala an annex to his own salon; Guido, an inventive and eccentric amateur musician; Giuseppe, and Giovanni. Shortly before the old duke died, Toscanini had asked that his salary be raised from 12,000 to 20,000 lire a year. Uberto inherited the issue, but before he could settle it, Giovanni happened to run into the conductor in a Scala corridor and told him his pay had been raised to 18,000 lire. Annoyed by this compromise, and by these aristocrats' airy off-handedness, he turned on his heel and, without a word, stalked away from the embarrassed young count.

The issue soon came to a head. In the spring of 1903, during a performance of Verdi's *A Masked Ball*, the audience called for an encore by the tenor. As usual, Toscanini signalled to him to ignore it. After another round of calls, the performance continued, but at the end of the act a prop man came out to announce that the conductor had suffered a haemorrhage and had left the theatre. The next day, before sailing for South America, Toscanini sent off a telegram vowing never to set foot in La Scala again.

Three years passed, marked by, among other events, the resounding flop of *Madame Butterfly* in 1904; Puccini was as roundly lambasted as soprano Renata Storchio, Toscanini's lover. When an untimely breeze swelled Butterfly's kimono, a wag in the audience shouted, 'She's pregnant! It's Toscanini's child!' The remark was rewarded with an astonishing chorus of guffaws, whistles, groans, bellows, giggles and shouts.

Yet, after considerable hesitation and laborious haggling with La Scala's manager, Carlo Gatti-Casazza, the conductor agreed to return to the theatre for two seasons. A brief visit there in 1905 told him how much the discipline and the atmosphere had softened since he'd left. Falling back into what Luchino Visconti later called the 'old Italian habit of considering the theatre as a big drawing-room', his uncle, Duke Uberto, and his friends were now inviting their favourite singers and dancers to supper in their boxes.

So Toscanini stated his terms: he would not return to La Scala unless: 1) there were no more encores; 2) no one but the performers was allowed on stage (some aristocrats, including Count Guido Visconti, would sometimes assume disguises and mingle with the company on the stage); 3) an orchestra pit was built.

This, Ricordi grumbled derisively in his magazine, was just a new fad, aping Bayreuth; he 'forgot' that Verdi had made the same demand in a letter to his publisher in 1871: 'Making the orchestra invisible. This isn't my idea, it's Wagner's, and it's a very good one. It seems incredible that in our day we still tolerate those miserable tail-coats and white ties mixing with Egyptian, Assyrian or Druidic costumes, and what's more, having the orchestra, which belongs to the world of make-believe, almost in the middle of the stalls among whistling, applauding spectators. Add to all this the repugnance of seeing the harpists' heads, the bass-players' shirtcuffs and the contortions of the conductor.'

Two brief but memorable Toscanini seasons were to supply the musical background for Luchino Visconti's first two years of life. Later he would remark of this period that at home 'no one did anything, no one even was born, without first glancing at the Scala show bills'. The dark fires of *Carmen*, the disturbing perversions of *Salome*, the 'infernal voluptuousness' of *Tristan*, sweet nostalgia in Gluck's *Orfeo ed Euridice* were the sparkling constellations in La Scala's 1906–7 season. All four would later inspire and fecundate work by Visconti. In the following year, *Götterdämmerung* again, and a triumphant *Pelléas et Mélisande*. Wary of Milanese chauvinism, Toscanini had been fussier than ever in preparing Debussy's opera, even wrapping stagehands' shoes in felt to muffle extraneous noises.

The maestro and the Viscontis clashed again, however, when Count Guido, chairman of the Concert Committee, asked Toscanini to conduct a work by a friend of the count's, Milanese composer Gaetano Coronaro, who had just died. Toscanini refused, whereupon the Committee gave one of the two concerts he was to direct to another orchestra leader, Ettore Panizza. Toscanini sued, and lost. Again he stormed out of La Scala, leaving behind him an atmosphere made steamier by the poor reception given Richard Strauss's *Ein Heldenleben*, which Toscanini had premièred in the one concert he did conduct. The work was being dismissed locally as 'music for madhouses'.

The maestro did not return to Milan until 1911, this time to move into a palace on Via Durini, near Via Cerva. The majestic eighteenth-century building with its rusticated walls and elegant wrought-iron balcony became and forever remained his favourite dwelling. It was a comfortable, conventional residence, resplendent with old panelling, crystal and silver, all watched over by tutelary painted gods. At the entrance hung a reproduction of Boldini's famous portrait of Verdi in a black top hat and a knotted white silk scarf. On the grand piano were mementoes, letters from Verdi, Wagner, Puccini. A photograph of Debussy was dedicated to 'the maestro I can never thank enough'; on the back the composer had jotted down the opening chords of the third act of *Pelléas* and written: 'From which Toscanini emerged victorious after all. Debussy. *Pelléas et Mélisande*, 2 April 1908 at La Scala.'

As a boy, Luchino carried Wanda, Toscanini's younger daughter and Visconti's first actress, through the streets of Milan on the handlebars of his bicycle at speeds that terrified the maestro. Their friendship frequently brought the boy into the magical ambience of the palace on Via Durini, saturated with music and ghosts and warm, poetic intimacy.

An old Chekhovian governess, Nena, served in the house for fifty years, 'becoming . . . an institution in Milan', said the journalist Camilla Cederna; in the 1950s, Luchino would re-create her to the life in his direction of Giuseppe Giacosa's *Come le Foglie* (*Like the Leaves*). 'So that her little masters could get some fresh air, she took them, after arming them with a brioche and a bar of Theobroma chocolate, to play in the Monumental Cemetery. First she led them to the grave of their little brother Giorgio, who had been lying there for some years. Then she sat down and knitted while the children played hide-and-seek among the tombs, stroking the romping bronze cherubim and the glum bronze angels and vying to be the first to touch the granite piano decorating a composer's grave . . .'

Nena sometimes escorted little Wanda to the Viscontis' to join a frenzied gang of fifteen kids: Duke Uberto's children, Count Giovanni's three boys and three girls, and the three Castelbarco youngsters, the children of Donna Carla's sister. Together they turned the old Cerva palace into a gigantic hive of games. When they came home from the shows they attended every week, they improvised tragedies or comedies using all the clichés of opera and silent films – heroes and traitors, women murderers and women sacrificed, grim conspiracies and thwarted love, ghastly killings and grislier punishments.

In the 'memoirs' written by the Viscontis' French governess, Mlle Hélène, and shown to us by Uberta Visconti, she noted: 'Every Thursday the children were freed for the afternoon and we went to the cinema to see endless serialized films such as *The Mask*

With the White Teeth and *The Red Circle*. The children came home very excited from these films and, with their cousins, they acted out all the episodes they'd seen. Naturally, there was a hero and a traitor, the one defending the heroine that the other pursued and persecuted.

'They took their parts so seriously that one afternoon, when the bell rang at five o'clock to signal that the play period was over and they were to return to their rooms to do their homework, I heard groans as I walked down the gallery. I stopped in surprise, trying to discern where the sound was coming from. As I drew near a wardrobe, I heard another moan. I opened the doors and Luchino, gagged, tied up like a sausage and half suffocated, fell into my arms. He must have been either the traitor or the hero to be trussed up like that.'

An imposing company of servants, maiden ladies both Italian and foreign, and tutors was recruited for the children and housed in the Cerva palace. 'At Count Giuseppe's there was a very large staff to look after the whole tribe of youngsters,' Mlle Hélène remarked. Her list, referring to the war-time period when households were smaller, did not include the two nannies hired after the births of the two 'little ones', Ida Pace in 1916 and Uberta in 1918. She did mention 'the gate-keeper (a fat Swiss in livery) and his wife; a gardener, formerly the coachman; Antonio, the driver; Luisa, the countess's personal maid; the count's valet; the children's maid; two laundresses; three people in the kitchen; Miss Esther, the boys' governess; myself for Anna, and Bozelli, Guido's tutor, who did not live with us, but who came for Guido every day and also for the others, whom he drilled in gymnastics.'

The weeks and months passed in a round of the same activities, the same pleasures and parties. Free days, Thursdays and Sundays, were as crowded and as ordered as school days: 'On Sundays,' wrote the French governess, 'we attended mass in the Duomo: Anna, the boys, Miss Esther, me, plus Countess Castelbarco's three children, their governess, the "three blondes" (Count Giovanni's daughters), sometimes their brothers and their governess. That made a troop that could not pass unnoticed when, after mass, we walked back up Via Dante to stroll in the park behind the Castle . . . In the afternoon, we often went to the races. The children were mad about horses. Sometimes we went to the theatre, alone or with the count or countess, or we made an excursion to an estate near Milan called La Librera.'

In the evening, the whole family gathered in the dining-room for dinner served in silver dishes by a majordomo and two liveried, white-gloved footmen. Don Giuseppe was meticulous in preserving the solemn, immutable ritual that his son would later recreate in *The Damned*. Punctuality and elegance were mandatory. Donna Carla and her daughter Anna wore evening dresses, the count and Guido dinner jackets, and the children were encased in black velvet suits and spotless white silk shirts.

Years later, long after the war, the ceremoniousness that Uberta remembered from her childhood was still intact: 'In his films my brother often showed these big family tables and there is certainly something of us Viscontis in those pictures . . . In fact, terrible duels took place under those tables, furious battles were fought. And my father, an infinitely gentle Gattopardo, never noticed a thing. The majordomo, old, lovable, patient Linetti, was "humiliated" by Luchino, Luigi and Edoardo, and he just stood there in despair with all the frogs torn off his fine coat . . .'

The count was roused from his benevolent placidity, however, when the boldest of his children spouted obscenities, more out of playful defiance than real vulgarity. 'Who said that?' Don Giuseppe would thunder. When no one replied, his disorderly sons were immediately sent to their rooms.

All his life, Luchino would respect the family tradition of having meals served on Irish lace tablecloths by white-gloved servants in black and yellow livery. Every evening he and his cook settled on the next day's menu, always scaled for seven or eight people. 'The cook,' Uberta says, 'posted the menu every day, sometimes adding: "Excellency" – that's what he called [Luchino] – "I've run out of money!" And Luchino would write: "So have I." '

The film-maker drew some general conclusions about life from this household ritual: 'Life is a hive. Everyone lives and works in his own cell. Then we all gather in a central nucleus around the queen bee.' That, he added, 'is when the tragedies erupt' – as in *Sandra* (*Vaghe Stelle dell'Orsa*), and in *Conversation Piece* (*Gruppo de Famiglia in un Interno*).

None of these dramas erupted early on at the Visconti palace. In the first fifteen years of this century, no clan was more united, no atmosphere more propitious to the flowering of an artistic temperament. As hobby or passion, every art form was cultivated and practised on Via Cerva. Count Emanuele Castelbarco was a patron, a lover of literature and friend of countless painters and poets. In Milan he founded *La Bottega di Poesia* (The Poetry Boutique), where the first Milanese showing of Modigliani's painting took place.

Don Giuseppe, who was passionate about painting, would shut himself up in his studio for hours, and would climb scaffolding to decorate his various residences with Renaissance-style frescoes. King Victor-Emmanuel once asked him, Uberta says, to create a diptych by painting a group of women to match an eighteenth- or nineteenth-century painting of a cluster of men. 'He imitated the original painter's style so skilfully,' Uberta recalls, 'that an expert appointed by Queen Helen to examine the two canvases finally pointed to my father's copy and announced, "I guarantee that this is the original." For my father, it was a triumph.'

Along with a handful of extremely wealthy noblemen drawn to everything that seemed modern, and excited by fields in which everything was still new, still to be invented, the Viscontis turned to the youngest and most plebeian of the muses, the cinema, which in the early years of the century could only be seen at the fairs and festivals held annually in the city's outskirts. So, on the board of directors of Milano Films, along with a number of Milanese princes, marquesses and counts, sat Count Giovanni Visconti di Modrone, Duke Guido's youngest son.

Eager to make more illustrious films than anyone else, these aristocrats embarked on ambitious projects, went in for such sweeping historical tableaux as the 1910 *Joachim Murat*, its credits listing the flower of Milanese aristocracy, including Giuseppe Visconti. No wonder, then, that on Sundays, Count Giuseppe often accompanied his children to the Centrale Cinema, where Luchino went wild over the early American gangster movies.

But it was the stage with which the boy first fell in love. 'The city bubbled when a new play opened,' he later recounted. 'Given my boyhood, how could I have helped being smitten with the theatre?' At bedtime, he left notes for his mother on his night table

'Dear Mom, may I please go and see Alda Borelli tomorrow, or *La Gioconda* at the Carcano, or else go to the Centrale Cinema?' On the same sheet of paper his mother would reply: 'I would gladly have let you go, dear, if you hadn't gone roaming around on the roof,' or 'if you hadn't quarrelled with your brother Guido'. The theatre! 'I was born with the smell of the stage in my nostrils,' he would say. 'The private one we had on Via Cerva, and the astonishing, exciting one at La Scala.'

The Palazzo Visconti, like the palaces of Renaissance princes, had a charming little theatre of its own. It exclusiveness did not prevent the newspapers of the period from reporting in minute detail the shows presented there on behalf, in the purest Milanese social tradition, of such charitable organizations as the Committee for Abandoned Children and Queen Helen's Asylum. Goldoni plays were staged, along with vaudeville shows, satirical revues plotted and written by one Josef von Icsti, a Germanized anagram of Count Giuseppe Visconti. The titles of these displays of theatrical fireworks, these light, joyous and ephemeral butterflies of stagecraft, were emblazoned on silk fans struck with the Visconti arms: *The Peopling of the Pole*, *A Little Love*, *For a Kiss*, *Someone Teach Me the Game*, performed by Milan's aristocrats and wealthy commoners in lavish costumes.

In the days following a performance, the *Illustrazione Italiana* listed the actors' names and titles: Countess Durini, Marchioness Anna de Villahermosa, Countess de Albertis, Marquess Ponti, Count Alberto Locatelli and, minus the aristocratic handle but ennobled by her vast fortune, Ada Baslini. Also mentioned were the organizers of these sumptuous private productions: Count Castelbarco; Duke Uberto (an impenitent lothario who was the darling of Milan); Count Giuseppe and, finally, 'unanimously admired in the show, the ravishing lady of the house, Carla Visconti di Modrone, tall, pale, slender and always so elegant'.

Carla drew applause in a series of guises: as a powdered, beribboned and bewigged marchioness dressed in ermine and gold lamé; as a Renaissance dame trailing finery like a figure in a pre-Raphaelite painting; as a pushcart vendor selling herbs and vegetables, insolent and pert, with her fists planted on her generous hips. When she played a commoner her voice could go harsh and her accent thick with the inflections of the slums, a voice almost as coarse as that of the Duchess of Guermantes, 'in which lingered the fat and indolent gold of a pronvincial sun'. Perhaps, after all, she was merely reproducing the voice and dialect of her grandmother, who had pushed a barrow of medicinal herbs through the populous Porta Garibaldi district in northern Milan.

To Luchino, his mother *was* theatre – and his father even more so as manager of an actors' company headed by Marco Praga, author of many dramas about the middle class, among them *The Ideal Woman*, in which Duse triumphed in 1890.

Music, however, remained the art that held pride of place in the Visconti family. In 1911, Duke Uberto spent the notable sum of 50,000 lire at the Hôtel Drouot, the Paris auction rooms, to acquire paintings and archaeological remains connected with La Scala. These formed the basic collection of the Scala museum, which he headed from 1912 to 1918.

Count Guido, called Guidone, or Big Guido, because of his imposing stature, was generally considered an eccentric who cruised the city on a bicycle with his heavy black beard floating in the wind. It was only fitting that Guido should invent a strange, monumental harpsichord that, to his great satisfaction, produced the most bizarre of sounds. He had met Schönberg and Webern and displayed a predilection that was rare in Milan for the new trends in modern music. He loved Debussy's compositions, and played passages from them on the piano while abstract coloured images were projected on the walls around him.

Young Luchino's most profound and lasting aesthetic emotions, however, were connected with his mother more than with his uncles – specifically, with the lessons in harmony and counterpoint she gave her children promptly at six o'clock in the morning even if she'd been out on the town and had only got to bed a few hours before. 'This may be my dearest memory,' he said; 'I can still see the dim early light shining on my cello. I can feel the light weight of my mother's hand on my shoulder.'

On spring evenings, along with the purplish aroma of wisteria, there rose to his room 'where I had long gone early to bed' the sound of the music Donna Carla played on the first floor: selections from *Boris Godunov*, airs by Ravel and Debussy and, especially,

César Franck's *Toccata and Fugue*, which the mother in Visconti's film *Sandra* could not remember. There were memories of La Scala, too, with little Luchino and his mother together following the scores of works, often while Toscanini was conducting them.

The boy was less than six years old when he first watched a performance from the family's box in the first row to the left of the stage, directly above the 'mystic pit', an orchestra-level salon lined with red damask and hung with mirrors. 'We were at home in La Scala, and our box was just what was needed to fire our imaginations, which were probably more oriented towards plays; it was Number Four, close to the stage, with the orchestra pit at arm's reach and the blare of the brasses instantly reverberating among the timpani.'

No one could resist the show, that great festival of ritualized gestures, melodramatic movements, colours, odours and brilliant voices. 'My first recollection of La Scala,' Visconti said, 'is not musical.' It was connected with a ballet entitled *Pietro Micca*, based on the glorious sacrifice of this Piedmontese hero of Italy's struggle for independence: he had sent his companions away and then blown himself up, destroying an underground gallery dug by French sappers and thus saving the fortress of Turin from capture. 'The truth is,' Visconti went on, 'all I remember of this ballet is the glowing, curling fuse, the explosion, the acrid smell of gunpowder that spread until it even invaded our box . . .'

An 'explosive' place, La Scala, full of thunder and lightning that was more theatrical than musical. The roar of applause there echoed long afterwards in Luchino's ears, and he would always remember the house 'full to bursting, with a tremendous din'. His childhood was marked by the exaggerated, magical lighting, the gaudy glare that bathed operas by Verdi, Puccini, Wagner, Strauss. Like the French novelist Michel Leiris, but earlier than the author of *l'Âge d'homme* (*Manhood*), he had 'wept for the death of the couple in Verona, exulted at the ballerinas in tights, the gilded cardboard silhouettes, the lighting and other grand effects of Walpurgisnacht, had quivered when the clown Rigoletto mistakenly slew his daughter, shared the horror of Rhadames and Aïda doomed to suffocation in their underground prison, quit Mount Salvat with the Knight of the Swan, drained the cup of madness with Hamlet . . .'

The mythology of the major repertory operas 'fired the imagination' of the young and ardent Luchino. Its influence was reinforced by silent films, with their processions of great historical figures – Agrippina, Brutus, Julius Caesar, Garibaldi, even ancestor Marco Visconti – and their grandiose dramas of antiquity (*The Last Days of Pompeii, Quo Vadis, Cabiria*) in which the stars whom people were beginning to call divas glittered in an aura of doom.

Of all the Visconti brood, Luchino was the most passionate, and the most disconcerting. 'He would sometimes come in like an avalanche,' his governess said, 'hurl himself into my arms, then, shoving me away, would race off as fast as he had come. I shrugged and laughed and treated him like a lunatic. His reactions were so unpredictable . . .'

Count Giuseppe had a soft spot for Luigi, and Donna Carla for Guido, her eldest and most delicate child. Luchino worshipped his mother totally, jealously, anxiously. As a child in Cernobbio he would search the house if he lost track of her, Uberta tells us, opening every door in the huge mansion; when he finally found her, he would shout 'She's here!' with an air of breathless triumph. He was only three in the marvellous photo that he would keep with him throughout his life: Donna Carla kneeling and smiling, her eyes lowered, her cheek against his, hugging her son to her, and he, looking fierce, standing with her hand pressed to his heart, his eyes glaring at the camera as if challenging anyone to try to come near them or separate them. 'He was very jealous of mother's affection,' his sister Ida says, 'of her demonstrations of affection.'

Every evening, like the narrator of *Remembrance of Things Past*, and especially on party evenings, Luchino waited to hear his mother's footsteps and the silken swish of her gown on the stairs. Then would come that instant when, exuding the subtle scent of Chevalier d'Orsay, her shoulders veiled in masses of pastel-coloured tulle and with fresh flowers in her hair, she would bend over him and he would feel her soft cheek and the reassuring warmth of her pearl necklace.

Every evening at midnight Donna Carla came into her children's rooms, her fingers brushing their foreheads, covering them if they had uncovered themselves, kissing them lightly, being careful not to wake them. Luchino would duplicate these gestures, displaying the same maternal tenderness, with the two 'little ones', Ida, nicknamed Nane, and Uberta. 'When he came in late,' Uberta says, 'he always stopped in our room. He tucked us in and asked us, "Are you thirsty? Do you need anything?" When he finished fussing over us we kicked off all our covers to make him stay with us.'

Yet there was rebellion and conflict, too, in Luchino's relationships with his parents. As much as his outrageous pranks, these earned him the nickname Luchinaccio, or Chinaccio, 'naughty Luchino'. He often hid, sometimes in the attic, after a row with his father or someone else in the family, but occasionally he simply hid for no particular reason. Once he climbed high up into a tree and calmly watched people searching for him below.

People who live on Lake Como know about its deep whirlpools. When he was nine, Luchino, whose 'imagination was always working', said Mlle Hélène, 'was excited by the idea of taking a small dinghy tied up at the Cernobbio villa's landing stage and going to the whirlpools. He had read *Malombra* and seen the movie version played by Lyda Borelli, a famous actress of the period. Romantic as he was, he was fascinated by the story; when we stepped out in the evening, he always wanted to go on the water at sunset. So whenever Luchino went missing a bit too long, everyone ran to see if the dinghy was still at its mooring.'

Antonio Fogazzaro's novel *Malombra*, written at the end of the nineteenth century, is set against a background of violent storms on Lake Como; it tells a tragic story of an aristocratic family's revenge. Luchino was as mesmerized by the atmosphere of mystery and morbid passion as by the 'satanic' Countess Marina de Malombra, a character haunted by the 'evil shadow' of hereditary madness. Once, when all the children were innocently playing, one of the nannies noticed that Luchino had disappeared again. The countess was informed, the dinner bell was rung, the lake was searched with poles, as at the climax of the Visconti movie *Ludwig*. Luchino was finally found happily devouring strawberries and raspberries in the kitchen garden.

'I have never seen the countess so angry,' the governess wrote. 'She roundly boxed Luchino's ears and sent him packing to the house. She railed at him to herself: "Little monster! Insufferable child! Heartless! Dangerous lunatic! I'll send you to boarding school –" She told me: "Take him away or I'll kill him. He is to go to his room and stay there." For several days, we saw Luchino only at his window. He was in quarantine, eating alone, not speaking to anyone.'

Such stern punishments were rare in the family. Luigi had once locked the cook in the ice-box, allegedly for refusing to feed him. Worse still, he hid the key and refused to tell anyone where it was. Luchino finally found it in a vase the children often used as a hiding place, and the cook was released, suffering nothing worse from his ordeal than a bout of bronchitis. As Luigi's sole punishment, he was deprived of movies and the theatre.

Did Luchino, more anxiety-ridden, more jealous than the other children, feel less cherished than they, more harshly treated? Art for him was primarily a way to charm people, an assertion of personal superiority that showed itself in his precocious musical gifts.

The Visconti children's teacher of harmony was among the first to notice this talent. 'Professor Perlasca,' reported the French governess, 'had devised a special method for studying music. Each of the children had a big box containing a large cardboard musical staff folded into three panels. Also in the box were closed compartments of notes – whole notes, half notes, quarter notes, quavers, etc., clefs, sharps, flats, rests and crotchet rests, in short, everything used in writing music. The teacher sat down at the piano and played four or five bars. Then the children literally hurled themselves at their boxes, competing to be the first to note down the melody, with its rhythm, tone and accents. Luchino was certainly the most gifted for this exercise. He literally played with the notes, so he became the teacher's pet even though he teased the man. He had noticed that the teacher was a bit sweet on me, and in the middle of a lesson he would say things like: "A golden thread comes out of Professor Perlasca's heart and goes to meet Mlle Hélène's."'

At fourteen, Luchino was already up to playing Benedetto Marcello's *Sonata in Two Quarter Time* at a public concert in the Milan conservatory; his 'splendid mastery' of his instrument, said the Milanese daily *La Sera* on 9 June 1920, foretold a promising career as a cellist.

His most notable early successes, however, were in theatre. 'Very early on,' he recalled, 'we tried to create theatre at home, in a cloakroom. I directed and acted. *Hamlet* was my favourite role. The leading actress was little Wanda Toscanini. We rehearsed for an hour every day and on Sunday we gave our performance.' Luchino had the last word on casting, set design, the choice of plots and plays.

Before tackling abridged versions of Shakespeare plays in which the young actors did more improvising than reciting, he staged shows he wrote himself – *The Tyrant*, for example, which won, for the first time, what he considered top honours: his mother's applause. Then came an opera, *The Rose of Bengal*, for which he wrote the words and music and which was produced in the family theatre in 1914.

'Even today,' he later commented, 'I don't see how I did it. The problems were greater than any I've encountered since then. I turned my same old brothers and sisters and cousins into singers, and the scores were difficult, complicated. There were betrayals, thefts, brawls and duels, an endless series of situations that crossed and interlocked and unravelled. And with it all, there was the music!'

Mlle Hélène adds some details on the show: 'Luchino, who had a pretty voice and a peach-fuzz complexion, was a perfect prima donna. Luigi was the conquering knight. He was the tenor. Didi played the noble father. As small as he was, he sang in a basso profundo. Bobolino, the eldest of the Castelbarcos, had to be the traitor who wanted to rape the heroine, the Rose of Bengal. It was very dramatic. There were lots of rehearsals. We all helped out. Anna and I made the costumes on Luchino's instructions. Since it all happened in Bengal, the costumes were oriental. The countess ransacked her wardrobe of evening gowns to provide fabrics for us. Luchino, as a dancing girl, wore billowing chiffon pantaloons and a long veil, but we didn't know what to do about the long hair the role required. All these preparations amused the count, and he finally saved us. He brought some tow from which we made a magnificent blonde wig with long braids.

'When everything was read, we sent invitations to the family (who paid admission). It was such a success that we lugged suitcases (containing the costumes) to several friends' houses to give performances.' What Mlle Hélène did not say, but Luchino mentioned later on, was his princely, highly theatrical gesture the next day: 'I was lounging in the sun on the balcony while my brothers and sisters and cousins were playing in the courtyard. So I grabbed the [box-office] receipts and threw them down shouting, "For my actors." After that outburst I was confined to my room with my pug.'

Through the theatre, Luchino could rival his father. Like the count, he wrote plays – not comedies, like his father's, but nobler tragedies and even opera librettos. On such occasions the entire household, including the servants, was mobilized. In his film *The Damned*, the young cellist Gunther plays before the assembled family on grandfather Joachim Essenbeck's birthday, in a scene that conveys beautifully the homely magic of performing in company, of putting on a show. A slow, intricate flow of images and music, nocturnal and meditative, begins with an inset portrait of the dead father, linking him to aristocratic old Joachim and then to the rest of the household – the servants in their goffered caps, Uncle Konstantin, the aunt, the little girls – until the camera stops in a close–up on the governess's tormented face.

Music binds Gunther to his family, especially to his mother, who in many ways resembles the mother of Thomas Mann, the venerated author of *Buddenbrooks*: in her distinctive beauty, her worldliness, the fondness for luxury – which she (like Donna Carla) never allowed to intrude on the care of her children – and, finally, in her love of music, especially Chopin's. Mann, too, spent hours listening to the 'practised, sensitive and delicately sensuous playing of his mother, who most truly and fully expressed herself in Chopin's études and nocturnes'.

When Luchino's mother died, he inherited her piano. He kept it all his life. The passion for music that linked mother and son never faded, especially their love of romantic music, which novelist André Gide's mother so feared would sicken her son's nerves and senses.

A fascinating and ambiguous figure, Donna Carla. She was a commonsensical, rational, realistic, orderly woman. Yet co-existent in her with these strong, sober traits were the passionate excitement, the unfulfilled aspirations and wild dreams she transmitted to Luchino. 'From *Bellissima* (*The Most Beautiful*) to *Rocco and His Brothers* and *The Damned*,' he later remarked, 'the doting mother transmits her enthusiasms and her errors to her children along with her problems, her traumas and her aspirations.'

A single image of a woman secretly loved and desired unites the idealized maternal figure in *Death in Venice* – the veiled, morally spotless matron watching her still childish son run laughing towards her across the Lido beach with his gift of seashells – with the night-roving, demoniac Sophie von Essenbeck abetting her son Martin's perversions and vices in *The Damned*. In *Venice* this figure remains unassailable, enveloped in a platonic aura of adoration; in *The Damned* she withers and dies in the profane throes of incest.

On her converge all of life and all artistry. Around her revolves all ceremony, as at the Christmas festivities in *Ludwig*, in which Cosima Wagner, holding her newborn child in her arms, receives her husband's musical tribute, the *Siegfried Idyll* (which Toscanini found on the back of the original score of *Parsifal*). The children gathered around the huge, lighted tree recall the Christmases of Luchino's disciplined but gilded childhood, when trees were raised in the courtyard and gifts piled at their feet. The day would come, however, when the spell would break; tragedy would erupt around the Mother, the 'Queen Bee', and the two sides of the family would separate forever.

IV

THE TWO STRAINS

*Nothing could be more different than these two
families . . . I often told myself that I was
forced to make works of art because only
through them could I harmonize these too
disparate elements – which would otherwise
have kept on battling, or at least debating,
within me.*

ANDRÉ GIDE, *"If It Die . . ."*

Summer interrupted the orderly household routine. The excitement
of imminent departure filled the house. In a soft rustle of tissue
paper, summer clothes were carefully folded and laid in trunks.
With its inevitable escort of nannies, footmen and housemaids, the
family left the stifling city to while away the summer at one of two
large estates, the paternal castle in Grazzano, or Villa Erba, at
Cernobbio, on the shore of Lake Como.

In Grazzano, nine miles from Piacenza, the medieval castle is
covered by Virginia creeper and screened by poplars. It is massive,
square, with round towers at the four corners linked by crenellated
walls looming above a dry moat. The grooves that once housed the
drawbridge chains are still visible in the main gate.

Legends galore enshroud the castle's origins. There is, for example, the picturesque and rather cosy story of the White Lady, who
was caricatured in a small statue that used to greet visitors at the
entrance: a dwarf, round as a keg and wearing a hennin. Her neck
and arms were covered with jewels of all sorts that no one dared
filch for fear of angering her; since the Middle Ages, it was said, she
had roamed the castle halls at night, vengefully troubling the sleep

of those who failed to pay her a ritual tribute of jewellery – bazaar junk or solid gold, she didn't care which.

Other stories more in keeping with the castle's history told of murders and hasty hangings and the bloody suppression of peasant uprisings against their tyrant masters. Some say that Gian Galeazzo Visconti, that industrious builder of castles, erected this one for his daughter Valentina, and that it was the scene of her marriage to Louis d'Orléans, brother of France's King Charles VI, towards the end of the fourteenth century. It was from Grazzano that the princess is believed to have left for France, escorted by a thousand horse and bearing in her train part of her prodigiously rich dowry. She was nineteen, her husband seventeen. With her for her triumphal entry into Paris was Charles's queen consort, Isabella of Bavaria, her cousin and sister-in-law.

Charles soon began to show signs of insanity; periods of delirium alternated with calm spells in which he recovered all his faculties. Before long it was being whispered in the queen's entourage that the king was bewitched, or was being poisoned. Valentina, the Italian woman whose voice and words, whose mere presence, so mysteriously tranquillized the mad sovereign, was of course suspected of being the witch who was poisoning him and causing him to lose his wits.

The rumour served the dark ambitions of the Bavarian queen. 'The common gossip runs through the kingdom of France,' reported the chronicler Jean Froissart, 'that Valentina employs such arts that so long as she be near the king, and the king see her and hear her speak, he will not be rid of the ills that consume him.' She was confined to the castle at Asnières. Her husband was assassinated. She then was exiled even farther from Paris, to Blois, where she lived on for a few years with her son, the future poet Charles d'Orléans. On the funnel she chose as her emblem she inscribed her melancholy motto: '*Rien ne m'est plus, plus ne m'est rien*' – 'I have nothing, I value nothing.'

We do know that the Visconti castle in Grazzano was the object of battles and bitter rivalry in the early fifteenth century with the Anguissola family of Piacenza, who, in fact, were bound by numerous marriage ties to the Viscontis. We know it was the scene of bloody clashes between rebellious peasants and Francesco

Sforza's troops. In the sixteenth century, Count Giovanni Anguissola plotted there against Pier Luigi Farnese, who took revenge by confiscating Giovanni's fief; it remained in Farnese hands until it was restored to Count Alessandro Anguissola for his bravery and skill at the battle of Lepanto and in fighting in the Low Countries.

Not until the end of the nineteenth century did the fortress revert at last to its original owners, the Viscontis. In 1870, the last of the Anguissolas, Marquess Filippo, was caught in the teeth of a mechanical harvester and died. His mother, Marchioness Fanny Anguissola, a Visconti Litta di Modrone, inherited the castle, and she willed it to her nephew, Duke Guido. In 1902, he in turn left it to his son, Count Giuseppe, on whom King Victor-Emmanuel soon conferred the title of Duke of Grazzano.

Giuseppe was not satisfied merely to restore the fortress to its original state. He razed the hovels around it and, some distance away, laid out a complete village, with homes, public buildings, parks, statues, a theatre and a chapel. On all of these he sought to impose the medieval style of the family castle. Henceforward, not only visitors and tourists, but the villagers themselves, for whom he designed a suitably historical costume, mingled in a kind of stage set: houses had pointed or clover-leaf windows, loggias, Gothic-style balconies, crenellated towers, timbered porches; wall niches sheltered statues of the Virgin. There were fountains and wells, porticos and arcades. The charade continued inside the houses, with vaulted chambers, coffered ceilings and Gothic furniture made by local carpenters and blacksmiths.

'I often stayed at Grazzano, near Piacenza,' wrote the Duchess of Sermoneta in 1947, 'a fine old pile of grey stone with four massive towers at its corners. Tall poplars grew in the moat and the Virginia creeper hung in garlands of flaming scarlet round the courtyard where the white pigeons fluttered near the well.

'Giuseppe Visconti took great interest in his home and had rebuilt the entire village of Grazzano that stood outside the park gates. Once it had been a squalid conglomeration of ugly houses and now it was so picturesque that passing motorists constantly stopped to admire the little piazza and campanile, the inn with its signboard bearing the Visconti coat of arms, the small shops under the porticos, all this festooned with creepers and every window gay with flower pots. Visconti had even established a school of drawing at Grazzano in which the village boys received training and were afterwards given a start in various workshops, making furniture, wood carvings and wrought-iron work. Everyone was hammering away contentedly and earning good money; they could not execute orders fast enough.

'The Duke was his own architect, and supplied designs and ideas to the various artisans and craftsmen. When he walked about his village, so tall and handsome, with his iron-grey hair and fine features, it was remarkable to see the affection with which he was greeted on all sides . . . He knew every soul in the place, and no decision was taken in any family without consulting him. His three daughters had many friends in the village and would walk about with them on the piazza in the evening, while their father sat in front of the inn, talking to the local men.

'Giuseppe Visconti had designed a picturesque peasant costume that the women of Grazzano wore every Sunday and when there were dances at the castle or other festive occasions. There was a delicate thought behind this rather theatrical institution: he wished his daughters and the humblest girls in the village to be dressed alike . . . He looked after [his people] when they were sick, amused them on feast days with the pageants or lotteries he organized, and was always ready to help them with his wise advice . . .'

So to this miniature fief, which today has some 300 inhabitants, the Viscontis brought not terror, as their ancestors had done, but prosperity, hospitality and courtesy. It is a place where allegorical statues consort with votive columns topped by a madonna or a benedictory angel or Saint Francis talking to the birds. In the centre, imitating a medieval town hall, an imposing crenellated building houses the Visconti Modrone Institution, the count's crafts school. From the bluish stone clock tower beside it, shrouded in ivy and Virginia creeper, a carillon sounds the hours.

Everything in Grazzano celebrates the glory of the Viscontis: the family arms recurring on the houses' pink brick walls, the family emblems of a serpent devouring a babe* and of a radiant sun, and

*See the section on *The Guivre*, p. 419.

buildings commemorating the family's more recent history. The Luigi Visconti Day Nursery, for example, was built in gratitude for divine grace granted to Donna Carla: when Luigi fell severely ill soon after his birth in 1905, his mother detached a pearl from her necklace and donated it with a vow to build the nursery if the boy recovered. He did, the building went up and a motif of pearls decorating the outside of the building recalls the event.

The whole village was dedicated to the Virgin Mary, beginning with the frescoes painted by the count – the retable in the small marble chapel and, especially, the composition decorating the crafts school, in which Don Giuseppe pictured himself, surrounded by his family and friends, offering his Foundation to the Madonna like a Renaissance lord.

Was the count an 'enlightened' feudal lord who had strayed into the twentieth century, a bit like King Ludwig II of Bavaria? Or was his village simply an extension of his love of theatrical décor, of masquerades and Carnival balls?

Every year when the wine grapes were harvested, a grape festival was held. The men of the village dressed in velvet, their wives and daughters in red-and-white dresses embroidered with scarlet carnations, the emblem of Grazzano. Everyone watched the cortège of lords and their ladies (the castle's noble guests) go by in their long-veiled hennins, their jewels of gold and precious stones and their gowns of velvet and brocade. Everyone escorted the castellan's lady to her throne, where she received the ritual tribute: a basket of gloriously sun-ripened grapes.

The village of Grazzano was, in fact, more than a prince's whim, more than one of the period's most worldly and exclusive gathering places for such guests as stage stars, royal courtiers, even the queen, who endowed the chapel with a gold filigree cross in memory of a stay at the castle. For Count Giuseppe was also a shrewd business-man, the richest of the Viscontis, and he turned tiny Grazzano into a flourishing tourist centre with its craftsmen and souvenir shops dispensing GiViEmme scents (*Gi*useppe *Vi*sconti di *M*odrone), the count's own brand, and a gastronomes' haven, the Serpent Inn. Anticipating possible criticism from visitors, the count had inscribed on the inn's façade an enigmatic motto in Gothic lettering on an escutcheon showing a red carnation:

Otla.ni.ad.

raug.e.eneta.

pipmi

Imitating Leonardo da Vinci's mirror writing, the cryptogram reads, from the bottom up: *Impipatene.e.guarda.in.alto* – Go ahead and scoff, and then look up.

To the children, the castle with its towers, spiral staircases and dim corridors, its galleries and armory and its fierce dogs was a marvellous playground, a setting for adventures and dreams. A haunted castle amid centuries-old trees! Perilous forays on to the roofs, despite repeated warnings from the children's parents! The mysterious emblems and legends and history! In such a setting, the young Viscontis could not help feeling as if they were reliving *Hamlet* or *Il Trovatore*. In Grazzano, their mother wore gowns that looked like costumes and recalled Mariano Fortuny's historical paintings. Once she posed in all her finery for a photograph beside the well emblazoned with the Visconti arms; in her midnight-blue gown misted over with pale blue veils, and with her regal carriage, she *was* Leonora, the heroine of Verdi's *Il Trovatore*, beloved of both the Count de Luna and the rebel chieftain Manrico, one of rebellious Luchino Visconti's favourite characters.

Through such scenes the boy could peer into the shadowy Middle Ages in which his ancestors had been so eminent and which Verdi had re-created. From earliest childhood he was familiar with the dense web of history that binds the centuries together. His enormous sensitivity to the colour of each epoch, to the vanished codes of customs and manners that his directing would later re-create on film stemmed neither from scholarly research nor mere vague romanticism. He had been presented at birth with the keys to the kingdom of time.

No place was more nurturing than Cernobbio, the pre-eminently maternal stronghold. 'Everywhere,' André Suarès wrote about the shores of Lake Como, 'mountains enclose a world walled into its own happiness.' The French writer Paul Morand told of stopping there in 1908 to wait out 'the dog days in that Lombardian hell that roasts even the leaves of the willows on the banks of the Po'. And he recounted a foray into the Tremezzina chestnut groves, where the air was as cold as marble, and where he breathed the same fragrance that Fabrice del Dongo smelled while crossing those very woods on his way to Waterloo in Stendhal's novel *The Charterhouse of Parma*.

No setting is more conducive to great flights of imagination. Here, in the late eighteenth century, came the liberal aristocracy of Milan and Venice to plot against the Austrians – the Melzis d'Eril, the Arconatis, the Arrivabenes and the celebrated Christine Belgiojoso, whose republican fervour earned her the nickname of Citizeness Guillotine. In their splendid villas bordering the lake they welcomed the French as liberators.

This is a region of wild and unpredictable storms, of bald mountains and tumultuous waterfalls, of deep woods filled with the slow, grave tolling of monastery bells; from here sprang those proud heroes of fiction, Stendhal's aristocratic Fabrice del Dongo, and Manzoni's silk-worker, Lorenzo Tramaglino.

And here, in the vast grounds, stood the two houses of Luchino's maternal grandmother. The larger of the two, Villa Nuova, was built at the end of the nineteenth century to certify the Erbas' new social grandeur. A lawn dotted with neo-classical statues ended at the lake and, in the 1920s, tourists might, with a little luck, suddenly see the statuary come to life. For on fine summer days, Luchino and Edoardo loved to strip naked, roll themselves in talcum powder or flour and then, already relishing the sensation they knew they'd make, they would race down to the lawn, topple the statues from their pedestals, climb up and assume their poses. Just as the lake steamer came level with them, they would dive into the water.

Villa Nuova was a square Palladian house with stone steps leading to a colonnade topped by the upper-storey balconies. The lines were massive, imposing, hardly lightened by the sculptured garlands and lion's-head consoles over the doors or the stone flames rising from pots crowning the cornice balustrade.

One came into a vast, square entrance hall and peristyle showered with light from high windows. The interior was laid out in a style that might be called neo-Renaissance Pompous. Everything was incredibly rich and refined: floors paved in blue and gold mosaics, honey-coloured marbles, painted foliage and flowers and masks, stucco angels cavorting in the mouldings. On the first floor was an immense ballroom and a procession of chambers with painted walls and ceilings framing pious masks and medallions. This was a whirl of colours and arabesques; Venetian crystal chandeliers glittered in tall, gold-latticed mirrors, glowing on consoles and seventeenth-century paintings, on door-frames in peach-coloured marble, on the blond marquetry of parquet floors and on gleaming, twisted black columns topped by chalk-white corinthian capitals.

So many rooms! There were studies lined with old books bound in gold-stamped leather and guarded by statues of Saints John the Baptist and Mary Magdalene. An old dispensary that Duke Giuseppe had personally painted with his coat of arms – the familiar radiant sun and the serpent devouring a babe – had been turned into a music room; mandolins, lutes and violins now filled the tall, bluish marble cabinets that, at the end of the eighteenth century, had held the jars filled with Carlo Erba's medicinal herbs.

The second house was called Villa Vecchia, the Old House, because it had been built in the Napoleonic era. It was less emphatic, more charming; its yellow ochre façade and blue shutters and statues composed a sober and harmonious whole. But for a long time, Uberta reports, it had stood empty, spoiled by its wooden facing. No one lived there; it served as a stable for grandmother Anna Erba's horses. Years later, Donna Carla set up an embroidery workshop on the first floor, where nuns worked. 'My mother had a shop in Paris,' Uberta says, 'but the woman who ran it was a swindler . . . We've always been surrounded by thieves.'

This was the house, with its neo-classical and Lombardian Gothic furnishings, to which Luchino Visconti always returned. Here, every summer, he saw his brothers and sisters, even during the second world war when, his sister recalls, she 'planted a whole lot of vegetables in the garden to have something to eat; since the villa was built on an old monastery, I always harvested bagfuls of bones'. In Cernobbio he finished editing his film *Ludwig* while recovering from the cerebral haemorrhage he suffered in 1972. In this house that was so much a part of his childhood dreams he slept in a boat-shaped bed on whose posts sat stylized swans straight out of the symbolic bestiary of Bavarian Ludwig. And when he opened his window at dawn, all the memories and ghosts of his childhood came to life.

'The power mower,' he said, 'couldn't cut the grass under the trees. I recognized the old sound of a scythe being sharpened. I walked with my sister [Ida Gastel, who owned the house] along a narrow path we had used as children; all the plants that had watched us go by so many years ago are still there. I found the book we were reading. I remember the old fears, the doubts that drove us to spend whole nights talking feverishly.' And here, in the first-floor hall-way, he learned to walk again after his stroke, in a sort of rebirth.

More than Grazzano, even more than the palace in Milan, the Erba villa ranked as the Mother House, through whose rooms and corridors he moved as naturally as blood through veins. Luxurious yet intimate, both a theatre and a nest, this was the archetype of all the homes in which he had once, long ago, been happy. It held the poetry of holidays, of a still united family: a childhood paradise, with the household awaking every morning to familiar noises, the dogs barking, servants' footsteps on the stairs, the beloved lilt of maternal voices, and, always, music.

Cernobbio, Mlle Hélène wrote, 'was paradise for the children. The grounds were so big that there were three gate-houses at each end. The count had a small African village built for the children. There were five tree houses where they could entertain, give dolls' dinner parties, make themselves at home.' All sorts of creatures roamed the grounds – peacocks, jays, horses, especially dogs.

Dogs came and went in the house. They weren't the tall, slender Russian wolf-hounds one expected to find in an aristocratic home, but hulking, powerful Newfoundlands whose 'eyes and pendulous, blood-red lower lips' terrified the French governess: 'They were almost always at the feet of their mistress' – the very authoritarian Grandmother Erba – 'who controlled them by tapping their muzzles lightly with her cane. The children played with them, pulling their tails and their ears, climbing on their backs as if they were lambs. I looked on, petrified.' The whole day was spent careering wildly about on bicycles, swimming, going on outings on the lake, staging battles and ambushes that the count liked to plan and lead. By evening, Luchino later recalled, the children, happily exhausted by their games, 'held sleepy faces up to their parents'.

The year-round rules and rituals of daily living remained intact in Cernobbio. There was no let-up in the social whirl in this elegant colony where Milanese high society summered; squadrons of rich foreigners as prominent as the Viscontis came as houseguests to the famous Villa d'Este: the Noailles, the Beaumonts, Russian princesses, as well as Sergei Diaghilev, the tsar of the Ballets Russes, Misia Sert and, soon, Coco Chanel.

'In Cernobbio, life was ample and comfortable,' Mlle Hélène wrote. 'We had lots of visitors and we made lots of visits, too.' Yet Villa Erba's charm remained intimate and domestic. Over sixty years later, Visconti was to recall that 'green paradise', those 'happy hours on the lake shore, when we made plans with my brothers and, from time to time, storms broke. Annoyed, we pressed silently against the rain-streaked windows. A storm knocked down the finest tree in the garden.' At such moments there was nothing for it but to expropriate one of the 5,000-piece jigsaw puzzles their grandmother had already begun to lay out on the green baize of the billiard table, ignoring her indignant protests.

'It's all still alive and real in me,' Visconti said. 'Sometimes we'd fall asleep in the grass in a late-afternoon slump, amid the rustling of grasshoppers and crickets . . . Then autumn came, grape-harvest time, and, saddened by the approach of the new school term, we harvested our crop of emotions and images and dreams.'

Of memories, too. Luchino's earliest memory is of a summer holiday when he was taken on an excursion into the Engadine mountains. He recorded it in his diary: 'Automobile trip to Chiavenna, where we had lunch while waiting for the car that was to take us up beyond Maloja (it was still hot in Chiavenna, but cool up above). Stopped at Cernobbio. The porcelain washbasin with slate-blue flowers. Porcelain dolls in the gutter at Chiavenna. All along the road, the heavily fragrant mountain pinks. *My mother* on the high rear seat, where we all took turns sitting with her. The others in the open car . . . We visited [Countess] Casati . . . Edoardo fell and hurt his chin . . .'

Other places would soon enlarge his holiday landscape (Paris, where his mother and grandmother loved to go), and especially the beaches on the Lido in Venice, at Rimini and Forte dei Marmi. But Cernobbio and Grazzano remained the home bases, where

Luchino's roots were. After his parents' final separation, the differences between the two places became still more symbolic of the division Visconti felt between his Erba and Visconti sides, between the two extremes of his sensibility.

It would probably be an oversimplification to stress the harmony which, for fifteen years, seemed to prove how perfectly Carla Erba's common – indeed, peasant – stock blended with Giuseppe Visconti's aristocratic lineage.

The nobleman, as we have seen, also had a middle-class flair for business; he had not merely 'taken the trouble to be born', and he taught his children that their birth did not confer unlimited rights on them. His generosity to the poor was exemplary. And the commoner who so often donned an apron, rolled up her sleeves and helped the caretaker's wife cook risotto had been brought up to the subtle code of fashionable society. The easy assurance with which she wore her elegance and culture was unmatched even by Queen Helen, whom she served as lady-in-waiting into the 1920s.

Moreover, both parents agreed on how much personal time and care they would devote to their children. 'What still surprises me,' Luchino later said, 'is how successfully my father and, especially, my mother managed to divide their time among business, their social life and their children.'

Donna Carla had a vitality her husband lacked. She was the one in the family who drove the others to venture, to face life, to look to the future. The Visconti di Modrone Foundation was a functioning enterprise, true enough, but it was primarily aimed at recreating the past. So much distinguished Don Zizi from his wife: his love of disguises and pseudonyms, of the theatre and the social whirl, his frivolous life, his interest in occultism, in spiritualist séances, in dreams (he tried but failed to persuade his children to record their dreams) – in other words, his flight from reality, and his flightiness, which extended to his morals and his love affairs.

Where Donna Carla was permissive and understanding with her children, Don Giuseppe was strict and apprehensive. 'In my family,' Uberta says, 'everyone rode horses well. That included my mother, a true Amazon. But I didn't. My father always kept me from learning. Mother profited from his absence during the war to train all her children to the saddle. By the time he came back, they all knew how to ride. Mother was infinitely less timorous; she thought people have to take chances.'

The Count's overanxiety made him a martinet regarding punctuality at table. Lateness might be a bad sign, might indicate an accident. An empty place at table worried him, as if it signified a death. For his superstitiousness was proof even against his wife's commonsensical arguments. The Viscontis had always loved dogs, cats, monkeys, all animals. But when the count was a child, a brother died the day a bird was brought home. From then on, Don Giuseppe tolerated no birds in his house; Uberta reports that caged birds had to be left outside.

Said the French governess: 'He had only one fault: he was superstitious and highly impressionable . . . Once, during a meal, a painting of one of his ancestors suddenly fell off the wall. The cord it was suspended from had snapped. The count rose and went to his room. For two days he awaited the misfortune he was sure would fall upon the house. Nothing happened, of course, and he got over it, but we had to be very careful not to do things that brought bad luck.

'At Cernobbio, one day I found some blue and black jay feathers I thought were so pretty that I gave them to Nane to play with. The count happened by. When he saw the feathers he blanched, took them out of her hands and asked who had given them to her. "I did," I said, embarrassed, "I didn't know."

'He didn't say anything, but I could see he was extremely vexed, and so was I to have worried him unwittingly.

'On another occasion, a little bird flew into the palace in Milan. He took this as another evil omen. The countess, who was not at all superstitious, tried to convince him that just as the cord on a picture frame might well break after so many centuries, a foolish little bird might well fly in through an open window without bringing bad luck. But he remained worried and upset for several days.'

How would he have behaved had he been present on an outing to the country that Mlle Hélène described? 'We had spread a tablecloth on the grass for a picnic when suddenly the cloth began to dance. There was a nest of snakes underneath it, and our cries brought everyone running, including the servants. We armed ourselves with clubs to kill [the snakes]. There were about twenty of them, but luckily they were all tiny. Only the mother was bigger. After the massacre, we burned the corpses . . .' This happened during the war, when Don Giuseppe was away from Milan. Expert as he was in reading signs and omens, how would he have interpreted this country picnic that had turned into a slaughter of snakes? For, call them snakes, serpents, vipers or dragons, they were inseparably associated with the Viscontis, on whose coat of arms they figure.

'And,' we asked, 'was Luchino superstitious?'

Uberta smiled at the question. 'No,' she said, 'not really. But he pretended to be. He defied such terrors.'

The screenwriter Suso Cecchi d'Amico, on the other hand, says Luchino had bouts of superstition. 'A medium lived next door to me and he would consult her, but he always came away disappointed. While he was working on *Rocco and His Brothers* he sometimes resorted to the pendulum.'*

In fact, doesn't toying with the occult forces require at least a modicum of belief? In 1939 Luchino had seen his birth on All Souls' Day rather than All Saints' as an ominous, 'shocking coincidence', an evil presage. But shortly before his death more than a quarter of a century later he declared: 'I belong under the sign of Scorpio: decision, coherence, struggle against the destruction of feeling . . .' Henceforward, reason and serene contemplation of his fate triumphed over the threat of the 'unlucky star', the 'evil shadow' whose malignant influence he had felt for so long and whose reflection he sought in characters of fiction whose very names bore the stamp of a hereditary malediction: Fogazzaro's Countess Malombra, for example, and Verga's Malavoglias.

Throughout his life he probed for meaning in the worrisome conjunction of the stars at his birth. Through his art he tried to exorcise the destructive forces connected with gloomy November, with the autumnal celebration of death and with everything commonly associated with the sign of the Scorpion: torment inflicted and suffered, an attraction to the abyss, an obsession with time, which destroys as it passes. In the empire of signs, however, Visconti had to face an even older and more mysterious monster:

---

*A form of divination based on the vibrations of a pendulum in the hands of an initiate (translator's note).

the fierce Serpent of the Viscontis, which again had obliterated the snake-entwined, fortune-bearing caduceus of Mercury, the reassuring symbol of the Erbas.

V

THE TWILIGHT OF EUROPE

An age of gold ended, another arose, edged in black.

PAUL MORAND

In 1971 Visconti declared that because he was 'born in 1906, I belonged to the period of Mann, Proust and Mahler'. A glaring anachronism that dismissed the time span covering his formative years and adolescence.

He was only nine when the first world war broke out, but he was sixteen when Mussolini seized power. Yet he claimed to belong – along with, say, Stefan Zweig – not to a time long past, of course, but to yesterday, a period that 'pursues us'. Visconti was born thirty-one years later than the youngest of the artists (Thomas Mann) with whom he asserted his affinity; all of them were born in the twilight of the previous century and they identified with something that was ending. Visconti's lapidary phrase also attempted to close a generation gap that might distinguish and isolate him from his parents. 'The world around me, artistic, literary, musical, was that world. It's no accident that I feel attached to it.'

To Zweig, this lost epoch was summarized in the Vienna of his youth, with its ritual, its rigidly hierarchical social structure, the great theatrical and religious celebrations which excited the city far more than politics or the army. Vienna then was Emperor Franz-Josef's impregnable fortress, where thousands of children gathered every year at the foot of the grand staircase at Schönbrunn Palace to sing Haydn's *God Save Emperor Francis* to him.

Visconti saw the period as less pompous, more cramped, a tissue of strict rules brightened by 'the pleasant life before the revolution' that seemed to guarantee the preservation of what he supposed was his parents' indestructible marriage. In hindsight, those years before the first world war, before Fascism, seemed a golden age of security. But this notion only came to him much later, after a myriad images, 'thousands of experiences, encounters, voices, sounds, colours, minute by minute' had been 'distilled' in his memory. Only then would he bring the period back to life in *Death in Venice*, to music by Austria's Gustav Mahler.

Venice as Luchino first saw it with the wonder-struck eyes of a child was no decrepit, decadent city with 'canals as black as ink'. It was still haunted by the shade of Wagner, by the memory of the torchlit funeral described by D'Annunzio in *The Flame of Life* and that Visconti later considered re-creating in *Ludwig*. Venice was not yet a capital of aberration, a meeting place for homosexuals who here, more completely than anywhere else, escaped society's condemnation of the 'accursed race', strolling, said Paul Morand, 'ringed and cooing like the pigeons in Saint Mark's Square'.

In D'Annunzio's novels, Venice was a mirror of countless *fin de siècle* eccentricities. Those of Marchioness Casati, for example, with eyes like embers and a mouth like flame, who walked the city with her Afghan hounds and her ocelots; the balls and masquerades she gave sometimes overflowed her palace of Non Finito into Piazza San Marco, which she had lighted by black torch-bearers in costumes copied from Tiepolo's paintings.

In such a setting, the aristocratic beauties of the day could safely wear the gowns designed for them by Mariano Fortuny, inspired by the paintings of Carpaccio and Titian: sugar-loaf doges' caps, velvet cloaks encrusted with antique gems, brocade coats streaked with elaborate gold arabesques, chiffon scarves floating over sparkling fabrics. All this harmonized with their palaces 'leaning like courtesans under the weight of their necklaces'.

The courtesans were, indeed, top of the line. There was Countess Morosini, who had made the Kaiser pine for her. And Luisa Casati, whom D'Annunzio boasted of having possessed in a gondola, 'nailing her to the silver coffin'. Even though Morosini was well past her youth, the two women sneered at each other in catty rivalry. At their first meeting, Casati told Morosini, 'When I was a child, my father used to tell me how beautiful you are.' To which the countess nonchalantly replied, 'We needn't go that far back: your husband used to tell me every evening how beautiful you are.'

Donna Carla was of the same world as her friend Luisa Casati, whose father, an extremely rich Viennese banker, had married her to a Milanese nobleman while she was still very young. It was a world in which gossip writers delighted in retailing the latest scandals and extravagances. Not even Countess Visconti's dignity, piety and charity could shield her from scandal-mongering. It was whispered that her beauty had exposed her to pressing attentions from admirers, that she had not been perfectly faithful to her husband, himself a confirmed Don Juan. Some less restrained reporters even added details to these vague but persistent rumours.

In the eyes of her children and her friends, however, she never betrayed the maternal image that her son was to project of her in *Death in Venice*. According to Luchino's boyhood friend Manolo Borromeo, in Venice in 1912 'Carla Visconti, Marianna Brivio – Donna Carla's mother – and my mother had two or three beach huts and they arrived on the beach with an escort of nurses and servants. In the evening they danced at Chez Vous in the Excelsior, or they might run across young Barbara Hutton and Princess San Faustino.'

A single scene in *Death in Venice*, capturing the light, the Lido beach, children at play, the watchful nannies and the children's attentive, imperious mother, sums up the bright joyousness of the holidays the Visconti youngsters spent with their mother and grandmother on the Adriatic, in Venice or in Rimini, beginning in 1912, the year after Thomas Mann stayed there. The Grand Hôtel des Bains had all the luxurious elegance of Proust's Grand Hôtel in Balbec – on which Visconti would have opened his planned adaptation of *Remembrance of Things Past*. And it had Venice's special brand of cosmopolitan charm, that of a society which, wrote Morand, 'was living its last hours between the Quadri and Florian cafés' before 'the old tree, Franz-Josef, buried everything in his fall'.

Venice was, first of all, where Europe met the East, 'the summer extension of the Ballets Russes'. It was the magic melting pot in which water and stone, past and present, even civilizations blended. Above all it was the sheltered gathering place of the great families. In that Hôtel des Bains, Mann wrote, 'one heard all the earth's principal languages spoken in hushed voices. Evening dress, the uniform imposed by custom, covered the divergences of humanity and reduced them to an accepted type. One saw Americans with long, lean faces, Russians surrounded by their big families, little Germans with their French governesses . . .' Had he come a year later, Mann could have added to his list the family group of the Visconti children, their German governesses and Donna Carla.

Only a few years later, Morand found another Venice, 'the walls of the Doges' Palace cracking. Saint Mark's [Basilica] smothered under fifteen feet of sandbags supported by beams and steel cable, the quadriga★ horses gone!' Gone, too, were Diaghilev and Nijinsky and Cocteau and Proust, who once strolled through the Piazza in white flannel trousers, with gardenias or tuberoses in their buttonholes, to the sound of orchestras playing Strauss waltzes.

Nothing foretold, however, that the radiant summer of 1914 would be different from any other. Or, even less, that a sudden storm would sweep away the pre-war civilization, shake most institutions, dismember empires, alter the map of Europe and even radically change the Europeans' way of living and thinking – that an unprecedented crisis would, as Zweig put it, bring about a complete break with the world 'my parents had inhabited as in a house of stone'. Years after the tempest, the pens of those writers most firmly planted in the pre-war world still trembled at the memory of the historic eruption that had hurled them 'into the maelstrom of life, uprooted from everything that held us, we – both the victims and the willing servants of mysterious powers – for whom comfort had become a legend, and security a childish dream . . .'

While agreeing with those he styled his 'contemporaries' that the first world war was a fundamental breaking point, Visconti always avoided the bathetic nostalgia, the rhetorical posturing that, in 1919, bewailed the death of a civilization with its 'millions of ghosts on a vast battlement of Elsinore stretching from Basel to Cologne, reaching the sands of Nieuport, the swamps of the Somme, the chalky earth of Champagne, the granite of Alsace'. The 'decadent' Visconti never fancied the role of an intellectual Hamlet. At most, he conceded in a diagnosis stripped of pathos, 'roughly between 1911 and

★The four sculptured Greek horses over the basilica's main portal (translator's note).

1918, in those fundamental years for understanding subsequent events, those years of complex cultural upheaval . . . for the whole European bourgeois culture, all the old difficulties came crowding in, all the old problems arose again in new guises, for the war swept away all the old solutions and the old ideals'. He refused to mourn that enlightened, middle-class Europe.

Luchino was still months away from his eighth birthday when the summer of 1914 began – too young to see the importance of the strikes and unrest that paralysed Italy during a week in June that came to be called 'Red Week'. They marked the rise of Socialism in the northern cities, especially in Milan, where Benito Mussolini, the most dynamic of the writers for the socialist daily newspaper *Avanti!*, had just won a victory in a municipal election. On 28 June, the day on which a Serbian student named Gavrilo Prinzip shot dead Archduke Franz-Ferdinand in Sarajevo, a small town in Bosnia-Herzegovina, Luchino was in Rimini with his mother, brothers and sisters. A month later, Austria–Hungary declared war on Serbia, the nations of Europe mobilized their forces and, one after another, entered the war.

The Viscontis returned to Milan under a changeless blue sky. They found the German fräuleins in a state of trepidation and the children wildly excited. Would Italy enter the war?

Premier Giolitti at first opted for neutrality; under the 1882 Triple Entente, Italy was not obliged to support Germany and Austria unless they were attacked. But for nine months, the country – especially Milan, the peninsula's most incandescent city because of the intensity of its political passions and the influence of its parties and newspapers – was plunged into feverish and stormy debate between neutralists and interventionists.

The war reawakened Milan's hereditary hatred of the Austrian invader and the Germans – *i Tedeskh*. The flame of the Risorgimento was rekindled. Donna Carla, a patriot and ardent Garibaldian, argued for Italy's entry into the conflict. Toscanini, whose father had been buried in his red Garibaldian shirt, blew up when his friend Puccini, bitter at French incomprehension of his music, spoke up for the Germans. The two men spent a good part of the summer together in Viareggio, and the conductor's daughter,

Wally, remembers that 'on the eve of the war, their discussions grew very heated. One day Puccini complained that things were terrible in Italy, that the whole country was in chaos, that everyone cheated, that the authorities were guided entirely by their own self-interest and that it was always the poor who paid. He concluded his speech by saying, "Let's hope the Germans come and put things in order." Dad flew into a beastly rage, leaped up, ran off and shut himself in the house. He said he wouldn't come out again because if he met Puccini he'd hit him.' The two friends finally made up their quarrel, but only by avoiding the prickly topic and confining their discussions to music.

Partisans of the war represented it as a crusade against the barbarism and injustice of authoritarian empires, but few were as inclined as Toscanini and Puccini to forbearance and compromise. The announcement on 3 August that Germany had invaded Belgium was seen as an intolerable violation of a nation's honour and independence. In Milan, shops and homes owned by Germans were sacked.

Reassertions of the great Risorgimentist principles were soon mixed with irredentist claims to Italian-speaking cities and regions still under foreign domination: Corsica and Nice, as well as Trento and Trieste. Perfervid orators advanced lyrical arguments for violence and war. Among the most fiery were the Milanese futurist writers. They abandoned their usual targets: tangos ('slow and patient funerals of dead genitalia') and the 'polyphonic purulence' of Wagner's music ('the candy floss of desire' that released floods of mystical tears). Instead they leaped aboard their old warhorse and declaimed verses glorifying 'the love of danger' and 'the cultivation of strength and courage'. This was a marvellous chance to exalt 'aggressive gestures, febrile insomnia, quick-step walking, mid-air somersaults, slaps and punches'. In September 1914 they gave a demonstration of aggressiveness by interrupting a performance of a Puccini opera to burn an Austrian flag on the stage.

This was the moment D'Annunzio chose for his flamboyant return from five years in exile (for debt) in France. On 5 May 1915, the anniversary of Garibaldi's departure from Quarto, near Genoa, on the Expedition of a Thousand to conquer Sicily, a monumental bronze memorial was inaugurated there. D'Annunzio, the 'bald sybil', made a vibrant speech heralding the coming of a new dawn: 'It is towards . . . this dawn that heroes arise from their graves . . . With their burial shrouds we shall renew the white stripes in our flags.'

A week later, after a series of poetic perorations in the same vein, he was welcomed to Rome by a throng of more than 100,000. Addressing them from his balcony in the Hotel Regina, he bawled: 'We want to confront cowardice with heroism. Italy must arm itself, not for a heroic parade, but for stern combat. Romans, here is the challenge!' And he flung his white glove down to the petrified crowd.

At the same time, Mussolini was also haranguing a crowd, this one in Milan's Piazza del Duomo, in an atmosphere so inflamed that people came to blows and gunshots rang out; one person was killed and eighteen were injured. Then representing the spearhead of the left, Mussolini had gone to prison in 1911 for promoting a general strike in protest against the war in Libya; in July 1914 he had head-lined an editorial in *Avanti!* 'Down with War!' Yet within two months he had come around to a belief in the need for armed conflict, which he saw as the best road to a proletarian revolution. Sacked from *Avanti!*, which he had edited since 1912, he started his own news-sheet with French money supplemented by contributions from a number of Italian businessmen.

On the masthead of *Il Popolo d'Italia* he balanced Auguste Blanqui's motto, 'He who has the weapons has the bread' with Napoleon's remark that 'Revolution is an idea that has found its bayonets.' From this new tribune, Mussolini threatened the king: 'We want war, and you, Sire, are empowered under Article Five of the Statute to send our soldiers to the front; if you refuse, you will lose your crown.'

And the king, with the complicity of his premier, Antonio Salandra, disregarded the opinions of the Parliament, of Giolitti, of the Vatican, the socialists, the liberals and the vast majority of the country. Instead, he heeded an ill-assorted minority of unrealistic, old-line pro-French conservatives, of men sincerely enamoured of freedom and justice and of diehard nationalists, all financed by the big munitions-makers. They were joined, in the person of young Mussolini, by a tiny fraction of the socialists.

In Queen Helen's retinue, interventionism was obligatory; she had been raised at the Russian court, where she had many relatives. And as a Montenegran, she lost no love on Austria–Hungary.

So Garibaldism, combined with loyalty to the House of Savoy, aligned the Visconti family in support of a conflict for which neither the country nor the army was prepared. On 23 May 1915, Italy finally declared war on the Central Powers.

'It wasn't our fault,' Visconti later said, 'that to us children the war was just a game . . . Day after day infantrymen marched cheerfully up the main streets and we were thrilled.' The German governesses were dismissed; Mlle Hélène would henceforward supervise the children's education. 'Our life was comfortable enough, if busy,' she wrote. 'It was because of the war. The restrictions prevented the family from operating on its usual grand scale.' The salons, the big dining-room and the count's office and workshop were closed. Everyone moved into smaller rooms that were easier to heat. Although the count had not been called into the army, he left for the front with an ambulance 'paid for', Mlle Hélène noted, 'out of his own pocket'.

The children, more excited than frightened by the parades, the bands, the drums, were alone for the first time with a woman who was now a wife only when her husband was home on leave. They didn't see their father for months on end, and they were living in a reduced household where the rules had been eased. Still they went on playing their old games, with Luchino obeying his impulses in organizing fancy-dress charades, impromptu concerts, games of hide-and-seek and sliding contests on the corridor floors.

Sometimes, says Manolo Borromeo, Luchino would suddenly issue a decree during the afternoon snack: '"No charades today, I want to play you something," and all the children had to listen to a Brahms recital.' When Donna Carla asked him that evening if his day with the Viscontis had been fun, Manolo replied glumly, 'No, Luchino played the cello all afternoon.'

Once, when Donna Carla went to meet her husband in Udine, she took Guido and Anna with her, leaving the remaining three boys with an elderly aunt and the servants. Within hours the place was a madhouse: children raced through the halls, ambushed the nannies and almost drew blood when Edoardo, the youngest, plunged through a glass door.

The youngsters knew virtually nothing of what the war was really like. When their father came home, his orderly told stories of his gallantry, of how he had rescued wounded men from the flames and from under rubble. Occasionally a young and pretty cousin, Maria Grapallo, came to visit wearing a cavalry badge on her gold bracelet. This started heated arguments among the children over the respective merits of the Novara lancers and the Saluzzo light horse. 'Luchino was for the latter,' wrote the French governess, 'and so was Didi. Luigi, Anna and Guido supported the Novara lancers.

'Later on, Guido, faithful to his favourites, became a lieutenant of lancers. There were endless discussions, and no one ever missed an opportunity to praise his favourites and criticize the others. The countess laughed and sometimes injected an ironic remark into the squabble when it grew too lively.'

The children's reveries about the war were fed by the more intense, more excited atmosphere in which they lived. Even at La Scale, a bustling Toscanini arranged performance after performance for the relief of air-raid victims and of musicians thrown out of work by the war. *La Traviata* (Teresa Storchio's farewell appearance), *Tosca*, *A Masked Ball*, *Falstaff* – Luchino didn't miss one of them.

Donna Carla was determined that she, like the Toscaninis, would take part in the war effort. With the governesses and her daughter Anna, she knitted gloves, scarves and balaclava helmets for the soldiers at the front. She took cigarettes, money and provisions to the wounded in the hospitals. Best of all, as far as the delighted children were concerned, she established a new custom: every Sunday, ten Italian soldiers were invited to the Visconti palace; she served them a copious breakfast (in the kitchen) then distributed money, cigarettes and gifts. Better still, she authorized her sons to bring home Allied soldiers they met in the street or at La Scala. After the youngsters fought a battle of confetti with five British soldiers at a gala in honour of the Allies at La Scala, the countess, who spoke fluent English, invited them to Via Cerva.

Another time, the guest was French. The children had noticed him, Mlle Hélène recalled, looking into a shop window one Sunday after the theatre. He was 'a little French soldier', she wrote, 'who disappeared under a helmet that was too big for him and that he wore rammed down almost to his eyes'. An oversized sky-blue cape swallowed up the rest of him. He was too good a prize to pass up, the children agreed; they decided unanimously that he was 'ploché', a word they invented for those they considered especially amusing and appealing and thus worthy of an invitation to Via Cerva.

The 'little soldier' turned out to be a spellbinding talker. 'Poetry spouted from him like a geyser,' Luchino later said. 'He told us about his friends huddled in holes full of mud and water trying to protect themselves from bullets and bayonets and to kill other young men crouched in similar holes and impelled by the same urge to kill rather than be killed.'

After dinner, the children and their mother gave him a recital of chamber music. Then Donna Carla and Luchino played a piece for piano and cello. At the end of the evening, the soldier fell all over himself thanking his hostess while, behind his back, the children wickedly imitated his gestures and his respectful bows. A few days later, flowers were delivered to Countess Visconti, along with some poems. One, dedicated to Luchino, was entitled *The Soul of the Cello*. They were signed by Léon-Paul Fargue.*

However, the war was not being fought, as Luchino might have imagined, in immaculate uniforms and polished boots. Conclusive proof came in the autumn of 1917, when Milan was invaded by ambulances carrying wounded men from the battle of Caporetto.

Toscanini had returned from the front horrified by the disaster that had swept over the Italian forces. A few months earlier, fed up with tacking little flags on a big map to follow the progress of the war from the communiqués in the newspapers, he had enlisted in the army. At the head of a marching band, he went off to accompany troops in training to the vigorous music of his military airs. But when the Italian high command, in the panic and disorder of defeat, ordered its forces to retreat, it forgot the orchestra in Cormons. Toscanini went on imperturbably conducting the prelude to the third act of *La Traviata* until the Austro-German advance forced him to flee. His daughter saw him when he returned. 'He

*One of France's best-known modern poets, Fargue was a disciple of Mallarmé and a friend of Gide and Paul Valéry (translator's note).

opened the door to the servants' entrance, ashen and filthy, his eyes swollen with tears. Mum, thinking something had happened to my brother, rushed to him shrieking "Walter! Walter!" My father murmured: "No, it's Italy. Italy is lost."'

Caporetto: 40,000 dead, 293,000 captured, 91,000 wounded, 300,000 soldiers wandering in the Veneto, two-thirds of the army's supplies and equipment lost. Because of the Austro-German break-through, which was finally stopped at the river Piava, the king considered abdicating. Some 700,000 soldiers were driven back nearly a hundred miles. Images of the collapse were registered by Morand in *Venises*: 'It was the end of the retreat on the Tagliamento, a front 300 miles long between Lake Garda and the Adriatic . . . In Brescia, Verona, Venice, French divisions tried to revive the Italians' courage . . . In the Red Cross trucks, wounded Senegalese and Neapolitans in hospital bathrobes mingled with bersaglieri whose plumes had been decidedly plucked, Austrian prisoners, Tyroleans in grey-blue uniforms, carabinieri who had swapped their three-cornered hats for helmets like Colleone's;* Russian prisoners rescued from the Austrians swept the quays with corn-husk brooms; on the walls, threatening posters ordered deserters from Caporetto to rejoin IV corps or risk being "shot from behind, like a pig".'

The shock to the public, heightened by the extreme privation they suffered during the last year of the war, was appalling, so strong that not even the victory of Vittorio Veneto a year to the day later could wholly relieve it. 'Heroes don't interest me,' Luchino Visconti would later say. In *Senso* he transposed the atmosphere of the Caporetto disaster to Custoza, where Austria defeated the armies of King Victor-Emmanuel II in 1866. Both victories were fruitless. The speech of Lt Franz Mahler, the deserter in *Senso*, to Countess Livia Serpieri could apply to both battles: 'What do I care if my fellow-countrymen won a battle today in a place called Custoza . . . when I know they will lose the war. And not just the war . . . And that in a few years Austria will be finished and a whole world will disappear – the one you and I belong to.'

*In Andrea del Verrocchio's equestrian statue in Venice, Bartolomeo Colleone, a fifteenth-century condottiere who for a while fought in the pay of the Vis-contis, wears a heavy, shell-like helmet (translator's note).

Another backward glance, this, at a war whose horror Luchino could only feel in flashes. Throughout those three years he went to the theatre, attended parties, went on holidays. Not to Grazzano, which remained closed, or to the Adriatic, but to the mountains, to a village near Bergamo called Cantoniera della Presolana, where they joined Carla Toscanini and her daughters. Or they went to seaside villas rented for a few weeks on the Ligurian coast, first in Alassio, then in Santa Margherita Ligure. Both were beach resorts with huge, pink hotels where Donna Carla went to treat the early symptoms of the lung disease from which she was beginning to suffer. But the children knew nothing of that. For them, as for the recently born 'little ones', Ida Pace and Uberta, the Riviera simply meant sheltered, radiantly sunny summers before the golden season of the grape harvest in Cernobbio.

Italy did not greet the end of the war with the explosion of enthusiasm that peace touched off in France. Those first weeks of euphoria could not erase the memory of 600,000 dead, the drop in the general standard of living, unemployment, the climate of disorder and insecurity that settled over the country after the troops were demobilized. Italy had hoped the war would bring it increased grandeur and prestige. Over the Treaty of Versailles, which granted the Italians some not insignificant advantages, arose a howl of protests joined by the Futurists, the Irredentists, Mussolini, Filippo Marinetti and D'Annunzio. Claims to Italian-speaking Fiume [modern Rijeka, Yugoslavia] and Slavic Dalmatia grew more strident after D'Annunzio proclaimed that 'Dalmatia belongs by divine and human right to Italy!'

Milan was again the scene of the most violent of these debates. La Scala became a political forum where moderate voices like that of the socialist leader, Leonida Bissolati, who championed the Allies, were drowned out by a chorus of insults, whistling and shouting orchestrated by Marinetti and Mussolini.

In *Goliath: The March of Fascism*, Borgese wrote: 'There had always been a measure of tolerance in modern Italy, at least in the big cities and in debates between political leaders . . . One often had the impression that the most inflamed political discussions, even strikes, were more play-acting than real conflicts, and that as soon as they ended everyone would go off to drink together and slap each other on the back. It is unheard-of that a man as respectable as Bissolati, considered an Aristides whose moral probity was held up as an example by his opponents as well as his disciples, should be treated as cruelly as he was that night at La Scala. It is as though a mortal blow had been struck at freedom of speech and of thought, and as if the foreign war had been followed by a bloodless civil war.'

First blood in that civil war was shed three months later, in Milan, with the burning of the *Avanti!* newspaper plant on 14 April 1919. On 23 March, Mussolini had founded his revolutionary 'anti-party', using the columns of his paper, *Il Popolo d'Italia*, to summon 'the surviving members of the interventionist party' to Number 9, Piazza San Sepolcro, in the heart of Milan, not far from the Visconti palace. Around a hundred people responded: nationalists, syndicalists, students and, of course, Futurists. In the three weeks following the formation of a 'combat group', brawls broke out between Socialists and Fascists all over the city.

Sunday, 13 April, was tumultuous. Socialists pillaged shops, stoned public buildings and traded shots with troops who charged the crowds. A general strike was called for the following day. After a rally near the Sforza Castle, a procession of some 10,000 demonstrators moved towards the Duomo. The Fascists were certain they were marching on *Il Popolo* to burn it down. Socialists and Fascists waged a vicious battle. That very evening, Mussolini resolved to torch the headquarters of *Avanti!*. Approximately one hundred men invaded the building, sacked the offices, burned the paper's files and pursued printers and journalists.

Had the Revolution come? 'We were all worried,' Mlle Hélène reported, quaking like Mlle Dombreuil in *The Leopard*, one day when the count came home later than expected. 'That was the troubled period when Mussolini was campaigning against the nobility and loudly declaring that the time would soon come when the rich would live in the attics and the poor would come down to the *piano nobile*, the comfortable first floor.'

Street brawls, strikes and riots marked the year 1919. Mussolini was by no means the most conspicuous of the small-time condottiere in those troubled times. D'Annunzio, disappointed that the war had ended so soon, abhorring the smell of 'the stinking peace', had already made headlines with his bold flights over Trieste and

Vienna, for which the king had awarded him silver and gold medals. Now he embarked on the tragic-comic epic of Fiume.

Under the motto 'Fiume or the sea' he formed a private army of twenty officers and two hundred men recruited from among the *arditi*, deserters and demobilized regulars dreading return to civilian life. On 11 September 1919, D'Annunzio boarded a convertible red Fiat 501 and led a line of thirty-five trucks out of Venice. Volunteers joined the column all along the road. At eleven o'clock the following morning, without offering the slightest resistance, Fiume fell to the fiery 'Poet of Beauty'. From a balcony he made his first speech: 'Italians of Fiume! In this mad and vile world, Fiume today is the sign of liberty. In this mad and vile world, only one thing is pure, and that is Fiume! Fiume is like a beacon shining over a sea of abjection . . .!'

Soon he announced that he was going to turn the city into a centre for world revolution. He wrote in a letter: 'Nowhere on earth does one breathe the air of liberty as on the Quenaro [the Kvarner Gulf], which is like a sea of the future . . . The true novelty in life is not there where Lenin's doctrine loses itself in blood but here where the bolshevik thistle becomes a rose of love . . . I am completely outside the code of sterile institutions and dessicated laws.' Everything he did affirmed his indifference to law: having 'I don't give a damn' embroidered on his personal banners, his piratical capture of ships loaded with food, and his attempts, so outrageous to the British, to invade the Dalmatian coast.

To apprise the world of his programme, he outlined his foreign policy in leaflets dropped on Paris from a plane. On another occasion, he sent aloft a pilot named Keller, a giant with a fiery red beard, to fly over Rome on a dual mission: to drop a chamber pot full of carrots on the Parliament on a day when Giolitti was to speak there, and a wreath of red roses on the queen mother's palace.

In *Il Popolo* Mussolini hailed 'the revolution, necessarily political in its first phase, which is already under way. Begun in Fiume, it can only end in Rome.' But he did everything he could to prevent D'Annunzio from reaching the capital, and to that end he appropriated some of the cash contributions his paper solicited for the 'regency' in Fiume.

On 26 June 1920, under threat of an Italian bombardment,

D'Annunzio at last capitulated. He withdrew to the shore of Lake Garda to bury himself alive in a villa called the Vittoriale, later described by Visconti as 'a pharaonic tomb where the poet sought more obscure obscurity'. Mussolini went to see him there on 5 April 1921, as if in tribute to the man who had supplied him with the liturgy and ritual of Fascism: the marching militia, the black shirts, the skull-and-crossbones insignia, the Roman-style salute and the war cry, 'To us . . . Eïa, eïa alalà!' D'Annunzio, too, had set the pattern in almost daily orations for the huge Fascist rallies at which the throng in massed chorus answered the orator's exhortations.

'To whom does Fiume belong?' he screamed.

'To us!' the throng shrieked back.

'To whom does the future belong?'

'To us!'

A future that had no place for D'Annunzio, and would ignore Fiume. The future belonged to a new dark age, one that began in Milan.

VI

YOUNG VISCONTI

How is it that the clouds still hang on you?

HAMLET, Act I, Scene ii

The family: a sort of inescapable fate.

LUCHINO VISCONTI

'A sort of flight to Varennes.'* So Visconti called the alarming trip that finally brought the procession of automobiles containing his family and its usual retinue of servants, nurses and governesses to the Italian Riviera in the summer of 1920. Since the end of the war, the spectre of the Russian Revolution had hung over Italy – a spectre given more than a semblance of reality by an economic depression, a rise in prices, especially of bread, the introduction of ration cards, turbulence in the countryside and a hardening of labour relations in the big industrial cities.

In Milan, the incandescent capital of Lombardy and a bastion of socialism, Mussolini was plotting his grab for power, on which Italy's destiny pivoted. Red or black? To the editor of *Il Popolo d'Italia*, black in 1920 was still the colour of the Vatican, and of Don Sturzo's People's Party. 'Today, two religions are fighting for dominion over minds and the world,' he said, 'the black and the red. Encyclicals are being issued from two Vaticans, one in Rome and the other in Moscow. We are the heretics of these two religions.'

After the war, all the parties had demanded a fairer distribution

---

*King Louis XVI of France, attempting to escape from his Revolutionary captors, was recognized and arrested in Varennes, in eastern France, in June 1791 (translator's note).

of the nation's riches through estate and wealth taxes, land redistribution and institutional reforms. 'The fall of the Hohenzollerns in Germany,' Mussolini said, 'the disintegration of the Habsburg empire and the flight of its last emperor, the Spartacus League in Berlin, the Soviet revolution in Hungary and in Bavaria – in short, all the extraordinary and resounding events of late 1918 and early 1919 – strike the imagination and arouse hope that the old world will collapse and humanity will reach the threshold of a new era and a new social order.' While he refused to wave the communist flag, as the Socialist Pietro Nenni did, Mussolini did formulate a democratization programme for the municipal election campaign in November 1919. His platform seduced Toscanini into adding his name to the list of Milanese Fascists, along with those of Mussolini and Marinetti.

So far, however, the fascist day had not yet really dawned; until 1921, the Socialists seemed to be triumphant. Little King Victor-Emmanuel shuddered when his speech to the new Chamber of Deputies was interrupted by the 156 newly elected socialist deputies shouting 'Long live the socialist republic!'. They then marched out of the Chamber singing *Bandiera Rossa* (*The Red Flag*).

'Revolutionary Italy Is Born!' proclaimed a headline in *Avanti!* the next day. Strikes flared all through the year 1920, on the railroads, in factories, the postal service, among schoolteachers. In Turin, Genoa, Milan, the red flag floated for weeks over occupied factories – more than three hundred of them in Milan alone in August 1920. Walls bloomed with revolutionary graffiti: 'Long live the Soviets!', 'Long live the Revolution!', 'Long live Soviet Russia!', 'Long live Lenin!', 'Power to the workers!' and 'The dictatorship of the proletariat!'. Over a thousand men in the carabinieri, the national police force, and in the Royal Guard, a new police corps formed to combat growing violence, died in street fighting between April 1919 and April 1920.

Public agitation, possibly spurred by businessmen eager to see the government use force, increased with the formation of the *squadre*, fascist goon squads armed with clubs, daggers, pistols and shotguns. Almost every night they rode out of the cities in trucks to commit mayhem. Sometimes they raided a socialist meeting place, beating up the occupants and burning down the building. The Erbas

certainly could never have foreseen the use these shadowy comman-
dos would make of the family's cod liver oil: they would invade the
home of a politician, preferably a Socialist, force him to swallow
glass after glass of the purge, then either leave him tied naked to a
tree several miles away or murder him on the spot.

What did the king and the government do about *squadre* terror?
Nothing. As early as January 1921, the Socialist deputy Arnaldo
Matteotti had denounced the authorities who, he said, 'look on
impassively while the law is massacred'. In June 1924, less than two
weeks after he had publicly denounced fascist fraud in the
parliamentary elections, he went missing. Consulted about what
attitude to adopt, the king merely remarked that his daughter had
bagged two quails in the sky over Rome that very morning. Matteotti's body was later found in a shallow grave outside Rome.

In fact, the police had been sitting on their hands since 1921.
Judges, prompted in advance to consider the 'patriotic motives' of
arrested *squadristi*, turned a blind eye to the sacking of cooperatives,
the arson attacks on Socialist Party offices and labour exchanges and
the killing of Socialist and Christian Democratic journalists. The
murderers were set free.

No one protested, for example, when Fascists in their black
shirts bearing the death's head symbol again set fire to *Avanti!* headquarters on 3 August 1922, and then ousted the socialist city government. D'Annunzio, strapped into a uniform weighed down with
medals, materialized on a balcony at the city hall and harangued the
crowd. On the following day, the most liberalist of Italy's
newspapers, Milan's *Il Corriere della Sera*, congratulated
Mussolini for so vigorously uprooting bolshevik subversion. The
Socialists capitulated in the newspaper *La Giustizia* on 12 August:
'The fascist squall is raging with the same destructive violence in all
the major centres. We must have the courage to admit it: the Fascists
are now masters of the field.'

Two months later came the March on Rome, blackmailing Victor-Emmanuel III with the threat of an insurrection that his army
could easily have put down.

On Sunday 29 October 1922, a telegram signed by General
Cittadini was sent to Mussolini at *Il Popolo*: 'His Majesty the King
requests you to come to Rome as quickly as possible because he

wishes to entrust you with the task of forming a cabinet. Respects. General Cittadini.' At 8:30 that evening Mussolini, wearing a bowler hat, spats and a stiff collar, boarded a train in Milan. He was later at pains to depict the March as a heroic conquest, but he marched on Rome in a sleeping car.

'Your Majesty,' he told the king on his arrival, 'I am bringing you back the Italy of Vittorio Veneto.' After an interview lasting three-quarters of an hour, the 'fascist king' and Il Duce appeared together for the first time on a balcony of the Quirinale palace. When a courtier asked Victor-Emmanuel what he thought of his new premier, the king replied, 'He is really a man of character and I can assure you he will last for quite a while.' Many young people then felt, like the writer Curzio Malaparte, 'ready for anything', burning to 'enlist in the service of the proletariat that yesterday was red and today is tricoloured'.

Luchino Visconti was just sixteen years old. He looked on as his Milan plunged into civil war; not a day went by without its ration of pillaging, violence, bomb blasts and dead bodies in the theatres. He saw red flags flying and blackshirts marauding; with pennants flickering above them like candle flames, bands of heavily armed *arditi* forced passers-by to doff their hats to fascist insignia. But to Luchino the crushing of Socialism, the rise of Fascism, the new dictatorship were all distant, like grotesques in a play. Patriotism and nationalism briefly drew him to the Mussolini he later saw as a 'clown'; for a while he wore the blue shirts of the young nationalists, who were soon incorporated into the ranks of the Fascists.

But where was this young Stendhalian to find his Bonaparte? Certainly not in D'Annunzio, whose books he devoured, but whose charade as the hero of Fiume 'horrified' and outraged him. Nor in his wrinkled little king with the quivering jaw and the badly tailored general's uniforms, whom he met at the Quirinale and at San Rossore, near Pisa, where he rode with the king's son, Umberto, also known as *Sciaboletta*, 'little cardboard sabre'.

Luchino never talked about politics. His father, like most aristocrats, felt a visceral loathing of the blackshirts, especially of Achille Starace, who became secretary of the Fascist Party in 1931. A war hero who had won so many decorations that Mussolini called him our 'walking medal', Starace joined the party in 1919 and had become a living caricature of Fascism and the Duce. He was in charge of all the theatrics designed to create a mystique of the new government. Short, skinny and arrogant, he embodied everything that Duke Giuseppe warned his sons against: vulgarity, ignorance and brutality. When the duke saw Starace's name in the paper, or when he met him at the Quirinale, he held up his index and his little finger in the sign of the horns, as an exorcism.

Duke Giuseppe's aversion to the man was not shared, however, by all the Viscontis. Uberto's son Marcello, Luchino's much older cousin, was to serve for six years as *podestà* (mayor) of Milan in the Thirties. Uncle Guidone – bearded, bicycle-riding, facetious Guidone – who now lived in Florence, would become a senator. In 1930 he organized an art exhibition at the Royal Academy in London. His opening address was a full-fledged defence of Mussolini who, 'taking the reins of state in his hands with the sole aim of rendering them to his king', showed himself 'worthy of his country's great historical tradition'. And more: 'Perhaps, outside Italy, public opinion as a whole does not realize how close to the brink Italy came after the war, when it was threatened by the most insidious dangers from Bolshevism . . . I think of Fascism as essentially romantic. No, it is not merely a dictatorship, it is a new social and political doctrine to which Italy owes its complete regeneration.'

Years later, Visconti would depict the split that Fascism caused in his own family by portraying the conversion of the aristocratic Essenbeck clan to Nazism. For the time being, however, his ideas were fuzzier, and he never missed a chance to discuss the issue with his father. Those sombre years of his anxious adolescence were, he said, 'full of uncertainty and rebellion'. His doubts did not filter into the shapshots of the period, in which he assumes haughty, disdainful poses and glares fiercely and defiantly at the camera. But sombre and rebellious they surely were, so much so that his parents finally lost patience with his poor grades in school – especially in subjects that did not interest him, notably science. Don Giuseppe and Donna Carla decided that a term at boarding school would do him good. They sent him along with his brother Luigi to a secondary school on Lake Como run with an iron hand by monks of the Salesian order. Instead of the expected quarterly report, Giuseppe received an astronomical bill from the local tea-room. He asked for an explanation from the good fathers. It was true, they confirmed, that a man came to the visitors' parlour almost every day to meet his two 'nephews', the Counts Visconti; he invariably brought them quantities of cakes which they generously shared with their schoolmates. How were the monks to know that the 'uncle' was merely a tea-room waiter abetting the fraud? The two boys were sent home to resume classes at the Berchet school.

'When I was young,' Visconti remarked, 'I rebelled against constraint of any kind. I always sat in the back of the classroom. I had a decided preference for literature and I lay awake whole nights reading – at fourteen I had read through Shakespeare. My room was buried in books, especially French books.' He plunged alone and excitedly into a prodigious cultural maze where no teacher could boast of leading him. Awesome bills from the Baldini and Castoldi bookshop, which Luchino raided for reading matter, arrived on Don Giuseppe's desk at the Visconti palace. 'When it comes to books,' he pleaded, 'forgive my impulses.'

At the same period, with classmates Corrado Corradi, Ignazio Gardello and the son of a musician named Gnecchi, he founded a small literary club and, at his own expense, published *Repliche* (*Retorts*) a volume of their writings. It included one of his pieces, a 'horrible' tale, he later said, called *The Blind Man*, a pathetic story of a man blinded in the war. A plan to adapt it for film was shelved because of his grandmother's death.

One day in 1922 he found his father deeply absorbed in a novel that had just been sent to him from Paris. 'My amazement at his interest,' Luchino recalled, 'made him interrupt his reading, and he told me he was pained at every page he turned by the thought that this marvellous novel had to end.' The book was *Swann's Way*, and Luchino followed his father on this long journey through *Remembrance of Things Past* that he would make again and again in his lifetime: 'I must have been around seventeen . . . It was really a fever . . . And that's where I remained: with Proust, Stendhal and Balzac.'

The duke was more interested in fashions and elegance than in politics. It was he, says Fabrizio Clerici, who gradually taught the queen – 'a beautiful woman, but who knew neither how to dress nor how to behave' – to act her part. He also produced shows for her at the Quirinale, living tableaux in which his own children acted. 'Luchino played in them too,' Uberta tells us. 'At the Quirinale there were some superb sixteenth-century tapestries; Luchino and Luigi, dressed as pages, came in and looked at the figures in them. The queen then said, "Ah, if only those figures could come alive." As she did, a moonbeam fell on the hangings, which opened to reveal another scene, this time with flesh-and-blood people. And butterflies, too; they were us, Ida and me, and we tried ponderously to fly.'

Visconti never spoke of these shows. What he always remembered were the performances Toscanini gave during his ten-year reign at La Scala: an unforgettable lesson, the only revolution that could have won his full support then. For on 14 July 1920, Toscanini had been granted absolute power at La Scala and had set about renewing it from top to bottom.

He began with an attack on privilege, banning the old associations, restoring the four rows of boxes to the public and abolishing the directorial monopoly formerly held by the boxes' hereditary owners, the old *palchettisti*, among them the Viscontis. At Christmas 1921, having single-handedly chosen his staff, set up a permanent troupe of singers and auditioned every member of the orchestra, the maestro opened the season with his favourite opera, *Falstaff*, the same one he was to mount thirty years later at the Piccola Scala in a version staged by his daughter Wanda's old playmate, Luchino Visconti.

After a moment of confusion caused by a bomb scare, the curtain rose on a bigger, better-lighted stage and an expanded orchestra pit. This kicked off a series that included, in addition to Puccini's *Manon Lescaut*, all the Verdi operas in which Visconti himself would seek inspiration: *La Traviata* in December 1923, *Il Trovatore*, which achieved unprecedented popularity in the spring of 1925, and *Otello*, *Don Carlo* and *La Forza del Destino* between 1927 and 1929.

Toscanini demanded more of his singers than just technical prowess; he also insisted on acting ability, the naturalness he wished to restore to opera. 'When you listen to Wagner,' he once said, talking about *Siegfried*, 'you can hear the leaves rustling . . . And then you look at the stage and all you see is painted cardboard. It's ridiculous! We can't present operas without murdering them. There is genius in the music; on stage we see fat singers in transports of emotion. What a fake!' Like Visconti later on, he attended every rehearsal, supervising all the details of acting and staging, teaching the singers how to move, what gestures to make.

Toscanini's influence on Visconti was probably enormous, says the composer Franco Mannino. 'They had similar ways of seeking the truth, the same love of authentic little details; neither ever accepted improvisation. They had inordinate energy, which they devoted to an uncommon ideal of perfection. They were giants who towered over us dwarfs.'

Said Visconti: 'Toscanini was La Scala. He was the idol of the Milanese.' He was Visconti's idol, too, and not only as an artist. Luchino had to admire the civic courage of a rebel who refused to post portraits of the Duce and the king in La Scala, standard practice in all other theatres and public places; who broke his conductor's baton and stalked off when, in December 1922, a group of Fascists wanted the fascist hymn *Giovinezza* sung before a performance of *Falstaff*. 'La Scala's artists are not vaudeville singers,' he fumed, 'and they will not sing that piece of buffoonery!'

Visconti would always remember him as the artist who 'was slapped because he refused to begin a concert with the fascist hymn'. That was in 1931. When he arrived with his wife and his daughter Wanda at the theatre in Bologna where he was to give two special concerts devoted to the music of his friend Martucci, his car was surrounded by young Fascists. Would he conduct the *Giovinezza*? He barely had time to answer 'No' before he was slapped in the face and roughed up. He went back to his hotel, where he was asked to give up his room before six o'clock the next morning.

He wasn't even safe in Milan any more. Blackshirts taunted him by singing the fascist anthem under his window on Via Durini. He had to wait another month before his passport was returned to him and he could leave Italy. He would not wave a baton or even set foot in the country until the second world war ended.

Relations between the Toscanini and Visconti families had nevertheless deteriorated during the Twenties. Not for any political reason. Why, then? Because of Wally Toscanini.

In 1920 the conductor's eldest daughter was twenty and a raving beauty. Since her childhood she had gazed in fascination at the Viscontis' box at La Scala, where Donna Carla appeared so swathed in 'clouds of mauve and grey veils' that Don Giuseppe's face was blurred by this ethereal mist. 'Countess Visconti,' Wally later said, 'was so beautiful that I tried to imitate her.' Like the countess she hid behind big fans of black and pink ostrich feathers and draped yards and yards of chiffon around herself. And, like her, she set shockingly daring fashions. She was one of the first girls bold enough to wear lipstick. She scandalized Milan by appearing at a ball with bare arms, and shocked it even more by becoming the mistress of Emanuele Castelbarco, Visconti's uncle and the husband of Lina Erba. She was one of those women, the film-maker said, 'who bring an element of disorder into life'.

Toscanini was extremely strict with his children, insisting that they be obedient and punctual. But Wally? 'She's the only work I was never able to direct,' he later admitted. One day Countess Lina Castelbarco came to him and, her voice racked with sobs, told him that Wally was wrecking her marriage; he learned that his daughter had been hiding her behaviour from him for years, that half of Milan knew about her affair and that Count Castelbarco had filed suit for divorce. The peaceful house on Via Durini was suddenly rocked by the Jovian thundering of paternal rage.

'He slapped me,' Wally recalled. 'That was the first time he'd ever raised a hand to one of his children.' Wally married Castelbarco in Hungary in 1930, but her father was not present. Even after the birth of his granddaughter Emanuela, Toscanini would have nothing to do with his son-in-law. They were not reconciled until 1933.

The affair scandalized Milan and profoundly disturbed the Viscontis. One day Wally came across a photograph of herself on which Luchino had written: 'Wally, in the days when she wasn't yet a countess.'

'What would you say,' she asked him, 'if someone wrote that on a picture of your mother?'

'That he was an oaf,' Luchino replied.

'Exactly! That's what you are.'

Their quarrel was soon made up, but it did show how sternly young Visconti felt about the 'disorder' Toscanini's daughter had brought upon her family just when the harmony between his own parents had gone sour.

'I don't know exactly why they separated,' Uberta told us. 'My father was a charming man, perfectly sweet, but quite frivolous, and he led [my mother] a terrible dance. [She] put up with it at first, until, at last, she'd had enough. She was very intense, and the break was final. It's hard for us to imagine since nowadays separated couples continue to keep up with each other, to see each other.' But Donna Carla broke for good with her husband, and with Milan, where she henceforth spent only a few months a year. When her daughter Anna married at Grazzano, the countess refused to cross the castle's threshold, and the ceremony took place outside.

While Carla Visconti's reputation may not have been immune from scandalmongering, and she lived a fairly free and easy life, Don Giuseppe, like Count Castelbarco, was reputed an impenitent Don Juan. When he founded GiViEmme, his scent and cosmetics firm, the names he gave his perfumes and colognes – Blue Countess, Narcissus in Love – were said to have been inspired by his most recent conquests. When he was named a gentleman of the queen's household, people whispered that he was Queen Helen's lover. He spent more and more time in Rome, in the house on Via Salaria that he had built alongside the royal Villa Savoia.

At the same time, other predilections were ascribed to this Lothario who wore powder and mascara to La Scala: not just women, it was said, succumbed to Don Zizi's charms. Gossips spoke of the impressive number of his young protegés who showed up in Grazzano when he died, and who were politely asked to go away. A story went that he not only refused to tell his name to one of his lovers – who probably knew it and spread the word – but warned him that 'if he ever learned his name he would disappear like Lohengrin, in a skiff drawn by a swan'. A skiff we would find again in the cave of the languid bears in Luchino's film *Ludwig*.

The countess, now Duchess of Grazzano, left the palace on Via Cerva and went home to mother on Via Marsala. Her three eldest children were to live mostly with their father, while the youngest, Luchino among them, went with Donna Carla. 'We, the two youngest, spent five months in Cernobbio and five months in Milan,' Uberta said. 'We didn't go to school; tutors came to the house. For the December holidays there were two Christmas trees, my father's and my mother's. The trouble was that when we were with my father we'd rather have been with Mother. And Father was jealous of that attachment; he was worried that we might prefer Mother to him. To Luchino our parents' separation was no tragedy. He'd probably have preferred that the family stick together, but he was already old enough, and we were too young; I must have been five at the time.'

No tragedy? The observation is contradicted by the obsessive theme of family disintegration running through all Visconti's future work. Disintegration, what's more, that inevitably entails the family's economic decline, and that is explained by a domestic crisis, a conjunction of moral corruption and mortal illness. In the 1950s Visconti considered filming a *Buddenbrooks* set in Milan that would have been an X-ray portrait of his own family. He planned to paint its grandeur and decline by following the story of three generations. The first was to be that of the pioneers, of Carlo Erba, if you like, and grandfather Guido Visconti, whose fortune was connected with the typically Lombardian silk industry which, after reaching its peak in the period just after the first world war, suddenly collapsed in the Thirties.

In Visconti's outline, the fall of the 'House' was not so much caused by external hard times as by disregard of its founding fathers' rule: be united like the fingers of a hand. 'The germs of the break-down,' Visconti wrote in the screenplay, 'are already in the family itself, where wealth, the children's faulty upbringing, the weight and pride of a tradition of opulence, are beginning to sap the relationships among family members, to dig a dangerous ditch between the new events in the world and our characters.' Gradually 'the sense of family is lost, of the Corporation formed by a whole body of deeply experienced interests and affections, and in which a child's birth, a marriage, deaths, founding a new factory and signing an important contract were all dates that lived on the same plane in the family's affective memory . . .'. Instead, the factory becomes more and more a machine for making money, and 'when the last member of the second generation dies, all sense of responsibility to the Corporation is finally lost by the family, too'. Deterioration accelerates, reversible only by someone from outside, someone uncontaminated by the family germ.

The Erba and Visconti sides split. Carla, who had transferred to her husband some of the shares in the flourishing drugs company founded by her uncle, now insisted that she and her sister resume the sole management of all Erba resources. They were later joined by Edoardo, the only one of the children, according to Uberta, who had a keen business sense that kept money from slipping through his fingers.

There was a lawsuit, a painful row over the litigants' interests. That was in 1923, a year before the scandal broke that led to Lina Erba's divorce from Count Castelbarco. Luchino was then seventeen. The banquet for five hundred guests given in honour of Puccini when *Manon Lescaut* was revived in February 1923 was the last function Carla and Giuseppe attended together before they broke up. In the Visconti palace there would be no more of the grand balls, worthy of those in *The Leopard*, that Luchino saw as a child. 'The guests,' he was to recall, 'had eyes only for my mother. I watched her, not losing sight of her for a second. I wanted to remember every detail of that vision for as long as possible. It was a grandiose sight. Then I woke up, livid: the servants were putting things away, sweeping up the plumes and the sequins. It was the end of a world.'

From then on Donna Carla would live in semi-reclusion, abandoning a social whirl which, according to Uberta, she had never really enjoyed: 'She thought of it more as a duty. My father, on the other hand, really loved to entertain and to go out.' Every evening, however, even when she was alone, she put on evening dress and came downstairs, scented and imperial, for the dinner served to her in the big, empty dining-room.

For Visconti, and for Italy, 1924 was a grim year. It was, as we have seen, the year of his parents' separation. At dawn on Easter Monday of that year, Eleonora Duse, the heart and soul of an epoch, died in a Pittsburgh hotel room. And June 1924 was when fascist gunmen murdered the socialist leader Matteotti and, with him, all freedom in Italy.

'Alone, alone' were the last words the heartbroken Duse said on a stage. A supreme interpreter of plays by D'Annunzio and Ibsen, she had rivalled and surpassed Sarah Bernhardt, had felt and expressed all the subtleties and torment of a woman's heart; she had brought a breath of almost religious emotion to the stage. Bernhardt had been the femme fatale, resplendent in her sparkling jewels, her costumes, her artistry. But Duse remained herself, and she was inimitable.

After a long absence she had returned to the stage, first in Turin, in May 1921, in Milan a month later, to act in Ibsen's *The Lady from the Sea*, a drama of waiting, loneliness and renunciation. In it, a woman, Ellida, although in the grip of an incurable longing for the infinite sea, refuses to leave with a roving sailor, the Stranger, who had come back for her. Duse, with her slightly heavy, irregular features, her too-wide mouth and broad sweep of brow, was no beauty and did not pretend to be. 'When I appear before the public,' she said, 'my first achievement is being ugly.'

When Luchino, with his mother, saw her for the first time she was sixty-three years old. Her hair was grey, she wore no make-up. What reached him first, from the wings, was her light, vibrant, anxious voice, like music, yet an everyday voice, unrhetorical, unaffected, perforated with silences and imperceptible pauses. 'I felt enormous emotion, I was spellbound, I don't know how to say it,' Visconti later recalled. 'When I heard her – I was very young – she literally took my breath away. I couldn't understand how anyone could act like that. I remember asking my mother, "Is she acting, or what?" Because she didn't seem to be acting. She played the first act of *The Lady from the Sea*. "Is she acting or talking with Zacconi – what's she doing?" She was acting, all right, she said things, drew things in the dirt with her umbrella, things a lot of people did, but they did them a long time after she did.'

Visconti watched D'Annunzio's *The Dead City*, a gloomy celebration of incestuous passion. He saw Duse play the part of the tormented mother in Ibsen's *Ghosts*, marvelling at the indefinable modulations of her voice, the soft lights and sickly shadows in her face, the irony of her smile, and those hands with a life of their own. When the final curtain fell, the applause was endless, flowers rained on her and there were shouts you heard in no other theatre. Visconti would always hold inside himself, like the lovelorn narrator of *Remembrance*, the recollection of that voice stripped naked by suffering, that frail body bearing the whole weight of the tragedy, of the anguish of loving. And he would always associate her with his mother, she, too, 'alone' and suffering.

Toscanini, Duse, theatrical footlights were all beacons in the murk of dismay, of 'uncertainty' through which he moved. His family was no longer a haven for him, but a torment. He dreamed of adventure, of freedom, and he ran away from home three times. 'I had always been a roaring rebel,' he said in 1972, 'even if I only slowly clarified my political ideas. I was sixteen the first time I broke loose from my moorings. I got as far as Rome. My father came to find me and he told me: "Now that you're here, stay here. But at least profit from it by getting a little education. Have a look at the sights." And off he marched me to San Pietro in Vincoli to see Michelangelo's *Moses*, the "marble colossus bearing the Tablets of the Law" that, seven years earlier, Sigmund Freud had called the very image of authority and of the "eternally judging and irritated Father".'

This encounter with the Law did not discourage him from running away a second time, from Grazzano, where he was supposed to be cramming for a school examination, to Rome during his father's absence. This time he took with him a girl of old and illustrious Venetian lineage: Roberta Masier, much sought-after in Roman salons and reputedly impossible to seduce.

'No one would have noticed,' Uberta says, 'if my brother hadn't taken Titi to the smartest restaurant in Rome, and if Don Giuseppe in person hadn't sat down at the next table. But my father had a strong sense of humour, and it all struck him as so funny that he burst out laughing and didn't have the heart to scold [Luchino].' Titi, who was much older than Luchino, was soon to have a much less amusing, more tumultuous love affair with Curzio Malaparte, whom she met at a party given by the Fascist Militia leader Italo Balbo. Malaparte fought a duel with Roberta's brother. After an unsuccessful suicide attempt, Titi went off to live in Paris.

Finally, when Luchino was eighteen, a third escapade, which he called 'mystical and romantic', climaxed briefly in the monastery in Montecassino. This, says his friend Giorgio Prosperi, who confirms the facts of the episode, 'is an element not to lose sight of in trying to understand Visconti's character and future evolution – anxious, emotional, romantic, but profoundly serious, concerned with fundamental problems, eager to pursue to the end every new path he struck out on. He may have had unhappy experiences in his life, but you don't find any semi-experiences.'

VII

MILAN-MUNICH-PARIS

What could she desire? Fortune, high birth,
wit, beauty, so others said and she believed, all
had been heaped on her by the hands of chance.
STENDHAL, *The Red and the Black*

In 1925, at barely nineteen, Luchino Visconti brilliantly displayed all
the gifts that sum up distinguished birth and character: lively and
impertinent intelligence, physical beauty that, as Wally Toscanini
put it, 'made you drop your bread', prickly pride combined with
tact and generous impulses, exquisite urbanity and an iron will,
fierce courage and repeatedly demonstrated physical endurance.

At great moments in history in the days of earlier Viscontis such
a combination of acquired elegance and instinctive mettle would
surely have boosted this 'well born soul' to worldwide fame. But
these were petty times; the laurels and the titles had already been
distributed to a boorish new culture, without elegance or soul, that
paraded in black shirts and yawned or dozed at Wagner's operas.

The vulgarized court around dwarfish, cautious King Victor-
Emmanuel was merely an anachronistic caricature of royal
splendour. The king went to his Quirinale palace every morning as
to an office, to ratify Il Duce's decrees rather than to govern. 'I am
blind and deaf,' he would say at the height of the Matteotti crisis.
'My eyes and ears are the Chamber and the Senate.' Every morning,
after checking the temperature in his office (it had to be precisely
sixty-six degrees), he read his mail like a punctual office-clerk, then
granted audiences while sitting on the edge of a red damask sofa and
straining to keep his feet touching the floor; if he forgot himself and
leaned back, his legs dangled in the air.

He had always practised his kingly trade like a bureaucrat. He did not like exceptional people, but at least he disdained the bombast that had invaded everything around him. 'What are heroes good for?' he asked. 'Stealing chickens?' Only fishing and coin collecting excited him. Court life was reduced to a strict minimum; most of the time, the Quirinale was merely a pompous setting, a line of empty reception rooms inhabited only by footmen in red livery, aides-de-camp and a few gentlemen who looked as though they had stepped out of another time.

Now and then a ceremony would revivify the palace – when Luchino's close friend Prince Umberto, for example, married Marie José of Belgium, kin to the Wittelsbachs of Bavaria, in January 1930. But the routine receptions for diplomats and foreign celebrities passing through Rome remained hopelessly lacklustre. Starace once went so far as to appear at the palace in his black shirt. This seemed revolutionary at first, but was soon widely adopted at court. How Duke Giuseppe Visconti must have hated that!

What place was there for a fiery young aristocrat in a society that had lost its aristocratic values, in which the fascist hymn *Giovinezza* had replaced the *Royal March* and the emblem of the fasces overshadowed the cross of Savoy? Donna Carla's fortune doubtless made the problem easier to deal with, but the Viscontis had never encouraged their children to look forward to a life of idleness. Given Luchino's poor showing at school, his parents hoped to make him understand reality by giving him a job in a family enterprise. This turned out to be a disaster.

'I must admit I didn't take any of that very seriously,' he said. 'I started such a revolution among the employees and made such a mess of things that I was fired almost instantly . . . I was by no means unhappy. And the women had such crushes on me!' In fact, Visconti's charm won him a great many women admirers. Everyone but he agreed that this homosexual was a great ladies' man – but so were his father, and his friend Umberto, Prince of Piedmont, and Saint-Loup, and Baron Charlus. 'When I was young and rather handsome, women's admiration struck and flattered me,' he said. 'I admit it: I still enjoy seeing beautiful women.' Helped by the prestige of a fine uniform and the suave moustache he allowed to grow, not to mention the straight, chestnut hair, pale complexion, regular features and 'Grecian nose' described in his military record, this student officer made women's hearts beat faster.

On 22 February 1926, he enrolled as a cadet to beat the draft. Since he had no school degrees and so could not immediately gain officer status, he attended the school for non-commissioned officers from April to December. In 1927 he entered the aristocratic Pinerolo school a few miles south of Turin.

Even here, the ghost of Proust pursued him: like Doncières in *Within a Budding Grove*, Pinerolo was 'one of those small, aristocratic and military towns surrounded by great stretches of open country over which, in fine weather, a kind of intermittent mist of sound often floated in the distance. This indicated that a regiment had moved on manoeuvres, that the very atmosphere of the streets, the avenues and squares had finally contracted a sort of perpetual, musical and warlike vibratility, and that the most commonplace noises of carts or trams echoed vaguely like bugle calls ...' This second Saint-Loup had just turned twenty-one when, with the rank of senior corporal, he entered the Savoy Cavalry regiment, whose emblem bore the crown of Savoy and the heraldic winged figure of Pegasus.

From the start, Visconti the rebel took to military life: the manoeuvres in the field, the discipline, daily contact with the men, the exercise of command, which appeased deeply rooted aspirations in him. In all this he regained the discipline and order he had known as a child. Promoted to sergeant, then staff sergeant, he controlled the men in his regiment with an iron hand. He also managed to maintain the pleasures of civilian life through a new friendship with Princess Gerace, whose Rolls was frequently parked near the Hôtel de France, where he usually stayed.

If his two years at Pinerolo awakened any passion, however, it was for horses, not women. 'In Pinerolo I gave free rein to my love of horses and of military school ... In the barracks I was very authoritarian, I made the men in my regiment quake. I loved military life, I was in the saddle all day long ... This was pleasure, not duty.'

When he returned to live in Milan in 1928, he began feverishly making plans, starting projects he never finished. With his friend Livio Dell'Anna he outlined a play, *The Play of Truth*, a comedy of manners; it ended up in a drawer. Following in his father's footsteps, he enlisted Dell'Anna and Corrado Corradi in an upholstery-fabrics business, the CLV, that rapidly went bankrupt.

Just for fun, as an amateur, he helped stage Goldoni's play *The Wise Wife*. Duke Giuseppe, who financed the show, used it to introduce a young and beautiful actress he had just discovered, Andreina Pagnani. She was struck by the exceptional care Luchino took in choosing the furniture and objects to be used in the sets. 'When I met Luchino,' she said, 'his father was organizing an [actors'] company, and since he preferred to launch a young actress, he picked me . . . Luchino was passionate about the theatre and he worked without pay, "for friendship's sake". He even brought furniture and paintings from home. He was almost obsessively precise, and if he had a specific object in mind, a certain kind of chest of drawers or a certain kind of vase, he couldn't rest until he found it.'

Duke Giuseppe was then dividing his time between the court in Rome and his theatrical life in Grazzano and Milan. In the palace on Via Cerva he continued to entertain, organizing parties and putting on shows in his small private theatre that were rather naughtier than any he'd done in the past. He could feel it: none of his sons were as close to him as Luchino, who was even more gifted than he in all the arts, drawing, writing, directing, music.

Don Giuseppe was deeply disappointed, therefore, when his son announced that he, like his brother Luigi, wanted to devote himself to horses, that he was planning to found a racing stable and stud farm. The father knew it was useless to try to dissuade the boy. Luchino was as stubborn as they come; when he made up his mind to do something, he did it, and better than anyone else. All Giuseppe could hope was that this ambitious project would be as short-lived as so many of Luchino's whims turned out to be.

In 1929, Luchino bought his first racehorse, Esturgeon, and rode it himself in the winter races at Saint Moritz. Against all expectations, he won, although he failed to collect the prize: he could not yet officially call himself a gentleman rider.

At first he knew practically nothing about the dressage and training of a thoroughbred horse. So he hired a steeplechase jockey, a Florentine named Ubaldo Pandolfi. 'Luchino,' his brother Luigi said, 'was the opposite of people like the Aga Khan, who went to see their horses at eleven o'clock in the morning, getting out of their Rolls in their raccoon coats.' He moved into an apartment on Via Domenichino, near the San Siro racetrack, and went every day to the near-by stables. Tirelessly, month after month, every morning at dawn and every afternoon he observed his trainer at work. He asked no questions, but watched everything Pandolfi did until he could do it all himself. He was soon able to take his trainer's place. 'At first, I was the trainer at his stable,' Pandolfi said, 'then he took it all over himself.'

Several times during those three years, Pandolfi stayed at the villa in Cernobbio, where he took care of the horses belonging to Luchino and Luigi. He saw Donna Carla, 'tall and haughty', dressed in black and white, and Madina, Luigi's young wife, who could jump as well as ride. And he witnessed the Viscontis' excursions on the lake, 'such an incredibly elegant group'.

That summer of 1929 was the last of Luchino's placid summers. 'He was our "Grand Meaulnes",*' Uberta says, recalling her brother's unexpected arrivals at Cernobbio, the games he organized, the adventures on which he led the little girls and their friends up trees and across roofs. Madina Arrivabene remembers the extraordinary atmosphere at the house that summer, the interminable conversations between the young count and the Cernobbio parish priest: 'I can still see us sitting on huge yellow brocade sofas . . . Uberta and Luchino on the rugs, with their dogs. Luchino spoke of God, of physics, of solar energy; from time to time the old priest raised an objection . . . .'.

From Cernobbio, the family caravan moved on to Forte dei Marmi, a beach resort near Viareggio which had inspired painters (including the Swiss Arnold Böcklin and the Italians Carlo Carrà and Ardengo Soffici) and had been the setting for D'Annunzio's love affair with Duse. 'It was enchanting,' Uberta says. 'My brother's films are never, strictly speaking, autobiographical, but details in them sometimes evoke an atmosphere; when we went to Forte dei Marmi, where mother rented a house, we always stopped in the Cisa mountains; we got out thermos flasks, wicker baskets of

*In *Le Grand Meaulnes* (*The Lost Domain*), a poetic novel published in 1913, author Alain-Fournier (Henri Alban Fournier), wrote of mystical love in a dreamy summer landscape (translator's note).

food and spread tablecloths on the grass for lunch, as in *The Leopard*. The trips were wonderfully lively because we took along a lot of animals that got sick, cats that escaped. It was at Forte dei Marmi that Luigi and Edoardo first met Madina and Nicky Arrivabene, pure beauties descended from a very old Mantua family, whom they later married.'

Motorboats, fast cars, racehorses – the descendants of the Dukes of Milan adored speed. In the autumn of 1929, Luchino bought a Lancia Spider. During a weekend at Grazzano, he was seized by a whim to test his new car on the race circuit at Monza. He asked the family's long-time driver, Macerati, to go with him. 'I can't,' the driver said. 'My son is sick and I don't want to leave him.'

Irritated and annoyed, the young count ordered him through clenched teeth to be ready to leave in a quarter of an hour. Luchino took the wheel. The road was slippery, fog cut his visibility. Suddenly, around a curve, a cart loomed ahead of him. He swung out to pass. Macerati raised himself up and turned to make sure no other vehicle was coming. As he did so, he ran smack into a beam sticking out of the back of the cart. He died a lingering death.

Visconti was grief-stricken. He felt so responsible for his servant's death that until his own death he paid Macerati's family a pension. Not long after that fateful 20 September, he decided to put Italy as far behind him as he could, and he left for Tripoli, where his brother Guido had lived alone since the break-up of his marriage to Luciana della Robbia. But Luchino didn't stay there. With two Tuareg guides he went off to the Tassili plateau in the Central Sahara. The silence, the stony ground, the pure and boundless sky appeased him. He wanted no absolution, no consolation, no diversion, but only an orgy of loneliness and expiation until they wiped out everything he had been. No punishment seemed great enough to fit his offence.

When he returned to Italy, he shut himself up in the splendid stables he had built in Trenno. He had resolved to live there forever after, among his stable lads and the horses (some thirty of them) he was breeding. Few visitors were allowed into this forbidden kingdom, only his family and his closest friends, among them Prince Umberto.

The architect Pietro Necchi had faithfully carried out Visconti's instructions in designing the main building roofed with green tiles and used as living quarters, the horses' stalls each bearing the name of the man who looked after its tenant, rooms for the jockeys, trainers, grooms. Still cited today as a model, the Trenno stables became a sort of abbey dedicated to a pagan, earthly cult, a fairy kingdom of centaurs and gnomes that echoed with the cracking of whips, the clatter of horses' hooves, with snorting and whinnying. It was the opposite of the romantic castle in which Duke Giuseppe delighted in Grazzano. Here there were no benedictory angels, none of the suave scents exuded, so the tourist leaflets tell us, by 'the Virginia creeper, the red and pink geraniums and the carnations dripping from every balcony, the countless roses and jasmine that made Grazzano a flower and a song of harmonious poetry'. Trenno smelled of saddle leather, sweat, horse piss and droppings, all the effluvia of powerful and headstrong animals.

'It was a bit like a retreat in a monastery,' Visconti later said. 'I began at four in the morning. I inspected all the horses, one by one. By eight o'clock in the evening I was in bed. In those days I had dropped everything, even the theatre.'

And yet . . . Despite nephew Luchino Gastel's remark that Visconti enjoyed the thoroughbreds' dressage and training even more than he did the races, the stables at Trenno were like a theatre backstage: each race, like every theatrical performance, had its stern preparatory routine. Grand Prix days were marked by what the author Michel Leiris, himself a devotee of racing since childhood, calls 'a ritual procession': the jockeys in multicoloured silks on horses with gleaming coats, the announcement of the owners' colours, the lining up of the horses at the starting gate as they 'stamp like cocks and bob like swans, then the sudden gallop and the sound of hooves on the earth . . .' It is theatre, but true theatre. 'For here,' Leiris goes on, 'nothing is false: whatever the importance of the staging, the sporting show itself, with its theoretically unpredictable ending, is a real act, not a make-believe in which all the vicissitudes have been pre-ordained.' Painstaking, patient preparation, anxiety multiplied by the risks and the obstacles, the flashing dash to triumph or defeat – these would be, for Visconti in later years, the perils of true theatre as well.

All of Visconti's options were determined by the goads of

daring, of risk, of impossibility challenged. At the 1931 autumn sales, he paid the leading breeder of the period, Federico Tesio, a pittance for a bay horse named Sanzio that everyone else considered incorrigibly flawed. In a matter of months he had 'put it back on its feet' and entered it, under his own colours – green and white – in the Milan Grand Prix.

The weather was overcast, promising a heavy track, the most unfavourable conditions for Sanzio. 'The count,' Pandolfi says, 'kept repeating: "If only it doesn't rain! We'll do all right if only it doesn't rain!" On the afternoon of the race, only seconds after Sanzio crossed the finishing line, the sky was suddenly shredded by a storm which turned the turf to mud.'

For Sanzio, 'Count Luchino's pure creation', had won – to the astonishment of breeder Tesio, suddenly rueful about the miserable 1,500 lire he had asked for the horse. Visconti's fetish horse went on to win many other races, including the Ostend Grand Prix the same year, 1932. When that event ended, a deliriously happy Visconti threw a memorable champagne party for everyone who worked in his stables.

It was with thoroughbreds, he frequently insisted, that he learned to make actors work. By making actors work, he meant bending them to his will, doing what he wanted with them, 'creating' and 're-creating' them. Dogs as well as horses aroused in him an ardent desire to bear directly on the process of conception and birth through careful study of pedigrees and blood lines, arranging carefully calculated crossings to produce breeds that, his trainer said, were 'purer, wonderfully select'.

'The Viscontis have always had a strange understanding of animals,' says Fabrizio Clerici. Everyone in the family maintained a constant relationship with them that was both affectionate and tyrannical. In Uberta's big drawing-room in Rome, which one expects to find filled with portraits of illustrious Viscontis against dark wainscoting and old gilt, dogs with gentle, almost human eyes pad across the brick-red carpet amid a forest of plants; cats stretch in sunny windows, roll up in balls on the piano, glide among huge bouquets of fragrant flowers and sometimes accost Uberta, who brushes them off impatiently, almost distractedly.

'We've always had animals,' she says. 'All kinds of animals. The only ones I'm afraid of are wasps, because they always sting me. It was the same for Luchino; aside from the horses, he even had a lion, and a bear. But they got too big and had to be put in a zoo.' In all the family homes, in Rome, Ischia, Torre San Lorenzo (fierce) dogs cohabit with cats strictly confined to a single storey, even a single room.

Each of the Visconti's fetish animals was named for something he worked on. The huge Pyrenean sheepdog he bought in 1974 was named Konrad, like the protagonist of *Conversation Piece*. A contemporary, a pink female cat was dubbed Manon and its son Lescaut because the director was mounting the Puccini opera at the time. 'The day Luchino died,' Uberta reports, 'a bitch puppy was born. The mother had smothered all the rest of the litter, but we managed to save this one. We called it Teresa Raffo, in memory of *The Innocents*.'

A Visconti home is never a mausoleum, a temple of memories. People in it turn their backs on death, they exorcise it. The past burns on only in the secrecy of their hearts; what they assert is the continuity of life, its power, smiling or brutal. This begins with the sparse, vibrant, unaffected presence of nature. In her great gondola of an apartment on Via Fleming, high up among the umbrella pines looking down on Rome, Electra-Uberta's grief pulses unconcealed.

'When he died, my life stopped,' she told us, her almond eyes suddenly filling with tears. But her voice, broken only for a moment, went on stubbornly reviving the past. Her parents, for example, so handsome, always so young that she thought them invulnerable. 'I don't know how old they were when they died. To me they were ageless.' The celebrations, too: Christmas in Milan, and later at her brother's home in Rome, with a tree bent under the weight of the gifts on it; the lovely parties on her mother's birthday, 18 August. Laughing, she recalls the pieces of Chinese porcelain Guido gave her; since he was often away, the bills invariably came to Donna Carla. Uberta recalls Luchino's wonderment at the birth of his nephew, whom he called, in the Venetian dialect, the *puttin*, the little cupid. And, in her childhood, the little theatres and the puppet shows Luchino spent weeks preparing for the two 'little ones'. 'He used dolls' clothing, furniture from my sister's doll's house. He tore out, ripped up, took whatever suited him for a show that, in the end, remained only a project. My sister was crushed. Not me. I had much more fun with my pet marmoset than I did with dolls.'

Two years of reclusion in the Trenno stables may have been as much an effort to prolong the games-playing and security of Visconti's childhood as to purge his conscience. But they failed to satisfy his confused aspirations, or to do more than partially relieve his growing exasperation with the bleak, stifling monotony of provincial Italy under Mussolini. 'One fine day,' Visconti said, 'I realized that love of horses wasn't enough any more. I had to express myself some other way. When that happened I sold everything, stable and horses, and left for Paris.'

That 'one fine day' was actually five years long, five years of wondering, of temptation, of uneasy wandering. The industrious, puritanical Milan of the Thirties was too cramped for him, and so was regimented Italy, where the Duce was 'always right'. So he travelled ceaselessly, to Britain, Germany, France, Austria, other areas of Italy. To tour the racetracks at first and find broodmares for his stables, and then for very different reasons.

He was in Germany at the time of the Reichstag fire that later opened *The Damned*; he was there to watch the parades of élite troops, and witness those nazi super-spectacles that so thrilled Pierre Drieu La Rochelle,* who had 'felt no artistic emotion like that since the Ballets Russes'. Uberta recalls a violent dispute between her brother and her father, probably in 1934. Luchino had just returned from Germany and 'he went on and on describing the beauty and strength of those young men on parade carrying I don't know what, a very heavy staff, I think'. Less objective than, say, his friend Prince Umberto about nazi and fascist pageantry, Visconti was attracted as much by their demonstrations of strength as by the human ideal that Drieu said Fascism embodied, an ideal of 'a man who believes only in action, who combines the virtues of an athlete with those of a monk, a soldier and a militant'. The photographer Horst, a close friend of Visconti's for a while, reported that as late as 1936 Visconti 'swore by *Siegfried*; that was his hero'.

*A pro-Nazi French novelist and apologist for the German occupation of France who committed suicide in 1945 (translator's note).

Yet there was a contrast to Germany, to [Leni Riefenstahl's Nazi-glorifying film] *Triumph of the Will*, to its cathedrals of light, its brown-booted storm-troopers and the *Horst Wessel* song. The contrast was in France, the Paris of the Roaring Twenties depicted by Fitzgerald and Hemingway as a feast, a whirlwind, a wild dream of pleasure, where the charms of pre-war life now danced to swing music and strutted to the *Lambeth Walk*.

Whatever the pull of Berlin and Munich, Luchino Visconti remained a spectator and a tourist, a stranger in a country whose language he spoke badly. France, on the other hand, had been familiar to him since childhood. 'French culture,' he was to say, 'was very formative for me because from boyhood on I lived a lot in France. I discovered German culture much later.' In Paris he naturally returned to the area around the Place de la Concorde and the Faubourg Saint-Honoré, stopping in its luxury hotels. At first he favoured the Vouillemont, home of one of Rasputin's murderers, the mysterious Prince Feliks Yusupov. Then he switched to the Hotel Castiglione, minutes away from the Tuileries Gardens where he had played as a child, and from Rumpelmayer's tea-room with its pink-and-blue paintings of the Italian Riviera and the ghost of Marcel Proust drifting past its mirrors.

'Paris still wore the perfume of *Remembrance*,' Visconti later recalled. True, the day was long past when Proust's Odette de Crécy went out in her barouche along the roads in the Bois de Boulogne in the spring. Diaghilev and Bakst were dead, Nijinsky had gone mad. But Misia Sert, whom Proust had called 'the young godmother of all these new great men', the Polish muse of the Impressionists and the Ballets Russes, friend of Vuillard, Bonnard, Renoir, Diaghilev, Alexandre Benois, Stravinsky and Picasso, still reigned over the city.

Then in her sixties, the woman Paul Morand had crowned 'queen of modern baroque' was still collecting geniuses, 'hearts and pink-quartz Ming trees'; she still 'launched fads that became instant fashions when they were picked up by her followers, exploited by decorators, talked about by journalists, imitated by empty-headed society women. And she went on lavishing advice and financial help as she had always done, passionately and generously. When she sat down with Marcelle Meyer at the piano in the grand salon of the

Hotel Continental one evening in 1933 and played Chopin preludes and mazurkas, and Serge Lifar danced Debussy's *The Afternoon of a Faun*, the Belle Époque* came to life again; a breath of Things Past floated over the crowded room. At that moment, Jean Cocteau said that in Misia he could see again Proust's Princess Yourbeletieff, she of "the huge, quivering aigrette . . . the aigrette of Scheherazade, reigning over the royal box at the Ballets Russes and filling theatre sets and violent dances with her magical influence, as once she did in sun-speckled Impressionist gardens . . .".'

Around her and her dearest friend, Gabrielle Chanel, Visconti easily recognized the lights and shadows of the Venice he had known, of the Hôtel des Bains where, in 1912, Stravinsky had played the opening of *The Rites of Spring* for Diaghilev; it was there, too, in 1920 that Diaghilev, the tsar of the Ballets Russes, and Grand Duchess Maria Pavlovna, the daughter of Grand Duke Paul Romanov, had invited Chanel and the Serts to their table; shivering with cold on that stifling June day in 1929, Diaghilev, the dying 'enchanter', looked one last time at two forms bent over him, Misia Sert and Coco Chanel, 'so young, all in white, so white'. Not long before that, on the Lido, Diaghilev had given his protégé, Anton Dolin, a copy of Mann's *Death in Venice*.

'Between Paris, London and Rome the world maintained contact and mingled in a tight little circle,' the dancer Lifar remarked. 'I was received in Paris by a social set that I met again in London, Rome, Venice.' On the shores of the Venetian lagoon, the dancer met Madina and Nicky Arrivabene Visconti, whose name, fortune and elegance opened for them the doors of Paris's most fashionable salons; when Lifar saw them again in the French capital, they introduced him to their brother-in-law, Luchino Visconti.

As in the days of Baron de Charlus, society was still ruled by 'a few dominant families'. Not the Greffulhes or the Montesquious or the Castellanes any longer, but the Beaumonts, the Polignacs and the Noailles were still supreme. In all these houses, said Lifar, 'sovereign ukases decide what is elegant and what is not'. Here women wore the colours, scents and dresses of two great rival Paris fashion designers.

*The French designation for the idyllic period between the turn of the century and the start of the first world war (translator's note).

One was Italy's Elsa Schiaparelli, 'Schiap' to her friends, who courted scandal with her bizarre creations: her famous 'shocking pink', her Daliesque hats shaped like shoes or chickens, her long black gloves with gilt fingernails and her sequined and brocade jackets. The other: France's Coco Chanel, who made clothes of classical, almost Jansenist sobriety, who was accused by the designer Paul Poiret of inventing 'luxurious poverty' and transforming 'the women of yesteryear, as architectural as the prows of ships, into underfed little telegraph clerks'.

These 'eminently womanly women', Cocteau said, who 'brought into the temple a spirit of havoc, a spirit of gowns and scissors', also costumed the countless masked balls, those facetious and grandiose gatherings of a social élite more concerned with dressing for the Thousand and One Nights and the last nights of Schönbrunn than with such unfashionable issues as the Stavisky scandal, the February riots in 1934★ and the rise of the leftist-dominated Popular Front.

Luchino Visconti was no social butterfly. He scrupulously boycotted certain salons, especially the one on Rue Boissière presided over by the gossip-mongering 'janitress of Paris', Marie-Louise Bousquet, whom he called 'a silly old cow' to be avoided like a fever. But in Paris he rediscovered the atmosphere of frivolity and refined hedonism that, after the war, had deserted Milan forever.

And the cosmopolitan Paris salons offered an added attraction: the presence of picturesque but never conceited celebrities, not a few of them geniuses. Salvador Dali would later look back on the delightful private recitals given by Jeanne Lanvin's daughter, Marie-Blanche de Polignac, and 'the string quartets played by candlelight beneath paintings by Renoir'. Christian Bérard, the comic decorator nicknamed Bébé Chien-Chien (Baby Bow-Wow) who was the darling of Paris society, functioned as a dirty, bearded jester for Marie-Laure de Noailles, the high priestess of the Paris *beau monde*.

Marie-Laure put together the components of her salon according

★The case came to light in December 1933, when bonds issued by financier Alexandre Stavisky proved worthless. Stavisky died a month later, under mysterious circumstances. Government attempts to hush up the scandal led to rioting by French fascist groups on 6 February in which fifteen people were killed and 1,500 injured (translator's note).

to an artfully balanced formula that everyone tried to imitate: 'a minimum of titled people sprinkled with a few royal highnesses', lots of stimulatingly exuberant artists, all spiced by a dash of exoticism, supplied first by White Russian refugees, then, after 1933, by such German refugees as composer Kurt Weill. In her celebrated salon on Place des États-Unis, the destitute Duke Fulco della Verdura, now reduced to designing bracelets for Chanel, rubbed elbows with Russian grand duchesses and princesses washed up by the Revolution and surviving as models or workroom supervisors in the big fashion houses.

This, then was the 'Red Viscountess', who as late as 1968 was bringing snacks to mutinous Sorbonne students whom she greeted with a familiar 'Hi, kids'. She was 'the soul of vulgarity', said the novelist Roger Peyrefitte, 'but dazzlingly loony and intelligent'. Married to Charles de Noailles, who, she noted, 'is even richer than I am', Marie-Laure was the granddaughter of Laure de Chevigné, the model for Proust's Duchess of Guermantes. Cocteau, being his usual catty self, remarked that to draw his marvellous character with her wheat-coloured hair and cornflower-blue eyes, Proust had 'left out the foul language, the cheap shag cigarettes, yellow teeth and parrot beak' of the original.

Marie-Laure was also the daughter of an immensely wealthy banker named Bischoffsheim, whose fortune she willingly inherited, but whose Jewish blood she denied, asserting that her grandmother Bischoffsheim had had enough fiery Spanish blood in her veins to have had her child by someone other than her husband. She was proud, however, to be descended from the Marquis de Sade.

Flaunting her outrageous non-conformism, she even came to blows with the very stuffy Mme Arbelot de Vacqueur at a lecture on Fascism by the ultra-rightist Henri Massis. She made no attempt to hide her love life, a medley of aristocratic affairs (with Alexis de Rédé and the Prince de Beauvau) and less blue-blooded adventures (with the orchestra conductor Igor Markevitch and the sculptor Oscar Dominguez). Her penchant for woman was no secret to anyone except, perhaps, highly tolerant Charles, who, in his youth, had been tossed out of school for his 'special friendships'.

Apparently getting on splendidly together, the couple lived in separate wings of their palatial mansion, surrounded by a cohort of turbulent artists. Both were enthusiastic patrons who bought paintings by Picasso, Dali and Bérard to hang beside their family portraits and their Goyas. They gave Cocteau a fabulous sum for the period – over a million francs – to make his film *The Blood of a Poet*; in a box at the theatre, they laughed along with their friends at a controversial scene in which a child is killed by a snowball.

A few months later, scandal marred another motion picture, the anti-clerical, anti-bourgeois *L'Age d'Or*, made by Dali and Luis Buñuel, when members of the ultra-rightist League of Patriots, the Anti-Jewish League and the royalist Camelots du Roi interrupted a showing and wrecked the theatre. The film's insolently profane, sacrilegious spirit earned its financier, Charles de Noailles, expulsion from the strongly Catholic Jockey Club and threats of excommunication from the archbishop of Paris.

The era's blithest spirit was Cocteau, the eternal *enfant terrible*; his scintillating intelligence could appreciate the genius of Proust and the throaty voice of Marlene Dietrich, the beauty of the circus and that of the Ballets Russes, the blood-red hair of Marianne Oswald and the grace of boxer Al Brown. His admirers were mad for cinema and theatre; it was not at all unusual to see men in dinner jackets and women in evening gowns leave sophisticated dinner parties and end smart evenings by lining up at one of the small cinemas off the Champs-Elysées to see *The Blue Angel* or *Camille*.

Everyone dreamed of making movies, beginning with Nicky Visconti and her friend, the Russian princess Natalie Paley, a close friend of Cocteau, who was soon to make her début in the film *L'Épervier*, directed by her brother-in-law (?), Marcel L'Herbier. 'Our group went to the cinema almost every day,' the princess said. 'We had to. It was a kind of contest. We asked each other questions like, how many times have you seen *Shanghai Express*? Then we began talking to Jean (Cocteau) about it. His apartment on Rue Vignon was a sort of sanctuary, with a Chinese valet, a tray of opium and pipes. A lot of us smoked with him. Occasionally there was something stronger than opium – was it cocaine? Jean never let me try it, but I'm sure I'd have loved it.'

These people whose lives were half fiction wove incredibly intricate love stories for themselves. Luchino Visconti had set tongues wagging in Milan in 1935 by bringing with him to Paris, Proust's setting for *Sodom and Gomorrah*, a young Milanese boy named Umberto Monaldi. The youth's tutor rushed to France to fetch him home. Yet Luchino was also in love with his sister-in-law, Nicky, as well as with Natalie Paley, after whom Cocteau, Lifar and Marie-Laure de Noailles also lusted.

Who was this woman of thirty whom the Arrivabene sisters had met in Venice? She charmed people with her delicate, china-doll face – perfect nose, prominent cheekbones, ash-grey eyes – and her sudden shifts of mood that took her swiftly from inconsolable sadness to unquenchable giggles. And, too, with her story-book life.

She was the daughter of Olga Karnovitch, Countess of Hohenfelsen, Grand Duke Paul's morganatic wife, whom the Duchess of Guermantes in *Remembrance* ironically persisted in calling 'Grand Duchess Paul'. Not until 1911, when she was eight, did Tsar Nicholas II rescind his decree of exile against her mother, allowing Natalie to leave France with her brother Vladimir and her sister Irene for her father's palace in Tsarskoye Selo [now renamed Pushkin]. They remained there until the Revolution.

In 1917 the whole family was arrested. In July 1918, two days after Nicholas and his family were slaughtered at Ekaterinburg, Natalie's brother was hurled down a mine pit along with Grand Duchess Serge, the Tsarina's sister. Six months later, despite his liberal ideas, Grand Duke Paul was shot. Natalie's mother, who had vainly tried to intercede for her husband, then joined her two daughters, who had managed to escape to Finland.

From there they took refuge in France, where, like many other White Russians, they lived from hand to mouth, yet hobnobbed with Parisian high society. At the same time, they belonged to another social group which, according to the dancer Lifar, 'had its churches, its newspapers, books, theatres, universities, secondary schools, conservatories, operas and nightclubs, forming a real state within a state endowed with every means of expression. A society that combined such varied minds as those of the Nobel prizewinner [poet and novelist] Ivan Bunin, Rachmaninov, the Romanov grand dukes, the famous Yusupov, the Tolstoys, Ivan Mosjoukine, the Pitoëffs, Chaliapin . . .' Natalie's sister Irene remained true to her origins in marrying her cousin, Prince Fyodor of Russia. Natalie wed fashion designer Lucien Lelong in 1927.

Mme Lelong nevertheless insisted on her independence. When Visconti met her she had just concluded an 'idyll' with Cocteau. At the same time, Lifar declared himself madly in love with her. 'I lived a difficult, complex, impetuous and by no means happy love affair with Natalie Paley,' he admitted. It was Lifar who took her to a showing of *The Blood of a Poet*, where Cocteau saw her for the first time.

The princess's affair with the poet lasted long enough to inspire the rumour that she was pregnant by him. In his diary, he blames Marie-Laure de Noailles for the abortion that kept his son – it could only have been a son – from coming into the world. 'Marie-Laure de Noailles learned from Bérard that I was living with Natalie Paley Lelong. Bérard was sketching [Marie-Laure's] portrait. He told me later he [told her of the romance] to bring some animation to her face. He animated her so much that she smashed everything in the house . . . then came to break everything at my place on Rue Vignon. Marie-Laure later told me that she would become Natalie's intimate and that she would come between us "like a Medusa", and that is what happened.' Indeed, he depicted her as Viscountess Medusa beside Princess Fafner (Natalie) in *La Fin du Potomak* in 1940.

Natalie's version of the story differs sharply, casting a harsher, more sordid light on their affair: 'I was mad about Jean's wit and charm, but the appeal I held for him was purely physical. He wanted a son, but he was as effective with me as a confirmed homosexual stuffed with opium can be. It was all unworthy and shameful. There was no love at all. I didn't inspire him to write a single poem; I was not a good influence on his work – everyone knows that was the least fruitful period of his life. There was a lot of nasty gossip and my husband asked for a divorce. I finally went to Switzerland to think things over because, in fact, Jean was always with [Jean] Desbordes, and I saw him become interested in a handsome Algerian. He said he wanted to marry me, but I don't think he'd have done it.'

Cocteau's biographer, Francis Steegmuller, said that Cocteau always kept a photograph of Natalie by his bed. But behind it,

Steegmuller reported, was another picture showing a young man agile enough and well enough hung to practise on himself what doctors call by the ugly word fellatio; that second photo was a kind of talisman to counteract the dangers of the first, the biographer remarked.

The freedom that prevailed in those circles, and which aroused so many passions and tragedies, was contagious. Madina Arrivabene told of being at a party and suddenly noticing, among all the men in dinner jackets, a man sitting alone in a corner. He was, she said, 'a horror, in a grotesque blue suit, with stripes . . . And he was wearing a red tie! I felt sorry for him, so I went and sat beside him. "I'm Giacometti," he told me, "I'm a sculptor and I live in Montmartre." He asked if he could do my portrait. In those days, Natalie's brother-in-law, Fyodor of Russia, was pursuing me. To make him jealous, I asked him to drive with me to Giacometti's, which was in a horrible place, and Fyodor, who was madly handsome, waited for me in the car while I posed.'

For Visconti, however, Paris's climate of constant inventiveness and creativity was inspiring. 'Today I look back on those years,' he said, 'as so astonishing for their boldness, their picturesqueness, their bohemianism, their creative power . . .'

When he returned to Milan, he bought a camera and made a few amateur 16-millimetre films, adventure and detective stories, with his brothers, sisters and friends as his cast. In 1934 he assembled his first film crew, including a cameraman and an assistant, to make a more ambitious film in 35-millimetre. The intensely melodramatic script he wrote for it was centred around three women whom a boy of sixteen meets on arriving in wicked Milan from the provinces. He has a baby with a young girl who dies in childbirth. A prostitute leads him into vice, while another young woman, ideally lovely, represents the purity he cannot attain. When all the boy's dreams sink into the slime of reality, suicide is the only way out.

These three woman characters symbolize the impossibility of loving, the gap between carnal desire and ideal love. Visconti gave his dream woman the face of Nicky Arrivabene, with her hair and make-up done in the neo-classical style popularized by [film director Georg Wilhelm] Pabst in L'Atlantide and by Cocteau in Antigone, an androgynous beauty with a Greek shepherd's tight blond curls on a statuesque mask. A young man whom Visconti had noticed in a fascist parade completed the small cast, recruited mainly from among his friends.

Extensive research along the banks of the Naviglio enabled him to draw the prostitute directly from life. He showed her as she was, except that her hair was dyed a fiery red. She had to be a real prostitute: the evil element could only come from outside, from her world, as seductive as it was repugnant, dangerous, forbidden – from the streets, from life. To Visconti this was still unknown territory.

VIII

GOTHA

I don't give a damn about the Gotha.

Coco Chanel

A road bordered with snowdrifts, snow-covered chalets and pine trees, a road sign: Kitzbühel.

These are the opening images in *The Witch Burned Alive* (*La Strega Bruciata Viva*), filmed by Visconti in 1967 as the first of three episodes in the movie *The Witches* (*Le Streghe*). In this sketch, an unknown young actor named Helmut Berger appeared for the first time; Berger lived in the fashionable Austrian winter-sports resort of Kitzbühel, where his parents owned a hotel.

Coincidence? It was in Kitzbühel that, thirty-two years earlier, in the winter of 1934–5, Visconti had met the only woman to whom he ever proposed marriage: Princess Irma Windisch-Graetz.

Forty years after this 'wonderful' but ill-fated love affair, which his parents said marked Visconti forever, the princess, to 'help perpetuate his memory', partly raised the veil on one of the most intense and tormented periods of his life. A few days after Luchino's death, she consented to be interviewed in her home in Oxford by reporter Peter Dragdze.

Beside a roaring fire she took the relics of her romance with Visconti out of a chest: a small gold cross he had given her, a few snapshots, some letters. And the memories came surging back 'as if it were yesterday'.

'Luchi was twenty-nine when he came to Kitzbühel with members of his family, his sister-in-law Nicky, and a gang of exuberant, lively Italians. We all knew each other, since in those days things happened in a closed social circle . . . I was at tea with friends. Luchi, who wasn't crazy about the mountains, had just arrived. He was so handsome, and talking to him was so interesting. Not the usual society gossip, but about art, music, theatre, a host of subjects that interested me, too. It was sudden, love at first sight. We saw each other that afternoon and we made a date for that evening.'

The girl's parents bore names as illustrious as Visconti's. Her mother was Princess Leontine Fürstenberg, her father was Prince Hugo who descended from one of Austria's oldest families and included among his ancestors the Alfred zu Windisch-Graetz who, at the head of a Habsburg army, had crushed the revolutions of 1848 in Prague and Vienna, and had then gone on to capture Budapest from the Hungarians.

At twenty-one, their daughter had the kind of beauty that would always conquer Visconti, and that he would see again in actresses Maria Schell and Romy Schneider. They were Austrians too: blonde, with light, bright, laughing eyes, a freshness hoarded from childhood – looks that inspired the princess's nickname, 'Pupe' (Doll). In Visconti's 1962 sketch called *The Job* in the movie *Boccaccio 70*, he gave the name to the young German countess, portrayed by Romy Schneider, who is married to and deserted by a rich Milanese count – the sort of couple Luchino and Irma might have made had their 'great love' not remained, as the princess put it, an 'unfinished symphony'.

He had always been wary of women and he always would be. 'Do you know,' King Ludwig II of Bavaria asked his cousin Elizabeth, 'when Siegfried felt afraid for the first and only time? When he saw a woman . . .' Women, Visconti said, 'are wonderful, passionate creatures. But because they're irrational they often cause disorder and trouble.'

All the more troublesome in that since childhood Luchino had always competed for love with his brothers, first for exclusive possession of their mother. Then there was Wanda Toscanini, for whom the three brothers vied and who would finally grow fondest of Edoardo, the baby of the family.

'[Edoardo] was the most attached to Wanda,' Uberta says. 'Father couldn't so much as say her name without [Edoardo's] turning as red as a peony. When he died, Wanda – who had become Mrs [Vladimir] Horowitz – came from the United States for his funeral.' Then there had been Madina and Nicky Arrivabene, especially the secretly adored Nicky, who became Edoardo's wife in 1931, after Luigi married Madina. Even love affairs were kept inside the family circle. Scriptwriter Suso Cecchi d'Amico tells us that all three boys were initiated into sex by the same courtesan, Pinuccia, who was famous in the Twenties and whose clientèle included all the scions of Milan's aristocracy.

As a foreigner, Irma Windisch-Graetz escaped this incestuous fraternal rivalry. She resembled none of the women Visconti had met in Milan, in Pinerolo, in Rome or Paris. In Kitzbühel's picture-postcard setting, she glittered with snowy purity. She spoke the language Luchino always loved, and which only Donna Carla, in his family, spoke fluently. Every morning he would stop under her window and whistle three times to let her know he was there. She slipped on a coat, went downstairs and they walked for hours 'on the fresh snow, with the sun appearing and disappearing between the trees and casting long shadows' ahead of them. He talked about himself, about horses, about his stables 'which weren't going too well', about his artistic plans.

'His intelligence and his vast culture were obvious even then, and our conversations ranged from books to figurative art, from philosophy to religion. He was very different from the other young men of the socially prominent families who came there. He had much deeper interests. He discussed essential problems that never occurred to the others. Holidays didn't appeal to him much. For most of the people we associated with, he was rather a difficult man. He was not a man-about-town.'

Luchino would spend days locked into his reticence, displaying an awkwardness that, despite Irma's efforts to teach him the waltz and the polka, made him a poor sort of escort. They could only see each other evenings, properly chaperoned, at the Goldener Gans, a small but smart nightclub, or the Praxmier, where people danced Austrian folk dances.

At last, one day, he broke free of his 'irreproachable propriety': 'We were coming back from the funicular one afternoon and Luchi, without a word of warning, kissed my hands for ten minutes saying

126

"I love you." A few days later he left for Milan and Paris, promising me he'd be back as soon as possible.' He gave her a photograph of himself inscribed: 'From Luchi, Kitzbühel 1935, so I can always be near you.'

For months they were restricted to brief meetings separated by long absences. 'He travelled a lot, but when he was far away, he wrote to me often . . . Beautiful letters, but he often forgot to date them. Or he'd just give the day of the week. On the other hand, he underlined some words. Here's the first letter he wrote to me:

> Pupe, my love
>
> I am so sad and lonely without you. And I can still see your dear, sad little face when I left you at the station in Kitzbühel. I think of you and I am near you at every instant of every hour. All these thoughts make me sad, and not being able to be with you fills me with pain . . . I feel that I love you so much, and that this love is *true sincere sure and forever*. And that consoles me for being so far away. Don't be too sad, dear Pupe, I'm with you, as on the evening *when it rained*, as on the evening *when it snowed*. It won't be so long before those lovely moments return, and then we'll be happy together *for always*. Can it be true? I believe in you and you must believe in me.

For him, love could only be absolute, but there was less sensuality in it than tenderness and sentimentality. When he dreamed of the future, the comfortable, solid and reassuring image of Home overrode all others:

> I did so much thinking last night! I made so many plans for our future, yours and mine! My house here . . . seems too small, not beautiful enough for you. From my window I see the horses galloping on the track, and it makes me happy to think you'll like them . . . I hope you understand Italian, which I write without too much difficulty. Anyway, even if you don't understand it perfectly, you will always and especially understand that I love you, that I understand you, that I'm dying of impatience to see you again, that I kiss you and hold you to me, so tight, so tight . . .

By his second stay in Kitzbühel, in February 1935, he wanted to marry her. He told her, the princess said, that in her he had found 'something clean, something he'd never known before, so different from the world he'd lived in until then'. He told her his fears, his plans: 'He had not yet decided to devote himself to the theatre and the cinema, but he was already thinking about it. Show business was already one of his main centres of interest. We often talked about it. I did what I could to help him. I told him: "Why not forget about breeding horses, which you don't like, and follow your real bent? As soon as you get back to Paris, try seeing what you can do to work where you like, even if it's only as an assistant director."'

Irma shared Visconti's love of music, of art in general. She wanted to marry him, too. And if the families objected and raised obstacles, knowing Visconti's character and what the princess called 'the terrible passion he brought to everything he wanted and loved', it would have been surprising had those obstacles prevailed over Luchino's fervour and self-assurance. 'I always do what I think is right,' he wrote to his future fiancée, 'and what I feel I can do sincerely.'

He blamed the failure of his marriage plans on the bourgeois prejudices of the Windisch-Graetz family. When he revealed his plans to Donna Carla, she was all love and understanding, as he expected. He had a harder time convincing his father, who, Luchino said, 'never thought of the possibility of marriage for his son. At first, he was startled by the notion that, with my character and my mentality, I could think of marriage.'

Luchino's manifest determination finally won him over, however. Despite his concern over his son's oddness and instability, his possible homosexuality, Don Guiseppe wrote to Queen Helen to ask her, as was the custom then, for information about Irma. And Luchino soon announced to his fiancée that if she came to Milan, his father would be happy to meet her.

Prince Hugo, on the other hand, did not feel at all welcoming towards young Visconti. Marriage was out of the question, he decreed, at least for the moment. Irma's father had been asking questions too, and had learned that his prospective son-in-law was handsome, cultivated and charming; but just what did he want to do in life? There would be no marriage unless Luchino announced firm plans for his future. The Windisch-Graetz family had its feet on the ground. Irma was later to marry Franz Weikersheim, who offered all the necessary guarantees: he belonged to one of Austria's oldest aristocratic families, the Hohenlohes, and – the icing on the cake – he was one of the richest bankers in Vienna.

Throughout this ordeal, Visconti's letters showed his alarm at the idea that Irma's parents might be hearing unflattering things about him. 'Has the information arrived from Rome? It'll be terrible. But I'm used to people not liking me much . . .' When Prince Hugo asked him to postpone the marriage, his pride was deeply hurt. 'I wanted to die,' he told a friend. And Irma added: 'Luchino was deeply offended by the idea that my father objected to our being married right away. Aside from the fact that we were madly in love, it was a matter of pride to him. After his interview with my father, Luchi told me: "Either we get married right away, or it's all over. I can't wait. It's impossible." I begged him on my knees to be patient, but he was a difficult man, his moods were always changing.'

The tone of his letters gradually changed from gushing sentimentality and urgent beseeching to weariness and ill-repressed rancour.

My dearest Pupe,

    The Milan I returned to is monotonous and not très gai. I've had a lot of business problems and I am busy *all day long*. But I want to get everything arranged, and quickly, as soon as possible . . . When are you coming? Hurry, hurry. I'm very eager to see you. It's already 6 March! You should already have left Kitzbühel, which makes you sad. Come to Italy. There's lots of sunshine. Spring is here. And you should come with it, like the flowers, like the warm air, like love. Come! Your Luchi is waiting impatiently for you.

    Don't let too many days go by, too many hours be lost for nothing. Life isn't long enough when you're in love. And every minute is a wasted eternity when we're far apart.

    Ciao, Pupe. See you soon, soon. I kiss you, I take you in my arms and press you lovingly to my heart, little girl. And I am deeply your

Luchi

Dearest Pupe,

Last night I went to a concert of Beethoven symphonies at La Scala. They played the I, the IV and the V. I spent three *divine* hours and I thought of you, of us, of the possibility of a life together. The Adagio of the IVth symphony, which you surely know, is so full of tenderness and sweetness that I felt it vibrate like words of love you would have spoken to me.

I'm leaving with friends for Paris this evening. I'll be away until Wednesday. I'll write you from there. I'm going to see some plays that interest me.

Thursday, 21 March

Pupe, it's unpardonable of me to have written so little to you these days, but you must forgive me. I returned from Paris last night . . . Paris was very pleasant, if brief. I managed to see four plays and two films, one of them magnificent. That was *Lives of the Bengal Lancers*. I wept all the tears in my body. The weather was marvellous, springlike, and I adore Paris at this time of year.

I found fine weather, sun and warm air here, too. But Milan is so dreary. And you can't make up your mind (or rather, you can't even stop on your way through).

I read Anet's *Mayerling*, as you recommended. I didn't like it much. He sees the characters too romantically, they have so little life, they're scarcely human.

Ciao, Pupe darling. Write to me. Your letters in the morning are dear things that mustn't be taken away from me. I hug you lovingly to my heart.

Luchi

Monday

Pupe, I got your letter today. What can we do? Your family's indecision is heartbreaking. I'm not coming to Kitzbühel because I don't want my arrival to alarm everyone. If you came to Italy, things would be different. Lots of people here are talking about us, and I'm very annoyed that others do everything long before us . . .

This situation is intolerable, . . . I saw Lella Bassi at the races yesterday and she asked about you, if you were coming, etc. I said you were supposed to come, but that I knew nothing about your decisions and, especially, about your family's.

I wake up every morning in a foul mood. I hope that every letter of yours will bring me the sun, hope – in short, good, comforting news. But we're still at the same point.

Tomorrow I'm going to another Beethoven concert at La Scala, the Sixth and Seventh Symphonies.

But I want to go to it with you. Our souls would surely speak profoundly to each other through the music, I'm certain of it.

On the contrary I'm alone here and you are alone there. I am still discouraged, but not completely, never fear. Only I don't think life is gay, do you?

Loving kisses from your

Luchi

Irma's submissiveness was natural: she was the docile little girl who conformed to her family's wishes and to the prejudices of her circle. In a letter written late in 1935 her suitor conceded that he couldn't hold it against her. Wasn't her docility in the order of things? At the worst it demonstrated a conformism of which he by no means disapproved. 'I wrote you a very long letter yesterday. But then I tore it up because it wasn't right on some points . . . I thought that you, poor darling, have nothing to blame yourself for in all this, that in fact you were irritated by these things too, and so it wasn't *chic* of me to reproach you.'

Oddly, Luchino's first reaction was not to fight, but to retreat, to go away, to seek refuge in religion or in the army. The temptation to withdraw into religion seemed obsessive enough to him to make him tell Irma 'half joking, half serious' that 'Pupe, if I weren't so much in love with you I'd probably become a priest.' Then, when the Italian army's drive into Ethiopia began in the autumn of 1935, he wrote to her: 'You know that a War Ministry decree was issued yesterday announcing that all those who want to go and fight in Africa, from the 1880 to 1910 list, can join up. I thought about doing it. If it didn't risk causing you too much unhappiness, and Mum, too. The idea would appeal to me. We young people who weren't in the other war think we are not worthy of our fathers, of the generation that preceded us, because we've contributed nothing to making the Fatherland bigger and stronger.'

To be or not to be a man, that was the question for Visconti at a time when he was reaffirming his childish attachment to a society of mothers and fearful women. At no time did he envisage coming of age outside the established laws and institutions: marriage, with the parents' consent, the Church, the army. Although he repeatedly urged Irma to come to Italy, and suggested a few stratagems for getting herself invited to Rome, he never toyed with any of the romantic schemes traditional for thwarted lovers: eloping with the girl, marrying her, doing 'what he thought was right' without worrying about anyone else. But, in fact, marriage and the sexual and social 'normalization' it implied demanded scrupulous respect for taboos and customs, and coincided with his announced resolve to 'put my affairs in order as quickly as possible'. His thinking at the time was extremely conservative, his dreams of happiness thoroughly sentimental and middle class.

So, for a while, he went along with all the irritating pre-liminaries to a marriage between people of good family. He tolerated – with some impatience, it is true, and perhaps exaggerat-ing its importance – the gossip about him that ran the length of the peninsula. 'My father arrived from Rome today,' he wrote, 'and I will certainly talk to him about us. I hope no one has said anything to him yet. But I'm afraid they have. Because the day before yesterday, the Prince of Piedmont' – Prince Umberto – 'came to dinner at my place . . . and *immediately* asked if it were true I was getting married, because in Naples it was being talked about as a certainty.' And: 'At lunch today I'll see one of my two kid sisters, who are back from Rome, where they saw [General] Infante. I know he has already said I'm "pleasant, but that I don't like to talk", what nonsense! I hope he didn't say anything else, however. Because I wouldn't want Dad to hear anything else before I talk to him about it personally.'

Precisely when his freedom was being most distressingly monitored and curbed in both Italy and Austria, he gulped great breaths of non-conformism and creativity in Paris. More and more French words stud his letters. In Paris he lived fully, marvelling at

the dynamism he saw working everywhere – in the theatre, during
the period that Jean-Louis Barrault called 'the enlightened years', in
films, fashions, music, ballet. And Paris was alive with the impulse
to live, to live *now*, which he so strongly wanted to do and which is
normally checked by adults' eternal admonition to children: 'Wait.'

On the French side of the Alps he met people his own age for
whom the war had been merely 'one long holiday' followed by an
explosion of euphoria, freedom and moral laxity. 'What do they
care about morality, bourgeois morality?' wrote Maurice Sachs.
The author of *Sabbat* (*Day of Wrath*) listed this generation's virtues:
'Enthusiasm, real and profound generosity, an immense avidity for
life, an extreme sense of veneration, wonderful rapidity of every
reflex.'

Its faults? 'An orgiastic desire for enjoyment, terrible slackness
towards everything but pleasure, basic instability, perpetually scattered wits, a frenzy for loving that generated indiscriminate crazes,
impatience, slightly flabby tenderness and constant wonder at
everything that glittered a bit.' Happiness was not a slowly ripened
fruit; pleasure alone sufficed. They had to live, now, so life 'was not
grasped, it was pillaged like a conquered city'.

While Visconti shared this impatience for life, he was neither
that naïve nor that immoral. At a time when his own class rejected
him, demanded total allegiance from him, the sacrifice of a whole
part of himself, this craze for individualism, this frivolity and this
creative fury might have seemed dizzying: perhaps, after all, it was
in this ferment that he could find *his* way, *his* reality, not cloistered
in a palace with a wife who was irreproachable, perhaps, but so
conventional.

The camera's iris closes on Pupe's 'sad little face'. The next scene
opens on a road across a broad plain that might be the one in
Obsession, or in a Chaplin film – the path of electrifying encounters
and of loneliness that Visconti was to call his 'road to Damascus'.

Along this path, two men and a woman would determine the
direction his life would take. One of the men was blond, with
laughing blue eyes. He spoke with a German accent that denoted his
birth and childhood in the small Thuringian town of Weissenfels-
an-der-Saale. He was Visconti's age, but he had burned the bridges

to his family and his country earlier. He went to Hamburg, where he studied art history. Hoping to become an architect, he wrote a letter to Le Corbusier – almost for fun, without really believing it would accomplish anything – offering to work with him. And Le Corbusier accepted his offer. Now there he was, in the early 1930s, in Paris, where he knew no one and spoke bad French.

His work with the architect being spasmodic and not very absorbing, he had plenty of time to look around him, to meet people, to drift wherever life's currents carried him. On the terrace of a Montparnasse café he met a fashion photographer, George Hoyningen-Huene, born in Saint Petersburg in 1900 to an American mother and a father who was Tsar Nicholas II's personal equerry. With George the blond man would work for the better part of his life. At *Vogue*, where he would soon develop his extraordinary photographic gifts, the editor spoke of 'that little Kraut, Orst – what a bear', a French pun on his name, Horst. In German, however, the name conjures up eagles, and while he had an eagle's keen sight and independence, along with the fiery mettle and quicksilver reflexes of a racehorse, there was nothing bearish about him. He melted smoothly into Parisian high society, his camera capturing its refinements and eccentricities better than anyone else's.

As a friend of the theatrical designer Christian Bérard, Horst gained access through Huene to the colony of Russian exiles, grand dukes, princesses and dancers such as Lifar and Leonide Massine, who, in Monte Carlo, carried on Diaghilev's work. Like his fashion pictures, Horst's photos of them paid tribute to a social élite that was frivolous but inventive even in its games and stratagems.

'We considered ourselves,' Horst said of Hoyningen-Huene and himself, 'he a Baltic Russian and myself of German birth and both self-exiled from our native countries, as observers of a world in transition and not as critics of a society or of "committed" artists . . . Because we had to earn our living, we mainly took pictures of people whose pictures we were paid to take. If we happened to know them personally and like them, that was even better. But we didn't care how posterity judged our models and their way of life. What mattered to us was recording part of the contemporary, local, human scene.

'One of the most attractive and memorable aspects of Paris life in the Thirties was what can only be called the rare communion of the most creative minds – painters, writers, musicians, choreographers, dancers, actors, decorators and fashion designers – with some of the most intelligent people in "Society". Most of them were friends. Even those who were enemies were intimate enemies.

'Chanel worked closely with Dali, Cocteau and Balanchine for the theatre and on ballet costumes. Karinska (the Ballets Russes' costume designer) now made costumes for private masquerade balls. Dufy, Bérard and [Pavel] Tchelitchev designed the sets for [Jean] Giraudoux's plays. Georges Auric and 'the Six'* gave frequent concerts with Mme Lanvin's daughter, Countess Jeanne de Polignac . . . Matisse designed tapestries and Giacometti made lamps and tables for the decorator Jean-Michel Franck. Louise de Vilmorin, the novelist and poet, created jewellery. The surrealist artists tried their hands at everything, even films. Almost all the nocturnal conversations I remember hearing then were fountains of new ideas.'

Horst, the son of small shopkeepers on the Judenstrasse of an obscure German town, needed only a few years to win admission to this circle of princes and millionaires eager to patronize the arts, a society in which talent and daring counted for far more than titles and wealth. In 1936, on his return from New York, where he worked part of the year for *Vogue*, he was invited to lunch by the Viscountess de Noailles. Although they had a mutual friend, Princess Natalie Paley (she and Horst played a pair of tongue-tied lovers in a short amateur film that Huene began but never finished), this was the first time he had ever climbed the grand staircase in the Noailles town house, where guests were greeted in the vestibule by a Cellini statue of Saint George and the dragon. And this was his first meeting with the distant, incredibly handsome young Italian, Count Luchino Visconti di Modrone, still considered no more than an extravagantly rich playboy crazy about horses and racing cars.

Shortly before the luncheon, Visconti had phoned Marie-Laure de Noailles and asked her if he could stop by for a moment and say

*The group of young French antiromantic composers guided by Jean Cocteau and Erik Satie in the Twenties. Besides Auric, it included Germaine Tailleferre, Louis Durey, Arthur Honegger, Darius Milhaud and Francis Poulenc (translator's note).

hello before he caught the afternoon train for Rome. Beside a blaz-
ing fire in the great fireplace, the two men exchanged a few words –
enough to start a compelling, instantaneous current flowing
between the blond, wilful-looking 'little Kraut' and the Italian
wrapped in Byronic gloom.

'He hung back,' Horst recalls, 'he didn't smile easily and seemed
constantly to be reining in his Latin temperament . . . For some
obscure reason, I was sure he was attracted to me. There was something mysterious in him, something that was simultaneously close
and distant. I had lived long enough on the fringes of fashionable
society to know that foreign aristocrats, even the English, as lordly
and snobbish as they may be in their own country, tend to be far less
cocky in Paris. And maybe the fact that I now lived mostly in
America led me to affect a kind of indifference to European titles
and customs.

'Whatever the reason, when Luchino apologized to Marie-Laure
for having to leave to catch his train, I suddenly found myself
interrupting their goodbyes to announce firmly to him: "You're not
leaving Paris this afternoon. Tomorrow at one o'clock you're
lunching with me at the Crillon bar." To Marie-Laure's somewhat
amused surprise, and to my delight, he motioned his agreement and
left. And the next day, when I reached the Crillon bar at one o'clock
– without much hope, but you never knew – he was there, waiting
for me. We lunched together, as agreed. Luchino remained at his
hotel for a week or two, and we saw each other every day.'

Horst remembers that Visconti used to carry three books around
with him everywhere. They were printed on bible paper and bound
in red leather: a volume of Proust's *Remembrance*, *Death in Venice* and
Gide's *The Counterfeiters*. The Mann story represented homosexual
temptation, the Proust concerned roots and love of family, and the
Gide, like an antidote, stood for alienation, praise of bastardy and
hatred of family. Horst says Visconti said little about his family, but
he gave the impression that he was not very close to his father, that
his family ties rather weighed on him, but that 'he felt a duty
towards it'. He never alluded to his parents' separation, or to the fact
that his father was generally believed to be the queen of Italy's lover.

Comparing his two aristocratic friends, Hoyningen-Huene and
Visconti, Horst remarks: 'Because I saw Visconti far less often than

I did Huene, and rarely spoke to him about our respective careers or of ordinary, boring details of daily life, my relationship with him took on a more romantic cast than with George. But there were mysterious areas in Luchino that I never tried to explore nor dared to intrude into . . . I think neither he nor George really fit into the aristocratic world they were raised in. But each reacted to this fact differently. Huene rebelled against his past like a disobedient kid; Visconti transformed his past into art.'

In those days, reports Horst, Visconti still kicked against his homosexuality. While he allowed himself what Oscar Wilde called the terrible pleasure of a double life, he feared gossip. Throughout the three years they were together – and that included frequent separations – he tried to keep their affair a secret. When they travelled to Tunisia together in the spring of 1936, to the Moorish house Huene had built in Hammamet, he was horrified to glimpse one or two appallingly familiar faces among his fellow passengers on the boat.

'To me,' says Horst, 'homosexuality was anything but a problem, but it wasn't the same for him. I made him more sure of himself, precisely because no one could have tormented him less on the subject than I did. He didn't talk much about himself, didn't tell me his life story. Sometimes he tried to explain his character, which was prickly: he was always right, I was always wrong.'

Not even escape to Tunisia, which had overcome the puritanical scruples of many other homosexuals – beginning with Gide – seemed fully to still the skittish Visconti's inner torment. Years later, in 1970, Horst sent him a photograph he had taken of him in Tunisia. 'Thank you,' Visconti wrote back, 'for sending me that image from my memory. The picture you took of me in Hammamet – believe me, I remember exactly "when", I mean the exact moment when you took the picture. I can feel again how it was, with that glass in my hand, in that doorway that gave on to the garden full of flowers, white flowers, strongly scented, jasmine and lilies. Those were happy days with you and I've never forgotten them. How could I forget them?'

In the picture he wears a silk scarf knotted up to his chin, and his eyes are deep in shadow, but he is not showing even a ghost of a smile.

Their affair was stormy, made more intense and passionate by Visconti's repression of his Latin temperament. 'His whole life was the product of his imagination,' Horst says. 'He knew nothing about sex, even though he was very passionate. But puritanical, too. There was something rigid about him. He went into terrible rages, and he was full of contradictions. An iron fist in a velvet glove . . . He had no sense of humour at all, and he couldn't laugh at himself.' An odd mixture of Latin sensuality and Prussian stiffness, born of his mother's stern ethics, a military and aristocratic sense of duty.

The photographer tells of a day in Tunisia when Visconti was twiddling his radio dial and happened to hear the announcement of a victory in Abyssinia retransmitted in Italian and followed by the fascist hymn. He bounded up and insisted that his friend stand up too. Horst, seeing how ridiculous this all was, retorted that he was not Italian and they were not in Italy. 'In that case, I'm returning to Rome,' Visconti allegedly said. 'Call me a cab so that I can catch the first plane.' On the way to the airport he accused Horst of deliberately trying to get rid of him, and only let himself be persuaded to return to Hammamet by his friend's vehement protests.

Friends the director made later have questioned this account. But it is in keeping with the patriotism expressed in his letters to Irma Windisch-Graetz, its sincerity reinforced by the fact that his brother Guido was then fighting in Ethiopia. The romantic drama it provoked fitted in with Visconti's notion of love as a way of tormenting himself and others, of embittering feelings, awakening and exaggerating deep conflicts.

All this was the very opposite of Horst's offhandedness. When he accompanied Visconti to Rome, their stay at the Ambassador Hotel on Via Veneto was again, and egregiously, disrupted by his tyrannical friend's moods and fits of jealousy. At one point, despite his aversion to scandal, Visconti allowed his jealousy to show in public when an Italian friend began chatting with Horst in English. The exasperated German warned that he would take the train to Paris that very evening, which he did. But Luchino travelled with him in a neighbouring compartment.

Because the work he still did with Huene frequently took him to the United States, Horst was never with Visconti for very long at a time. Yet, 'strangely enough, this only deepened our ties'. The war separated them, and they did not see each other again for ten years. In 1953, Visconti learned that Horst was staying in the Hotel Excelsior, in Rome. He immediately invited his old friend to his home on Via Salaria. 'We had aged, of course,' Horst says, 'and we had led very different lives in the interim. Yet it was as if time had stood still. We didn't say much to each other, but there was still a special intimacy between us.'

Maurice Sachs wrote: 'We are only responsible for our lives starting on a specific day. And each of us can remember the date of his or her birth as a man or woman . . . when free choice began to exert its influence and thread new strands into the fabric that childhood and heredity had woven for us on the loom of life.' But we are not born alone. It is true that Horst helped Visconti to live with and accept his own homosexuality. 'When I knew him in 1937,' the actor Jean Marais told us, 'homosexuality was no problem for him; he simply avoided flaunting it.' But a much older woman, whom he admired and befriended for the rest of his life, was to be his advisor, passionate lover and surrogate mother, tougher, less feminine but just as strong, energetic, realistic and combative as his real mother: the 'Grande Mademoiselle' of the Rue Cambon, fashion designer Coco Chanel.

Only three years younger than Donna Carla, Chanel had, like her, been born in mid-August, the ripe, hot season. Like the Milanese, she was both non-conformist and disciplined, unpretentious and munificent. She was lonely, too, despite the incredible numbers of people she knew, of friendships and love affairs she had. This twilight child seemed destined for loneliness; fate appeared determined to rob her of everyone she loved and who might have helped her to put down roots.

There had been Boy Capel, killed in an automobile crash, then Paul Iribe, who in 1935 had suddenly collapsed of a heart attack in the summer sun near La Pausa, the house amid olive trees where the 'bohemian' Chanel went every year to rest and touch base. There had been so many burial processions in her life: Raymond Radiguet's white funeral in December 1923, escorted by the black band from the nightclub Le Boeuf sur le Toit; the Venetian convoy bearing the body of the 'magician' Diaghilev on its ceremonial bier to the small, pink cemetery bristling with dark cypresses on San

Michele, in the middle of a lagoon, in June 1929. And, in September 1935, the black-plumed horses drawing Iribe's hearse in Barbizon, south of Paris. Chanel had paid for and staged them all.

Even the image her mirror returned to her seemed funereally black: 'My eyebrows in a menacing double arc, my nostrils flaring like a mare's, my hair blacker than the devil, a mouth like a crevasse from which pours a generous and angry soul . . . my body as juiceless as a vine without grapes.' She saw herself perfectly in the quick sketch the caricaturist Sem drew of her – as a black swan.

But this Fate past fifty who dressed only in white, with her slender figure and her youthful face 'topped by a little girl's big bow', her spirited mind and lively gestures, her 'golden-brown eyes commanding the entrance to her heart, where you see she is a woman', was the very image of lust for life, for passionate life. She was like the Russians she loved so well: 'They are at the extremes of heat and cold. At 70 degrees they are dead.'

'I love or I don't,' she said. And she loved Luchino Visconti because his excesses, his generous impulses, his brutal, sometimes coarse honesty, his love of absolutes, his intolerance combined to match her character. 'No one,' Horst remarked, 'could have been more fascinated than Chanel was by Luchino. He held back. She was mad about him and made him drunk with the sound of her voice.'

As soon as he arrived in Paris he rushed to see her, first in her luxurious apartment on the Faubourg Saint-Honoré, then on Rue Cambon, climbing the grand, mirror-lined staircase to her enchanted kingdom: beige velvets and silks embroidered in gold; coromandel screens; a library crammed with the works of the seventeenth-century moralists and manuscripts by her lover, the poet Pierre Reverdy; Venetian Renaissance blackamoors and a fantastic bestiary of bronze does, crystal toads, ivory and ebony ducks and monkeys.

Beside the fire, between a small Dali canvas – a golden ear of wheat on a black background – and an antique head of Hypnos, she talked for hours. Her voice was cracked and, Claude Delay noted, 'always [grew] hoarser in the evening . . . She talked without let-up so as not to hear the silence.' Coco spoke to Luchino of racetracks, of his broodmares, of the smell of the grass, the races when the 'lightly gaitered, delicate hooves burst from the starting gate with tendons straining, and the mounts, only a nose apart, arriving at the finish line with the jockeys standing in their saddles'.

In her 'torrential' voice, Paul Morand wrote, 'the words crackled like dry twigs' as she jeered at and mocked 'the smart set', calling it 'that divine, stinking body . . . The amusing evenings were the ones on which you flayed people alive. You see them devouring each other. We need a worldly language that is not given over to slander.'

Chanel needed no such thing; she savagely shredded the 'celebrities, passé and potential', whom she knew, supported and sometimes financed: poet-novelist Radiguet, 'a dry fruit, which is why he died so young'; Cocteau and 'his antique bazaar . . . charming, beautiful manners – so nice that you forgave him everything . . . Very little money, so I paid . . .' She could be ferocious, outrageous: 'A very petit-bourgeois who kept trying to steal everything new . . . An insect, an amusing insect, if you like.' She didn't spare Picasso, whom she accused of becoming a mere 'clown whose black eyes had petrified her, forced her to turn herself inside out, troubled her'. Or Dali, not so handsome as he had been, 'with a carnation behind his ear; he ate sardines and put some on his hair, so he smelled of sardines'.

She was the queen bee in a buzzing hive, financing Cocteau's plays and Diaghilev's *The Rite of Spring* and feeling wary of success. Money and titles didn't impress her, either; she had lived for years with the Duke of Westminster, had received the cream of Paris society in the reception rooms on Rue Cambon, had been accused of trying to humiliate great figures of world aristocracy by putting them to work for her. Better than anyone else around her, this intruder, this outsider, had observed the comedy of the world.

She rejected everything that was frivolous or flashy or merely decorative. In 1922 she dressed the actors in Cocteau's adaptation of *Antigone* in brown and beige and red, her favourite colours – 'beige because it is natural, not dyed; red because it is the colour of blood and we have so much of it inside us that we really must show a bit on the outside'. With their faces whitened and with black brush strokes underlining their features, Genica Atanasiou, Charles Dullin and Antonin Artaud appeared in costumes of coarsely woven stuff. 'Greece,' Chanel said, 'is wool, not silk.'

Uberta Visconti says that through the long and faithful relationship Chanel maintained with Luchino, 'I don't think they were more than friends. Yes, she was very much in love with Luchino. He was above all charmed by that very strong character of a woman who did things, who worked.' Like Visconti, she hated dilettantism; she imposed iron discipline on her models, frowned grumpily, moved too quickly. Her hair was a mess. At the head of her 2,000 employees, wrote Sachs, she was 'a general, one of those young generals ruled by a spirit of conquest'. When she walked down the great mirrored stairway, said Claude Delay, 'under the merciless floodlights, she was fighting her battle. No private ring could have held a fiercer one.'

Like Visconti, too, she was a despot at heart, a Pygmalion. She sculpted on the model, adjusting a hem, cutting, draping, sticking pins into a wobbly living statue. She would no sooner spot a flaw than she grabbed back the dress or gown or suit, plumped down on the floor tailor fashion, unstitched it and reassembled it. That was how Horst saw her in the wardrobe department for the *Knights of the Round Table*, remaking Jean Marais's costume a few days before Cocteau's play opened. She had 'worker's hands, [adorned] with cabochons like fake brass knuckles', and those hands were never idle. As she talked her busy fingers shaped mastic into the forms her jewellery would take.

Chanel also liked to play the role of good fairy, of a Fate weaving destinies for the people she loved. In 1936, for example, Visconti tried several times to interest two film directors in letting him adapt two items for the screen, *Mayerling* and *November*, based on a story by Flaubert; he was turned down by both Alexander Korda and Gustav Machaty, the Hungarian film-maker who had surprised and shocked moviegoers with a frank portrayal of physical love two years earlier. When Luchino complained that his plans had gone up in smoke, Coco replied flatly: 'You're going to meet [Jean] Renoir. He's a serious man.'

IX

THE ROAD TO DAMASCUS

Each arrow is for our welfare.

GABRIELE D'ANNUNZIO

'It was in fact my stay in France and my meeting with a man like Renoir that opened my eyes to a lot of things. I realized that films could be the way to touch on truths we were very far away from, especially in Italy. I remember seeing Renoir's *La vie est à nous* soon after I arrived in France; the film impressed me deeply. During that burning period – that of the Popular Front – I subscribed to every idea, all the aesthetic principles, and not only aesthetic, but political, too. Renoir's group was distinctly leftist, and Renoir himself, although he was not a card-carrier, was undoubtedly very close to the Communist Party. I really opened my eyes then; I came from a fascist country where it was impossible to know anything, to read anything, to learn anything or have personal experiences. I had a *shock*. When I went back to Italy I was really transformed.'

Precisely when did Visconti undergo that shock that was to determine his direction 'artistically and morally'? In Paris in 1936, as he repeatedly declared in statements to the communist press? Or when, encouraged by his sister-in-law Nicky, he sold some of his horses to try with his limited means to make movies? Was it specifically in the summer of 1934, when, listed vaguely as a 'trainee', his name appears in connection with the making of a film called *Toni*? He denied seeing the film at the time, despite the echoes of it evident in his first film, *Ossessione* (*Obsession*), made eight years later.

Obviously, the only background he wants for his meeting with the artist who exercised 'a major influence on me' was the red springtime of the Popular Front and its procession of revolutionary images: factories occupied by workers; the 14 July Bastille Day parades in which giant portraits of [communist leader] Maurice Thorez and [socialist] Léon Blum were carried alongside those of Robespierre, Saint-Just and Émile Zola; the leftist flags flashing scarlet, the joyous throng singing *La Carmagnole, La Marseillaise* and the *Internationale* through the heart of working-class Paris.

In 1936–7, Renoir held the banner high, making two films that won him praise in the leftist press – *L'Humanité, Ce soir, L'Avant-garde, Regards, Commune* – as the left's 'leading director'. His film *La vie est à nous* was directly commissioned as election propaganda by the Communist Party; the following year the party gave its all-out support to the man who made *La Marseillaise*.*

For years, since his 1931 picture *La Chienne*, Renoir's name had been synonymous in the film industry with scandal and failure. Producers turned their backs on a director who 'makes movies in which people spit on the floor'. He refused to take his ostracism meekly. In the fellow-travelling magazine *Ciné-Liberté* in March 1936 he unleashed his vengeful fury against censorship and the subservience of French film-makers to the movie industry trusts, the American and German production 'mastodons' like UFA and Tobis, controlled by Hitler and Goebbels, whose clutches he, like Marcel Pagnol, was among the few to escape. He derided young directors he identified as 'elegant riff-raff' who 'worship the photogenic golden calf' and who 'resolutely embark on a career by coldly undertaking a *Purple Heart*, a drama in five acts, or *All Those Ladies in the Parlour*, a rousing military farce . . .'.

Remaining independent meant having a united, incorruptible crew to rely on, he said, for 'you cannot venture into the cinema world unless you know you are surrounded by accomplices. A film is a lot like a burglary. It is also an exploration. A professional [thief] would never dream of robbing the Bank of France, any more than an explorer would venture alone into the jungle . . .'.

Une partie de campagne (A Day in the Country) – in which Luchino Visconti's name appears in the credits along with those of Jacques Becker and Henri Cartier-Bresson as a lowly third assistant director

*A 1936 film tracing the historical sources of the Popular Front (translator's note).

and again as assistant prop man – is a perfect example of a film that would never have been made or released without the combined efforts of men and women linked by friendship and devoted to Renoir. Such people as Yves Allégret. Becker and Cartier-Bresson, passionately attached to the director; Pierre Lestringuez, 'more than a childhood friend, a pre-childhood friend, since my father and his were intimates'; the actors from the October Group who consented to work without pay. On the set, says Cartier–Bresson, 'everybody did a bit of everything' and no one worried about rank or job definitions. What was *A Day in the Country*? Replies Renoir: 'We were a group of friends, and it was like a kind of happy holiday on the banks of a very pretty river.'

Completely happy? No, since, among countless other problems, the sun refused to come out, in defiance of Renoir's script. Scheduled to last for two weeks under a radiant sun, filming went on and on under a relentlessly grey sky from 15 July until the end of August. As the days and weeks dragged on, other storms darkened the atmosphere of happy innocence customarily encouraged by games, jokes and bibulous feasts. The film had been tailored for actress Sylvia Bataille, but her relationship with Renoir went from idyllic sunshine to storms, frost and, finally, to a deep freeze. Visconti declared that 'the film couldn't be completed because of an infinity of things: actor Georges Darnoux's teeth, the rain . . . I went back to Italy.'

His handwritten annotations in the script attest to how attentively he followed the filming. He was especially concerned with the costumes, showing a keen eye for details that, according to Miss Bataille, 'derived from an infallible knowledge of French fashions in that period' as well as of French culture and 'the profoundly French nature of the story. Even details like the vest; I don't think Italian peasants in 1886 wore that kind of thing. We once went to the Samaritaine [department store] together to look for a lace corset, and I found that Visconti know the store like the palm of his hand. He was exceptionally precise.'

His taciturnity and reserve were equally exceptional; he had a way of watching every retake without ever asking a question. He wasn't shy, no, but 'he had no sense of camaraderie, he wasn't the kind of person you'd have a drink with after work . . . I had the impression that he didn't like mixing with people, that it made him a bit uneasy'.

That uneasiness may have been due, at least when filming got under way, to prejudices he ascribed to the young people who 'belonged to the Communist Party' and who 'opened my eyes'. 'The whole group that gravitated to Renoir,' he declared, 'was made up of Communists. At first, naturally, I was looked on with suspicion. To them I was an Italian, I came from a fascist country and, to top it all off, I bore . . . the weight of an aristocratic name. That suspicion melted almost at once, however, and we became fast friends.'

Cartier-Bresson flatly denies that the crew felt any such suspicion based on ideology: 'That never intruded on the set,' he told us, 'or in our relationships with one another. In Renoir, as in all [poet Jacques] Prévert's friends, there was a fundamental streak of anarchism. It is wrong to say we had any bias against Visconti.'

Indeed, Renoir was the last man to accept or reject a friend or a fellow worker because of their political affiliation. There were too many personal contradictions for that in this strange man, this Jacobin aristocrat, described as 'half rebel, half snob in a tramp's hide' who mingled with Parisian society at the Jockey Club and flirted with the Communist Party; he once lamented that 'the fruit trees in the grounds of Plessis-lès-Tours were no longer bent under the weight of hanged rich men' as they were in the time of Louis XI.

One of Renoir's 'accomplices', the scriptwriter Charles Spaak, remarked in 1945 that 'men's ideas interest him far less than their instincts, their cravings. Imagine Renoir with some champion of the left; he'd befriend the fellow not for his ideals or his viewpoints, but, perhaps, because he had a connoisseur's knowledge of tobacco or horses . . . Renoir attached much more importance to people's professionalism, to the precise knowledge they acquire through contact with their work or with nature, than he did to their ideology. The instant he found something authentic in a person, he was charmed. He would like a mechanic in overalls in the same way he liked a marquess who wore the right tie at the right time . . .'

The strong political colour Visconti gave, in hindsight, to his first meeting with anti-fascist groups again demonstrates how intent he was to present his sudden conversion, his illumination, as exem-

1909. On a path in the grounds at Grazzano: Luchino, aged three, in the arms of his mother, Donna Carla.

1909. A family portrait that made all Milan envious: the Duke and Duchess Visconti di Modrone at Grazzano castle with their first five children, (left to right) Anna, Luigi, Luchino, Edoardo and Guido.

Tempestuous love, wrenching separation: Luchino's own family tragedy is echoed in his last film, *The Innocents* (1976), with Laura Antonelli and Giancarlo Giannini.

A poster for Carlo Erba's milk of magnesia. Luchino's mother was heiress to the Erba fortune.

The courtyard of the palace in the heart of Milan where Visconti was born to his illustrious name.

Above: A mirror of an idyllic childhood: Visconti (right) with Bjørn Andresen as Tadzio in *Death in Venice* (1971).
Left: Milan, 1920: Luchino, at fourteen, beginning his 'years of uncertainty and rebellion'.

Right: Luchino, looking like Proust's character Saint-Loup, in the uniform of the Savoy Cavalry Regiment in Pinerolo (Piedmont) in 1927.
Below: Visconti (right) leading his thoroughbred Lafcadio into the winner's circle in 1929, when he began racing horses under his own colours.

In their mother's ever-present shadow: Luchino and his favourite sister, Uberta, in 1950, before Antonio Arquani's portrait of Donna Carla.

Above: An explosive friendship: the 'red count' and Anna Magnani, the 'she-wolf', in 1951, the year in which Visconti filmed *Bellissima.*
Right: 1943: Visconti's film *Obsession* shocked Mussolini's Italy.

The tyrant Luchino Visconti (1287-1349).

Visconti, a cinematic condottiere every bit as imperious as his ancestor Luchino, directs his troops before the ruins of an old Visconti fortress in *Senso*.

plary and emblematic. 'I had always lived in Italy, in Milan, among anti-fascists,' he told the communist newspaper *Rinascità*. 'The anti-fascism there was diffuse, but passive . . . Then I went to France, where I worked as an assistant to Renoir. That was where I first came in contact with forces of whose existence I had never even dreamed. When you arrive in Paris from Milan, you really feel as if people in Italy live with their eyes blindfolded and their ears plugged . . . In a way, my friendship [with Renoir's group] became my road to Damascus.'

And again: 'In 1936 I was in Paris . . . to work in films . . . A real idiot . . . Not a full-fledged Fascist, but a fascist fellow-traveller . . . Someone who knew nothing and understood nothing. Someone whose eyes, in politics, were as closed as those of newborn kittens. But my friends made sure I opened them . . . They were all Communists, all party members . . . At first, naturally, they looked at me suspiciously. What's he after, this "rich, titled imbecile? What's this little idiot after?"'

There is no doubt that Renoir helped Visconti 'define his aspirations'. Not because the 'fellow-travelling fascist' aristocrat thought of him as a spiritual guide. He had no need for that. But, for the first time, he saw a master movie craftsman at work, he whole-heartedly admired Renoir as a man and an artist, 'his rich humanity, his affection for people and their work, his extraordinary skill at directing actors, his meticulousness, his technique'. Visconti identified with Renoir, saw himself in the film-maker: 'I felt that I was talking to him like a brother' – a brother with more freedom than Luchino had.

Renoir's childhood, after all, had been bathed in the same cultural climate as his own, in touch with painters, writers and society women who came to pose for his father Auguste in the 'Palace of Mists' in Montmartre. He, too, had run away time and again to escape from the schools to which his parents, exasperated by his turbulence, had finally sent him to pursue studies that turned out to be as chaotic and inconclusive as Luchino's had been.

And Jean had waited a long time before choosing a career. 'Horrified' at first by his father's fame and genius, he had considered 'being a grocer, or a farmer in Algeria', anything but an artist. The first world war had made him a cavalry officer, 'a dragoons officer, in fact'. But war soon stopped amusing him, and he resigned his commission. The next four years were spent making pottery. Then he happened into a cinema that was showing Erich von Stroheim's *Foolish Wives* and he realized he had finally found his way, even if he had to sell his father's paintings to raise money to make movies. He had been twenty-nine then, about the same age as Visconti when he met Renoir and began thinking seriously of directing films.

Sealing this 'fraternal' bond between the two men was a common attachment to their roots, a shared love of the turn of the century, of old family picture albums and a return to their well springs. What was *A Day in the Country*, filmed in 'one of the major settings of Impressionism', if not Renoir's past revisited? He had set up his camera at precisely the spot on the banks of the Loing river where his father, alone or with Claude Monet, had so often set up his easel. Specifically, in the village of Marlotte where, in 1866, Auguste had painted his *Cabaret de la Mère Anthony*; his son could personally remember everyone in the painting, from Sisley to Pissarro – even the three-legged mongrel poodle Toto. Where else could he have found authentic Renoir landscapes, the open-air riverside dance-halls, the banks of the Seine that we see in *La Grenouillère* and *The Luncheon of the Boating Party*? 'In 1936 the Seine was already a Seine of factories and steamboats and a lot of noise . . .'

The painter had met Guy de Maupassant in an inn much like the one in *A Day in the Country*, which was based on a Maupassant story. 'They liked each other,' Jean wrote, 'but they admitted they had nothing in common.' Auguste Renoir said the writer 'sees everything as black'. Maupassant said the painter 'sees everything as rosy'. They did share one notion: 'Maupassant is crazy', Renoir had said. 'Renoir is crazy,' the writer had declared. The wonder is that, despite his father and Maupassant, Jean managed to remain himself, and that although he opened his film to a maelstrom of influences, including suggestions from his friends and his cast, he created a work of art that was his alone.

Stress has been laid on the freedom Renoir left his actors to improvise lines, on his tendency to alter a scenario to match the circumstances (as he did in *A Day in the Country*, which he was forced to adapt to what he called 'the disorder, the traps wrought by the light, by the sun so dear to the Impressionists', as contrasted with the disciplined light of studio painting). Much has been said about his profound anarchism, apparently so different from the attitude Visconti would later show.

In fact, like Visconti, he always knew exactly what he wanted; he built fully developed scenes, laid out complete outlines of his films, carefully planned shooting schedules and rehearsals. He manipulated his actors shrewdly and skilfully, letting them believe they were inventing their own characters, making up their own lines, that they were in control, never realizing that he was taking them exactly where he wanted them to go.

'With him,' said Dalio, one of his favourite actors, 'work was a tissue of lies. He treated us like a mother sheltering her children. He fed us a little too much mother's milk, a little too much caramel. He made us do the same scene over twenty times, but we never realized it because we knocked off after each take. He wept, he asked the crew – he called them "comrades", not only because they were all Popular Front, but because we were all his comrades – to applaud us: "Wonderful, it's so beautiful, like being at the Conservatory." But there was no way of knowing what he wanted. All we knew was that we were well placed, spatially, which kept us from falling over each other. We all took turns crowing about how great we were. With him, we were creative, the words came easily. We were always correctly positioned. It all added up to truth.'

Truth – the truth that the Russian director Konstantin Stanislavsky sought in the theatre, that 'rough fabric' of life as people really live it, 'harsh, despairing, fated', from which Stroheim also fashioned his films. Visconti would seek it under the influence of the same teachers; it could be attained only by ridding acting of all the absurdly sentimental and romantic conventions over-exploited in traditional light comedies and melodramas. In *Toni*, Renoir had sent his actors without make-up into a southern French landscape of rocky hills and dark lakes, to the very spots where a murder really had been committed a few years earlier. Released after the run of Marcel Pagnol's reassuring film *Angèle, Toni* seemed unbearably cruel despite scissoring by the censor. To Visconti this was a significant lesson in cinema.

It was, first, a lesson in absolute control and consistency, instead of haphazard, risky improvisation. Renoir saw actors as cardinal elements in his films, and for them he devised a whole catalogue of tricks designed not merely to strip away the stock of conventional gestures and intonations a player might accumulate, but also to make him live the situation deeply, make him 'play the character and not the moment'. The long-shot sequences so typical of Renoir's and Visconti's work, like their tracking shots and pans and meticulously arranged backgrounds, were designed so exactly that the characters – and the actors – were never cut off from the real world or isolated from everything around them.

Did one really have to leave Italy to acquire that sort of training? Not if we remember that, beginning in 1928, the distinguished fascist film-maker Alessandro Blasetti had also been exploring 'the path of truth and reality' with his big films (*Sole, 1860*) and his teaching at the film school. Believing that actors should rub up against reality rather than huddle among library shelves, he took his students on field trips to insane asylums, prisons and morgues to show them real lunatics, real jailbirds and real cadavers. He, too, filmed in authentic settings – the Pontine marshes in *Sole*, Sicily in *1860* – and used actors and extras co-opted from real life, unorthodox in those days of 'white telephone' movies (sentimental comedies about the smart set).

References abounded in Italy to the great figures of Russian cinema, Vsevolod Pudovkin, Sergei Eisenstein and Nikolai Ekk, whose films Visconti saw in France, with Renoir, in a small cinema called the Panthéon, where he recalled seeing *Chapayev*. This film by Sergei and Georgi Vasiliev strongly impressed Blasetti at the Venice Film Festival in 1934. When the Experimental Film Centre was opened a year later in Rome, it was theoretically subject to tight fascist control, but the courses taught by Umberto Barbaro, a notorious Marxist and a colleague of Blasetti's, were based mainly on the theories and works of Soviet movie-makers.

'I didn't look at colours,' says Luigi Chiarini, the Centre's fascist director. 'The Centre was an open school, open to everyone with a serious knowledge of cinema. I showed Béla Balázs, who was Hungarian, Jewish and a Communist. I showed Pudovkin and Eisenstein, and my right arm was Umberto Barbaro, who was a Communist . . .' For the young people who flocked to the first major Italian cinema school – Sicily's Pietro Germi, the Roman

Luigi Zampa, Dino de Laurentiis from Naples, Ferrara's Michelangelo Antonioni, Giuseppe De Santis from the working-class
Rome suburb of La Ciociaria – this buzzing hive operating in the
shadow of Fascism was an opening on to real life, on to a foreign
world that represented the future.

Visconti, however, was not one to sit meekly at a school desk.
Besides, following a teacher like Renoir meant denying his own
past, breaking out of his provincial shell of institutions, prejudices
and conventional morality, escaping from the yoke of family tradition and duty and his 'aristocratic name, so heavy a burden'. It
meant choosing a clearly alien way of life under the guidance of a
new family, the Communists grouped around Renoir. The objective smacked of Gide: to 'be reborn as a new being, under a new
sky, amid things that were completely renewed'. This meant straining against the petrified knot still holding him to his real family, his
past, his old constricted self.

He never referred to the work he did with his father in the
theatre in Italy as key experiences – not G. Traversi's *Carità
mondana*, or Jay Mallory's *Sweet Aloes*, presented in the public
theatre in Como and the Manzoni Theatre in Milan in the autumn of
1936 (for which, at the request of the actress Andreina Pagnani, he
designed costumes that were praised by reviewers). It was in Paris
that he really went exploring, that he made his major personal and
artistic acquisitions.

In the spring of 1937 he was reunited with Horst, back from
America to photograph the spring fashion shows. Escaping from
the worldly tumult of the International Exposition of Arts and
Techniques, his German friend introduced him to the mysterious
Gustave Moreau Museum, where surrealist writer André Breton
longed to be locked up for a night; behind its long walls and high
windows seethed all the Symbolists' *fin-de-siècle* fantasies and
enchantments. Visconti still remembered the experience twenty
years later, when he sent Horst a small copy of a sketch for
Salome. Soon afterwards, for his staging of the Strauss opera,
Luchino borrowed Moreau's bizarre architecture, his bloody,
lunar expanses, and that chaste and lonely painter's burning
sensuality.

At the time one might have thought, like the characters in

Giraudoux's *Tiger at the Gates*, that peace was at hand, one might have seen a victory of tolerance and freedom everywhere – had it not been for the Spanish Civil War, cruelly recalled at the Paris World Exhibition by Mirò's *Still Life with Old Shoe* and Picasso's *Guernica*, and had it not been for the swastika on the red flag atop the German pavilion's 175-foot tower; 1937 was, after all, the year of Renoir's *Grand Illusion*. And the year was a kaleidoscope of parties, masquerades, fireworks.

Poetry flourished in the theatres 'without organ music or vocal embellishments', a product of the 'Four' directors' collaboration with old-fashioned playwrights (Louis Jouvet with Giraudoux) and new ones (director Georges Pitoëff with playwright Jean Anouilh). The theatres were hothouses of creativity – Bérard's spangles and baroque fantasies, for example, for the Jouvet production of Corneille's *L'Illusion comique*; Pitoëff's mistily nostalgic version of Anouilh's *Traveller Without Luggage*, and Jouvet, again, doing Giraudoux's *Electra* on a bare stage under the clear, direct lighting appropriate to the rites and times of tragedy.

That summer, Visconti went in search of the clear light of ancient Greece, not with Horst, but with his Milanese friend Corrado Corradi. 'Luchino wasn't crazy about the sea,' Corradi said, 'but we went off to discover the classical world. They were marvellous days . . . Luchino had a feeling for nature. Maybe he was more impressed by groups of things than by any single sight, even if it was superior.'

After his feverish activity in Paris, Visconti needed the restorative purity of that summer to regain his bearings, and he found it in his reactions to the Aegean islands, the wild, mythical setting sacred to Apollo and Artemis. Corradi said Luchino felt the spell of the place 'in an extraordinary way, almost overreacting'. What's more, he felt a need to summarize them and express them in lyrical, sensuous prose rather like the language in Albert Camus's *Noces* (*The Wedding*). His stylistic ambition is evident in these travel notes that, like his diary and the few pages of his unfinished novel *Angelo*, betray his concern with private feelings, his need to analyse and solve the enigma of his identity, his innermost being. Visconti's journey into the lost Grecian world was also a voyage in search of himself.

Tinos. I recall the interminable, sunbaked stairs with their broad, high steps leading to the sanctuary. In the main courtyard, four enormous cypresses, gnarled and black, stand guard over a dry fountain. I made that implacable journey twice, stopping at the uphill ranks of merchants' stalls offering silver icons and sacred scenes carved into seashells, all covered with a warm, brilliant varnish.

Mykonos. Mykonos is not a dragon with a long, scaly tail and fiery maw lying on the shore of an island in wait for lost seamen. Mykonos does not demand the answers to riddles and does not feed on human flesh. Mykonos is a small, irregular breast, a palm's breadth of green water, innocently crowned with a scattering of houses ranging downhill in terraces to the sail of a windmill. At the foot of the bright hill, herds graze, dispersed like stacks of freshly cut hay . . .*

A transparent and lovely landscape, a lost paradise still bearing the traces of sacred maternal 'innocence'. Going back to the cities meant tearing himself away from this 'measured perfection' and plunging once more into the cursed world of febrile, evil, mortal men.

En route to Piraeus. And we sailed tonight for Piraeus. The cruise is over. I lie down on the deck to sleep and all I see before me is the sky, the sky my sole horizon. This is the last sensation of infinity I'll have . . . The Milky Way runs like a huge vein patched with half-shadows and thick clots of diamonds, the world of the stars; elsewhere in the sky drift lonely flakes bright as nebulae . . . infinity is a great, liquid package barely pulsating above us.

Here we are in Piraeus, a horrible ant-hill on the sea, a pile of bones where smoke rises in long, funereal scarves from bristling, blackened chimneys. A fine ash falls in a constant cloud over this swollen, misty loaf. Farewell, peaceful pagan countenances of islands left far away at sea. Farewell to the measured perfection of gulfs of dark water, precise, climactic encounters of our sensitivity with your unfailing beauty. Farewell, ghosts rising amid the purple hay like the scrawny cats of Delos . . . Timolos,

Grecian Diary, Athens, August 1937.

the stairway on Tinos. The silken sky over Nios. Santorini, the raving of a mad titan. Now we must go down into the dinghy bobbing on the oil of the port that will take us back to land – a dry mouth to which, panting like sad asthmatics deprived of the sea wind, we will return to live in airless corridors.*

Back to the clustered grey stones of Milan after the brilliance of 'shining' Delos. Horst was in Austria, near Salzburg, on the banks of the Attersee, where Klimt painted so many landscapes. Visconti would later film the 'Night of the Long Knives' sequence in *The Damned* there. And there Eleonora von Mendelssohn, a friend of Bertolt Brecht, of Kurt Weill and the director Max Reinhardt, bought a castle to which to flee from Germany on Hitler's rise to power (her mother, the singer and pianist Giulietta Gordigiani, had named her after Giulietta's friend Eleonora Duse). At the end of every summer, Horst was invited to stay at her Schloss Kammer. Eleonora, the composer's granddaughter, had two passions: the theatre, where she made her début as an actress under Reinhardt's direction, and music, which would soon send her flying into Toscanini's arms. 'Bérard taught me to see,' Horst once said. 'Eleonora taught me to listen.'

Nevertheless, of the three women who mattered most to the photographer in those years – Natalie Paley, Eleonora, and Coco Chanel – 'Chanel was certainly the greatest actress'. He was closest to her in 1937, when she finally agreed to pose for him, allowing him to capture as no one else did the profound sadness she cherished.

Together, on 14 October 1937, they attended the opening of the *Knights of the Round Table*, a medieval fantasy staged against a back-drop of purple hangings; it was the occasion for Cocteau's latest discovery, Jean Marais, to shine in all his twenty-year-old splendour. After the performance, the actor met Visconti, whose unusual, aristocratic good looks had already struck him at a Chanel fashion show. 'He liked our play so much,' Marais says, 'that he came almost every evening. Horst, he and I saw each other often. I didn't even know he wanted to make movies, or that he had worked with Renoir.'

Grecian Diary, Athens, August 1937.

At the time, Visconti had in mind a film biography of Chanel. In the winter of 1937–8 he rushed to the United States in search of a producer, making a pilgrimage to Hollywood, which the rag trade called 'the Mont Saint-Michel of bums and boobs'. Most of his time, however, was spent in New York, not to meet Horst there, but for a stormy and unhappy affair with the wealthy young dime-store heir, Donague Woolworth, who then had vague ambitions to be an actor. Luchino not only returned empty-handed, without a contract, but, Uberta says, 'he was yellower than he would have been with jaundice. Hollywood made a terrible impression on him.'

But he did return home with more travel notes, a hodgepodge in which odd analyses of the 'musicality' of American speech – 'liturgical' song, 'a flow of honey' – are mixed with paeans to New York, its 'majestic gothic cathedral' and its titanic sprawl. No personal portraits, no individual details, no effusions, merely a small, bitter fable about loneliness: 'When penguins are left alone, they die. Once upon a time there was a penguin that was left alone and, to keep him from dying, he was given a mirror, and the penguin, believing he was no longer alone, did not die . . . So many men are like that penguin and escape death by developing illusions about a friendship, a companion who is merely their own image, a reflection in a mirror.'

Back in Milan, in March 1938 he designed the sets for his friend Henry Bernstein's play *Journey*, directed by Andreina Pagnani. And that March, the curtain fell on the first act of another tragedy. On 13 March, Hitler entered Vienna, scene of his humiliating failure as an architect and painter, which he had left thirty years earlier. 'This is the end of Europe as we have known and loved it,' wrote the novelist Julien Green in his *Journal*. 'The German armies entered Austria without firing a shot. Neither Britain nor France nor Italy turned a hair.'

After a brief intermission, the second tragi-comic act of Munich began, ending in the pompous white marble setting of the Führerhaus with the sacrifice of Czechoslovakia and the German annexation of the Sudetenland. After a moment of panic, with mobilization posters going up everywhere, France 'returned to its belote and Tino Rossi',★ the playwright Henri de Montherlant growled. But the play was not over yet.

That summer, Horst and Visconti consulted a clairvoyant. 'You,' she told the German, 'will grow like a flower . . .' For the Italian she forecast fame, but prison first. In any case, she assured them, there would be no war.

The time for fairy tales was over, however. With financial backing from Chanel, Cocteau turned a final hand to promotional razzle-dazzle by bringing black boxer Al Brown back to the ring, afterwards showing him in a circus act backed up by a black jazz band. Then he retired from the Paris scene to a hotel room in provincial Montargis to write a 'modern and naked' play dispensing with optical illusions, superfluous props and 'decorative subterfuges'. The set was to consist of a door 'so that misfortune could come and go' and a chair so that 'fate could take a seat'.

This climaxed, on 26 November 1938, in the shocking *Les Parents terribles* (*Intimate Relations*), a stifling, morbid drama of incest in a disintegrating middle-class family. Yvonne, the jailer and prisoner in this tragic enclosure, both mother and mistress, dies calling despairingly to her son, who betrays her by becoming a man. Visconti was never to forget its language, these nightmare corridors where evil roamed. It would be his final social event in Paris and, five years later, the first play he staged in Rome.

Meanwhile, the last strand binding him to his past snapped.

In mid-January a telegram from Italy called him to the bedside of his mother, who was dying in a villa in Cortina d'Ampezzo. 'She had to live in the mountains or by the sea,' Uberta says. 'There were no antibiotics then; the fever couldn't be broken. The disease had completely rotted her lungs and she was in great pain. It was a terrible shock; we didn't think she could ever die. Luchino was in Paris, I think, but he made it back in time.'

Donna Carla, that latter-day Isolde, had made a pact with her son. 'If something serious happened and I was far away, she would wait for me,' he said. 'I would reach her bedside in time to hear my name on her lips.'

---

*Belote: a popular French card game played with a 32-card pack; tenor Tino Rossi, the Corsican heart-throb, was a musical-comedy and film star (translator's note).

X

THE BLACK ROOM

Mindful of the lesson of the past, I expected
nothing of yesterday but the ordained, the
predetermined. Then, suddenly, the thread
broke. I was sprung from the unknown: no
past, no model, nothing to lean on; everything
was to be created: country, ancestors . . . all to
be invented, discovered. I was to resemble no
one but myself.

ANDRÉ GIDE, *Oedipus*

On Thursday, 19 January 1939, at ten o'clock in the morning, the funeral cortège left Casa Erba, at 3 Via Marsala, where Donna Carla had been born fifty-nine years earlier, and moved via the church of Santa Maria Incoronata to Milan's Monumental Cemetery. In keeping with the duchess's wishes, the ceremony was simple – 'no flowers or wreaths' – but the mourners included a host of friends, the leaders of that frivolous and extravagant society she had deserted more than ten years earlier. For one last time the newspapers extolled her haughty beauty, the refinement of her culture and intelligence, and her devotion to the many Lombardian charities she had headed or supported.

The loss to Luchino was crushing. There was no one he could love as he had cherished, idolized his mother. 'Without her,' he said, 'life wasn't worth living any more.' In his new apartment in Porta Nuova she was everywhere, in the furniture, curios and books she had given him. Photographs made her image omnipresent. He remained in mourning for months and, said his friend Corradi, he was sunk in grief. 'I felt terribly sorry for him and I phoned him every day before lunch. He went through a crisis of religious faith, or rather, a strong upsurge of faith. Donna Carla had been very pious, and he inherited her deep feeling for religion.'

Milan, the scene of his youth, the setting for happier days, was now unbearable for him. He went to Rome. That summer was spent aboard a sailboat with Uberta and Edoardo. In Edoardo he again encountered the zest for life and the practicality that had made their mother both strong and charming; in beautiful, wild Uberta, the freedom and rebelliousness that brought them so close together. When still very young, Uberta had married without her father's consent, choosing a young Venetian named Renzino Avanzo, whom she had met during one glorious holiday at Forte dei Marmi and who was crazy about automobile racing.

'Mother was pretty understanding,' she says, 'but my father was a stickler for principle; he insisted on a fine patrician match: "Wait," he said, "wait." So I left. And it didn't last. In fact, none of the marriages in my family lasted very long – only a few months for Guido . . . Luchino was right to steer clear of it.'

Henceforward, only one woman was to reign unconditionally over his life: Uberta, to whom he transferred most of the love he had devoted to his mother. The affinity between brother and sister went beyond words. If he grew doubtful or worried, she sensed it at once without his having to tell her. Luchino was twelve years older than her and stood in for her parents; he showered her with gifts, 'especially clothes – he tried to deck me out like a Madonna, but I didn't like that'.

He monitored her friends, too, sometimes directing her away from people he thought were not good enough for her. 'Once, for example, we were at the races,' Uberta recalls. "Turn around," he told me, and went off to greet a woman who also owned a stable. When I asked him why he hadn't introduced us, he told me, "They're not your kind of people." The woman giving herself such airs was an ex-actress who had played soubrette parts in second-rate plays and had then married a successful businessman.'

As anxious about her as his father had been about his children, Luchino worried about everything. After an evening at his place, he would gaze apprehensively after her when she drove off alone to her apartment on Rome's Via Cortina d'Ampezzo. He was intent on protecting her from dangers she disregarded, especially now that war clouds were gathering on the horizon.

There was cause for alarm. The political climate worsened, grew stifling. At court and in aristocratic circles, Mussolini's wooing of Hitler stirred mistrust and alarm. When the Führer visited Italy in the spring of 1938, he was offended by the cool reception he received from King Victor-Emmanuel. At the Quirinale palace, where he was lodged, Hitler was annoyed to find no blackshirts around him, only elegant gentlemen of the royal household and monarchist generals and admirals. 'This place reeks of the catacombs,' Himmler grumbled. Hitler wondered how the Duce could allow himself to be outshone by the courtiers, 'these arrogant good-for-nothing aristocrats'.

After the Pact of Steel was signed in 1939, Mussolini openly showed his impatience and his growing weariness with the caution and pacifism of the king he called 'the dwarf' and 'the silly little sardine'; in conversation with his son-in-law, Count Galeazzo Ciano, the increasingly pro-aristocratic foreign minister, the Duce used a cruder term: 'your old asshole friend'. The monarchy, he complained to Ciano, 'is blocking acceptance of fascist doctrine by the army . . . I wonder if the time hasn't come to get rid of the House of Savoy . . . I'm tired of dragging empty wagons behind me, with their brakes on at that!'

Awed by the strength and discipline of Hitler's armies, the Duce, with Starace's help, drew up a new code of conduct that governed even the language of fascist society. On the pretext of a return to the customs of ancient Rome, he abolished the *lei*, the practice of addressing people in the third person singular, as a sign of courtesy and respect, which he said prolonged 'centuries of servitude and abjection'; for it he substituted the democratic *tu*, 'you'. Handshakes were out, in the theatre and in films as well as in daily life, to be replaced by the stiff-armed Roman salute. Using foreign words was outlawed, even in restaurant menus. Fascist Party leaders were expected to set an example of the dynamic, energetic, healthy 'new man' by participating publicly in three sports, long-jumping, riding and swimming. One cabinet minister who emerged brilliantly from the first two trials bravely undertook the third; he dived, but failed to resurface. He couldn't swim.

It's no wonder that Prince Umberto, so imbued with aristocratic principles, so anxious to maintain a personal elegance that became the rule in every regiment, sometimes burst into odd, harsh laughter, more nervous than amused, when he watched Mussolini and other fascist leaders review the Militia at an athletic pace. Like the rest of the nobility, however, he remained passive – especially since the Duce kept a file on his private life, particularly his homosexuality.

Stifling provincialism, the sinister omnipresence of the police, the new race laws, the blustering belligerency of Mussolini and his henchmen: Italy had become a caricature of Nazi Germany. After the wild, carefree effervescence of Paris, Visconti felt trapped, mired in a dreary world with no future. It was one of those decadent periods that, as Ernst Jünger noted in *On the Marble Cliffs*, 'blurs even the form our inner life should take'.

An unexpected telegram from Renoir at the end of the summer announcing his impending arrival in Italy roused Visconti from his gloomy torpor. It was incredible but true: the creator of that *Grand Illusion* that had been banned by the censor, the polemicist who made *Ce soir*, the film voice of the Popular Front, had received a personal invitation from Il Duce.

True, Mussolini was particularly anxious to develop the Italian motion-picture industry. He had worked to make Rome the movie capital of the world, had inaugurated the Cinecittà studios – seen as the new Hollywood – with great pomp in the spring of 1937. A strict system had been instituted to supervise and control the circuits of movie production and distribution. And he had encouraged his son Vittorio, a film fanatic, especially of American films, to publish a movie magazine, *Cinema*, with a press run of 20,000; its influence would prove decisive for the future of Italian motion pictures. Almost every evening, private screenings were held for father and son in Villa Torlonia. Among the films shown was *Grand Illusion*. Instead of angering the Duce, it moved him to ask its creator to teach at the Experimental Film Centre, to help increase the centre's prestige.

'The Italians had not yet entered the war,' Renoir explained, 'and the French government was anxious to do everything it could to keep its indecisive neighbour neutral . . . I was a soldier. I had to follow orders.' Deeply disappointed and embittered by the failure of his film *The Rules of the Game*, he accepted the invitation and also agreed to film 'anything at all'. The 'anything at all' proposed by producer Michele Scalera was *Tosca*.

That was the first time he had set foot in Italy. With him he brought his German assistant, Carl Koch (who did noteworthy work on *La Marseillaise*), his future wife, Dido, and, of course, his favourite actor, Michel Simon, who was to don the powdered wig of the infamous Baron Scarpia in the film. As soon as he arrived, Renoir asked Visconti to take charge of the script and return to work as his assistant. The offer was immediately accepted.

While Simon spent his days photographing the frescoes in Rome's baroque palaces and exploring the city's brothels, Visconti guided Renoir and Koch through Hadrian's villa and other places that might serve as sets for *Tosca*. Because of him, Renoir later said, 'that stay in Rome was a revelation. My comprehension of this very sensitive Italian world I owe to him.'

But in September, France's entry into the war forced him to return to Paris where, as a reserve lieutenant, he spent three months in the French Army's film unit. On Saturday 16 September he sent a letter to Visconti, who was still living in Milan:

'My dear friend, I just received your letter. It is not cheerful, yet it was like a ray of sunshine in this grey month of September. I recalled our excursion to Hadrian's villa when we were thinking of filming *Tosca* in those Roman ruins. Dear Lucchino (*sic*), I haven't lost all hope and I still think we will make films together. I send you my best wishes. Very affectionately, Jean Renoir.'

Suspension of work on *Tosca*, combined with his loneliness and the growing horror of the international situation, plunged Visconti back into a mood of disenchantment and weariness that he described in a letter to Horst on 14 November.

My dear Horst,

I can't tell you how happy I was to receive your dear letter this morning.

My life, as far as I am concerned, is not too unhappy, even though the atmosphere now prevailing in Europe is not of the best . . . But I myself am no longer the person you knew.

Too many sad and serious events have occurred, and when I
think of the good times spent in Paris and even in America, it's
like a kind of impossible dream.

Nevertheless, I'm alive, as you see, and busy at all sorts of
things. Films as always – slightly compromised by the international situation, alas, and by my horses, etc.

When can I see you? I am not optimistic enough to think it
will be next year.

The fact is that here I am more in contact with the atrocious
things happening in the world, and with the kind of madness
that has gripped humanity! How I regret having taken the
Nazis' side, even if it was only for a brief moment of my life.
Perhaps you can understand that to me this leaning was essentially aesthetic. The time for penchants is past now, however,
and I hope that whole brood is destroyed (except for a few
people I could name). Do you agree?

Naturally, everything I've written here is foolishness.
Reality is much harsher than that. I send hugs and kisses, my
dear Horst. Don't think I'm mad. I have an immense desire to
see you again.

Ciao. Ciao.

Luchino

People in Italy were beginning to talk about the Nazis' persecu-
tion of the Jews, some of whom managed to reach Milan and then
sail from Genoa. Mussolini closed his eyes to all this. But wasn't he
going to plunge the country into war? Ciano, like the king a
champion of neutralism, felt his father-in-law's mistrust of him
grow steadily, and saw the chances for peace dwindling. 'The king,'
Il Duce told his foreign minister, 'would like us to enter only in time
to pick up the pieces. I hope they don't break things over our heads
in the meanwhile. Besides, it's humiliating to stand by idly while
others write History ... To endow a people with grandeur you
must send it into battle, even if you have to kick its arse to make it
go.'

When Renoir returned to Rome, political tension was at its
zenith. In the spring of 1940 the newspapers ran his picture with an
announcement that filming had begun on *Tosca*; the photo was

taken at the Castel Sant'Angelo and showed the smiling director standing beside his producer and Vittorio Mussolini. But he had yet to choose his cast, or his locations, hadn't even reviewed the script. In fact, he would never get to film more than the first five shots. 'One evening,' he recalled, 'in a brothel, Michel Simon found his favourite little divan occupied by some civilians speaking German. He complained to the madam, demanding his usual place, but she refused to get involved. He went home in a temper . . .

'But the German conquest of the Eternal City continued. Their method was simple. The sole newspaper favourable to France was the Vatican organ, *L'Osservatore Romano*. The Nazis hired a bunch of thieves, thugs and muggers. This army of hoodlums was told to survey the news-stands where *L'Osservatore Romano* was sold. When anyone walked up and asked for the paper, he was immediately attacked and beaten. Within twenty-four hours even the newspapers that had maintained a cautious neutrality became supporters of the alliance with Germany.

'I got out of this comedy with a good scare. I had asked for *L'Osservatore Romano* in a restaurant and was duly set upon. I'd have had my skull broken there if I hadn't invoked the name of Mussolini, who, after all, had got me into this mess. I reported the incident to the French ambassador, who advised me to leave on the first train out . . .'

Only hours later, on 10 June, Italy entered the war.

Visconti took Renoir to the train. The situation was too tragic to allow for making plans together, certainly not for *Tosca*. Their parting, Renoir said, was 'heartrending'. The film they were making? Carl Koch and Visconti would finish it. When it came out in January 1941, Visconti pronounced it 'horrible'. His father and his friends were no kinder about *Tosca*. Only the magazine *Cinema* praised the restraint and austerity of the framing, a discipline Koch had learned not only from Renoir, but also from his mentor, Bertolt Brecht. Noted, too, were the unusually long-held shots, stylistically typical of Renoir and, later, of Visconti in *Obsession*.

Tosca at least provided Visconti with an occasion to meet most of the young intellectuals who, under such pen-names as Scaramouche, Puck and Nostromo, were writing insolent, iconoclastic articles in *Cinema* and who would soon become his accomplices in his experiment with *Obsession*. Renoir's visit had been an event for them; he had come from a free country and he personified the creative freedom and freedom of thought that was denied to them. His were among the foreign films that had been banned from Italian screens, but that could be seen hurriedly at the Experimental Film Centre before they were confiscated. Films, even more than books, were their window on the forbidden world abroad. 'We lived in the dark,' said the *Cinema* critic Gianni Puccini, 'but we felt that someday there would be a bit of light, and we loved the cinema as a presage of a different future.'

The house Koch took over on Via Settembrini with his wife, Lotte Reiniger, who made cartoon films, became a tiny French enclave, an oasis of freedom, first to celebrate Renoir's coming, then simply as a place to meet in a refreshingly conspiratorial counter-cultural atmosphere. The people who met there did not all live in the same world, but their references were to Marx, Pudovkin and Eisenstein rather than to Mussolini and the fascist director Carmine Gallone. There Visconti met Umberto Barbaro and Rudolf Arnheim, two of the film centre's most independent-minded teachers. More important, he met their young students, including Gianni Puccini and Giuseppe De Santis. Another of them, Pietro Ingrao, was hoping to become a director, but movies were now his secondary passion; first came the clandestine political struggle he was waging with his friend Mario Alicata, a Sicilian-born philosophy teacher recently converted to Communism.

Without realizing how deep their political engagement went, Visconti was drawn to the ferment of rebellion he felt in each of these men. They, in turn, were intrigued by the puzzle he presented, this aristocrat, a friend of Prince Umberto, who was nevertheless on familiar terms with Renoir and consorted with anti-Fascists. Still more tantalizing was his stated determination not only to make films, but to devote part of his fortune to it. In the first meeting at Koch's, there he was, floating ideas, looking for co-workers. But a lot of prejudices had to be dispelled before his plans could be taken seriously.

Puccini, very obviously a novelist's son, later pictured the beginnings of the friendship that was to lead the group from dreams and theories to action. His technique for this was to describe Visconti's meeting with De Santis against a white-hot background of war preparations.

'It was during the 1940 Easter holidays; there was already war in Europe; the one in Spain had been over for a year and soon after the fire had blazed up again even hotter. For the moment, Italy was "non-belligerent", an ambiguous status that used a dazzling illusion to conceal the fascist jackal's plans for imminent aggression. Still, life went on; there were still holidays, and among the passengers aboard the vaporetto to Capri, one day in April before or after Hitler's invasion of Holland and Denmark, were two young men, one of them perhaps thirty-four years old, the other twenty-three. They didn't know each other, but during the crossing they soon fell into conversation, found affinities and became friends.

'They did not talk only of films; perhaps they talked mostly about the war and about anxiety, and it was important to both of them to talk about these things and to understand one another. The older one was tall, dark, with magnetic eyes in a tortured face that recalled those in Renaissance equestrian statues. His hands were like wings, his gait was odd, light and ponderous at the same time, one of those walks that reveals character and in which one sees controlled strength, restrained impulsiveness, gentle firmness.

'The other was blond, slender, almost frail until you noticed the harsh jawline, and the eyes, at once attentive and ironic, in which gleamed a constant, pinpoint light of sly peasant suspicion.

'The older of the two had gone bohemian, rebelling against a prearranged future and a boring present; he had bred horses, had been a dilettante film director, an assistant, forever searching feverishly for his way. He had even written a novel, which had then been abandoned in a drawer. The other invented stories full of strange melancholy, situated in vast and fabulous landscapes, and he was to become the most influential film critic of the period.

'They understood each other at once, established a pact of common and fervent work. In Capri they drafted and in Rome they wrote – ignoring everything, the sea, people, the holidays – a translation of [Alain-Fournier's] Le Grand Meaulnes which never became a film. That is how Luchino Visconti met Giuseppe De Santis.'

De Santis, who would later make the film Bitter Rice, rectified only the dates in this account. He had indeed crossed with Visconti in the vaporetto from Naples to Capri. But they had met before. 'We spent the whole crossing talking,' he reported. 'Luchino was surrounded by homosexuals and made fun of them, derided them, as he always did.'

Giuseppe De Santis had grown up in the orange groves and marshes bordering the Mediterranean between Rome and Naples. He had eaten the prickly pears growing wild in the ditches, had pastured buffalos with the daughters of farmers and workmen, had learned in a smithy how to shoe horses. 'My friends were barbers, butchers, blacksmiths, masons and cobblers,' he said. 'A kind of innate mistrust had always kept me away from rich kids. The only times I had anything to do with them was when I fought them behind the old cemetery wall.' His articles for *Cinema* were imbued with a violence, outrageous polemics and rash destructiveness that he may have inherited from his forebears, Turkish, Moorish and Arab pirates who roamed the seas and ravaged coasts and countryside. 'A bastard, that's what I am,' he said, 'small, swarthy, hawk-nosed, touchy, suspicious, with a pride and insolence that constantly tear my guts trying to mask the mysterious inferiority complex that assails all bastards when they're honest with themselves.'

For the editor of the magazine *Vi* (Vittorio Mussolini), whom he only met two or three times a year, he felt more pity than fear. Vittorio, as his father's son, also suffered from an inferiority complex, but he never rebelled, never tried to assume the freedom with which De Santis and his friends charged into life, raided bookstores, devoured the work of Proust, Alain-Fournier and the Americans, talked far into the night at the Caffè Rosati with writers like Mario Pannunzio and Vitaliano Brancati. They swam in the Tiber and, on Sundays, 'went to church to squeeze up against the thighs of rich girls from the posh neighbourhoods'. Class differences didn't matter. Visconti burned with the same fire, the same restless passion for freedom, the same disputatious intelligence in combatting bombast and affectation and the viscous sentimentality of Fascism.

'We met because we were anti-fascist, so ideology played a definite part,' says the communist leader Mario Alicata. 'I personally met Luchino one evening when I was invited to see

Renoir . . . There was a small group of anti-fascist intellectuals paying tribute to that democratic intellectual who was forced to leave our country.'

A common sensibility did more than ideology, however, to bring Visconti and his new friends together. They shared a mutinous spirit, defiance of prudence and obedience, a passionate interest in everything happening outside Italy. All Visconti's plans, all the scenarios he created, were inspired by foreign writers. One was Alain-Fournier, whose novel, had it not been for his heirs' opposition, would have become Visconti's first film; Uberta thinks of her brother as a kind of Grand Meaulnes: impulsive, enigmatic, adventurous. Another was Julien Green, whose novel *Adrienne Mesurat* (*The Closed Garden*) was translated into Italian by Visconti (the contract can still be seen).

Despite his friends' opposition and incomprehension, Visconti asked Alicata to turn *La Dame aux camélias* by Dumas fils into a movie script. Alicata again, along with Gianni Puccini and the scriptwriter Cesare Zavattini, was asked to adapt for film Maupassant's story *Les Tombales* (*Gravewalkers*). Massimo Puccini, Antonio Pietrangeli and Umberto Barbaro were put to work on Mann's *Early Sorrow*. This avalanche of projects – all duly paid for – also included work on George Bernard Shaw's novel *Cashel Byron's Profession*, and Melville's *Billy Budd*.

The only jarring note in this eclectic and cosmopolitan panorama was the work of the Sicilian novelist Giovanni Verga, and his verismo – the Italian form of literary realism – would become *Cinema*'s stock in trade. It exemplified what Alicata and De Santis together called the 'trust in realism and in the poetry of realism that we expect of Italian films, which are still hemmed in on one side by the rhetorical and archaeological D'Annunzianism of *Cabiria*, and on the other by escapism into illusory petits-bourgeois heavens . . .' After all, Renoir had opted for realism by going to Maupassant and Zola for his subject matter.

Gianni Puccini remembered seeing Verga at his home a year before his death in 1921: 'an old tree', a man with 'an honest moustache' who had been his father's friend. 'One evening just before Mussolini entered the war,' Puccini recalls, 'Luchino came to the house to talk about Verga with my father. Verga represented a step forward, a consciousness, a reference point in the common effort we had barely begun and which was to continue, with unwelcome interruptions, until 1944. At the time, we saw Verga as a guide to realism and to a still hazy understanding of the Italian masses.

'That evening, my father gave Luchino an old postcard from Aci Trezza, the fishing village near Catania where the action in Verga's great novel, *The House by the Medlar Tree*, takes place. Visconti told me that "the landscape on that card made me want to make *The Earth Trembles.*" He always kept it in sight in his office, and it's true that, although it was fifty years in advance, it looked like a shot from [Visconti's] film.'

In the following year, Visconti went off to discover Sicily, that harsh land of silence, of daily humiliation, of immemorial suffering. What he saw there confirmed his notion that no art can be called 'revolutionary' unless it depicts faceless humanity 'suffering and hoping'; he saw this as 'the only road to understanding the essentials of our humanity'. This aristocrat, favoured with all the gifts heaven can bestow, was moved to pity and love by the greatness and nobility of total poverty of the struggle waged anew every day against sterile, sun-scorched earth and fierce Mediterranean storms. This 'Lombardian reader accustomed by tradition to the structured clarity of Manzoni's imagination' was overwhelmed by Verga's mythical world.

'One morning when the sirocco was blowing,' Visconti wrote, 'and I was wandering idly through the streets of Catania and across the Caltagirone plain, I fell in love with Verga . . . My image of the primitive and gigantic world of the Aci Trezza fishermen and the shepherds of Marineo had always been violent, epic; in my Lombardian view – I am taken, I admit, with my native sky, "so beautiful when it's beautiful" – Verga's Sicily had truly seemed Ulysses's isle, an isle of adventures and burning passions, a fixed, proud bulwark against the slashing Ionian Sea.'

For three months, even before he took options on *The House by the Medlar Tree* and two Verga short stories, *Ieli the Shepherd* and *Gramigna's Mistress*, he and his new team worked on a film treatment of *Gramigna's Mistress*, a fine story of the love affair between a wild Sicilian peasant girl and the ferocious bandit Gramigna. He chose his cast: Massimo Girotti, whom he had met during the filming of Tosca, and the voluptuous Luisa Ferida. He picked his locations. All that was needed – this was in the late spring of 1941 – was approval from the Ministry of Popular Culture, or MinCulPop.

One day when Gianni Puccini was at the ministry, he happened to spot the scenario on Minister Pavolini's desk. On it in red pencil, in the minister's own hand, was the annotation, 'Enough of these brigands!' He quickly warned Luchino, who immediately requested an audience.

'The minister is being fitted for a suit,' the flunkey told him when he arrived. Pavolini finally appeared in the garment, a handsome white summer outfit. He was in an excellent mood. The audience progressed beautifully. 'The more Luchino talked,' Puccini said, 'the more convinced Pavolini seemed. But the annotation was never removed.'

By commissioning from his friends translations, scripts and reports on various works, Visconti provided them with tidy incomes during a tight-money period. Besides, a number of communist leaders had been arrested in 1939, leaving Alicata and Ingrao in charge of the communist underground in Rome. 'In dealing with the police,' Ingrao noted, 'writing scripts gave us terrific cover to meet for political work.' De Santis and Puccini had also gone underground, but so secretly that Antonioni, who began working for *Cinema* then, never suspected even though he spent most of his days with them. 'I heard them talk about Visconti as a friend whose ideas were close to theirs, but I never understood how this communion showed itself or what practical, concrete form it took.'

In fact, Visconti's personality still seemed hard to circumscribe, especially for Alicata and Ingrao. 'We talked about politics, about Fascism,' Ingrao said, 'but we still couldn't get a clear picture of him; he was an intelligent man, a cultured man, but with some weird traits. In short, he remained an aristocrat.' An aristocrat who probably surprised them, in that grim spring of 1941, by writing an obituary in the form of a satirical funeral oration over the 'corpses' of the film industry and the dying society they represented. That article in *Cinema*, Puccini said, gave his friends their clearest idea of what he was like. Visconti wrote:

In some movie companies it is not unusual to stumble on corpses that persist in thinking they are alive. Other people must have come across them as I have, but did not identify them right away, for they wear the same clothes as you and I. But the process of decomposition secretly afflicting them gives off a stench of decay that cannot escape a sensitive nose. In the ultra-modern buildings in which some firms are housed, all the offices open on to long corridors lined with doors, and on them all, identical plates bear the occupants' names: a cemetery columbarium.

In opening these doors at random, I have found myself witnessing memorable little scenes: a little old man hopping around the room in a fever of inspiration, under the gaze of a similar specimen with trembling wattles seated behind a vast blond-wood desk, chewing urethritis tablets and fixing him like a snake about to swallow a rabbit.

These characters meet in the late afternoon, with the exhausting process of digestion finally completed, to devise the scripts of melodramas that already exist without their knowing it.

If you have ever had occasion to speak to one of these gentlemen, to have to explain, with a touch of repugnance, your dreams, your illusions, your beliefs, they must have contemplated you with a sleepwalker's vacant eye; deep in that opaque orbit you must have seen the cold light of death.

Already dead, they live unaware of passing time, in the afterglow of dead things, of their faded world, where one walked unharmed on pavements of paper and chalk, where backdrops shuddered in the draught of a suddenly opened door, where crêpe-paper roses bloomed eternally, where styles and periods blended indulgently and art nouveau Cleopatras vamped fierce and sturdy Marc Antonys in whalebone corsets by whipping them . . .

Sometimes you run across them at night, between midnight and one o'clock, when furtively, with the ingenuity of schoolboys sneaking out, they race to meet a young girlfriend who lets them weep a bit on her shoulder. Then they flit up narrow stairways that reek of carbolic acid.

Later, in their sleep, they have terrible nightmares. At daybreak, wakened with a start by their livers demanding their tonic, they are uncertain in the room's dim light if they are still alive or if they have ever lived. They never go to the cinema.

There are so many young people today who survive for the time being by feeding on wild hopes, and who are impatient to say all they have to say; how sad for them to find this multitude of corpses stuck like spikes in their wheels.

Their time is past, and they remain, no one knows why. If only they'd allow us to put them in show windows we would all bow down to them. Why not? But how deplorable it is that so many of them still hold the purse strings and rule the roost. When will the day come when our cinematic young lions are allowed to proclaim loud and clear: 'Let the dead be buried'? You'll see how they rush, on that day, to hurry some heedless laggard along and, with all due respect, help him put the other foot in the grave.

Visconti was the last man to give up when someone tried to 'spike his wheels'. In the autumn of 1941, although all his plans had so far come to nothing, he dared to begin work on *Obsession*, the film that scriptwriter Cesare Zavattini said 'reflected our hunger for realism'.

Picking up a subject suggested by Renoir, Visconti was 'remaking *The Postman Always Rings Twice* in Italian', De Santis said. James Cain's 1934 thriller is about a woman, married to the owner of a ramshackle motel, who falls in love with a tramp and incites him to murder her husband in a fake automobile crash; in *Obsession*, De Santis said, the story was adapted to 'the true reality of our country'.

The subject clearly matched the *Cinema* group's aspirations as expressed in an article signed by Scaramouche: 'No men, not even Italian men, are plaster saints. Nor are women flowers of virtue. Yet go and find in our films, if you can, a man who is a bastard or a woman who is a bit of a whore. In Italian films they're all nice fellows, all honest, all above-board. But there is nothing shocking in the idea that detectives and courtrooms exist, that there must be guys around with slightly soiled police records, and there are still women who stretch the rules of marital fidelity . . . We are not asking that murder be glorified, still less would we excuse it. But films must move away a bit from the mandatory theme of goodness at all cost; the camera must probe wounds like a scalpel, must explore the darkness in the human heart, the pain of tragedy, the anguish of damnation, the screams of despair – not so much to set an example as to follow a path overgrown with brambles to reach the beauty of a work of art.'

Equally obviously, the subject of *Obsession* could not help but arouse the fascist censors' suspicions: it was lifted directly from the American literature – brutal, without consolation or hope – that was banned by the Mussolini regime. In that literature, every anti-fascist intellectual, from Cesare Pavese to Elio Vittorini, saw a mirror of his own experience, his own pain. Pavese, who translated into Italian the work of John Dos Passos, William Faulkner, John Steinbeck and Herman Melville, once wrote that 'America is not *another country*, a new beginning to History, but the gigantic stage, the giant screen on which, more frankly than anywhere else, our common tragedy is being played out.'

As though this were not trouble enough, the film's scriptwriters insisted on smuggling in an oblique anti-fascist message. For this they intented a new character, 'the Spaniard', Alicata's symbol of the struggle against Francisco Franco.

Preparing the movie was a long job, sternly regulated by Visconti. At eight o'clock every morning the whole crew gathered at his home on Via Kircher. De Santis called it 'an unimaginable world for us sons of the provincial petite-bourgeoisie'. And Puccini explains: 'There was a Polish butler named Janek. He was so imbued with the importance of his function that he insisted we all bear titles. He announced "Baron Alicata" and "Marquess De Santis".' They worked all day long, emerging dazed from their cage at nightfall to take long walks through Rome.

The scenario, with a working title of *Paludes*★ borrowed from Gide, miraculously slipped through the censor's net, probably because censorship was less vigilant then, with Fascism beginning to founder; only minor changes were ordered in the role of the priest, and they merely made the character more unctuous. In December, location scouting began on the banks of the Po, a desolate, foggy

★A term for alluvial coastal marshes in the Bordeaux region that were dried and planted in vines (translator's note).

landscape of poplars lining a muddy stream; it was a landscape, Visconti remarked, worthy of *The Phantom Carriage.*★

That was where he learned that his father had died. He went immediately to Grazzano, where the duke's funeral was held, in the snow, a few days later. The ceremony seemed so odd to Puccini that in his account of it this incorrigible romancer supplied some extra scene changes: the castle, the medieval setting and, in the funeral procession, dwarfs in scarlet coats against a spotlessly snowy landscape. 'Dwarfs! What an idea!' says Uberta. 'Besides, there weren't any dwarfs in Grazzano. My father simply wanted a dark pink or red shroud, one that wasn't black. And instead of a death knell, we heard the bells ring as usual.' In tribute to the duke's accomplishments, the citizens of Grazzano wore the costumes he'd designed for them.

According to Antonioni, Puccini had discussed at length with De Santis whether he, a communist atheist, could properly attend the religious funeral of an aristocrat. 'He returned from it with amazingly bizarre and luxurious tales, of people in medieval costumes, dwarfs swathed in red, music . . . Then Visconti got back to Rome. That was when I met him. He struck me at once as an imposing figure. He commanded respect, and his authoritarian ways were impressive . . . I saw him for the first time on the Via Veneto in 1942. He was sitting at a café table with Mario Alicata . . . Luchino was very thin, in mourning, wearing dark glasses. The first thing that struck me about him was the way he looked at passersby, as if he owned them all. Puccini, De Santis and I were middle class, and we felt the class difference with Visconti. He behaved like someone whose family had ruled Milan for two centuries.'

Four more months went by, during which Visconti found a production manager who suited him (Libero Solaroli, a connoisseur of French literature, especially of Laclos†), and received final authorization from the ministry, before shooting could finally begin on 15 June 1942.

For the male lead, the tramp Gino, he had chosen handsome

★A silent film by Swedish director Victor Sjøstrøm (translator's note).
†Pierre Choderlos de Laclos (1741–1803), chiefly known for the epistolary novel *Les Liaisons dangereuses*, published in 1782 and most recently adapted for film by Stephen Frears in 1988 (translator's note).

Massimo Girotti, whose blue eyes and sudden fits of fright had charmed him. In the role of Giovanna he wanted Anna Magnani, Anna the magnificent, who spoke with the nasal whine of the Roman slums. He had gone to see her over and over in nightclubs and music halls, frantically applauding her poignantly comic acts. A few months earlier at the home of her cousins, the Pariolis, in Rome's fashionable residential district, the explosive Magnani had made an outrageous scene with her husband, Goffredo Alessandrini, whom she had caught phoning one of her rivals.

She was eager to work for this unknown director; her infallible flair told her there was genius here, and she signed the contract without even reading it. The scenes in which she did not appear had already been filmed. But when she finally arrived, after a trying trip from Turin to Ferrara in crowded trains, she announced to Solaroli, with some pride, that she was 'in an interesting condition'. In other words, she was pregnant – four months pregnant, she specified. Solaroli told her she would surely have to drop out of the film: Luchino would never use an understudy, and besides, he worked very slowly. He could never do more than three shots a day. At that rate, he wasn't going to be able to finish the picture before November and by that time she'd come on the set carrying her baby in her arms.

Her interview with Visconti was emotional. She tried to persuade him that she was only into her fourth month of pregnancy – she was cheating by a month – but Luchino finally told her: 'That means that by the time we finish filming, every scene where you're not shot close up I'll have to dress you in a hoop-skirt.' They both burst out laughing, but it was all over. Magnani cried all night. She never got over losing the part that went instead to Clara Calamai.

Calamai was much younger than Magnani, and one of the period's most sophisticated leading ladies. In *La Cena delle Beffe* Alessandro Blasetti had caused a sensation by baring one of Clara's breasts, but he had left her peroxide-blonde curls and her filmy tulles unaltered. Visconti wanted her without make-up, dishevelled, 'realistic' almost to a point of ugliness. At their first meeting, in a hotel in Ferrara, he was pleased by her hoarse voice, which was in fact the product of a head cold. 'Perfect!' he said. 'But the perm is out.' He made her shake her head, rumple her hair, change her hairdo. He asked her to remove her make-up – let them see the fatigue, the wrinkles. That's how she ought to look with an apron wrapped around her hips facing a pile of dirty dishes after an exhausting day waiting on tables in an inn.

When she saw the first rushes, Calamai burst into tears and threatened to quit on the spot. The atmosphere on the set was gruelling, she said, she didn't dare so much as start to sit down, or show a moment's distraction. 'Listen when I talk to you . . . or go back to your whorehouse!' Visconti roared at the star, who would weep and hug her little dog to her breast. She remembered the endless rehearsals, Visconti's insistence that Girotti hit harder when he slapped her, the icy baths she took in the Po river, the atropine used to dilate her pupils in the murder scene that left her vision blurred for days afterwards.

In one scene, an actor was supposed to knock a glass over with his elbow so that it fell and shattered. 'The glass fell and didn't break,' Calamai reported. 'I don't know how many times we repeated that scene. In the end, Luchino lost his patience. There was a big tray of glasses on the table. He picked them up one by one and broke them on the floor, right at my feet. The splinters flew up in front of my face. There was a deathly silence. I was petrified, and anyway it never occurred to me to complain: I was madly in love with Luchino.'

And she adds: 'That's how Luchino was, he changed people. Massimo was gradually transformed, we watched him being tamed little by little.' But at what a price! Working with Visconti was a physical and psychological ordeal that generated 'almost unbearable fatigue'. Girotti, who had been pampered by Blasetti, literally collapsed twice during the filming. It happened once at the end of a scene in which he had to drink a glass of wine; the scene was reshot so often he was finally scooped up dead drunk. And he passed out again on the last day of filming: 'I fell down in a faint, overcome by nerves and fatigue.'

Visconti himself admits that there was more violence and cruelty in *Obsession* than in any of his other films. 'I'm interested in extreme situations, those instants when abnormal tension reveals the truth about human beings; I like to confront the characters and the story harshly, aggressively.' The violence was more inside him than in the world around him. De Santis and Girotti remember the astonishing peacefulness that seemed to reign in that part of Italy in that torrid, clear, dazzling summer.

And yet . . . that summer, Visconti's younger brother, Edoardo, as headstrong as Luchino, was thrown into prison for insulting some Germans; it took Luchino and Uberta a good month to get him out. Then, one afternoon in October 1942, an auto-pulled up on the Ferrara–Polesella road where the end of *Obsession* was being filmed. A cousin of Luchino's got out, waited until the scene ended, then took the director's arm and led him off down the road. Visconti, he said, had to be in Milan that very evening: his brother Guido had just been killed at El Alamein. 'He'd been a man from another age,' Uberta says. 'He died shouting "Long live the king."'

The whole company silently watched Luchino leave. Work went on the next day, directed by De Santis, who until then had been limited to preparing the backgrounds. Visconti was back on the following day.

It had long been supposed, even by the *Cinema* crowd, that the new director was merely an aristocrat dabbling in films for his own amusement. But evidence to the contrary piled up. He was confident with his cast and behind the camera; he showed no uncertainty about camera angles or movements or about the length of sequences. His discussions with De Santis, who had more technical training than he, bore uniquely on details or on the actors' diction. When the film editor Mario Serandrei saw the first sequences in Rome, he was stunned by their 'line', their 'spacious phrasing', which had nothing to do with Cain's crisp, rapid-fire style, but which already bore Visconti's stamp.

'I remember,' Serandrei said, 'that the first scenes were those filmed in the inn in which Giovanna is left alone with all the dirty glasses. To me it was a kind of shock. I realized I was dealing with a great director.' He wrote to Visconti expressing his admiration and adding: 'I don't know what else this kind of cinema can be called but "neo-realist".' Serandrei persuaded Visconti to let Blasetti do the editing. But when the director saw the result, he tore his film apart and re-edited it himself from beginning to end.

He was bolder than any of the later 'neo-realist' film-makers ever dared to be, especially in portraying love affairs, both heterosexual and homosexual. He wanted to depict them 'exactly', he said. But he never quite achieved that exactitude; the sensual passion with which the film overflows is too deeply scarred by murder and tragedy. Visconti's cruelty is sometimes reminiscent of Stroheim's, as in the scene in which, while Giovanna gives herself to her lover after he has murdered her husband, the camera moves from a close-up of a chamber pot under the bed to focus on the woman's hand grasping the dead man's watch chain.

In *Obsession*, Visconti recorded, reviewed and explored every phase of the couple's degradation and debasement in that hellish room. Twice the characters manage to escape their downfall – in the Ancona and Ferrara episodes – but they dwell on it incessantly, tormenting themselves in parallel laments, Giovanna bemoaning her past and her horror of growing old, and Gino taking up drinking and skulking behind closed shutters. Like the couple in his later film *Senso*, they live in a doomed world. The young 'dancer' Anita and the Spaniard have a chance, because they move rootlessly from town to town. But for the lovers there is no way out. Even as they leave the house by the side of the road, filled with wild new life and hope by Giovanna's pregnancy, the merciless hand of justice is closing around them.

The Spaniard could have pointed to a freer, more constructive way of life, since he is searching for a world where men are 'brothers'. For Mario Alicata this could only signify political brotherhood, and he accused Visconti of falsifying the meaning the character originally had in the script. 'He was a proletarian who had fought the war on the right side, not the fascist side,' Alicata said. 'A proletarian who had come back to Italy and gone on the road to promote Socialism and anti-Fascism. He should have been a positive character; he didn't turn out that way, and censorship may not have been the only reason for that.' In a word, the writer was blaming his friend for deliberately blurring things.

Visconti replied by claiming credit for the 'entire creation' of the character. For him, the Spaniard stood for essential ideas, 'social and poetic problems'. *Obsession*, he noted, 'was filmed under a fascist regime, and . . . the character was the arch-symbol of revolution and free thought'. And of homosexuality.

In fact, the Spaniard remains a very fuzzy character because of his suspect ambiguity, as is pointed out by the sternly moralizing Alicata, the puritanical Communist. 'If he is trying to turn Gino away from Giovanna, it's more because of his disturbed love for him' – we're quoting Alicata here – 'than because of any belief that he mustn't throw himself away on women, that there are other things to do in times like these.' That the Spaniard reported the pair to the police is clear despite the ellipses in the film; in this he anticipates the revenge the lovelorn Countess Livia Serpieri will take in *Senso*.

As a fast-talking barker at the Ancona fair he appears to be not so much a 'critical conscience' as the ironic and disabused spirit of the film. With a parrot on each shoulder (Barberousse on one side, Robespierre on the other) he pulls in the suckers by promising them a magic elixir and by selling them dreams in the form of lottery tickets. 'Fifty centimes will open the doors to the future, gentlemen. Robespierre, choose a forecast for these gentlemen. Green! A fine colour, the colour of hope. You're in luck, gentlemen – the colour of hope, the colour of strong men! As the proverb says, the other face of a lie is truth.' Visconti would return to this theme, of the artist as confidence trickster, in *Bellissima* and, later, in *Mario and the Magician*.

The film is balanced between the two extremes, of sarcasm and pity, cruelty and tenderness. Pity from Anita, the little prostitute to whom Gino, the new Stavrogin, confesses his crime; pity and pardon, perhaps, from little Elvira, who appears at the end, in the dark corridor, watching the couple through a keyhole; she answers 'no' when Gino asks her if she thinks he's wicked – but she also tells the police which way the two lovers have fled.

Many of the keys to Visconti's world can be found in this cruel film in which so many other people had a hand, including Alberto Moravia and Giorgio Bassani, but which bears no seal but its director's. Everything converges to pinpoint a personal 'obsession'. Love and life are seen as curses, death is omnipresent: the rabbits killed by Bragaglia; the appearance at the door of 'a dead man's house' of a black-clad farmer carrying a scythe, his eyes shadowed by a broad-brimmed straw hat; the murder, indeed, the whole tragedy, a slow, carnal return to the sources of life, which are also the sources of death. The river on whose bank Gino makes love to the pregnant

Giovanna returns to its primal state: the river of death, debasement, sterility.

'A dead woman at the side of a road, one of her stockings rolled down over her ankle. The man holds her up by the waist, as if she were a big doll, so that her feet drag against the pavement.' The idea for the film came from this image on which Visconti's version of *The Postman Always Rings Twice* ends. Death had indeed struck twice, in December 1941 and again in October 1942, at the beginning and end of *Obsession*. The work is charged with the anguish of this threefold family mourning, this long journey into the unknown to the music of *La Traviata*, the languorous and deadly music he was born to.

Was *Obsession* an unlucky film? Even before its first showing, in Rome in the spring, Visconti's crew was subjected to insistent questioning by the police. On 2 December, Alicata and the two Puccini brothers were arrested as subversives and sent to Regina Coeli prison. When Aldo Scagnetti heard the news, he contacted *Cinema* and tried to put pressure on Vittorio Mussolini to get them released: 'I kept telling him, "You remember, they were always here, either at the house or the magazine, the magazine or the house, so how could they have done anything wrong?" Vittorio began phoning, and what he found out finally made him blow up at Scagnetti: "House and magazine, you say, magazine and house. Gianni and Dario Puccini are Communists, that's what they are!"'

He blew up even more when he saw *Obsession*, a veiled thrust at Fascism's fake heroes, fake perspectives, fake optimism: it sneers at family life, flaunts adultery, homosexuality, instinctive brutality, depicts a world of jobless men, of tramps, of losers without hope or consolation. The small Arcobaleno Theatre was packed. Rome's social and intellectual élite thronged the overheated theatre where many of them had to stand through the film.

Girotti said that from then on, Visconti was looked at 'with the same astonishment as that of an astronomer observing Halley's comet'. 'Some women shivered with horror inside their fur coats,' Visconti remarked. 'What if they'd known that I had sold my mother's jewellery to make this film?' When the showing ended, however, the applause, hesitant at first, swelled to an ovation. Then the lights came up again, and the Duce's son rose, strode to the exit, boomed out an indignant 'That isn't Italy!' and stalked out, slamming the door behind him.

This had been a private showing, and *Obsession* was never booked into the regular distribution circuits. The versions shown in other Italian cities, Ferrara, Genoa, Bologna, were always sequestered for a while and then heavily cut before exhibition. Local authorities and critics invariably deplored the crudity of its language and its French-style naturalistic rhetoric, denouncing it as exaggeratedly, morbidly immoral. 'An insult to the Italian people,' or as Culture Minister Polverelli said, 'a film that stinks of latrines'.

Visconti would later tell of *Obsession*'s 'tormented existence'. 'It lasted two or three evenings in a theatre, then it was withdrawn by order of the local prefect,' he recalled. 'We got phone calls from all over: "It was shown in Salsomaggiore (or some other city) this evening and immediately banned . . . After two hours it was withdrawn from circulation . . . Not only that, but the archbishop went to exorcize the theatre . . ." Oddly enough, Mussolini, intrigued by all the controversy, ordered the film shown in his Villa Torlonia and then decreed, "No, might as well let it circulate." I never understood why.'

The movie went on living its 'hard life', hacked up and at the mercy of the moods of fascist local authorities. It came out in Milan, Florence or Turin in a version altered almost beyond recognition, and then not until the winter of 1943–4, with Italy occupied by the Germans. In the summer of 1943 another showing was organized in Rome, in the Braschi palace. But this was really a kind of trap, for in the middle of the film the police arrived and took the names of all the spectators. *Obsession* and Visconti had become arch-symbols of rebellion and anti-Fascism.

XI

ALFREDO GUIDI'S ADVENTURE

*I am leaving . . . I have made up my mind
and have seen the way to make this journey.
In the twinkling of an eye, all the sorrows
that, as you know, have been plaguing me,
especially on Sundays, seem to have been
blown away by a divine breath. I have seen
that great vision of Italy raising itself from the
muck in which the Germans keep it mired.*

STENDHAL, *The Charterhouse of Parma*

Summer 1943: Rome was a furnace. Visconti was preparing to leave
for Cernobbio for a brief stay with his brothers and sisters in the
Villa Erba, on Lake Como. He was still in his house on Via Salaria
on Sunday, 25 July when, a few yards away in the Villa Savoia, the
first act of Mussolini's fall, and with it the fall of Fascism, was
ending.

During the night, the Fascist Great Council, sitting in extraordinary session, had voted to ask the king 'to take command of the
armed forces and assume his full constitutional powers'. At the
request of Victor-Emmanuel III, Mussolini went to the Villa Savoia
for a private interview that lasted no more than twenty minutes.
The king briefly laid the facts before him: the army was
demoralized; only one member of the government remained faithful
to the Duce and that was the king himself, but he was not enough.
In view of the gravity of the situation, the crown must relieve
Mussolini of his duties as head of government. His resignation was
requested. The time was 5:20 p.m. The audience was over.

His Majesty accompanied the fallen dictator to the front steps in the oppressive heat. 'He was livid,' Mussolini later wrote, 'and he looked even smaller, almost stunted.' The two men exchanged a few more words, the Duce was assured he could choose his residence and that his family would not be molested. A long hand-shake. 'We were stifling, morally and physically,' Mussolini wrote. 'The sky was like lead.' Oddly, his car and personal driver had disappeared. He was ushered into an ambulance by a carabinieri captain and rushed, not to the Villa Torlonia, but to a barracks in Rome. Even then he did not realize he was under arrest.

The king could heave a sigh of relief: Il Duce had been disposed of smoothly. In Rome, in every city in Italy, portraits of Mussolini were burned in the main squares, posters bearing his picture were torn down and, in the euphoria of the moment, people shouted 'Long live the king', 'Long live Italy', even 'Long live peace!' The euphoria was short-lived. The new head of government, Marshal Pietro Badoglio, dissolved the Fascist Party – and banned all other parties as well. He freed some political prisoners, but not all. No pro-German military officers or government officials were dismissed. And he announced clearly that 'the war goes on'. While putting out truce feelers to the Allies, he promised German Foreign Minister Joachim von Ribbentrop that Italy's foreign policy would remain unchanged.

In the forty-five days he played this dangerous double game, the war increased in ferocity. German divisions poured into Italy. Thousands of Allied planes bombed the major cities: Genoa, Livorno, Naples; on 4 August they pounded Rome for an hour and a half. On the previous day, more than 2,000 tons of explosives had fallen on Milan, the most violent, most horrifying air raid yet recorded in Italy: thousands dead, houses gutted, ruins everywhere, the historic centre unrecognizable, with the blasted Galeria gaping roofless at the sky, the statues on the Duomo shattered, La Scala partly destroyed, the Manzoni Theatre reduced to rubble.

When the Viscontis heard the news they rushed home to find a nightmare scene. The palace on Via Cerva was in flames; throughout the night, Luchino and his brothers fought the fire to save what they could of the house in which they had been born. We are reminded of the feeling of despondency that gripped the author of *The Leopard*, Prince Tomasi di Lampedusa, when he, too, saw his bombed-out palace in 1943: this was a whole edifice of the past collapsing, a reopening of old wounds, nostalgia rendered incurable. It may have been then, in the midst of that political swamp, with truckloads of German troops streaming uninterruptedly through Milan, that Luchino felt what he later spoke of as a 'strange doubt' that 'even floated over my sleep . . . I stopped talking. Despair was for the weak. Had History become the decline of life, [become] misery . . .?'

For nearly a month the Badoglio government inched through negotiations with the Allies, scheming to obtain armistice terms favourable to the monarchy. The marshal finally had to agree to unconditional surrender; signature of the armistice was announced on the evening of 8 September. Before leaving Rome with the king and a handful of generals, Badoglio ordered Italian forces to support the British and American armies and to 'resist possible attacks from any other source', meaning, but not specifically naming, the Germans.

Abandoned by its government, at the mercy of Germans infuriated at their betrayal by what Goebbels called 'a race of gypsies destined to rot', Italy was plunged overnight into chaos. Everyone was on his own. Even before Mussolini fell, Visconti had decided where he was heading.

In an article – a manifesto – that appeared at the end of September under the now famous title of 'The Anthropomorphic Cinema' he declared that making films was 'the work of a man living among men', uninterested in artistic domination or superiority of any kind, laying claim to no 'so-called vocation, a romantic concept far from present reality'. Eluding contact with this pressing reality, with living, suffering people, meant being 'corrupted by a decadentist vision of the world', succumbing to a temptation Jean-Paul Sartre would later condemn and which Visconti was already calling 'vile abstention'.

This was his moral justification, an endorsement of a notion of labour which Visconti shared with his communist friends, that saw the artist as a 'worker', like any coal-miner or carpenter. Art's realistic mission was defined as 'a loving and objective examination of human experience', baring 'men's true humanity'. This could best be seen in simple people, he said, non-actors who were 'truer and healthier precisely because, as products of uncorrupted social groups, they are often better men'. Visconti further praised the cinema as a collective pursuit 'because in it the impulses and demands of many people combine to pursue an improved group effort. We see clearly how extraordinarily intense this makes a director's sense of responsibility towards humanity . . .'

Visconti's pact with Communism was really sealed in the months before and during the formation of the Italián Resistance Movement. After 25 July he publicly manifested his anti-Fascism by joining a committee organized to assist political prisoners and exiles returning to Italy. The committee was headed by Prince Doria, known for his unyielding anti-Fascism, who later became Rome's first mayor. Members included the communist painter Renato Guttuso, and Mario Alicata, who was released from prison on 6 August and took charge of the then clandestine communist newspaper *L'Unità*. 'We weren't being run by the party,' Guttuso said. 'We did all we could to obtain clothes, linen, ration cards; we found dentists for ex-prisoners who had been tortured and were left without a tooth in their mouths . . . That sort of thing.'

Laura Lombardo-Radice, Pietro Ingrao's future wife, says that a subcommittee went to Regina Coeli prison to obtain the release of the remaining prisoners before the Germans arrived. Alicata pushed Luchino forward to talk to the warden ('We'll let him be leader, he looks so distinguished'). At around the same time, Visconti was also asked to deliver a sum of money for the prisoners still in the prison. When the warden played dumb, insisting that he had never heard of the committee and didn't wish to know about it, Visconti delivered the funds in his own name.

The atmosphere, Guttuso reported, 'was euphoric. There were a lot of clandestine activists, plus those back from penal colony or exile, Negarville, Carlo Levi, Leone Ginzburg . . . We were expecting a German putsch at any moment. We had printed up an issue of *Il Lavoratore Italiano*, a magazine run by Alicata, which came out just as the Germans entered Rome, and we managed to distribute it . . . A drawing of mine was on the cover . . .'

Although he took no part in his friends' propaganda activities, Luchino made them welcome in his house. Who would suspect that behind the pink walls of the patrician mansion on Via Salaria, fiercely guarded by ten German mastiffs, clandestine meetings were being held? While artists no doubt attended them, many were card-carrying Communists who, like Guttuso, kept mimeograph machines to turn out flyers and subversive magazines. And who could have suspected that for two months, seven Sardinians newly arrived from Spain found food, shelter and safety there?

At least two key figures of the underground movement took refuge on Via Salaria: Luigi Longo, who also returned from Spain in the late summer of 1943, and Mario Scoccimarro, the Communist Party leader. 'We went to meet [Scoccimarro] at the station, Mario Socrate and I,' Guttuso reported. 'Our identifying signs: news-papers under our arms and dead cigarettes in our mouths. We took him to Luchino Visconti, on Salaria; that was where he'd be most comfortable. Scoccimarro was put up by L. Visconti while the other comrades found shelter in the Vatican or in monasteries.' Longo, still basking in the respect he had won under his military code name of Major Gallo, was preparing to take over fighting command of the Garibaldi partisan groups organized in Milan in early November.

Was Visconti aware of all these plans for action? He never asked any questions, at any rate. He was not a party member, but, accord-ing to Giorgio Amendola, he behaved like a 'comrade': 'As soon as Alicata got out of prison he spoke to me about Visconti, saying he wanted to see him and ask him to join the party. And when Alicata was assigned to find a hiding place for Scoccimarro, it was his idea to take him to Visconti's house on Via Salaria. Scoccimarro stayed there a week. I went to see him there twice, and we lunched with Visconti, who introduced himself as a comrade.'

The palatial villa Luchino had inherited from his father, an intimate friend of Queen Helen of Savoy, thus became a house of secrets, a safe house for conspirators. It can't help but remind us of the old professor's apartment in *Conversation Piece*, with its secret room in which he hides young Konrad, wanted by the police for his part in a neo-fascist plot in the early 1970s. The room is 'the product of fear'. Declares the character in the film: 'My mother was Italian and she was stuck here during the war. My father and I were in America, and I only returned to Europe with the Fifth Army. My mother had rigged up this secret little room to hide political refu-gees. Or Jews . . .'

Visconti's films are full of rooms, of hideaways where hunted men are sheltered, cared for, saved from the police, from the army, from authority. Whether real, like the house on Via Salaria, or imaginary, they all bespoke Luchino's feeling about this house he inherited; it was a place open to the rebellious, the guilty, to pariahs, a place diverted from the family and social functions for which it was built. A maternal place because it was a refuge, but a place of transgression as well, because those in it escaped from reality and its laws.

Luchino freely lent his keys to 'comrades' and gave them the run of the house. Maria-Antonietta Macciocchi says she took advantage of the offer to go and bathe in one of the five or six bathrooms, each done in a different colour. She was struck by the countless photos of film stars on tables in the drawing-room, 'Assia Noris, Isa Miranda, Alida Valli, Clara Calamai, all of them dedicated in a way that made you think they had all been madly in love with Luchino.'

Alicata often joked that Visconti had 'attempted in every way he could to demolish his fortune, but to no avail. First he tried with horses, then with films. All he succeeded in doing was piling up money.' His generosity was almost unbounded. To the list of Luchino's extravagances, Alicata could have added the money he contributed to the Resistance. 'One evening,' Maria-Antonietta recalls, 'Luchino waited for us in a café called The Bar just outside the city, in San Lorenzo, near the Verano cemetery. He looked lost, out of his element. He was wearing a pale trenchcoat and a trilby hat with the brim turned down . . . He had on a cashmere sweater. He told Rinaldo he wanted to drop out of sight completely, that none of us should try to find him, that we could still use his house if we were careful, keeping it shut up, never opening it or turning on the lights, as if no one were living there. Then he gave Rinaldo 10,000 lire for our resistance group to buy food for its members and help them improve their organization. It was an enormous sum.'

This, she says, was early in the summer of 1943. But not until autumn did Visconti 'drop out of sight'. After Badoglio's radio announcement of the armistice on 8 September, and the king's flight to Pescara, many Italian soldiers unwilling to fight alongside the Germans shucked their uniforms and put on civilian clothes. In two or three days before German troops flooded into the north, a Committee of National Liberation, combining the Christian Democrats, Liberals, Communists, Socialists and others – all the anti-fascist groups – had time to announce its formation and 'call on all Italians to struggle and resist'. Then it went underground. Approximately 1,500 men, most of them in the north, retreated into the mountains to escape the German invasion and await the arrival of the Allies, which they assumed was imminent. Some also joined for love of adventure, and, if they were dyed-in-the-wool anti-Fascists, as political activists.

Edoardo Visconti, like his brother Guido a cavalry officer in the Savoy regiment, was an adventurer. In 1943, after fighting in Albania, Edoardo deserted the regular army, returned to Lugano and joined the Resistance led by the National Liberation Committee. He, Stefano Porta, Guglielmo Mozzoni and Dino Bergamasco were assigned to liaison between the Milanese CNL and the Allies. They were called the 'four musketeers'. To deliver messages, orders and money, they had to cross the wire barriers along the frontier. They bribed the guards when they could, risked their lives when they couldn't, but they always got through. Edoardo crossed that border some sixty times without being caught, carrying money to Milan to help Allied prisoners of the Germans and to finance the Resistance, delivering the funds either to a businessman named Rosasco or to the church of San Fedele.

'Our ideals,' reports Mozzoni, an architect, 'were close to those of the Liberals and the Action Party. We met Ferrucio Parri,★ we risked our lives, but our choice was primarily a moral one. For Edoardo in particular it expressed a need to remain active.'

The Action Party was a collection of anti-Fascists and anti-monarchists of varying aims and social origins. They included ex-Communists, Socialists and Liberals like Edoardo who, holding strong ideals of justice and freedom, wanted to give Italy its chance for social and political renewal not through the proletarian revolution the Communists were promoting, but through the establishment of a modern, multi-party republic.

Parri was the leading spokesman for this ideal. On 16 Septem-

★Prime minister in the first post-war coalition government founded in June 1945 (translator's note).

ber, Socialist Party chairman Pietro Nenni offered him command of the rebel forces in northern Italy, and after the Allied landing at Anzio on 22 January 1944, Parri headed the northern wing of the CNL. He was a long-time anti-Fascist whose prestige rested on his record as a combatant, his experience as a political prisoner, and his stern sense of duty. Although his political ideas diverged sharply from those of the 'Garibaldist' Luigi Longo, Parri named the Communist as his successor to the command of the Resistance forces in case of his death. Because of his personal links to northern industrial leaders, however, Parri best represented the enlightened, pragmatic upper middle class to which Edoardo Visconti gave his allegiance.

Luchino's ideas were both more radical and more hesitant, but they coincided with his brother's in their rejection of the old values, even those embodied by his former cavalry captain at Pinerolo, the Piedmontese nobleman Giuseppe de Montezemolo, who in September took command of the Resistance in the Latium but remained loyal to Badoglio and the monarchy and ready to carry out their orders. Luchino would call him 'an obedient hero made for a period like that of the Risorgimento'.

However adventurous and respectable this might seem, it did not tempt Visconti. On 8 September he left Rome with Basilio Franchina and Mario Chiari, a Tuscan scene-painter full of verve and wit who had fought on the Russian front and was now intent on reaching the Allied lines as soon as possible. They were to join Massimo Girotti and Roberto Rossellini at Tagliacozzo, in the Apennine mountains, but Luchino soon returned to the capital to fetch Uberta and her son Carlo who, two years earlier, at Luchino's insistence, had been named Carlo Libero (Free Charles). The house on Via Salaria was to be inhabited now by actress Maria Denis, by the servants, and by Paolo Mocci, one of the seven Sardinians given refuge by Visconti. The other six had returned to their island, but Mocci had stayed on; officially he was the gardener who went with the house.

Luchino's plan was to join the Italian forces moving north on Rome with the Allies. He also wanted to leave his sister in a safe place. But the small towns in the Abruzzi mountains, including Tagliacozzo, were quickly occupied by the Germans. He persuaded Uberta to settle in the remote mountain village of Verrechie.

In a small pink house in the fields under a clear October sky, he spent two peaceful weeks with those he loved, among farmers who became so devoted to the family that even today their children, living in Rome, perform small services for Uberta and her daughter Nicoletta. 'I remember that in Verrechie we spent our days reading *War and Peace*,' Uberta says. 'I can still see the book passing from hand to hand as we read passages aloud.'

This was the calm before the storm, when the days were electric with the promise of coming action. At dawn on 27 October Visconti left the village inn with Franchina, Chiari and a guide who was to lead them into the wild mountains where herders kept flocks of black sheep and droves of mules, and where the deep woods sheltered the huts of the *carbonari*, the charcoal-burners who have figured in all of Italy's clandestine struggles for freedom. Visconti felt this departure as another, more crucial break with his former life; he carefully noted the date and exact time in the journal he was to keep, in three school notebooks, from 5:30 on the morning of 27 October until 5 December 1943.

These half-effaced lines still vibrate with that tender parting, with his eagerness to regain his freedom, to achieve a new identity:

Verrechie, 27 October 1943

I am leaving with B. and M. as soon as day breaks. The blue house of Mass. [Massimo Girotti] . . . I knock. Mass. comes to the door at once; the top half of it opens like a horse's stall. He woke up immediately. He is in pyjamas, his face puffy with sleep, his eyes small and his hair tousled. He shakes hands with us affectionately. There is a bit of sorrow in his goodbye at not being able to come with us. I entrust Uberta to him.

I am pleased with myself – a feeling of serenity on separating myself from everything representing the past. Separating means getting a clear fix on everything.

Above all, awareness of freedom in the first half-hour on the road. We reach the cross.

I salute Verrechie, where I stayed two weeks or more. The sprawling village is asleep in the light mist; it looks like an eye always open to watch the entrance to the valley of Cappadocia. Signora Paolina's house on the road in the distance, where

Uberta is. Higher up, the air and the green meadows and the
paving stones also visible from above, gleaming. Now, for me –
freedom of time – of action – and no pain over the separation,
but rather a keen and youthful joy. My only regret is for
Uberta, at not being able to stay with her longer . . . Fever of
preparation I hadn't felt for a long time, and so indifferent to the
rest. Massimo came to the door and stood there, watching me
get everything ready. I know so well the kind of fears he may
have . . . Then he said: '*Bon voyage*'.

Three Britons and four Americans, escaped prisoners who had
been hiding in Verrechie, joined the party. They, too, were trying
to get through the German lines and reach the Allies. Day after day
they walked for hours along steep paths through forests of beeches
and maples, 'huge, deep spots, yellow, red, on the flank of the
mountain, passing crucifixes at the crossroads'. Valleys were 'dotted
with white and grey stones', and 'as far as the eye can see, pastures
green as water, grey-blue mists . . .'. In this silent world where 'no
human or animal life seems to have appeared for eons', this 'free
landscape' of 'quick and brilliant air', he wrote, 'some facts, along
with the feelings that drive us and fill us with happiness, assume
their true proportions: microscopic'.

From time to time the party ran across other defectors from
Fascism. Not even their anti-Fascism, however, could protect them
from Visconti's merciless sarcasm. They were perfect targets,
aristocrats (real or pretended) and homosexuals (ashamed or
arrogant), his degraded doubles. A couple made up of a physician
and 'one Marquess Triomfi', who had also stopped for rest in a
charcoal-burners' village, were neatly pinned: 'I can't help naming
this marquess "del Faggio", Stendhal-style; they tell us, without
convincing me, that Venafro and Isernia have fallen. When they
leave, the marquess, who wears a little red beard and a permanently
bewildered look, rather strains our good humour. Very smugly he
delivers himself of a heap of nonsense, and the doctor assumes a
"young girl in flower" look that peeks irrepressibly through his
superbly black beard.'

At first the ten men progressed unimpeded through the mountains, walking parallel to the road along which the Germans moved

reinforcements to defend Montecassino. But to reach the Allied lines, this German-infested road had to be crossed. Chiari recalls the time when, just as they slithered down the slope towards the road, a group of German soldiers suddenly appeared. 'One of them looked back and he would certainly have seen us if a farmer had not come by at that moment with a cart of hay and given us time to hide.' Repeated attempts were made to cross over, but none succeeded.

As time went on, conditions grew more dangerous, the men's isolation more oppressive. They suffered from the cold, lice, fatigue, lack of food, the nightly search for shelter in abandoned farmhouses. Some farmers welcomed and fed them, others chased them off. Finally, because of the Americans' exhaustion, they left the valley and headed back into the mountains.

'What I wouldn't give to have a hot bath and sleep in a bed for a night,' Luchino told Chiari one evening. 'So I went down into a small village alone,' the scene-painter recalled. 'Because of the curfew, there wasn't a soul in the streets. I rang at the priest's house; in a small village, the priest is always a reference point. The usual sacristan came to the door, dying of fright, and I asked him to wake the priest. He was a typical old country priest, too, and very friendly. "I'm travelling with a celebrity who is very tired," I told him, "and before pushing on, he would like a hot bath and a bed, but I can't tell you who he is. In fact, neither you nor the sacristan must see him." And that's how Luchino had his bath. Then we devoured a whole chicken and we slept in the priest's bed.'

A comic interlude in a predicament that was anything but funny. For they had to find shelter for the British and American soldiers, to bring them food and clothing, sometimes to doctor them. The troopers were so worn out that at the end of November the party had to stop and rest. Their stay in the village of Settefrati stretched for an endless month. Visconti and Chiari found refuge with the village doctor; for security reasons, the soldiers had to hide outside the village, in barns, shepherds' huts, caves. Visconti's journal echoes with discouragement, with doubt about how this trip will end:

Settefrati, 23 November 1943

. . . I buy cigarettes and matches (last night when I went up, they couldn't make a fire at all, having used up the few matches

Mario had brought them the previous night). They were soaked, shivering with cold and fever in the dense darkness of the barn. P. said in the blackness: 'We must have fire – We must have fire,' and complained like a baby.

They told me what a terrible day yesterday had been. They had sheltered in a shepherd's hut above the Macchia Marina spring . . . Luckily for them, I had arranged with the German patrol's guide that he would not climb up beyond the spring; when he got there he said he was too tired and wet to go on, which convinced the Germans to go back down.

While they were in the hut, four Italians and a South African (the Italians were Air Force officers), vanquished by the cold, wet to the marrow of their bones, couldn't take any more and started down despite R.'s (Royal Guardsman Richard Edmunton-Low) telling them not to go back down into the valley where they might be caught.

From up top, the mist and rain completely hid them from view. In fact, R. and the others later learned that they had been captured . . . As were the character out of Jules Verne, with his children, and the Poles.

. . . Their shoes are really gone, the soles have completely disappeared . . . Their shoes [are] in shreds. I'll look for something for them in the village today.

R. admits that the punctuality and quantity of food I've sent him saved them from the exhaustion that would have driven them to surrender to the Germans . . . Indeed, they are unrecognizable, and their fatigue, weakness and misery can be read in their faces – aged and tired.

. . . Back in the village, I learn that the tanks that came in last night are already leaving today . . . What strikes me is how young the soldiers are.

If I had not formed the habit of this journal that I am glad I made myself keep, and [did not have] Rousseau, the days would weigh on me unbearably. Sometimes I even begin to think this operation is pointless.

Visconti, who had not fought in the war, felt especially guilty about this because his elder brother had died in it, and he had dreamed of receiving his baptism of fire as a rite of passage to manhood. He wanted to face danger, to achieve something that would be his own. But instead of confronting external obstacles and enemies, he had to fight himself, had to force his impetuous nature to accept the dreary limitations of an inglorious battle:

Settefrati, 5 December 1943

The fifth week of Settefrati is beginning. Seven more worrisome days of inaction, waiting, alternating hope and disappointment, even though a profound conviction tells me these will be the last. There remains the dissatisfaction of having had to wait here instead of making an attempt, of facing the danger, with all its unknown risks. Yet my conscience tells me we did the right thing – not so much for us – but to guarantee our friends' welfare. In fact, this caution that embitters me slightly was wholly dictated by the need to bring this operation to fruition for our friends.

If I wonder about it, I can tell myself with absolute sincerity that these days have weighed on me not so much because of boredom, but because they gave me no excuse to ask a little extra dash and courage of myself. If I look back – to the decision taken in Rome in the confusion of those first days, to the calm determination born in me to do this – I can say today I acted calmly and serenely, without giving way to impatience or eagerness, that I confined my utterly romantic impulses within the bounds of reason and morality. The coming days will give me further occasions to test this – call it sedative – discipline over my character, which I know too well is impulsive and sentimental.

Visconti's third notebook ends here, on that 5 December 1943. This testing of his patience and 'sedative' discipline was to drag on until the end of January 1944, when the Allied landing at Anzio raised new hope that Italy would soon be liberated. The landing sent Visconti back to Rome. More than a month had gone, then, in waiting, in discouragement, in humble and judicious effort: caring for the Americans who, Chiari says, 'were still in bad shape', keeping track of German movements in the area and packing the escapees off to safe hiding places at the first sign of danger, escorting them up into the mountains despite the snow and cold to the caves the shepherds showed them. On Christmas Eve they managed to attend midnight mass although the district was crawling with Germans. The priest spirited them into the church via the bell tower, so that they heard the service from behind a curtain near the organ while below them, across the church, some forty Germans sang in chorus.

By the time they reached Rome early in February, after being captured by a German patrol and escaping in the confusion of a bombardment, they were utterly exhausted. Visconti and Chiari managed to get their British and American 'friends' into a hospital. After the end of the war both the British and the American authorities expressed formal thanks. A British citation signed by Field Marshal Sir Harold Alexander was 'awarded to Luchino Visconti as a token of gratitude for and appreciation of the help given to the Sailors, Soldiers and Airmen of the British Commonwealth of Nations, which enabled them to escape from or evade capture by the enemy'.

Luchino nevertheless felt he had suffered a humiliating failure, had missed the trial of virility he so ardently desired. There had been an illusory swirl of his imagination, and now he was back where he had started. Except that now he was ten times as anxious to seek adventure, to enlist in a real struggle. His request to join a group of Catholic Communists was rebuffed: they were wary of him as an aristocrat and, worse, a homosexual.

No sooner had he moved back into the house on Via Salaria than he contacted his *Cinema* friends, who had gone underground. This was 'the most interesting, most beautiful, most coherent period of my life', he would say shortly before his death. 'The little I could give to the Resistance movement was the best thing I've ever done, and after that, my work . . .' In his commitment to the movement, his personal ambition, his heroic dreams mattered less than his wish to reshape his destiny, to burn himself out and be reborn. He even traded in his name, Visconti, so weighted with privilege and power, for a new one, a commonplace name with no resonances: henceforward he would be known as Alfredo Guidi.

The Allies landed at Anzio on 22 January. Sir Winston Churchill complained that he had hoped to let a wildcat loose on the beach and had wound up with a beached whale. The Romans, hostile to the German occupants but not at all anxious to fight them, simply hunkered down and waited for their liberators to arrive. Colonel Montezemolo, intent on keeping Rome peaceful at all costs, transferred Resistance operations out of the Eternal City. Five days after the landing, *L'Unità* issued a call to insurrection: 'Insurrectional general strike! People of Rome, to arms!' Nothing happened. The waiting went on.

In contrast to the partisan struggle in the north, operations in central Italy, especially in Rome, remained small-scale, badly organized and largely ineffective. The most active fighters were the Armed Partisan Groups, the GAP, recruited exclusively from among young Communists. They operated in teams of three or four, never more. In the cities, where hideouts were far harder to find than in rural areas, many of the teams were virtual suicide squads. In the winter of 1944 they stepped up their campaign of assassination, sabotage and terrorism.

Both the Italians and the Germans responded ferociously. There were waves of arrests; the Gestapo prison on the Via Tasso and the Regina Coeli prison held hundreds of political prisoners, people from all walks of life who had been denounced, or caught in possession of a leaflet, a poster, an underground newspaper. Some were simply swept up at random after a terrorist attack. Torture, deportation, death awaited them, as they did for the priest, Morosini, shot by a firing squad, and for thirty-four-year-old Leone Ginzburg, arrested in the printing shop where the underground *L'Italia Libera* was run off; his wife, the author Natalia Ginzburg, was informed of his death, but the cause was never stated.

In January 1944, Pietro Koch, a former carabinieri officer born in Benevento of German ancestry, set up a political police organization that operated alongside the Gestapo and the fascist police. Its offices, cells and torture chambers were housed first in the Pension Oltremare on Via Principe Amedeo, then moved to the Pension Jaccarino, a cluster of 'sad houses' of sinister reputation.

On his return to Via Salaria, Visconti learned that his house in particular had aroused the suspicions of the 'Koch gang'. In his absence the place had been searched. To complicate the situation, Koch, whose friends included such famous actors as Osvaldo Valenti and Luisa Ferida, fell headlong in love with the beautiful Maria Denis, who was living in the house. This gave the policeman two reasons to take a close interest in the mansion: suspicion that partisans were hiding there, notably the Sardinian Paolo Mocci, and the presence of the actress with the sweet, baby voice who had opened the door to him one evening.

Despite or because of the growing danger, Visconti continued to shelter partisans wanted by the police, and tightened his connections with the most dynamic Communist Party units. De Santis reported that 'Luchino, who felt cut off from activist life, asked for and was granted membership in the GAP at the most dramatic possible time.' He was credited with great courage and moral probity, useful assets for a member. But Antonello Trombadori, a party political leader who later exercised considerable influence over his friend Visconti, formally denies he was ever admitted into the group; homosexuality was no more acceptable to lay Communists than it was to their Catholic allies. Besides, how could so well-known a man, living in a house under surveillance by the police, be entrusted with assignments that required absolute secrecy?

In Rome, as in the other big cities in Italy, the GAP constituted a tiny fraction of the population, no more than thirty people, all carefully chosen. They were young, mainly workmen who could handle bombs, machine-guns or a P-38 automatic; all were party members. Luchino never joined the party, and De Santis admits 'he didn't have time for real Resistance activity, or to take part in sabotage operations, as he would have liked to'. He was, however, asked to find places where illegal publications could be printed, and to cache and deliver weapons.

He did this until March without arousing too much suspicion. True, one night at the end of the month, three SS men burst into his house, but they were after Mocci, not Visconti. Chiari remembers that Rinaldo Ricci, Renato Guttuso and De Santis were there. After a quick search – that missed the copies of L'Unità and the weapons hidden in Luchino's bedroom – the SS men asked where Visconti was hiding the suspicious persons in his house. They were chiefly interested in the count's so-called 'gardener'. No one said a word, but just then the door opened, and the Garibaldi Brigade officer Paolo Mocci appeared in the doorway. He did not resist when the Germans arrested him.

Visconti realized that it was time to leave Via Salaria. For a few days he stayed at Uberta's house. But things were moving quickly. At 3:30 in the afternoon of 23 March he was on Via Veneto with Chiari and Gianni Puccini when a terrific explosion was heard near by. The day was the anniversary of the founding of the Fasci, and a communist group had set off bombs in the SS barracks on Via Rasella, in the Quirinale district, just as a German division was entering. Thirty-two soldiers had been torn apart by the bombs or machine-gunned by GAP terrorists posted on a side street. The Germans, pursuing the gunmen, arrested everyone they found or who lived in the area. Central Rome was blocked off and reinforcements sent in to forestall an insurrection.

The repression was swift and merciless. A German communiqué published in the newspapers on 25 March announced that an investigation was under way and that no effort would be spared to wipe out 'the activity of these criminal bandits. No one will be permitted to sabotage with impunity the resurgent collaboration between Italy and Germany. The German high command has therefore decreed that for every German assassinated, ten communist criminals will be shot. This order has already been carried out.'

SS chief Herbert Kappler had selected all the prisoners on Via Tasso who 'deserved to die', Jews and anti-Fascists. Since his contingent did not reach the required number, the warden at Regina Coeli supplied the rest and even sent an extra fifteen, through over-zealousness or a mistake in arithmetic. Three hundred and thirty-five prisoners, three of them under sixteen years of age, were moved in canvas-covered trucks to the Ardeatine Pits, a quarry near the Catacombs. One after another they were coldly shot down as they entered the quarry, sometimes falling on the bodies of those who had preceded them. Then the Germans blasted out the rock face so that the victims' bodies could not be found. But they were unaware that there was a witness, a shepherd who had hidden when he heard the first trucks pull up, and who had watched the massacre from beginning to end.

Although Visconti didn't know it, among the dead were two

men he knew well: Colonel Montezemolo and Mocci, whose body, still wearing the sweater he had been arrested in, Luchino would later be called on to identify.

The vice was closing around Visconti and his friends. From then on they lived like hunted men, isolated and on borrowed time. On the murderous afternoon of 23 March he, Puccini and Chiari decided to split up and leave the area, where they would surely be arrested if they stayed. Chiari, however, rashly returned to Via Salaria that evening to retrieve his personal belongings. The house was surrounded by about sixty men, Germans and Italians. 'Where is Visconti?' he was asked. 'He's been in Milan since Thursday,' he replied on the spur of the moment. Maria Cerruti, a young woman who had always been in service with the Viscontis – indeed, was practically 'family', for Uberta thought of her almost as a sister – walked into the room just then. The police again asked. 'Where is the count?' Miraculously, her answer confirmed Chiari's: 'He left last Thursday for Milan.'

Mario says that when he went to his room to get his things, he found that his money and a gold chain had been stolen. He complained and, he says, 'while the SS was searching the Fascists, the telephone rang. It was Luchino. "I don't know where he is," I breathed into the phone, and hung up at once. He understood my message. Meanwhile, the SS and the Fascists had decided to take me to Via Tasso. But a little man from the Security Police said, "No, I'll take him to San Vitale," and that saved my life . . .'

That very evening, Visconti left Uberta's. For three weeks he sought refuge with friends, those – fewer every day – who had not yet been arrested or who were above suspicion. Keeping in touch with the group was out of the question; everyone was on his own. 'We were alone,' he said later, 'alone with our thoughts, with our dreams. Alone with an image, one image after another of our friends, who were God knows where. Some were workers, others were intellectuals. Every evening, their mothers waited for them to return home . . .'

Where were Chiari, the Puccini brothers, Rinaldo Ricci? Already in prison? Still at liberty? For how long? In Rome, people grew more and more afraid: giving asylum to a man wanted by the Gestapo could mean death for oneself and one's family.

Even Anna Magnani, the rebel, the tigress, was frightened when Alfredo Guidi showed up at her door on Via Amba Aradam. A few days earlier, a German officer had been wounded in the street, and all the surrounding houses had been searched. If it happened again and Luchino were found at her place, what would happen? She wasn't alone; her son Lucà, born in the year *Obsession* was made, was with her. Visconti talked to her, reassured her: only two days and then he'd be gone. Anna hesitated. Then, scowling fiercely, she told him: 'I'm scared, but you can stay as long as you like.' Luchino stayed there for a few days, then left to find another refuge.

He was at the home of Ricci's half-brother, Carlo Novaro, on Viale Eritrea on the evening of 15 April when Koch's men came and arrested him. They took him to the Pension Jaccarino, where they had already imprisoned another of his friends, twenty-two-year-old Franco Ferri. The house was in a garden; in it were Pietro Koch's lacquered desk, his thickly carpeted and softly lit bedroom, but also the blood-spattered corridors, the interrogation rooms, the stairs down to the cellars. An elegant man who loved art, pretty women and cocaine, Koch made it a point of honour to force his most taciturn prisoners to talk.

Before his victims were interrogated, he placed them in isolation cells just over one yard square, impossible to stand up in. 'I was arrested in an apartment in Rome by the Fascists in Koch's gang,' Visconti later said. 'One of the apartments we left from on clandestine missions. I was caught with a revolver in my pocket. They dragged me to the Pension Jaccarino and threw me into a cell; for days I was locked up in a small compartment, without food, to weaken me and make me talk . . . They told me: "Give us names or . . . you'll see."' When he refused to tell them anything, the words 'TO BE SHOT' were written on his record in red ink as he looked on. He viewed this process of intimidation as 'a poor piece of directing'.

He knew he wasn't the only one, and probably not the worst treated. 'I was not tortured,' he said, 'merely beaten . . . "Names!" That was what they asked my friends for, too. We gave them no names.' After being interrogated, the prisoners were taken back to tiny cells or old coal cellars with no light or air and left in a stench of excrement. 'They burst into the cell often, once, twice, three times a day, and beat us horribly. At night we helped those who had been strung up by their arms after interrogation, their bones dislocated, covered with blood . . . Some of us couldn't raise a cup to our lips because they had broken our fingers . . . I saw the most atrocious things in my life there.'

The images were so obsessive, the experience so horrendous, that after Rome was liberated, Visconti tried to make a film about it called *Pension Oltremare*, from a detailed scenario he wrote with Ricci and Ferri. His two co-workers deserted him to enlist in the army of national liberation, but he nevertheless said in October 1944: 'I am preparing a film entitled *Pension Oltremare*, which will be extremely realistic, with dramatic and psychological content as well as a polemical meaning. The story takes place in Rome during the cruellest period of nazi–fascist oppression.'

Long before he made *The Damned* he planned to do a film condemning the collusion between the Nazis and big business; long before Liliana Cavani made *Night Porter*, Visconti viewed German officers as weak, perverted and sadistic. One of the scenes he planned was built around a private party organized at the Albergo Bernini by a Piedmontese fascist businessman; among the guests were a Luftwaffe officer, 'young and already dead drunk', and an SS officer, 'cold, curt and stiff, with one wooden hand, the right hand, hard and rigid in a gleaming black glove'. The script has him 'gazing silently, with a cold, hard smile' at a young woman singing as she stripped in the middle of the room. 'At the end, he goes over to her and, with his stiff, black-gloved hand, slowly strokes her shoulder and breast.'

In counterpoint to this portrayal of corruption, perversion and decadence, Visconti planned to develop the story of a young man arrested at random and taken to the Pension Oltremare; his contacts with the partisans, with tortured anti-Fascists, give him so strong a political conscience that he can face his final sacrifice at the Ardeatine Pits with dignity.

In the twelve days Visconti spent in the Pension Jaccarino, his daily confrontation with violence, with the brutal suffering that wounds what is most human, most vulnerable in a man, brought about and confirmed his political maturity – a maturity achieved through pain, pity and horror rather than doctrine.

During those twelve days, two women did everything in their power to protect him from torture and to prevent Koch from turning him over to the Gestapo, as he threatened to do. Uberta persuaded her mother-in-law, Baroness Avanzo, to intercede for Luchino. And Maria Denis went to the Pension Jaccarino, playing on the passion Koch still showed for her.

On 27 April Luchino was transferred to San Gregorio, a prison hospital where conditions were distinctly milder. From there he could send notes to Maria Cerruti, yellowed, rumpled notes she has kept. Some are complaints ('Why hasn't Uberta come yet? If I had been shot, she'd have found me in a state of advanced putrefaction'), others thank the women who helped him and sent him money: the baroness and 'Miss Rica', perhaps a made-up name for Miss Denis, maybe invented less to shield her than to play a romantic identity game. This was the same game that led him to take the name Alfredo Guidi; the Alfredo may well have been taken from the character in *La Traviata*, as the Guidi may have been borrowed from his brother, who had died fighting for a cause that was not his own:

Dear Maria, thank Miss Rica warmly. My news needs only a few lines. I am well now. I'm the one who wants news, of Donna Uberta and all of you. But as long as Donna Uberta does not request an interview, it will be impossible. So I hope she'll come soon. She can request the interview from the police inspector here, who will in turn ask the special political police
. . .

Dear Maria, I have not yet seen the letters which the inspector must read first. Thanks for the things. I'd like a small bottle of ink, a pen and some blotting-paper.

Alfredo Guidi

Dear Maria, in my house, in my room, to be precise, there should still be some bottles of liqueur (cognac). Bring them. If you go to the cellar, there must be a bottle of whisky left. Can I have some Flit and a spray-gun? Ask Mr Massimo to give you two of my books that I would like to have here. One is a novel by Green. The other, a volume of Diderot. Money: I received

4,000 lire from the baroness, 3,000 or 2,000 from you, 2,000 from Mr Pagani. I would like some cough syrup. The plum cake was wonderful. Can you do an encore?

No mention of the war. Visconti seems as tranquil in his prison as Fabrice del Dongo was in prison in Parma; a few weeks later, in fact, he was to consider giving the role of Stendhal's hero to young Ferri. Uberta functioned for Luchino as the Duchess of Sanseverina did for Fabrice, trying immediately and by every possible means to get him out of prison. Koch, she says, was 'a terrible man who always sashayed around with a squadron of Fascists'.

He was intent on finding the hiding place of Maria Denis, who had disappeared to escape her shameful and sinister suitor. He attempted to blackmail Uberta. Figuring that the end justified the means and that the actress, after all, didn't have much to lose, she played along: '"Tell me where she's hiding or I won't let your brother go," Koch told me. So I said she was at the Acquasanta Golf Club . . . The place served as a refuge for many other people, too, but I didn't know that.'

Luchino was released from San Gregorio on 3 June, with American troops already at the gates of Rome. Chiari, who was imprisoned in Regina Coeli, says that on the morning of 4 June his cellmate, an old syndicalist who had spent most of his life in prisons and penal colonies, suddenly said, 'Look what's happening!' 'And I saw a scene out of Eisenstein: Republican Guards tearing off their fascist insignia and replacing them with little stars . . . At eleven o'clock, the warden (who was later killed in a horrible way, although he had not been one of the worst) told us: "I'm letting you go, but wait a while because the Germans are bundling all the men in the streets into their trucks, or taking pot shots at them."

'I saw the Germans in the streets, black and bloody. I also saw the famous hearse loaded with paintings and other stolen objects. I remember a little Wehrmacht soldier on the Via Lungaretta who couldn't have been over fifteen; in one hand he held a cluster of bombs, in the other three or four ice-cream cones. I went to the Sisto bridge, the only one open; Panzers were crossing over it while beneath it boys swam and sunbathed. Why get excited? This was just one more invader retreating.

'Luchino and I saw each other that evening on Via Veneto. How incredible, after all the running away and the terror. Being able to have a bath again – what heaven! We went to the Piazza Venezia, the moon was out and the first Allied jeep arrived. We dropped in at Via Salaria, with some friends . . . But so many others were dead. Then we went back to Via Veneto, to Rosati's, and drank two gins on the old café's red divans. In the streets, American loudspeaker trucks announced the landing in Normandy.'

Uberta still remembers 'that period of wild, unbridled joy . . . Incredible effervescence! And I had Luchino back . . .' Cesare Zavattini, the prolific neo-realist screenwriter, will never forget the hallucinatory sight he saw on 4 June: 'amid the throng overflowing the Piazza San Pietro, forming a chain with people he'd never seen before and radiant with solidarity' was Luchino Visconti the aristocrat, descendant of another Luchino Visconti who had waged incessant warfare with the Gonzagas for control of his native village. Zavattini cannot have been the only person, then and in the years that followed, to wonder about this living enigma: a Visconti, friend of that Prince Umberto who would briefly reign as king of Italy, and himself descended from the tyrants of Milan, transformed by the convulsions of war into a 'Red count', a prince of the Revolution.

XII

TRIAL

The truth, the harsh truth.

DANTON

*It is especially when all is false that one loves
the truth.*

DIDEROT

When the Americans entered Rome on 5 June, twenty-two years of
Fascism collapsed, twenty-two years in which, as Visconti put it,
'Italians' souls were suffocated, crushed by dictatorship . . . when
nothing true or genuine existed any more'. The nine months of
German occupation, and the continuing war, marked the final phase
of Fascism and ended it in a paroxysm of horror. But to intellectuals
hauled out of their ivory towers to work in the Resistance – even to
solitaries as stately as the Neapolitan philosopher Benedetto Croce –
the liberation of Italy seemed a renaissance, a new and purer
Risorgimento.

For months they had waited to realize their dreams, the plans for
social renewal they had argued over through many a night of clan-
destinity. But, like Vittorio De Sica, they had to admit that there
was very little to work with: 'It was not even worth talking about
making movies: there were no theatres, no cameras, no film. And
we didn't even acknowledge one another. Everyone lived for himself, thought and hoped for himself.'

Films were being made, but in the north, in Venice, under the
protection and control of Mussolini's puppet Italian Social Republic.
Quite a few film-makers, technicians and producers bowed to pressure or were lured by inflated promises that eventually brought

them – like actors Osvaldo Valenti and Luisa Ferida, accused of collaborating with Koch – before a firing squad. In Rome, the studios at Cinecittà, created by and symbolic of the Fascists, were turned into a refugee camp by the American military governor who set out to destroy every vestige of its film-making facilities, all its technical resources, in short, to destroy the Italian film industry. Italy, he explained, was an agricultural country, so what did it need with a movie industry?

Visconti was convinced that the film industry urgently needed restructuring and moral purification. In June 1944 he joined Chiari, the Communist Umberto Barbaro, the film-maker Mario Camerini and the writer Mario Soldati on a purge committee supervised by the Union of Entertainment Industry Workers. Its job was to black-list or arrange the prosecution of film people who had worked in fascist or nazi propaganda operations.

A few months later he helped make a group film, with the work coordinated by his old comrades-in-arms and fellow workers, De Santis and editor Mario Serandrei. The movie, called *Giorni di Gloria*, was a documentary montage tracing the high points of the partisan struggle starting with the 'Days of Glory' of the Resistance, from 8 September until the liberation of the north. It celebrated the exploits of the underground army and, in lyrical, emphatic, Eisenstein-type images, the reconstruction that was already under way.

Two sections of this communist propaganda film are free of bombast: Marcello Pagliero's investigation of the Ardeatine Pits massacre, and actual footage of the trial, on 4 June 1945, of the former Roman Police Chief Pietro Caruso and Pietro Koch, and of their executions the following day. Visconti actually testified in the trial, at Koch's request; the hangman of the Pension Jaccarino hoped the film-maker's testimony would soften his punishment, that his leniency towards this distinguished prisoner made up for the atrocities he was accused of. But Visconti's merciless testimony demolished Koch's case.

Among the moments of high drama in *Days of Glory*: first, the lynching of Carretta, the ex-warden of Regina Coeli prison. Visconti happened to be in the crowd, with his camera, when Carretta arrived at the courthouse. The jailer was recognized, wrested from the police and hurled into the Tiber. Boatmen joined in the

riot, beating at the man with oars to keep him under the water.
These wavering first-hand pictures of a murder are followed by the
slow, tense ceremony of the Koch-Caruso trial. Visconti's eye
isolated and caught the trial's climactic moments. Broad, slow
sweeps of the camera alternate brief shots of the crowd, especially
the women, with pictures of the judges (one of them the father of
the future Communist Party Secretary, Enrico Berlinguer), and of
the defendants' tense faces.

Throughout this sequence, which gives us a foretaste of Visconti's later movie Lo Straniero (The Stranger), the editing creates an
atmosphere of tragic ritual that is even more intense than the two
men's execution – clipped and rapid as a guillotine blade – filmed the
following day in Fort Bravetta. We see Koch's tall, black-clad figure
get out of the van in the glaring early-afternoon light. The camera
frames the fort and drops down to the chair where the sinister
proprietor of the Pension Jaccarino and many other 'sad houses' will
meet his end; we see the religious ceremony, the sign of the cross,
Koch kissing the rosary. Seated, hands bound, he refuses a blind-
fold. Death, the fall. The chair overturns.

'We watched Koch's execution,' Chiari said. 'Luchino was con-
scious of watching an act of justice. Luchino was first of all a philosopher.' Meaning a man who subjected his life to moral imperatives
and rational consistency, comforted by his brand-new subscription
to the principles of Communism.

Now, working night and day to make up for lost time, our stern
Dominican plunged into a sea of plans for which he summoned
scriptwriters, producers and actors. Antonioni was put to work, for
example, on a story based vaguely on Maupassant's Boule de suif,
commissioned by the producer Alfredo Guarini as a vehicle for his
wife, Isa Miranda. It was, said Antonioni, 'the story of a small
women's orchestra that went up to the front to play for the soldiers.
It's a pity: I think this film would have taken the place of Open City.
Vasco Pratolini, Gianni Puccini and I worked on it.

'In the mornings we went to Visconti's on Via Salaria. We met
in a room in the little tower. There was a fire burning in the fireplace
and a big boardroom table with notepads and pencils. Luchino sat at
the head of the table. He said, "Let's hear the ideas." It was a bit like
being in school when you're not prepared for the teacher's ques-

tions, and the others considered me a company scab because I got up early in the morning and therefore I felt less groggy than they did. One afternoon, after two months of work, Luchino said: "Boys, I've seen what you've come up with; let's say that so far it's been a joke." And under our horrified eyes he tossed the manuscript into the fire, burning the only copy.'

Lots of scripts suffered the same fate. Some related directly to 'very current subjects' about which Visconti said he was anxious to go on record. In May 1945 he signed a contract with Lux to make a film entitled *Furore*, on which he was to work with his usual team, Alicata and De Santis. At the end of 1945 he agreed on another film on the Resistance, adapted from Elio Vittorini's novel *Men and Non-Men*, the story of a Milanese partisan in 1944. Vittorini, a Sicilian, pressed him to find funding that did not come from 'just any capitalist film company'.

All these projects aborted more or less quickly. They were never completed, he said later, because of the hopeless timidity of producers 'who don't want to put a finger in the wound'. But other subjects, less topical and more ambitious, suffered similar fates: *The Charterhouse of Parma*, and especially *The Trial of Maria Tarnowska*, based on a real-life criminal case that had filled the newspapers in 1907; in the spring of 1945 he began nearly a year of hard work on the idea. Then he switched to a tableau of Milan's middle class as seen through the saga of a big-business family from the period of Italian unification to the second world war.

Was the fault all the producers'? Guarini was excited by the story of Tarnowska, 'the witch of Kiev' and a descendant of Mary Stuart, whom Annie Vivanti found in a women's prison in Trani in 1918. In her book *Circe*, Vivanti followed the track of this young Polish woman who, bedizened like an idol with lovers, diamonds and debts, aroused scandal, censure and worship wherever she went. All this ended after she enticed two of her lovers into murdering her 'fiancé', Count Pavel Kamarovski, in a palace on the Campo Santa Maria del Giglio, in Venice, on the morning of 3 September 1907.

Producer Guarini couldn't have wanted a more fascinating *femme fatale* role for his beautfiul wife than that of this hell-spawned Madonna. Both a woman and a blighted society on trial, with the action taking place entirely in the spring of 1910 on the quays of the Grand Canal, where the putrid water ate away at the splendid, decaying aristocratic palaces it mirrored – wasn't this a film made to order for Visconti?

What a whirlwind of passion and folly danced around Maria Tarnowska beginning on the day when, at seventeen, she escaped from home by marrying Vassili Tarnowski, a debauched, childish and violent Polish aristocrat. A few years later, at the end of a meal, Tarnowski began shouting drunkenly at his wife's lover, Count Alexis Bozevski, the handsomest officer in the imperial guard: 'I want to play blind man's bluff,' he bawled, 'blind man's bluff with the cavalryman! Bing, bang, blind man's bluff!' As Bozevski was leaving, Tarnowski shot him from behind, then bowed to Maria, whose gown was spattered with blood.

It was then that she began wandering through Europe, from one Grand Hotel to another. She travelled first with Bozevski, until he tore the bandages off the festering wound in his neck and died before her eyes. Then she took up with Donat Prilukov, a famous Moscow lawyer who the countess hoped would reunite her with her children. Prilukov became her lover, embezzled money for her, and suggested she allow herself to be kept by Count Kamarovski.

He probably urged her to arrange Kamarovski's murder by a young student, a relative of the writer Ivan Turgenev and a close friend of Kamarovski's, who was desperately in love with her. The young man, Nicolas Naumov, son of the governor of Orel, loved Baudelaire as much as he did Maria, and he relished the whippings his latter-day Circe inflicted on him.

A magnificent story of a sumptuous hell, perfect for Visconti, as *Remembrance of Things Past* would have been. Yet after the case was thoroughly researched, after Visconti assembled a detailed file that covered everything – court testimony, the psychiatrists' defence of Maria, statements by the defendants and the witnesses, summations by the attorneys and the judges, even press clippings from all over the world – he dropped the idea.

'I don't know why, but at the time Luchino had no money,' says Antonioni, who wrote a polished script for the project with Count Guido Piovene, Antonio Pietrangeli and Visconti himself. 'He had rented out his house on Via Salaria and taken two suites (one for himself, one for the servants) in the San Giorgio Hotel, a thoroughly dismal hotel on one of those squalid streets near the Termini train station. A terrifying place. We went there in the morning, meals were served in the room, and when Luchino had to go out he locked us in to make us work. We felt like caged animals. Out of boredom, Piovene stood at the window and spat on the heads of all the bald men who went by.

'Fortunately, spring came and we went to work on the beach at Ostia. We made a great expedition of it, we, Visconti, a friend of his who was a sort of master of ceremonies for him, and his scene-painter, Mario Chiari. We stopped in a trattoria, Gina's, got a basket of food and worked on the beach until dusk. It was all very beautiful – the sea, the sand (which was clean then), Luchino and his friend, who spoke French, the beach chairs, the white tablecloths. It was almost like the picnics that elegant bathers took on the Hôtel des Bains beach on the Lido, in *Death in Venice*.

'One day we faced the problem of writing Tarnowska into the Hôtel des Bains, along with the servants who brought her breakfast. Luchino said, "All right, what do you say is on the tray?" And I said: "No one can know that better than you do, Luchino. It's a scene only you can write." He wrote twelve pages. It took a mitteleuropean like him to catalogue the china, the toast, the butter and the little butter knife, the preserves, the flower, the silver on the tray. But that kind of accuracy was essential in this case; if we were wrong about the things on the tray, we were wrong about the whole film.'

Yet, says Antonioni, after months of hard work, Visconti, exasperated by Miss Miranda's childishness and affectation, announced that he no longer wanted to do the film. 'We tried every way we could, and we were quite sincere about it, to change his mind. He wouldn't budge. Getting Luchino to reverse a decision was impossible. In the meanwhile, we went back to Via Salaria, and one day he sent for Guarini. Guarini seemed to be an easy-going, jovial man. With us he was even more so because of the film with Isa. When Luchino told him the news, he blanched and began to teeter. We laid him on a couch and then we all went out, leaving him there as white as a sheet.' We can imagine Antonioni's understandable disappointment; he had seen himself as an assistant director to Visconti. Luchino later said he burned everything, including the stack of research material.

All of it? No, he was too interested in the story. Years afterwards, when he formed a close friendship with actress Romy Schneider, the obsessive image of Tarnowska resurfaced. He had not abandoned the project and would not, Antonioni insists, 'for as long as he lived'. In the character of Maria Tarnowska he surely saw himself mirrored; she had been apportioned beauty, nobility, a rebellious spirit and, too, that pervasive poison whose 'infection', she wrote in black pencil in a school notebook in Venice's Giudecca Prison, she felt spreading through her veins and into her belly. Like Luchino she was born in the shadow of the fateful serpent,* and of the poisons called sickness, neurosis, madness, death, an evil shadow that accompanied her everywhere and that 'every day, every night, grew and became gigantic'. Gradually they took the form of 'the huge monster' she bore within her, which the world will see, she wrote, on the day 'the flimsy walls of my brow explode'.

The same black blood flows in the veins of many other Visconti characters, giving them all a sort of family resemblance. It is there in Countess Serpieri in *Senso*, indifferent to the shame she has brought on her name, her class. It pulses in Ludwig II, the Moon King, an 'enigma to others and himself', born under the sign of Saturn, as Visconti was born under the sign of Scorpio the destroyer, and who, like Tarnowska, 'was denied the right to love'. Visconti's interests were astoundingly varied, covering the whole range between current events and the broader perspectives of history to which he was irresistibly attracted.

Well, relatively varied, on closer examination: his condemnation of the protagonists in the Tarnowska case – a judgement on an entire class before the court of history – is echoed in the works he was beginning to mount in the theatre. All of these, too, bring judgements on society.

At the end of 1944, the Turin businessman Riccardo Gualino, the richest producer of the day, offered to finance Visconti's staging of

*See the section on *The Guivre*, p. 421.

any show he chose for the Eliseo Theatre in Rome. A few feverish days of work resulted in the 'historic' production of Cocteau's *Intimate Relations*. In the preface to a French edition of the play he marked out in red the intentions proclaimed by Cocteau in 1939: 'To remain an accurate painter of an errant society, to write a modern and naked play . . .' At every performance – all matinées, from 30 January to 13 February 1945 – the dull growl of the power generator provided a constant reminder that the war was still going on along the Gothic line and on the Rhine. But in theatres transformed into tribunals the trial of 'errant societies' was already under way.

What is theatre? Visconti replies: 'A tribunal where one can also say things that might shock.' Late in 1945 he supported his definition by creating a series of scandals to celebrate his defiant reunion with his native city: *Intimate Relations*; Marcel Achard's play *Adam*, banned in Milan and Venice for 'corrupting the young', and Erskine Caldwell's *Tobacco Road*. He had left an aristocrat and returned a man of the theatre and of the left, 'Luchino the Red': the political colour that, said a Lombardian newspaper, 'so appeals to blue blood'. His new coat of arms? The unmade bed of incest, a man (the virile Vittorio Gassman) wearing make-up and powder, and a dead tree in a vacant lot where a family of rednecks vegetates.

Not all the plays he staged in the period were scabrous, not all exuded what many called a latrine stench, but all were exhibits in the prosecution of a discredited society. Cocteau's *La Machine à écrire* (*The Typewriter*) put on trial a stifling small town's conspiracy of silence towards a series of anonymous letters; the play re-created the atmosphere in Henri-Georges Clouzot's 1943 film *The Raven* and, when shown in Rome, implied condemnation of fascist Italy's suffocating provincialism.

Tyrannical orderliness was icily arraigned in Jean Anouih's *Antigone*, a funerary ritual in which the king, Creon, is presented as a sort of wax image, a puppet frozen inside a dark, stiff dinner jacket; between speeches the actors sit on benches on either side of the stage under a huge crystal chandelier, converting the scene into both a funeral chapel and a courtroom. The same judgmental spirit pervades Jean-Paul Sartre's play *No Exit*, also produced in Rome in 1945.

To audiences still in shock from the war and Italy's defeat,

Visconti set out to proclaim the truth, the harsh truth about the family, that sacrosanct nuclear cell of Italian society; about homosexuality, and about the Spanish Civil War, seen this time from the other side, the Hemingway side, in *The Fifth Column*, which Visconti also staged. Post-war Italians could not accept all this as the kind of sophisticated games played by Cocteau the illusionist, the *enfant terrible*, the whimsical darling of muses and countesses. Yet it was in Cocteau's wake that Visconti the gadfly made his entry into the theatre.

Even the communist critics shied away from this firestorm of home truths. They feared that by choosing such 'artistically and morally execrable works' as *Intimate Relations*, their new fellow-traveller would reinject Italy with the germs of Fascism. Conservatives howled that 'Italy is being poisoned', while the Socialists and Communists joined in deploring as exaggerated the realistic bias, the starkness with which America is portrayed in *Tobacco Road*. 'That's not America,' they protested, just as Vittorio Mussolini had protested that *Obsession* was 'not Italy'. In neither case did they see the ruins, the millions of unemployed or the grinding poverty they lived with every day.

But for Visconti, as for the Sartre of *No Exit*, the post-war era of reconstruction and bright tomorrows was, first of all, one of expiation, a time for purging past errors; in this period the theatre became the celebrant of a sacrificial and sacrilegious ritual. It is worth noting that Visconti's anti-Fascism went beyond personal revenge; it was not content merely to point a facile finger at fascist leaders or to pillory scapegoats. 'Whose fault is it?' asks Garcin in *No Exit*; everyone's, answers Visconti, you can see it in how they act if not in what they say. No, we cannot rid ourselves of the past simply by executing Caruso and Koch and Mussolini. Nor could post-war theatre simply be a fairground shooting gallery where comfortably seated audiences could laugh at the deflated windbags who had once oppressed and enslaved them.

Despite his communist sympathies, Visconti always hated to turn the stage into a political platform. Unlike Giorgio Strehler, he never mounted a Brecht play. Seeking rather to alarm people than to reassure them, he entered the temple with the iconoclastic, profanatory fury of a theatrical Erostratus.*

He chose his repertory for its explosiveness, which explains why, along with *No Exit* and *Antigone*, he presented *Adam*, a play whose inadequacies he was the first to recognize. But, he said, 'homosexualilty does exist; we cannot close our eyes to it and pretend it isn't there. Besides, the cases that have brought it back into the public eye have their counterparts in Rome; the subject that was once banished from conversation now fills the newspapers.' Through the fascist period, he noted 'Italian theatre took refuge in evasion, in plays that did not deal with certain plots . . . Even the subject of *Intimate Relations* was definitely dynamite for . . . unaccustomed Italian audiences.'

Visconti took the demon provocation as his guide. He loved to 'horrify the bourgeois', he said, just as he had enjoyed frightening his brothers and sisters by suddenly surging from a closet disguised as a grotesque and terrifying witch. 'The aristocratic love of displeasing' abetted his determination to throw a harsh light on everything Fascism had hidden and to darken everything it had celebrated. The family? A nest of hysterical, incestuous, criminal vipers. Virile, 'strong', heroic men? The theatre made dwarfs of them; they became the father in *Intimate Relations*, Garcin in *No Exit*, a false hero, really a deserter. Or the pathetic homosexual in *Adam*. What was real? The wretched, shocking, lunatic banality of *Tobacco Road*, with its tumbledown shack and its empty oilcans stacked at the foot of a withered tree beside a dead-end road.

Every play he drew from his bag of scandalous tricks in that period was a passport to perdition. Evasion in the theatre was impossible; this was a hall of crime and expiation, where the leprous and the possessed tore ferociously at each other in love and hate. The magma of repressed violence erupted to the surface under the pressure exerted by the defeat of Fascism and was conducted along the breaches the war had opened in society's harmonious façade. The cardboard sets of the old order collapsed. On stage and in the auditorium, Visconti unleashed a storm of violence never before seen in any theatre.

*Erostratus was an Ephesian who, to immortalize his name, burned the temple of Artemis at Ephesus in 356 B.C. He was executed, and all mention of his name was forbidden on pain of death (translator's note).

The opening night of *Intimate Relations*, on 30 January 1945, with its Freudian forest and twofold incest, inaugurated Visconti's 'Oedipal' entry into Rome's Eliseo Theatre; with its Freudian snarl and compounded incest it marked a decisive turning point in Italian theatrical history. A pistol shot in the middle of a concert could not have awakened the public more rudely from its torpor and its polite reserve – 'probably,' Visconti said, 'because the direction was simplified and everything was presented in a true and realistic way, which people were trying to get a little away from . . .'.

The actor Giorgio de Lullo recalls: 'It was as if we had suddenly swept away the dust, the old furniture, the trumpery, the false elegance and goody-goody sentimentality. All of a sudden, that stage, in a violent light, was plunged into darkness, and Andreina [Pagnani], without a hint of make-up, her hair obviously dyed – I was used to seeing her beautiful, a bit mannered . . . All of a sudden we were hurled into this violent, painful world where after five minutes we forgot we were in a theatre, or we [thought we] were in the theatre to be strangled by what we saw.

'And what did we see? A bed, the lighted toilet, a rumpled blanket, a bedside table and a lamp covered with a handkerchief to mute the light, and it looked like a drawing-room covered with mattress ticking, it was trying so hard to be true and essential. No sets, no beautiful staging, and actors I knew but whom I found unrecognizable because they had been changed from puppets – actors, anyway – into tremendously moving characters . . . I remember some bits of business: Andreina running her hands through her tousled, half-dyed hair; Pierfederici (in the role of Michel), who beat his legs against the bed (when had we ever seen such things in a theatre?) to protest against the speech his mother was making about the girl he loved – a whole pattern of truth I had never seen before and which, I think, had never been achieved in the past because verism was something entirely different.'

Every evening, Miss Pagnani's appearance caused a shock. Visconti had worked with her before, in the troupe her father had assembled in 1926. In this version of *Intimate Relations* the director completely transformed her. He left her nothing of the refined, sophisticated beauty that had so delighted Duke Giuseppe. To start with, he removed the 'pounds of junk she always had on her face'.

Without make-up, her hair dishevelled, with dark rings under her eyes because, as Visconti later remarked, she was exhausted by 'fourteen days of rehearsals during which the actors also performed in Irwin Shaw's play *The Gentle People*; I only rehearsed in the evening, and then only a few hours, with an already tired Pagnani'.

Rina Morelli, who was to become Visconti's first-string actress, looked down on him in the beginning. He had asked her 'to forget her career, an already brilliant, established career, and return to her sources, to bring up out of her gut the real feelings and passions she probably had inside her. And in fact she expressed them with a violence, a power that enormously impressed both critics and audiences.' Between these two women, Morelli and Pagnani, young, angel-faced Antonio Pierfederici padded about the stage in his bare feet and even – what a stir in the audience! – jumped on his mother's now mythical bed.

Visconti had dyed Pierfederici's raven hair blond to make him look more like Jean Marais, who had created the part in Paris and whose type of beauty the director constantly sought in all actors he liked. Changing his players' physical appearance was a device of his possessiveness. For when he directed, everything had to belong to him. He personally designed the set mock-ups and, typically, filled the stage with furniture brought from his home, along with his famous opossum bedcover; people who came after the show to finger it and poke into the closets on stage were bemused to find them full of clothing.

Visconti insisted on being the captain of his ship, independent of the conventions, of the 'iron laws' then ruling the theatre, and he made this clear from the first rehearsals by shaking up rigid cast hierarchies and acting habits. Miss Morelli, then thirty-seven years old, was given an ingenue's part. Lola Braccini had been typecast as a mother, but Visconti took the role – a leading one in this play – away from her and gave it to Miss Pagnani, who usually appeared as the female lead. Braccini had to make do with the secondary role of Leo. 'I ruffled a lot of feathers in the company that way,' Visconti said, 'but I didn't know this until long afterwards. All I knew at the time is that everyone gave me dirty looks. Gino Cervi, the father in the play, kept telling people "Patience, patience, kiddies, in any case the play falls on its face in the second act and that'll be the end of it."

On the contrary, it was a smash hit. Everyone still remembers it. At the end of the show, the audience scrambled up both flights of proscenium stairs and invaded the stage to kiss the actors, who were certainly more astonished than anyone else.'

The director had realized Cocteau's instructions: 'Don't give the actors or the audience a chance to catch their breath.' The spell, described by one critic as 'fetid and powerful', held.for every performance. Night after night, audiences surrendered to the disturbing spell of intense realism – piles of dirty laundry, shoes and socks on the table, dressing-gowns stained with grease and make-up – combined with a cloying atmosphere of dreams and madness, heightened by the oblique light coming from houses across the way, by shaded lamps in the room, and by periodic drops in the steam-driven generator's power output. Uberta thought she smelled ether. Chiari, who had designed his sets with two key directorial words in mind, 'sickness and misery', points to the telling clutter of medicines covering Yvonne's night table.

Visconti had worked out his direction in the lightning-fast time of twenty days – he insisted it was no more than sixteen – and its success surprised even him. On opening night he took fourteen curtain calls after the first act, sixteen after the second and twenty at the end. 'That was the most glorious evening of my life as an actress,' said Pagnani, who recalls being literally carried in triumph across the Eliseo Theatre on the crowd's shoulders.

Every time Visconti directed a play, a psychodrama was played out in the audience: enraged spectators stamped out of the theatre, frenzied applause called the cast out for endless bows while some people whistled and jeered. Fist fights broke out.

He sought this supercharged atmosphere, delighted in engendering it with every play. In the Sixties he would look back wistfully at the post-war public he had wrenched from its apathy, rekindling its passions with his agressive provocation. 'Today there is a kind of indolence, of laziness towards the theatre, almost a lack of interest in it,' he said. 'Perhaps because there is nothing explosive in it, none of the things that give it life. The theatre should be a continuing conversation between the stage and the audience . . [In those days] audiences reacted. There were opening nights when I remember telling the actors in the wings: "Stay calm, don't talk, don't move, let them howl and jump up and down; when that's over with we can get on with the play." I saw people fight and scream. All that at premières like *No Exit*, very new things for the period, that shook audiences.'

To shake up that public and awaken it from twenty-two years of treacly daydreams, Visconti opted from the start for the harshest kind of realism, Antoine-style naturalism.* And when he obliged his actors to dye their hair carrot red, to grow beards, to eat pounds of turnips on stage (as Vittorio Gassman had to do) and walk barefoot on real pebbles (in *Tobacco Road*), his rivals guffawed. Why turn fascination with reality into a vice by recruiting an old woman out of a home for the aged to portray the grandmother in the adaptation of Caldwell's play? This was sick, Visconti's critics charged, it violated the elementary laws of the theatre, of good taste and morality.

Which was exactly what he wanted: to release passion, to turn a dead theatre into a place of tumult, furore, excitement. In December 1945, shortly after the turbulent opening of *Tobacco Road*, he told the press: 'The support of a snobbish public that tends to applaud superficial and ambiguous beliefs pleases me less than the enthusiasm of young Milanese . . . They came looking for me on the stage, besieging me with questions, and I talked to them at length. I must say that it is among the young that I find the public most inclined to follow me – a quick understanding that only our community of problems and interests can explain. I am really working for them, by clarifying for myself concerns they share with me.'

A theatre of definitions, then, marked by iconoclastic fury, convulsive violence, a frenziedly agitated acting style. Visconti appeared in this as a 'terrible' magician whose craving for truth rolled like a groundswell, shocking audiences awake. Here was life unmasked: the light and the language were raw, sex suddenly appeared as incest and homosexuality and sadism. From it the theatre drew new strength, once more becoming an unclouded, exciting mirror of reality.

Visconti, closer to Artaud than to Cocteau, restored the cathartic function that theatre had in antiquity, arousing horror and pity, but

---

*André Antoine (1858–1943) was an actor, manager and critic who founded the influential Théâtre-Libre in Paris, specializing in naturalistic plays (translator's note).

also imposing critical detachment, mobilizing untapped resources, seeking to 'drain abscesses collectively'. By 'speaking the truth, the whole truth', the past was to be exorcized and assigned its proper dimension.

XIII

THE COMMUNIST FAMILY

Is he a Danton?
STENDHAL, *The Red and the Black*

'To Luchino, with friendship, from a very grateful Figaro, De Sica, 1946.' In the photograph Vittorio De Sica dedicated to his friend Count Visconti, he is dressed as he was in the palace grounds for *The Marriage of Figaro*, that 'mad spree' of lights and rainbow colours, of tinkling laughter and delicate eighteenth-century music, ballet and folk-dancing that the director, declaring a moratorium on rumpled beds and dishevelled women, had just mounted at Rome's Quirino Theatre. Figaro looks out at us wrapped in his sweeping black cloak, wearing patent leather shoes and silken hose. De Sica, too, was a southerner, from ramshackle, exuberant Naples, its heart brimming with tenderness even as its mouth spews out jeers and sarcasm.

Count Visconti-Almaviva had set so demoniac a pace for his fiesta, had commanded his Figaro to run, jump and prance so vigorously that the forty-five-year-old De Sica wound up winded. So many whims, so many orders, so much splendour and spectacle and expense. For the sets, to start with: a sort of pastry palace on two levels connected by a double sweep of stairs. On the upper terrace, a chamber orchestra to accompany the constant flow of dancing and singing and entries and exits. A crowd of actors transformed into grotesque, Goyesque puppets or charming Sèvres bisques à la Watteau. A monologue by Figaro altered, when De Sica went down into the auditorium, into a dialogue with the audience. And, as a final splash, a masked ball at which eight dancers dressed in black velvet embroidered in gold and silver removed their masks to reveal death's heads, while the orchestra played *La Carmagnole*, a folk-dance of the French Revolution.

'Visconti-Egalité,' sneered one outraged journalist, 'brandishes these death's heads in the midst of a joyous finale, while the conductor, in a powdered wig, leads his unionized orchestra through *La Carmagnole*.'

'It was an enormous hit with the public in Rome and Milan,' Visconti later recalled. 'Especially in Milan . . . De Sica was very good. I very much enjoyed working with him and he very much enjoyed working with me.' The actor was nevertheless disconcerted by all the agitation, this frenzied whirlwind. At one point he took Gerardo Guerrieri aside, making sure they were out of the count's earshot, and demanded, 'Sire, the lines! Sire, the lines!' as if to say, 'What's happened to the play?'

For the lord of Via Salaria, however, what mattered was the baroque intoxication of movement, the spectacle, a feast for all the senses. *Figaro* foretold many other directorial festivals in which Visconti resolutely turned his back on the currently fashionable bare stage and stripped-down sets like those that the actor-author Jacques Copeau was using at Paris's Théâtre National Populaire. A few months later, in his version of *Crime and Punishment*, three acrobats in sequined tights interrupted Marmeladov's serious conversation with Raskolnikov.

By 1948, his stagings reached a point of lavishness and excess that made his production of Beaumarchais' *Figaro* seem no more than a bubbly little vaudeville revue. Music, dancing, rich costumes and sets, the realm of dreams and delights – that was theatre to Visconti. What else did people need after the war, he retorted to his irate critics, 'but gay things that amuse them'? He reminded them that even before beginning to rebuild on the smoking ruins of Warsaw, the Poles first built a new theatre. 'I would be more disciplined today,' he later commented, 'but I don't regret *The Marriage*.'

Thirty years later, however, an obituary published by the communist newspaper *L'Unità* said Visconti had reached his peak in the theatre with his 'rereading of Beaumarchais' great revolutionary work'. In communist eyes it had been 'a brilliant declaration of faith', partly for his choice of a play banned by the Fascists, and also because of the dogmatic meaning that the 'Red Count' supposedly gave to his 'garish colours and incredible costumes'; by exaggerating what was monstrous and grotesque about eighteenth-century society, the newspaper said, he revealed its decadence and brought out the play's 'clear forecast of the collapse of the aristocracy'.

'A communist count?' the actor Paolo Stoppa had asked in surprise on learning that the former stable-owner he had met in Milan before the war had friends not only in high society and the theatre, but also among Communist Party members who had come out of hiding to become prominent political leaders.

Visconti certainly remained an aristocrat, a count; he never renounced his homes, his squadron of liveried servants, his packs of dogs or the money he threw around by the fistful. All right, then he was the 'Red Count'. Wasn't he merely obeying the law of his heraldic snake by changing his skin? Be that as it may, the public declaration he made on 12 May 1946, two weeks before the Constitutional referendum that swept away the Savoy dynasty, and only days before elections to a Constituent Assembly, was nevertheless a shocker. Running in *L'Unità* under the title, 'Why I Will Vote Communist', it was an unequivocal act of faith, a declaration of allegiance to the party then headed by Palmiro Togliatti. With a backhanded sweep, Visconti brushed away all the political, religious and personal considerations that might have prevented him from taking the jump:

Fear of Communism still stalks the land – fear of leaping into the dark, of a totalitarian state, of curbs on freedom, of stifling initiative and other such rubbish. Because we are heading towards a form of government that, for a whole body of historical, political and economic reasons, can only be socialist, and since the institution of the monarchy has proved to be merely the last 'vehicle' of the germs of Fascism, here is what I choose: a republic, and a parliamentary republic, such as the Communist Party has proposed in clear terms in its programme.

If any party can defend freedom against a rebirth of Fascism it is the Communist Party, which has made itself the bulwark of this defence not only today, but since 1921, by leading all Italians in the anti-fascist struggle.

Visconti was a Roman Catholic. Not only, he maintained, did the party respect 'a thoroughly sensible freedom of religion', but it aimed 'to realize a city of men that in no way denies the city of God'. He therefore found in the programme 'a vision of life, and of aspirations to justice, to honesty, to equity' that matched his own while satisfying his love of practical, organized, constructive action. 'In this struggle,' he concluded, 'I am co-operating, personally and in my work, and I plan to continue doing so in the future.'

Allegiance to Communism by Visconti the artist at the war's end is hardly surprising. His mentor, Jean Renoir, despite his anarchism and his basically aristocratic leanings, also campaigned for the Communist Party. To cultivated Italians from Moravia and Malaparte to the young novelist – and count – Guido Piovene and the elderly poet Umberto Saba, the party, with its then open cultural policy, held out a promise of freedom and progress. It was a chance not to be missed.

'Conversions' and declarations of sympathy were epidemic in the film industry. People of every political background, including some, like Blasetti, Rossellini and De Sica, who had not even been anti-Fascists, rallied to the left. In 1947, film-makers under attack by the Christian Democrats were fiercely defended by the Communist Party. When the Vatican newspaper *L'Osservatore Romano* assailed De Sica's *The Bicycle Thief*, Ingrao flew to the director's defence and accused the Church of trying to rekindle the fires of the Inquisition. Togliatti himself defended *Fabiola*, made by the ex-Fascist Blasetti, in an article entitled, '*Fabiola*, where all roads lead to Communism'. And the party would soon take over the orchestration and support of protests against the restoration of the preventive censorship the Fascists had instituted.

One of the left's pet aversions was the young Under-Secretary of Entertainment and Information, Giulio Andreotti, already considered the political heir to Premier Alcide De Gasperi. Andreotti's policies were constant irritants to the left. In 1952, the Sicilian author Vitaliano Brancati, in his *Return to Censorship*, had plenty of reasons to complain of 'the hatred of culture that in Italy has an office all its own; what used to be called, with unwitting irony, the

Ministry of Popular Culture is now the Under-Secretariat of Entertainment and Information. The head of this under-secretariat is a person who I am told is very young . . . But a young man of this stamp should not be placed in contact with culture, especially if the contact with culture consists in functioning as intermediary, not to say spy, between the author of a play or script and the police in charge of banning it . . . Books in Italy are still free, but the cinema and the theatre are already controlled.'

Visconti always insisted that he was 'instinctively opposed to anything that theatens freedom'. He never missed a chance, for example, to sign open letters protesting against the blacklists drawn up by the 'clerocracy'. But he was also a man of order, and a member of the Church. Nothing would weaken his fidelity in principle to the party, not even the uproar caused after the war by the contagious mutiny of Elio Vittorini, who said that leftist intellectuals should be fully independent of party shibboleths and who refused 'to enrol poetry in the service of theology', meaning communist orthodoxy. Vittorini spurned 'blowing the trumpet of revolution for an already questionable truth that leads to artistic suicide, but also to the condemnations inflicted in Italy on such writers as Kafka and Hemingway and, in the Soviet Union, on Dostoyevsky.'

Later on, the deeper convulsions that racked the communist movement – the death of Stalin, the revelations in the Khrushchev report, the invasions of Hungary and Czechoslovakia – would shake but not break Visconti's faith in the communist credo. Although he never carried a party card, Visconti, a traitor to his class, would remain a faithful fellow-traveller. He always felt especially irritated by people who, with a knowing smile, cast doubt on the sincerity of his commitment.

He would even allow party discipline to wreck theatrical plans that his friend Antonello Trombadori opposed as inopportune. When he founded his troupe in the autumn of 1946, he announced that in addition to staging *Crime and Punishment* and Tennessee Williams' *The Glass Menagerie*, he had his heart set on presenting a group of plays 'by writers of proven value' that he said should 'contribute to renewing the national repertory'.

But he produced neither Piovene's *The False Redeemers*, 'written expressly for my company', nor two plays by Sartre, *The Flies (Les Mouches)* and *The Unburied Dead (Morts sans sépulture)*, for which he had already chosen the cast, sets and music. Piovene, while a communist sympathizer, had been consigned by the party, along with Moravia, to the ranks of incorrigibly bourgeois intellectuals. *The False Redeemers* was called 'ambiguous . . . morbid . . . corrupt . . . unreal'. Sartre, the 'hyena typist', was a favourite target of Stalinists in France, Italy and the Soviet Union. He was one reason for the split between Togliatti and Vittorini, who in 1945 had founded the daring *Il Politecnico*,★ a publication whose spirit anticipated Sartre's *Les Temps modernes*.

Everything about Vittorini's experiment, even its up-to-the-minute page make-up, clashed with the Communist Party Secretary's tastes and cultural conservatism. Michele Rago, a disciple of the Marxist theoretician Antonio Gramsci, said the party boss had 'an old, obsolete vision of the middle class and the intellectuals who represented it. Togliatti thought like an old-fashioned humanistic intellectual with a classical education. Even his fondness for Latin and classical quotations proves this.'

Togliatti saw *Il Politecnico*, a rival to the strictly orthodox *Rinascità*, as dangerous to the policy of national unity he was promoting; it seethed with too much critical ferment, gave off a suspect smell of dissidence. Vittorini had, after all, opened his magazine's pages to the Gide who wrote *Return from the USSR*, and to key works of existentialism, surrealism and Italian hermetism, indeed, to all the currents of modern thought, including sociology and psychoanalysis. 'And when you start from Freud,' commented the highly Cartesian Togliatti, 'it can take you very far, into a madhouse, but certainly not to Marx or to our difficult socialist struggle.' Moreover, *Il Politecnico* analysed, annotated and criticized classical Marxist writings – including those of Lenin and Gramsci. And it frequently raised embarrassing topical issues, such as the Mafia and divorce. By contrast with the communist pope, Togliatti,

★*Il Politecnico*: Elio Vittorini's cultural revue was published in Milan in 1945–7. It was marked by visceral anti-Fascism, a keen receptiveness to all Europe and the rest of the world, and a vast range of interests (including philosophy, science, literature and social and political problems). It aspired to a new type of culture, not 'consolatory' but actively influencing the real world.

and his cardinals, the intransigent, Dominican-minded Alicata and the Jesuitical Sereni, Vittorini and his cultural standards appeared heretical.

It is through the filter of this quarrel, which ended with the suppession of *Il Politecnico* and a communist anathema against Vittorini in 1951, that we must see Visconti's decision to drop plans for a film version of Vittorini's novel *Men and Non-Men*, along with the Sartre plays.

In 1970, Trombadori, a communist leader and grey eminence behind the director, declared: 'It was recently written that I dissuaded Visconti from mounting *Dirty Hands* (*Les Mains sales*). It seems to me that such an incident did occur, but it was in 1946–7 and concerned another work by Sartre, *The Unburied Dead*, mainly because I could not tolerate the identification between the Nazi torturers and the tortured guerrillas. There was some oversimplification in my intolerance, I admit, but our armed struggle against the Nazis had been waged with just this kind of oversimplification. If I'd had to dissuade Visconti from directing *Dirty Hands*, I would not have done it with today's arguments – its encouragement of terrorists of the Red Brigade type – but with the Stalinist argument that it was an "anti-Soviet calumny".'

One thing was sure: the choice of a work would never be a mere whim on Visconti's part. Each would reply not only to the need for personal expression, but also to the need to clarify current problems, while allowing for a careful evaluation of the moral and political influence its film or stage production might have. He had no intention of blundering off into propaganda art; he saw Communism as the true way, and everything he did, even after he had supposedly become decadent, was consistent with his May 1946 profession of faith:

I believe that every form of art must be absolutely sincere, and that its highest goal is to clarify the position and feelings of men living among other men, to strengthen their unity through familiarity with their passions. In Communism I see a great opportunity for humanity and freedom in art, and I am fighting for both of these. I absolutely do not believe that strict observance of doctrine must be flat and rigid. On the contrary, I think the yeast of Communism is very much alive, and that it drives the artist towards reality, drives him to grasp life at its truest, and to know and exalt man's suffering.

His fidelity to this creed, reaffirmed throughout his life, has sometimes been ascribed to the attraction the party's power exerted on him. 'But he didn't need the party,' protests the screenwriter Suso Cecchi d'Amico. 'He had wealth and power of his own. No, he was morally committed to the Resistance, and he could go to any extremes to honour his commitments.'

His memory of the Resistance was also to dictate his choices in the elections on 28 April 1963: 'I will vote for the Communist list, as indeed I have always voted. But given the fierce confrontation this election campaign has become, and considering that we will soon mark the twentieth anniversary of the victory over Fascism and that it is worth looking back to survey the ground we have covered, I will say that I am voting Communist because I am an anti-Fascist.'

In the communist family, Visconti felt closest to young Trombadori. An art critic, Antonello would often comment that because of his Piedmontese mother's marriage to his Sicilian painter father, 'I am the son of Italian unity.' The nephew of a founder of the Italian Communist Party, he joined the clandestine struggle in 1939. Sent to a penal colony in 1941, he returned to Rome and was assigned in July 1943 to organize the activities of the Armed Partisan Groups. Arrested again in 1944 and sentenced to forced labour in Anzio, he escaped before the Allies landed and resumed his underground work. When Italy was liberated, Visconti and Trombadori became lifelong friends.

More chivalrous and less bureaucratic than Alicata, younger and less intolerant, he was open to the boldest experiments in modern art, which he consistently defended against the dreary platitudes of socialist realism. Less servile to the party's shibboleths, he even showed his sympathy for Vittorini. When he took over the direction of the magazine *Contemporaneo* in 1954, he managed without breaking with Togliatti to open its columns to cultural and political debates that grew particularly heated in 1956.

It was usually Trombadori who transmitted Togliatti's opinions to Visconti. He was the first to know of the director's plans, and often advised him on points of history. 'Not doing anything the party didn't like was very important to Visconti,' he says. 'This was a moral, almost a religious choice, very understandable in an aristocrat ... It was a sort of self-punishment, a limitation he imposed on himself. He had reached the point at which discipline is blind, but it always proceeds from a rational choice. This wasn't fanaticism. On the contrary, Luchino was a rational man.'

A lay religion, that's what Communism was for Visconti. It did not matter that he had no party card, any more than it mattered that this Catholic was no model of piety. His 'moral, almost religious' commitment constituted a solid support, a sort of spine that held his life together and gave it order and coherence. Visconti saw no contradiction between his communist faith and his belief in God, which he defined in a long interview with the journalist Costanzo Constantini in 1973 as 'a mysterious force, bigger than the individual, something stronger than you that you can't even judge, you don't know what it is, but you feel it's something you can trust. It's a bigger feeling than yourself, a feeling of love around you, of trust, of courage, of something sure in a word; whether we call it God or something else is not important.'

The basic principles of religion and Communism were more important to him than the mistakes made by the Church and the party: 'I have been a Communist since the Resistance. My ideas in this respect have never changed. Even today, I'm on the side of the Communist Party, although, to be truthful, not always. Sometimes I can dispute party positions. But in general I think it's a good thing to be a Communist, that you must be one. In some cases you must be one even if you are not completely convinced. You must be one on principle, even if you are critical in your own mind.' In an earlier interview he had specified: 'I condemned the invasions of Hungary and Czechoslovakia. I did not agree with what happened in Hungary. I argued about and suffered over the events in Prague. But I know mistakes can be corrected. What counts are the principles.'

If we leave these 'principles' aside, there is still the paradox of an aristocrat and, more important, a homosexual seeking his salvation in circles that, on principle, rejected him. For Communism is as sexually puritanical as the Church. No compromise was allowed with, say, Moravia's 'erotomania' or Pier Paolo Pasolini's 'lechery'.

But Visconti allowed himself to outrage people by staging plays about sexual deviation – *No Exit, A Streetcar Named Desire*, Achard's *Adam* – not to defend deviation but to exhibit its degrading tragedy. We could say of Visconti what the French author Robert Merle wrote of Oscar Wilde: 'This taboo was nowhere more powerful than in himself.' To Visconti, as to Ludwig of Bavaria, as to Proust, homosexuality was and would always carry a curse. In many of his opinions he was more the middle-class moralist than the libertine aristocrat, a puritan whose values included those of the family and of a traditional patriarchal society.

The party was consistently intolerant not only of Vittorini, but also of comrade De Santis, criticized for permissiveness and morbid eroticism in his 1949 film *Bitter Rice*. And of Vasco Pratolini, a great friend of Visconti's, who was excoriated for the mystical *crepuscolarismo* in his 1955 *Metello*. Yet the communist attitude towards Visconti, notwithstanding a few superficial reprimands, remained amazingly docile. In 1948, Togliatti intervened personally to prevent publication of a savage attack on Visconti's staging of *As You Like It* in sets by the 'dollar-hungry' Salvador Dali: 'You can't publish that,' he wrote to the overzealous journalist, 'you can't crush Visconti under that kind of criticism. You can't chop down a forest to cook an egg. I am especially opposed to the fact that, because of disagreement – questionable, in this case – with the performance of a Shakespeare play, we accuse an intellectual friend, one with progressive tendencies, of being the leader of the reactionaries, no less. Writing such things makes laughing-stocks of us and of Marxism. I advise A. to write on another, more directly political, subject and to turn his invective against real enemies and serious mistakes.'

It was Togliatti again, in reply to criticism from the left, especially from Alicata, of the 'decadentism' of *The Leopard*, who wrote to Trombadori on 2 April 1963: 'I saw *The Leopard* in Turin. A great work of art. If you happen to see Visconti, please convey to him my admiration and my unreserved approval. One has the impression that with each of his new creations he outdoes himself . . . And also tell Visconti not to make the cuts he's been asked to make. Above all he must cut nothing from the ball, the summit of this work of art, because in it he achieves the obsessiveness (I don't know if this is the right word) characteristic of great artistic creations.'

'Togliatti always considered Visconti's collusion with the party as something to be proud of,' Trombadori says. 'As a man of the avant-garde, he was anxious to show his opinion publicly, and there may have been a point of personal vanity in this. It is true that the diffuse thinking in the party about homosexuality was what it was (I'm in a good position to know, because in 1955–7 I defended Pasolini in *Contemporaneo*) and I don't think Togliatti's opinion on it was very different. But this gave even more value to his almost ostentatious shows of respect and partiality towards Visconti.

'Togliatti attended his theatrical premières and would go backstage with his companion, Nilde Jotti, to Visconti's dressing-room, not at the end, but during the first or second intermission to talk comfortably with him . . . Togliatti's predilection for Visconti was also specifically cultural, or rather, was linked to the cultural struggle within the Communist Party.'

The party secretary was a conservative, not an avant-gardist, and he rightly saw in Visconti's work a return to national traditions, to the humanistic and civic culture of which he, too, was a product. He could close his eyes to the director's homosexuality, since Visconti was a relative, if a distant one, of the communist family; as the saying went among the people around Togliatti, 'A mother doesn't beat her neighbour's children.'

The two men never developed close ties, never really became friends. But adoptive, omnipresent father Togliatti nevertheless influenced the artist's choices and moral dilemmas. The screenwriter Enrico Medioli said that 'Visconti only paid attention to the opinions and advice of two or three people, among them Antonello Trombadori and Togliatti.' When the party chief died in August 1964, Visconti insisted on keeping vigil at the bier of the man he thought of as 'another Cavour', a defender of national unity and, for him, a guide and model. Ten years later, shortly before Visconti himself died, he said:

Real greatness, it seems to me, is that of a man who identifies with his people. Palmiro Togliatti was such a man. At the end of his life he was young, more alive than most young people are today. Togliatti radiated candour, goodwill, kindness, ingenuity. He was a true intellectual, a rarity in politics. Many politicians today have nothing to say, not a word to bequeath to new generations full of uncertainty . . .

Togliatti was a great friend . . . He saw all the plays I directed. Afterwards he wrote to give me his impressions. Nor did he miss the openings of my films. And for these, too, he wrote with his opinions and impressions, in his small, precise handwriting . . . The last time I saw Togliatti was at a private showing of *The Leopard*, which I had just completed. He told me that our pessimism bore the stamp of our own desires, and that instead of regretting the feudal order he aimed at proposing a new order. Then he wrote to me: 'The ball in the film is an apotheosis and a disaster. People say it's long. That's not true. Don't cut a single centimetre of film.'

Togliatti was no Machiavelli. He was a Communist with a human face, an enlightened despot, like the philosopher kings of whom eighteenth-century writers dreamed. He was a political intellectual who managed to balance tolerance with a vigorous defence of humanistic values, discipline with freedom, morality with politics. An 'impossible' aspiration, would say the teacher in *Conversation Piece*, common to 'intellectuals of our generation' united in a search 'for a balance between morality and politics'.

Visconti's 'conversion' to Communism owed less to his reading of theoretical works – it was not until 1947, at Togliatti's insistence, that a start was made on publishing Gramsci's books – than to his connection with Trombadori and Togliatti, his spiritual advisers. It was rooted, too, in his image of an artist, whose mission is to 'grasp life at its truest', to stay in touch with reality and 'know and exalt men's suffering'.

'I could have been another Oscar Wilde,' he said – an aesthete like his father. He had escaped dilettantism and the pure cult of beauty thanks less to Marx and Gramsci than to circumstances, to chance encounters. To his moral vigilance, too, what Trombadori called his 'need for self-punishment'. What but soul-searching made him interrupt a triumphant theatrical season in the summer of 1947 and leave Rome?

He spent the end of the summer in a splendid villa in Ischia, the

Colombaia, which he would buy some years later. Every day he would 'isolate' himself in his peculiar style: setting himself up in an arbour to work while four or five friends conversed some distance away. The writer Giuseppe Patroni Griffi was a frequent Visconti guest at Ischia. He recalls that no matter how absorbed the director was in his work, if a friend, weary of the typewriter's relentless clatter, got up and moved around the garden, Visconti's booming voice would freeze him in his tracks and force him to wait patiently for a programmed walk along the beach or a foray into the port.

'And no one would dare ask him what in the world he was doing so secretly in those first days of autumn . . . What took shape were his modern Valastros and Malavoglias, the first of Visconti's great family sagas. When the summer house was closed, we all left the island. He no sooner returned to Rome than he left again, this time almost alone, with his sheaves of notes, to explore Sicily.'

Who went with him? Perhaps Francesco Rosi, a twenty-four-year-old Neapolitan whom he had met through Patroni Griffi, and who wanted to make movies; Rosi would be his assistant for *The Earth Trembles*. Perhaps Franco Zeffirelli, a Florentine actor with whom he had fallen in love a year before when he saw him play in *Intimate Relations*. Visconti had directed him in *Crime and Punishment*, but the contact soon aroused broader ambitions in the young blond with the charming smile.

Visconti left Rome with no regrets. This Grand Meaulnes felt a restless need to move, to embark on a new adventure into the perilous unknown, like the Rimbaud of *The Drunken Boat*. 'If I stayed here,' he wrote to Griffi, 'it would most probably be to chew things over uselessly and hurtfully, a "remembrance of things past". I say this in its broad sense, in terms of art, too. I cannot accept a castrated art. Adventure is a prelude to other griefs, other things, especially to other struggles. "And the stains of blue wine and of vomit – I wash off . . ."* Let them come, the new struggles and new griefs and new opportunities and then, again, the bitterness, the illusions. I expect that. But on condition that it all be new, disinterested and pure. Would you believe it? What a terrible need for

*Visconti is quoting here from Rimbaud's *Le Bateau ivre (The Drunken Boat)*.

purity, limpidity, intelligence, of the sort, however, that seems to me most precious, I mean that of the heart.'

Three out of four of the shows mounted the previous year had indeed been 'remembrances of things past'. Around the fragile characters in *The Glass Menagerie*, for example, float the shadows of things dreamed or vanished, like the soldier, dead or imprisoned somewhere, both absent and present in the Wingfields' small apartment when his huge photograph is projected on the wall. The picture was one of Rosi that Visconti, spotting him at once as 'his' character, had taken the day they met. In fact, Visconti himself lived amid countless splendidly framed photographs, his icons of memory: pictures of his family, his friends, all the actresses and artists who had moved him and whose presence he preserved as talismans against death, against absence.

There had also been the lunar sadness of Anouilh's *Eurydice*, attuned to the regular chiming of a funereal clock and the drawn-out whistling of trains in the night. And there had been the nostalgic portrait of a late-nineteenth-century American family, Clarence Day's *Life with Father*.

In the production of *Crime and Punishment* with which Visconti had opened his company's first season in November 1946, the characters' anxiety and alienation had been heightened by the expressionist sets used for the scene of the murder – the dark mass of the house with its gables, its peeling walls, its stairs and balconies hanging over empty space – against a vast, starry sky; crosses in a cemetery served as backdrops to the middle-class parlour where Paolo Stoppa as Raskolnikov borrowed from Fritz Lang's movie *M*, and Rina Morelli, candlelit in a flowing gown of pale taffeta, resembled the Scarlet Empress.

In his journey backward in time, Visconti even brought back to the stage actors he had loved as a child, but who had since disappeared from the public eye. 'At that time,' he later said, 'it thrilled me to unearth these actors.' Memo Benassi, who had played opposite Duse in *The Lady from the Sea* in 1921 and had later worked under Copeau and Max Reinhardt, was cast as Porfiri in *Crime and Punishment*.

And as soon as he read *The Glass Menagerie*, which Williams had sent him from the United States, Visconti pictured the great Russian actress Tatiana Pavlova in the part of the mother lost in her dreams and her nostalgia. Trained in the Stanislavsky method, she had brought the repertory of the Moscow Art Theatre, especially Chekhov's plays, to Italy in the Twenties. 'Pavlova is an actress I greatly admired in my youth,' Visconti said . . . 'I was at the theatre every evening. Whatever Pavlova did, I was there. I know her whole repertory, from Kossorotov's *Dream of Love* – that was her first thing – to *Adriana Lecouvreur*, and everything she did, *The Cherry Orchard*, and so on.'

She had married a fascist official before the war, and from then on no one had offered her work. She was considered washed up. Visconti went to see her in Milan and asked her to play Clytemnestra in *The Flies* and Amanda Wingfield in *Menagerie*. Later, when he told her he was dropping the Sartre play, she railed at him furiously and accused him of tricking her. 'She didn't realize,' Visconti said, 'that, on the contrary, I was the one who had put her back on stage and from then on she had been able to live a normal life again. I did it because I thought she wasn't to blame simply for being an official's wife . . .'

She did not, however, play in *Eurydice*, for which Visconti continued his scavenging by recruiting an old comic actor, Antonio Gandusio, then sixty-four, to play the role of Orpheus's father. He hadn't performed in years either. Visconti said he 'did a wonderful thing. I was delighted to watch him . . . In all those years I'd never had an actor as good as Gandusio in this play: so disciplined, so perfect, so amiable, so gentle, like a young man, enchanting. I remember that before the dress rehearsal in Florence, it was eight o'clock in the morning and we were all dead tired from last-minute preparation. At eight o'clock I told Gandusio, "Please, go to bed, get out of here." "Why? As long as you're here, as long as everybody is here, I'm staying." I was afraid he'd die on the spot, but he wouldn't leave. He was always the first one ready, every evening, five minutes before curtain time . . . I went to greet them all and I found him already on stage, with his cigar, at his little café table – it opens at the station café, right? – and he was already there. Perfect, the old school.'

Perfect, no doubt, but Visconti needed to grapple with reality again, to cast off his moorings and face 'new struggles', to visit the

Orphean inferno on Ulysses' isles. In other words, to leave the confines of the theatre for Sicily's limitless horizons.

In doing his early location spotting, he had in mind – as witness the notes he had feverishly made in Ischia – a vast epic in which the 'first disorderly and dispersed nucleus of a family of fishermen' developed into two parallel and complementary episodes in the struggles of Sicilian farmers and miners against the big landowners and tax-gatherers, who exploited their poverty. There are various examples of injustice, then the farmers' rebellion after a massacre of farmers during a country festival. They rush to occupy the land, and 'the earth trembles' under their horses' hooves. At that juncture, Visconti envisaged a resolutely optimistic and didactic finale. Surrounded by the police, threatened by the bosses, would the 'raging hawks hold out? Then comes the miracle: cities and countryside rally to the side of the peasants who have declared war on the age-old taboo. The battle is won, thanks to the solidarity of all other workers on the island. The government is forced to intervene to end the conflict.'

In writing these 'Notes for a documentary on Sicily', Visconti had recent events in mind, and especially the bloody incident at Portella della Ginestra on 1 May 1947. For years, a bandit named Salvatore Giuliano had been considered a local hero, a sort of Sicilian Robin Hood, holding the big landowners in the province of Palermo to ransom and distributing part of his loot to the peasants of Montelepre. But on that 1 May he had machine-gunned those very peasants, men, women and children, at a country picnic. The slaughter had been arranged by the Mafia and the landowners, who then murdered Giuliano, with the complicity of the authorities, as Rosi later showed in his film *Salvatore Giuliano*.

At the time, the problem of southern Italy was one of the Communists' stock causes; for Alicata, Trombadori and Guttuso the area's misery vibrated in their blood, in their roots. But what was Visconti, the Milanese accustomed to the muted landscapes of the Lombardy plain, doing in the village of Aci Trezza with its small white houses forming a wall between the violent sea and the harsh land, the volcanic *sciara* lorded over by Etna's snowy cone?

'On the face of it,' Antonioni commented, 'Aci Trezza has no

234

connection with Visconti's world. Its people are of a different race and blood.' Hadn't the race of northern factory owners made Sicily their colony beginning in 1860? What had Visconti the conqueror in common with Verga's 'defeated' Sicilians, those humiliated, offended people caught in the twin trap of nature and history? What link could he have had with Sicily, with the south, to make them 'one of the principal sources of my inspiration'?

A political link, obviously. In the financing of his film, to begin with. 'Only the Italian Communist Party,' Visconti said, 'believed in my project and helped me to carry it through by giving me three million (lire).' Second, in the part Alicata and Trombadori had in the film's genesis. In a letter written from prison in 1943, Alicata had warned Visconti against his overly lyrical vision of Sicily as seen through Homer; even Luchino admitted that 'it was still very much the unknown land discovered by Garibaldi and his Thousand'. As early as 1941, he had dreamed of adapting Verga's Malavoglia: 'A fabulous and magical scenario,' he wrote then, 'in which the words and gestures should have the religious contours of things essential to our sense of human charity.' It was a mystery play of the Passion, enacted against 'the monotonous booming of the waves against the Faraglioni [cliffs]'.

Trombadori, with Visconti's consent, wrote a foreword to the film, trying to justify the use of a local dialect that not even Sicilians in Syracuse or Palermo could understand: 'All the actors in the film were chosen from among the villagers: fishermen, housewives, day labourers, masons, fish wholesalers. They know no language other than Sicilian to express rebellion, grief, hope. The Italian language is not, in Sicily, the language of the poor . . .'

When Visconti explained the origin of the two other films – Rocco and His Brothers and The Leopard – that, with The Earth Trembles, make up his 'southern trilogy', he never failed to refer to his political commitments. He cited his 'illuminating' reading of Gramsci's works, the letters he received from ordinary people and his interest in all 'the profound reasons that disturb Italians' lives and leave them alarmed and anxious for change'.

Verga's 1881 I Malavoglia, a novel full of 'real tears', is a parable about a family of fishermen whose disintegration begins the day the most adventurous of them throws off his heritage of submission and decides to become his own man. It is meant to illustrate a law, a destiny: 'When one of these little people, weaker or more rash or more selfish than the rest, tries to break away from his people, out of longing for the unknown, or a desire for a better life, or out of curiosity to learn about the world, then the world, like the voracious fish it is, devours him, and his loved ones with him.'

Unlike Gramsci, Verga the pessimist laid down no 'precise, realistic course of action' to head off the destiny expressed in the very name Malavoglia.★ Visconti changed the name to the more lightly worn Valastro. His character 'Ntoni, unlike the Malavoglia, does not leave the family's village, but starts over again, still determined to fight, not alone any more, but with the others. 'Ntoni draws the moral of the fable: 'Water is salty everywhere in the world. When we pass beyond the Faraglioni, the current sweeps us away. It is here that we must fight.' The message obviously does not sum up the film's scope, nor does it tell us about the real need, more poetic than political, to which it responds.

Writing to praise the beauty of *The Earth Trembles*, Antonioni was among the first to warn critics to shed their political blinkers, but he also reproached Visconti for occasionally sliding too facilely into rhetoric. 'Visconti's ethic,' he said, 'is deeply humane and invests his art. But when a split develops between his humanity and his art, rhetoric intrudes with all its bad points. The rich fish dealers at a table groaning with food, the belly laugh of the man against a wall bearing a pro-Mussolini slogan, some of 'Ntoni's speeches – these images are not born of the same brilliant expressive gift as that which inspires the portraits of the two sisters and the brothers.'

Fortunately, the film's clarity and its message are contaminated by other elements derived more from emotions than ideas, from everything 'instinctive, illogical and unconscious' in Visconti's mind. 'Anyone who knows Visconti knows that his gestures are weightier and say more about him than his words,' Antonioni warns us. 'The gestures are so many scenes in the film, the voices and bustle when the fishermen go to sea at dusk, the mason's songs, the livid light of the storm, the vehemence of 'Ntoni and the

★The name means 'reluctance', 'unwillingness', but also calls to mind the Italian adjective *malevolo*, meaning 'malevolent' (translator's note).

mother's resignation and so many other things which, aside from
the inevitable social indictment, contain the sincerest tone and
timbre of Luchino Visconti's poetic voice'.

Reality counted for more than ideas. Any of the party's liegemen
would have provided a more optimistic and vigorous ending.
Togliatti noted with some surprise that the characters had no political conscience. That, replied Visconti, is how I saw them; 'There is
only one thing to do: pay more attention to Aci Trezza.'

After hours and hours of rehearsals, Visconti had asked those
fishermen whose lives he shared for six months to relive Verga's
situations, but with their own gestures, their own words, in their
own dialect. 'The scenario was not frozen,' he later said. 'I left it
entirely up to them. For example, I took the two brothers and I told
them: "This is the situation: you've lost your boat, you are reduced
to poverty, you have nothing to eat and you don't know what to
do. You want to leave, but you are too young and he wants to hold
you here. Tell him what's driving you to roam far from here." He
told me: "To see Naples, and I don't know what else . . ." "Sure,
that's fine, but go on and say why you don't want to stay here." He
replied exactly what he says in the film: "Because we're like animals,
we are given nothing, and I want to see the world." Then I turned
to the other. "What would you say to your brother, your real
brother, to hold him here?" He was already moved, he had tears in
his eyes . . . And with those tears in his eyes he replied, "If you go
beyond the Faraglioni, the storm will carry you away." Who could
have written that? No one.'

Verga could have written it, and he did, but in Italian. By letting
people hear it in the language of Aci Trezza, Visconti went against the
Communists' cultural principles, which opposed reconditeness, and
offences against public taste, which disliked anything disturbing.

'A film without concessions', Visconti was to say of The Earth
Trembles, either to party shibboleths or to aesthetic 'arabesques and
zigzags'. He strove for an absolutely stripped-down verity; he
slowly fused with characters utterly unlike himself who took on a
secret resemblance to him; he sacrificed the most visible part of his
identity – his luxury, culture and cosmopolitanism. And from all
this grew his commemoration of a world that he had made his own,
an insular world hedged within its music, beliefs, rites, dialect,

LUCHINO VISCONTI

within everything that came to it from the past and which became
muddled with its 'anxiety for change'.

The poetry of the Valastro family, of these characters full of
dreams and fables, is the poetry of Visconti's own family,
threatened and finally stricken by the haunting tragedy of its inevitable disintegration. And as accompaniment to his progress through
the realm of silent mothers who, wrapped in their long, black
shawls like the grim heroines of Greek tragedy, watched through
the night and the storm for their men to return, there could be no
music other than their dark and antique language. Like the ancient,
obscure Milanese dialect Donna Carla spoke, it was, Visconti said,
'as beautiful as Sophocles'.

'I spent Christmas with *my* fishermen,' he wrote to Antonioni,
who remarked on how the film-maker irresistibly reconstituted a
family around him. 'The characters are Visconti's adopted children,'
Antonioni said. 'He made them his during his stay in Sicily.'
Throughout those six months he had tried to experience their
poverty, their daily struggle at the most hostile season, late autumn
and winter. From 10 November 1947 to 26 May 1948, he forced
himself to live as an ascetic and made the crew of *The Earth Trembles*
do the same. The crew was reduced to a minimum: Rosi, Zeffirelli,
a few technicians, including the cameraman, Aldò (Graziati). It
faced what Visconti called 'almost insurmountable difficulties'
because of the cramped interiors it had to film, the violent storms
and the rudimentary, makeshift camera equipment. No money.
Iron discipline.

'You could have wept at times,' Rosi says, recalling the painstaking job Visconti assigned him of entering into four huge ledgers
the minutiae of all the scenes shot, everything from the weather and
the actors' costumes and gestures to 'technical notes on the choice of
lenses, the description and exact plan of each shot . . .'.

'He always found a mistake, and his rages were devastating . . .
[He] was shrewd enough never to let himself be caught in error,
even though he dragged a lot of doubt and uncertainty behind him.
But he solved his problems alone. When the work ended, he shut
himself in his hotel room, dined in bed and, at dawn, was the first to
face the day.'

The filming itself matched the movie's theme: both attempted

238

the impossible. 'Ntoni ventures to sea alone. But 'Briny is bitter', said the proverb, and 'Who has his fortune on the sea has nothing'; a storm soon sinks the defiant son's boat, *Providence*, and his hopes.

With *The Earth Trembles* Visconti also cast himself defiantly adrift, and while the venture was not a disaster, it was certainly a commercial wreck. He never managed to carry out his original plan – of which nothing remained but, as a reminder, a thoroughly enigmatic title. And the picture was a bottomless pit for production money. Time and again filming was suspended because Visconti had run out of funds and had to make lightning ascents to Rome and Milan in search of a co-operative producer. He finally found one *in extremis*, Salvo D'Angelo, a Sicilian connected with Universalia Produzione, on the set of a Hollywood-style epic called *Fabiola* that Blasetti was making on a billion-lire budget. In the meanwhile, Visconti had had to sell off securities, family paintings and even his mother's last jewels. 'The count is ruining himself,' the family's business manager murmured with a pained look.

When the film was shown at the Mostra, the film festival, in Venice in the autumn of 1948, it was greeted angrily by a shocked public and was not programmed for showing in the official theatres despite support from the Communist Party, which hailed *The Earth Trembles* as 'the masterpiece of the festival'. Rosi remembers the Venice première: 'Visconti and D'Angelo were dressed in white linen, but their faces were even whiter than their suits, Visconti's because he was nervous about the reception his work would get, D'Angelo's because he was probably thinking of the Bank of Sicily, which financed Universalia Produzione, and of what would be said and decided after this film came out. At the time, the Christian Democratic government was fulminating against the Italian film industry, which, instead of washing its dirty linen in the privacy of the family, did it abroad and in the full light of day . . .

'The film caused pandemonium. There was yelling, whistling, all kinds of protests and personal insults to Visconti. Why? It's the old story of festival audiences, but it was also about a degenerate "bourgeois" who had deviated and betrayed his class.'

And, too, of a man and a work that, recalled Antonioni in quoting Gide, had about it 'something disconcerting and surprising, which means something lasting'.

XIV

A THEATRE NAMED DESIRE

> *He suddenly abandoned his actors on the stage.*
> *'Go where you want and tell me what you'd*
> *do,' he said.*
> *And for two or three days he watched them;*
> *he stole their instincts.*
>
> ACHILLE MILLO

> *That is what I want, those are my orders,*
> *which means no more backtalk if you do not*
> *want to lose me, to lose me forever.*
>
> JEAN-NOËL SCHIFANO,
> *Chroniques napolitaines*

Obsession had marked the dawn of neo-realism, *The Earth Trembles* was its zenith. With his second film, Visconti had conferred nobility on a bleak 'people's' cinema. But he had no intention of becoming its prisoner. He had invented neo-realism, had pushed it to its outermost limit in reaction against the sham of bourgeois theatre, and because actors taken from real situations – like the fishermen of Aci Trezza – have more animal presence, they ring truer than professional actors with their 'complexes and reticence'; with real people you touch truth and suffering faster, you hear the cry of pain.

Equally Viscontian were other currents that crystallized in those years: intoxication with luxury, a love of spangles and artificial dazzle alternating with a need for simplicity, of self-mortification and abnegation visible even in his gaunt, ascetic-looking face when he returned from Aci Trezza. 'We find neo-realism,' he said in 1948, on the threshold of an outrageously lavish theatrical season, 'at the sources of our imagination and in our current experiments, and we

240

do not forget it any more than we forget the monks' dictum of "dust thou art and unto dust shalt thou return".' He was soon to put this humility into practice when he worked out the scenario for a new film with Vasco Pratolini, author of *A Tale of Poor Lovers*.

Three years earlier, Luchino had entered Galli's, the Milan pastry shop on Via Victor Hugo that was famous for its panettones, and noticed a slender, sixteen-year-old cashier with big, sad eyes and a carriage as aristocratic as that of any Visconti. 'You'll be in the movies someday,' he told her, 'I'm sure of it.'

On the following day the friend who had been with him returned to Galli's and ordered the ritual cappuccino brimming with cream and chocolate sprinkles. 'Do you know who that was talking to you yesterday?' he asked the cashier. 'Luchino Visconti.'

Visconti? She had never heard of him. She had been born on a farm near Milan, had spent her childhood in poverty and fear of bombing raids, and had been toiling since she was twelve. 'My world,' she later said, 'was behind a pastry-shop counter. To me, escape was tram line twenty-four, Monforte, Scalo, Porta Romana, Ripamonti, Porta Vigentina. There was Sergio, my first boyfriend, and the Idroscalo,★ and that was all.'

Until a year later, that is, when her picture appeared on newspaper front pages: she had just been elected Miss Italy by a beauty-contest jury headed and financed by GiViEmme, the Viscontis' famous cosmetics firm. Overnight she was swamped with gifts, invitations, offers. The dream of thousands of girls was coming true for her: '100,000 lire for a smile,' she said, 'a million and more for a pretty face . . . In those days that brought wealth and success. Italy, our Italy, then lived in hope of the million that could change a life . . . That was certainly when Lucia Bosé was born.'

From that time, too, dates her connection with the Visconti family. Edoardo fell for her and became her lover. Luchino cast her in the film version of *A Tale of Poor Lovers* that his brother was to finance, with Lucia playing alongside Gérard Philipe and Marguerite Moreno. Then things went wrong, for the film and for Lucia's love life. So Luchino took her into his home, watched over her – she was suffering from tuberculosis – and kept Edoardo away from her.

★An outlying slum district of Milan. The tram line ran through some of the city's poorest areas (translator's note).

Something of Lucia remains in the film *Bellissima*, which revolves around one of those beauty contests that so fascinated the mothers of Eleonora Rossi-Drago, Silvana Mangano, Silvana Pampanini, Gina Lollobrigida and Sofia Scicolone (better known as Sophia Loren), as well as the mothers of the younger girls on whom the cinematic ogre fed.

Visconti was more neo-realist than ever in the Fifties, when, with Pratolini, he made *Notes on a News Item*, a documentary about the rape and murder of a little girl in the outskirts of Rome. Yet he declared that 'neo-realism is merely a question of content' – a tone of verity suitable for directing works by Arthur Miller or for filming *Rocco and His Brothers*, but not for Shakespeare.

On 26 November 1948, the day *The Bicycle Thief* opened in Rome's movie theatres, Visconti opened 'a game' at the Teatro Eliseo, 'a musical entertainment', a 'coloured dream, three hours of fantasy in the very teeth of neo-realists more realist than the king'. The show was *As You Like It*, with magical sets by Salvador Dali. Make way for pleasure, he said, make way for 'a world of wonders whose paths the theatre abandoned ages ago; we want to return it to those paths and to the destination to which they lead: the public's enchantment'. With this began Visconti's period of big productions, of monumental sets and extravagant staging which, in those difficult years of reconstruction, recession and unemployment, were greeted with acrid disapproval by the champions of unalloyed austerity.

In *Rinascità* he replied to the criticism that his staging of the Shakespeare play had stirred, especially from the left:

There is a rumour that by directing *As You Like It* I have abandoned neo-realism. An impression created by the style of direction, the acting and my choice of Salvador Dali's sets and costumes.

I apologize to those who lean to vague terminology, but what does neo-realism mean? In films the word has served to define the concepts that inspired the recent 'Italian school'. It allied those (men, artists) who believed that poetry springs from reality. That was a starting point. It is becoming, I think, an absurd label that has stuck to us like a tattoo, and instead of meaning a method, a moment, it has become a boundary, a law. Do we need boundaries? Aren't boundaries suitable only for the lazy, for those who lose their balance easily?

. . . In the panorama of show business, the theatre has its limits and distinctions, and I'm not the one who discovered them. So let us allow it all its possibilities of movement, colour, light, magic. Not realism or neo-realism, but imagination, total freedom . . .

To Visconti's flamboyant and lavish imagination, inflamed by Dali's vision (which was steeped in piety and conveniently converted to Francoism) excess was the measure of all things. But in the spring of 1948, with the filming of *The Earth Trembles* barely behind him and his association with the surrealist painter still well ahead of him, the 'terrible' count had already concocted some grandiose theatrical plans. To Pariso Votto, director of Florence's arts festival, the Maggio Musicale May, he proposed a production of *Orlando Furioso* in the Boboli Gardens, to be staged in a series of scenes between which the audience could come and go as it liked. And a *Lorenzaccio* whose spectators would move from the gardens to the Pitti palace to follow the action of Alfred de Musset's play.

All this would not only require staggering budgets, but permission from the Historical Monuments Service, which handed down a categorical veto. By comparison with those two projects, the stagings of *As You Like It*, of Vittorio Alfieri's *Oreste* and a 'monstrous' *Troilus and Cressida* in the Boboli Gardens appear relatively sedate.

Yet nowhere outside of the Roman arena in Verona had so many actors ever been assembled on one stage, nor had there been so much music, so many costumes, such luxury. In his exile in Shakespeare's enchanted forest of Arden, the melancholy duke is surrounded by his entire court, clowns, princes and knights, not to mention a full complement of shepherds, disguised princesses, lute players, court ladies and pages.

Dali, whose fee reached a million lire, had designed sets of astonishing fantasy, splendour – and cost. 'I wanted a bizarre set designer,' Visconti later said, 'a magician . . . For a month, Dali immersed himself in the construction of his "geometrical" forest of "Raphaelesque" trees amid shepherds, courtiers, sheep and "atomic" pomegranates . . .' The painter recalled seeing Visconti often then, and said that he and his wife, Gala, frequently accompanied 'a guy whose name I don't remember' – Zeffirelli – to scour Rome for objects, fabrics, 'candies and cakes, because we wanted the actors to eat real cakes'.

Visconti's objective was not the faithful re-creation of an epoch, but the shaping of the sort of paradise he associated with eighteenth-century lightness and freedom. Only the music, written for Shakespeare, was absolutely authentic. Visconti said:

> Why choose the XVIIIth century when Shakespeare's play straddled the XVIth and XVIIth? I would reply with other questions, the ones I wondered about before beginning. Does 'historical accuracy' suit me? What purpose would it serve – to a teacher or a historian? Did I want to use XVIIth-century sets and costumes, puritanical, austere, so dignified in attitude and line? Or rather – since the story takes place outside of time and could have happened in Arcadian Greece or in the forests of Scotland or in the woods of Venetian painters – was I to favour a freer, more romantic, imaginative and pleasant century? That is how I got the idea of setting the plot and ballet in the XVIIIth that Dali envisioned as an autumnal XVIIIth century, full of colour, merriment and melancholy, an XVIIIth century that was not historical but imaginary, the innocent XVIIIth of the story. 'Puss in Boots' costumes, reflections of a rather en-chanted golden age.

The same unfettered, imaginative sense of spectacle was brought to Count Alfieri's *Oreste*, which Visconti mounted in the spring of 1949 with the sole aim, he said, of pleasing his 'pet', Vittorio Gass-man. He declared he didn't like the play, and in emphasis and artifice his staging matched the versifying in that pompous eighteenth-century tragedy.

In the completely remodelled Quirino Theatre he placed almost all his spectators in the boxes, since the stage far overflowed its usual limits and spread out into the orchestra. A vast eighteenth-century San Pietro crystal chandelier dangled from a black ceiling, sur-rounded by huge folds of scarlet hangings slanting down towards the floor. Stone doors opened like fantastic jaws flanked on each side by blood-red stairs and Mycenaean lions. Half hidden by a greenish veil and bathed in an aquarium light, the Santa Cecilia orchestra played Beethoven. The play's five characters wore outlandish costumes of feathers and sequins with a circus air and a glitter of fish scales, each of which cost Visconti the then huge sum of 500,000 lire. Gassman, as a solar Orestes, brandished a sword dripping with blood and sequins ('The blood,' Visconti insisted, 'we have to see the blood!'). Marcello Mastroianni played a melancholy, lunar Pylades at what looked like the court at a new Atlantis.

'[Visconti] reasoned this way,' says his assistant, Gerardo Guerrieri. 'Alfieri was eighteenth century and therefore he was the approaching Revolution, the monarchy swallowed up, everything swallowed up, in an underwater Versailles encrusted like an old galleon.'

The explanation goes too far in reducing Visconti's inspiration to a mechanistic, cerebral aestheticism. Why did he exaggerate Alfieri's baroque style, to the point of using the Fratellini brothers' spangled costumes, unless, as the critic Giorgio Prosperi suggested, he sought to 'free himself from it, cast it out of himself in a kind of auto-therapy aimed at ridding himself of a pervasive baroque sensuality'?

Visconti confirmed this when he said: 'My *Oreste*, which Gassman found so exterior, was in fact designed as a baroque spectacle, the construction of a world in which Alfieri's verses, so forced, so insincere, yet so heroic and furious, could resound and awake echoes in close harmony with their author's mind. I always try to bring out something the work suggests, I seek . . . a bridge between me and the work I am directing. Sometimes I deal with works that inspire my fullest confidence; sometimes, as in the case of *Oreste*, with works that I feel force me to be contentious.'

More commonly, his staging grew out of passionate feelings of identification with and possession of the lines, the characters, the actors. Visconti himself was an accomplished actor who related obsessively to specific characters, especially Dostoyevsky's Stavrogin. 'He talked about him constantly,' Guerrieri says, 'he was *his* character. He mimed the gesture of the young woman who hangs herself, raising his forefinger as if to say "Watch out!"'

But, he adds, 'at a performance he became all the characters. He was more actor than director. From the very first rehearsals around a table, that first physical contact with the actors, he felt a neurotic impulse to improvise on stage the roles they were rehearsing, making the actors his audience.'

An actor, then, must be a faithful, spotless mirror and not, contrary to Diderot's theories in *The Paradox of Acting*, a personage entitled to govern himself and bypass the sovereign director. This is why regular rehearsals were always preceded by countless group readings under the director's guidance. Actors were forbidden to learn their parts on their own before these sessions. The most docile and disciplined among them – especially Stoppa and Rina Morelli – bowed unprotesting to the rule. But more rebellious, more histrionic players were put through training sessions spiced by crude insults, rancorous remarks and deadly aspersions that tamed the most fractious of them.

At one point, while the cast was reading Chekhov's *The Three Sisters*, the actor Memo Benassi – 'who had extraordinary skills,' Visconti said, 'but who was terribly disorderly and confused' – slammed shut his script and spoke his lines without consulting it. He kept this up until the end of the session. 'Why didn't you read your lines like the others did?' Visconti asked him. 'Because I know them,' Benassi retorted, obviously pleased with himself.

He would pay for this slight to the director. For an actor was supposed to make himself forget everything he knew, everything he might have learned or thought about the character, thus clearing his mind to see the part through Visconti's eyes. 'Everyone probably has his own point of view,' he said. 'But since it is my work, I explain it and I shape it in my fashion, because I start with a plan and I am really the one who is responsible for the show. An actor may have doubts about something, the interpretation, say, of a detail, a line, a scene, but I convince him that the scene, viewed as part of my overall concept, must be done this way and not that way . . .'

He had the same attitude towards Gassman: 'When he joined my company, he told me, "I will gladly join, provided you do something for me. Let's both choose what you want to do." He settled on Alfieri's *Oreste*. "All right, I'll do *Oreste* with you. But I'll do it as I want to, as I see it, as I feel it, to dot the i's and cross the t's the

way I think it should be done . . .'" Gassman had too much character to let himself be led docilely by the nose; he bucked and kicked,
Visconti recalled, but he finally obeyed 'after a good dressing
down'.

By breaking him to the director's method, however, Visconti
merely accentuated Gassman's rebelliousness and ambition, until
the independent-minded actor finally broke away. 'I don't remember why any more,' Visconti said. Gassman proudly remembers the
day when the director, after twelve hours of rehearsal, yelled at him
from the back of the theatre: 'Wake up! Get moving! You're not
Talma yet.' To which the actor dared retort, 'And you will never be
Stanislavsky.'

'Cruel, he was cruel,' Clara Calamai would say. According to
Massimo Girotti, 'working in the theatre with Visconti was a real
ordeal. He established a church atmosphere, the gloomy atmosphere of a temple, in absolute silence. A depressing, obsessive
atmosphere. Irony was his favourite weapon; he made fun of the
actors, he ridiculed them, parodied them. He parodied what they
did and what they shouldn't have done. He managed to terrorize
everyone.'

On the other hand, as Adriana Asti later said, 'He could make
stones act.' And Mastroianni, whose first role was in Visconti's *As
You Like It*, said: 'He was disrespectful to a lot of actors. He used to
get a slight kick out of humiliating poor Marga Cella, an old actress:
he made her dance, he treated her badly, provoked her. He treated
almost everyone badly, including Stoppa, who was always wagging
his tail at [Visconti's] heels. But for me, and Gassman, whom he
knew had a gift for irony, he had respect.'

'His relationship with actors,' Guerrieri said in 1977, 'was a
mixture of tyranny and worship . . . He brought Sade into the
Italian theatre. An actor who was very close to him* says even now:
"Luchino was a tyrant. Working with him was always enormously
unpleasant. I can't remember an experience with him that was not
disagreeable. But remember the scenes he got out of Paolo Stoppa
and Marcello Mastroianni? Out of everybody, except Rina Morelli.
He vented his spleen on the first person who came to hand. It was an

*Without doubt Girotti.

electric, passionate relationship that on stage turned into a hysterical and paroxysmal portrayal of those years."

'But there was another side to the relationship: idolatrous worship. Actors were fetishes through whom he expressed himself and with whom he identified. He worshipped great actors – I was going to say the great actors of the past, those he'd seen with his mother when he was very young, and he had seen them all, starting with Duse; he remembered sitting on his seat and hearing Sarah Bernhardt's wooden leg squeak on the stage. He wanted at least one of them in every show: Gandusio in *Eurydice* (how he praised him: such an exemplary generation, such punctuality, not like you young people), Ruggero Ruggeri (who was so pale we nicknamed him "The Corpse"), Tatiana Pavlova . . . with whom he also had run-ins; he once called the stage manager and told him that "rehearsals will be suspended as long as Madam Pavlova continues to speak Turkish".' The remark was worthy of Toscanini, whom Visconti resembled more than he did Stanislavsky.

He demonstrated dramatically his dominion over actors in the Florentine festival in June 1949, when his net snared every big-name actor in Italy. 'All of them,' he said, 'they were all there.' And they were all in his *Troilus and Cressida* in the Boboli Gardens: 150 actors under his direction, 'a kind of national assembly of the Italian theatre. That's what they called it, because in addition to those in my company – Paolo Stoppa, Rina Morelli, Gassman, Mastroianni, De Lullo, Girotti – I brought in others: Renzo Ricci, Memo Benassi, Carlo Ninchi . . .' The greatest names in old-time theatre, people who were not only actors – and not just any actors, but the most famous in the first half of the century – but troupe managers in their own right, used to staging and playing in works by Shakespeare, Pirandello, Chekhov, and the like.

Commanding this army, organizing his troupers' manoeuvres – *Troilus* is, after all, a story of the Trojan war – demanded an energy that only a human whirlwind like Visconti could muster. Able while working to go for three nights running without sleep, he demanded the same endurance and devotion of his actors. 'I remember,' he later said, 'once when we were rehearsing *Troilus* – there were twenty-two days of rehearsals – we were doing an exterior in the Boboli Gardens, which was a huge space.' During a scene with

Benassi (playing Thersites, the fool and 'curer of madmen') and Girotti (Ajax), 'Benassi went up and down a hill with Girotti beating him. Benassi began laughing with the extras and I noticed. So I told him he wasn't to do that. And I made him redo the scene, twenty times. I think, until the poor fellow was almost dead from going up and down that hill. And he, with great strength of character, never weakened, he did it ten, twenty times, and then he said, "I'm dying, [but] I would have died rather than knuckle under."'

The show went on until two o'clock in the morning. It had cost thirty million lire. For a play that had been considered unplayable, that had discouraged many a director, an entire city had been built on Zeffirelli's designs, with ramparts, walled gardens, fountains, a labyrinth of alleys, stairways, terraces, minarets, hidden corners. Before the gleaming white walls of Troy stretched the Greek camp, with its heroes in spiked helmets, its battle flags, its caparisoned horses.

Audiences nevertheless gave this remarkable production a lukewarm reception. Yet Visconti was so attached to the play that in 1963, during France's war in Algeria, he thought of reviving this epic confrontation between two civilizations, archaic Troy, wedded to its traditional values, and modern, corrupt Greece. Into it could be read not only the opposition between northern and southern Italy, but also the struggle between East and West and the eternal rebellion of the vanquished against their oppressors. In 1963, Visconti vowed to update and accentuate the theme by clearly representing the Trojans as Algerians and the Greeks as French paratroopers.

Was he already thinking by 1950 of lavish costume films in colour? Probably, since he and Suso Cecchi d'Amico discussed plans built around two towering figures on whom Visconti bestowed unreasoning devotion.

One was his Imperial Highness Antonio de Curtis, count palatine, knight of the Holy Roman Empire, Duke of Macedonia, Prince of Constantinople, of Tenaglia, of Ponto, of Moldano, of the Peloponnese, Count of Cyprus and Epirus, Count of Drivasto, Duke of Durazzo, etc. Visconti doubted the lineage, but he recognized that, under the name of Totò, the man was a magnificent comic; Suso Cecchi said it angered Visconti to see how Totò was used, and he grew obsessed with the idea of showing him in the role of Antonio Petito, a Neapolitan actor and the nineteenth century's greatest Pulcinella.

The other project, around which a full-blown scenario developed, was a film version of Prosper Mérimée's play *The Coach of the Blessed Sacrament*, with Magnani in the role of Périchole. But Visconti became so bogged down in discussions with his producers that he finally withdrew the scenario. Magnani, however, remained under contract. Renoir's name was floated as the film's director, whereupon Magnani sought Visconti's advice. 'What should I do?' she asked him. 'What do you mean, what should you do? With Renoir, and you're hesitating?' The film was *The Golden Coach*.

Pulcinella and Périchole, Totò and Magnani: this was still Italian-style theatre full of movement and dancing and arabesques, a jubilantly corporeal theatre. 'Perhaps this is the twilight of the age of Ibsen and Chekhov,' Visconti said in 1948. 'Modern theatre likes dancing, not for aesthetic reasons, but as "liberated" movement. Perhaps a century is opening before us of shows in which characters express themselves more fully and more naturally and more sincerely than they do in the grey and over-subtle style of the bourgeois theatre.'

But between the winter of 1949 and the spring of 1951, Visconti was not interested in the wholesome, jovial harlequinades of the Commedia dell'arte. He was looking to America and the 'abnormal, wild' theatre of Lee Strasberg and Elia Kazan that would give us Montgomery Clift, James Dean and Marlon Brando – an actor who fascinated him then and would continue to later when Visconti was casting *Senso* and *The Leopard*. He even thought of him to play Baron de Charlus in *Remembrance of Things Past*. For the moment, he was working with Stoppa (whom he had moved out of his early comic roles into drama), Mastroianni, Giorgio de Lullo and, especially, Gassman, whom he spurred and excited, and whose violence he exploited to a point of paroxysm.

His body covered with sweat and shivering in fright, shaken by spasms of anxiety, brawling amid broken bottles – Gassman was so immersed in the part of Stanley Kowalski in the dress rehearsal of *A Streetcar Named Desire*, the first version, done in January 1949 – that he took a bad fall and injured himself. The stage looked like a lunatics' battlefield. This was also to be the tone of *Death of a Salesman* two years later, one of hysteria, of 'a violent obsession', said the critic Silvio d'Amico, 'aimed more at shocking than at moving'.

To Visconti, realism was violence: of language, so crude as to outrage prudish audiences and critics; of lighting, as in the spotlighting of the 'throne room' in *Streetcar*; above all of body language, the afflictions of anxiety, rage, madness, desire. Reality was these drifting, poignant characters created by Williams and Arthur Miller, these rejects of old Europe and young America, down-and-outers, exiles, failures, seen as moving shadows against a background of neon mirages. Or they were the beaten, like Verga's characters, who sometimes escaped into an infantile world where, at last, they were kings: in Alaska and the Cameroons, where salesman Willy Loman dreamed of finding gold; at Belle Rêve, Blanche's girlhood home in *Streetcar*, now furnished with little more than stacks of bills and worthless papers, but where, with an old pair of slippers on her feet and a rhinestone tiara on her head, she lives out memories of her family's vanished splendour.

All the works Visconti imported dealt in violence and nostalgia, his two muses; all of them spoke, or sang, of exile, as the barrel organ and Negro spirituals did in Williams' stifling New Orleans nights. Miss Morelli, playing both Blanche Du Bois and Linda Loman, managed to convey these nuances in a look, a sigh, a murmur, a silence.

We find Visconti's favourite motifs in the American mirror: a family's decline, the conflict between the triviality of life and the characters' dreams of happiness, in innocence, madness and failure. Blanche, that modern Traviata descended from an aristocratic old French family, a part-time whore living as a social outcast on the edge of reality, was Williams himself – Visconti called him Blanche – but she was Luchino, too. The two homosexual artists, living like their actors and their characters on the edges of 'normal' life and haunted by the notions of decline and fall, met frequently when Williams began spending more and more time in Rome. Visconti was so driven to identify with the playwright that he even grew the same meagre moustache, eventually coming to resemble him like a brother.

These plays also had social overtones in a period of widespread unemployment, when riots by laid-off workers in the winter of 1950 caused several deaths in Modena and Parma. Reality was also this tribute paid to the victors, the Christian Democratic governments which, helped by Andreotti and the Interior Minister Mario Scelba, had long ago activated the machinery of repression and censorship.

In 1950, Visconti joined the peace movement sponsored by the Italian Communist Party. A year later, on 3 October 1951, in an open letter to Pietro Ingrao published in *L'Unità*, he protested against Scelba's denial of an entry visa to the Berliner Ensemble headed by Bertolt Brecht. To emphasize his displeasure, he had his name removed from the playbills of the show he was directing for the Venice Festival Theatre, Diego Fabbri's rather weak play *The Seducer*, which he had saved in extremis by accompanying it with waltzes from the magical *La Traviata*.

Stubbornly opposed to the restoration of conservatism and puritanism in Italian government in the Fifties, Visconti was equally severe towards the boredom of cultural compomise, the return to routine that he was the first to detect on stage and screen. In the Communist Party debate on the decline of neo-realism, he was an early critic of the sentimental, folkloric imagery, the blandness of such reassuring comedies as *Bread, Love and Fantasy*, which offended no one. He did not even spare his friend De Sica, who deserted the rocky road of realism with his *Miracle in Milan*: 'At the end of *The Earth Trembles*,' he recalled, 'there is more hope and promise than there is in sending tramps flying off on broomsticks. We cannot and must not abandon reality. I am against escapism.'

The film *Bellissima* that he made in the summer of 1951 is both a tribute to Magnani and a trial of the neo-realistic school of cinema of which, since *Rome, Open City*, she had become the emblem, the reigning diva. 'I am certainly one of the first to have seen *Rome, Open City*, because Rossellini showed it, in an almost unedited version, in a small theatre in the Ministry,' Visconti recalled. 'There were about twenty of us. I remember that in the famous scene in which Magnani dies, I was so enraptured that I was among the first to lead the applause . . .

'In those days we were excited by a flag flapping in the wind, by

252

a cannon squarely hitting its target. The movement continued after *Paisan, Shoeshine, The Children Are Watching Us*, but I thought the legitimate exploration of certain themes, the search for a moral posture towards life, gave way quietly to comfortable compromise.' Yet everything about *Bellissima* – Magnani's presence, as well as the story written especially for her by the pope of neo-realism, the scriptwriter Cesare Zavattini – promised a return to neo-realism by Visconti.

The movement's leading films, from Blasetti's *Four Steps into the Clouds* to De Sica's *The Bicycle Thief* and *Umberto D*, were conceived in Zavattini's Roman retreat on Via Merici. The door opened and a little man in glasses appeared, his neck wrapped in a scarf. He began to talk, a flood of words interrupted by laughter and breathless ums and uhs and clownish digressions and romances, a tide brimming with memories, images, dialogue and incredible stories drawn from life. Visconti, too, went to this Aladdin's cave 'just,' he said, 'to take two or three nuggets from your big bag of gold'.

Among the nuggets was the plot of *Bellissima*. In the film, Blasetti, playing himself, is looking for a little girl to play in his next picture. A contest is held to choose the most beautiful little girl in Rome, and mothers hustle their daughters to Cinecittà. One is a working-class woman, Maddalena (Anna Magnani), who brings her daughter, Maria. This was one film, then, that did not start from a work of literature, which makes it unique among Visconti's pictures: from 1941 on, all the others, even *The Earth Trembles*, had been based not on some minor incident but on 'the great narrative structures of European classical novels'. The characteristics of *Bellissima*: rapid filming, 'natural' sets in Cinecittà and the working-class districts of Rome, with Magnani improvising as only she could.

The film was a Trojan horse in the neo-realist citadel. Zavattini quickly realized this when Visconti completely altered the end of his script, changed the characters and introduced new ones such as Iris – Liliana Mancini in real life, a film editor at Cinecittà. She tells her own story, a true one: film-maker Renato Castellani saw her in the street one day, stopped her and offered her the lead in his picture *Under the Roman Sun*. 'I was picked once, twice like that, because I was the type they needed. To tell the truth, it went to my head a bit, and I left my job and my fiancé. What I say is, if you are not really a professional actor you had better have a trade and not have any illusions . . . Illusions about working in pictures have made so many people unhappy.'

Visconti also asked Blasetti to play himself. 'Do what you please,' he told him, 'just be yourself.' But each of his appearances on the screen is treacherously accompanied by the theme from the charlatan's aria in Donizetti's *L'Elisir d'Amore*. When some charitable souls pointed this out to him, Blasetti, who Visconti said did not know the opera, sent him an irate letter.

'Why?' the director replied. 'We're the ones who put illusions in the heads of mothers and daughters. We pick people up in the street, and that's wrong. We sell a love potion that is not an elixir. As in the opera, it is only Bordeaux wine. I didn't use the charlatan's theme for you, but for me.'

In fact, the film pillories the whole motion-picture world as a looking-glass of illusions, an industry of escapism. And not just through its directors, but also through its hairdressers, fashion designers, photographers, drama teachers, all the parasites who buzz and croak around that gigantic hive of dreams. Annovazi, for example, played by Walter Chiari, one of the best paid and most mercenary actors of his day.

Cecchi d'Amico created the character thinking he was exactly Visconti's cup of tea. In the film, the fellow has no clearly defined function at Cinecittà, but he swindles Maddalena (Magnani) of her money by promising to recommend her daughter personally and to wangle her a screen test; once he has pocketed the family's savings, he buys a scooter, puts down half the price, then guns the motor and disappears. The scene was shot outside a film theatre showing an obscure film called *Every Woman Is Always Charming* and, more important, before a pharmacy with a lighted sign bearing the name of Carlo Erba.

It is hard to tell how much Visconti played at identifying himself not only with Blasetti, but also with that man who takes money from a woman, a mother – the situation recurs in the director's work – and squanders it frivolously. 'People say I wanted to show the film world in a bad, ironic light,' he remarked. 'That was only a consequence.' It was not, he adds, the important thing: 'The real subject was Magnani,' a woman he had known since before the war, explosive, disorganized, possessive, always under foot, with whom he was forever clashing, but whom he adored. So, for that matter, did Tennessee Williams, who spent many an evening talking to her or accompanying her to the Colosseum to feed Rome's stray cats, and who said he could never help putting an exclamation mark after her name.

Visconti was a witness to her tumultuous love affairs, first with Rossellini, but also with a string of actors and, during the *Bellissima* period, with a gorgeous electrician in the company named Lavoretti. She dragged him around with her everywhere, publicly jeered at his inelegance, even forbade his entering the street in Rome, appropriately named Panico, on which he had lived until then with his wife and two children.

Luchino and Suso Cecchi d'Amico tried to tone her down. They tried to talk her out of living with her lover by calculating what Lavoretti would have to pay his wife for deserting her. Magnani furiously attacked them as prejudiced, Visconti because he was an aristocrat, Ms Cecchi d'Amico because she was upper middle class. 'A fine pair you two are!' Magnani fumed. 'You only talk like this because he's an electrician.' Her life with her lovers was a series of scenes and explosions. Finally, in despair, she would summon her two friends, who rushed to her apartment high over the Pantheon to hear her complaints and submit to her recriminations.

'She was a little crazy,' Ms Cecchi d'Amico later said, 'but what tremendous charm.' The relationship the actress developed with Visconti was passionate, unbridled, one that he said clung 'in the forefront of my thoughts and plans'. How could he put up with her morbid jealousy? 'She was jealous of everything she felt excluded from, of every intimacy she couldn't penetrate. She was afraid of losing friends because they were too absorbed in other problems. She tried to combat this instinctive impulse, without much success. She could hold grudges over silly things. She lost control and devastated everything, like a river in flood . . . We reached a complete break-up . . .'

That happened at the Venice film festival in 1956, when Maria Schell won the best-actress award for her work in *Gervaise*. Magnani, who appeared in Luigi Zampa's *Sister Letizia*, was sure Luchino voted for Miss Schell. Suso tried to reason with her, assuring her that the jury's verdict was fair and that 'in this sort of thing, nothing could sway Luchino, not friendship, not even his father or mother'. She was nevertheless so aggrieved that she refused to speak to him for twelve years afterwards – until the day she happened to run into him in a shop and fell into his arms.

Possessive and difficult though she was, Visconti always showed infinite patience and affection towards her. As his scriptwriter notes, 'he understood women better than anyone did, in an absolutely extraordinary way.'

This was also the period of his equally turbulent relationship with the novelist Elsa Morante, the wife of Alberto Moravia. She had just completed *House of Liars*, which Visconti considered adapting for film. 'He was flattered,' Suso says, 'he loved to charm people, but she was the intrusive kind, following him around everywhere; she had given him a cat named Arturo, because of the novel *Arturo's Island*, then two pink Persian cats. The Elsa Morante period was also the cat period. In the end, however, the novelist's attachment to him and her demonstrations of affection grew too hard to take.'

While it lasted, their relationship was an odd one, of mutual fascination and provocation. Visconti would phone her at night and tell her to masturbate; she sometimes appeared before him with a bunch of grapes stuck in her panties and announced, laughing hard, that 'I've got one, too . . . .!' He finally grew tired of all this. Morante later referred to his 'nastiness'. Indeed, agrees Ms Cecchi d'Amico, 'in the end he was unpleasant, even nasty'.

Visconti was most drawn to this feminine, passionate atmosphere, almost animal in its irrationality, that Morante so intensely embodied, when it involved his actors and actresses. With Magnani, he said, he wanted to 'experiment with a "real character"', to express 'more internal and meaningful things'. The character was that of a mother, a 'modern mother' to whom still clung vestiges of the archaic mother in *Rocco and His Brothers*, with her superstitions – which Magnani shared – and her visceral attachment to her only child. The fictional role was intensified by Magnani's love for her son Luca, the child for whom she had been obliged to give up her role in *Obsession*, and who had been stricken with infantile paralysis in 1945. This screen mother, moreover, would be intent on seeing her child achieve everything she had never done.

In *Bellissima*, Magnani said, 'despite all Visconti's faults – and he had so many of them, oh so many! – I got on well with him. He gave me my head. Besides, he knew that was the only way to get me to work.' In fact, it is the only example of a movie in which Visconti really improvised, allowing a performer to ad lib without advance preparation, a performance 'full of working-class instinct that had nothing at all to do with the tricks of standard stagecraft'. She weeps, she laughs and, at the end of the film, the cry of a wounded animal rises up out of her guts as she sits alone on a bench at night beside her sleeping daughter, for little Maria, lisping, ridiculous in a tutu and a vacant stare, had sent Blasetti's crew into fits of laughter.

Francesco Rosi, Visconti's co-assistant, with Zeffirelli, on *Bellissima*, later spoke of this amazing chemistry of two artists, each highly individualistic, each known for his rages on the set. 'Watching them work together was magnificent,' he says. 'Never a blow-up, never even a clash. Magnani was very intelligent, and so was Visconti. He knew she'd bring him her personality, her acting genius, and naturally, as an experienced showman, he received (her gift) with the utmost respect. You had to know how to use that strong a personality while at the same time giving it free rein; the balance between these two demands was amusing to watch.'

'I was interested in finding out what kind of a relationship would grow up between me and Magnani the diva,' Visconti said. His resurrection of the diva cult, a new violation of the principles of neo-realism, was confirmed in 1953 in his sketch in *We, the Women*. Zavattini had envisioned the film as a series of 'naturalistic' portraits demythologizing the big stars of the period, Isa Miranda, Alida Valli, Ingrid Bergman; Visconti used it to highlight Magnani's outsized persona. At the time, the two artists who most fascinated him were Magnani, 'the she-wolf', and the 'vestal' Maria Callas; he had idolized her since seeing her in *Parsifal* and *Norma* in 1949. They both, he said in virtually the same terms, aroused deep emotion in him. The emotions stirred by Magnani related to his childhood and his ties to his mother, strong, realistic, authoritarian, but also protective and loving, adoring and jealously adored.

We, the Women is the only film in which the director depicted a child's anguish – the child-king, adorned, attired, disguised, photo-graphed in majesty in a straight-backed armchair that looks like a throne. This is the child-Christ, and the child-clown, too, wrested from his games, exposed to the merciless laughter of adults, the child torn between his quarrelling parents, weeping in the dark as he listens to their endless squabbling. Among the deep emotions the diva aroused in Visconti was his childhood anxiety in a family threatened with dissolution.

Magnani's face was so mobile, so changeable that, he said, it 'captured the expressions of thousands of creatures' plus the thousand expressions – suspicion and innocence, maturity and youth, ardour and irony, vitality and sadness – of a single creature, the venerated Mother. Instead of stressing the character's febrile, picturesque expressiveness, Visconti brought out her almost stoic dignity, contrasting it in the climax to the other women's hysterical cackling.

In that family, the father doesn't count, nor would he in any of Visconti's films except *The Leopard*. The person who matters is the mother: stripped of her petite-bourgeoise illusions, she spurns the impresarios' offers, rejects the mirages of fame and fortune for her daughter and herself, keeping jealous watch over the child, who lies, calm at last, sleeping between her reconciled parents while the charlatan's song fades in the distance. Transfigured, ennobled, beautified in this sentimental, utopian dream, Magnani becomes the Madonna with Child, serene guarantor of the family values she herself had so rashly disregarded.

XV

THE MASTER

*Unfortunately, I didn't know Visconti as well
as I would have wished. Those of us who
work in show business are like raindrops on a
sheet of glass: we follow one another, we come
together, we blend completely for a brief
moment, then we separate, sometimes forever,
sometimes to meet again before sliding away
and vanishing.*

EDUARDO DE FILIPPO

'Nobody lives like that today,' says the stage designer Piero Tosi,
'like on an island.' An island pounded by the waves of history,
however: after the great storms, the seemingly interminable low
tide of the Fifties. In that period, dominated by the Christian
Democrats, that led up to the boom, the Italian economic 'miracle',
the general mood was one of comfort, of confidence. 'Italy was
rightist,' says the director Mario Monicelli, 'and the movies were
leftist.'

That was the period of Marian pilgrimages, of Pope Pius XII and
the ubiquitous Andreotti. The air people breathed, Antonioni
recalls, was 'stifling. The atmosphere was provincial and stupid,
morals oppressive and politics repressive, clericalism was intolerable
. . . Censorship and moralism reigned.' Communists and their fel-
low-travellers were excommunicated. In 1955 Visconti denounced
this climate in his staging of *The Crucible*, Arthur Miller's parable on
Senator Joseph R. McCarthy's anti-communist witch hunts.

Count Luchino no doubt lacked a talent for martyrdom, but
neither was he among the officially blessed. Without government

support, he had to relinquish plans to establish a 'people's theatre' like Jean Vilar's Théâtre National Populaire in Paris. A more modest project also escaped him: a film to be called *Wedding March*, based on a real-life incident in Naples; it was to parallel the engagement and marriage of a working-class couple with the suicide of a society matron who, some months earlier, had leaped off the Posillip hill with her two children. Such plots were not to be tackled head-on at a time when, although loose living was customary in high society, Pius XII's Church kept a tight rein on the middle and lower classes. In 1958 the newspapers reported that an engaged couple had committed suicide on the eve of their wedding because, in collecting the necessary documents for the marriage, the girl had discovered she was illegitimate.

'If circumstances had been different,' Visconti later said, 'my work would have taken on another aspect.' Only four years had been needed to deflate the great post-war surge of artistic excitement. Visconti, to whom Chekhov represented the middle-class image of a stagnant, futile society weeping over the felling of an orchard, had expressed the excitement of that period when, in 1948, he wrote: 'This is probably more an age of Shakespeare than of Chekhov, who was certainly more alive in the days when we were awaiting the Messiah. Today the Messiah is among us, we feel he is everywhere, we feel him arriving from the farthest corners of the world . . .'

By 1952 the wind had changed, the Messiah was no longer 'among us'. This was a time of waiting, a Chekhovian time, and Visconti went on to stage the Russian's *The Three Sisters* (in December 1952), *The Evils of Tobacco* (March 1953), *Uncle Vanya* (December 1955) and, finally, *The Cherry Orchard* in October 1965. 'Stendhal,' he recalled, 'wanted the epitaph "He loved Cimarosa, Mozart and Shakespeare" engraved on his tombstone . . . On mine I'd like them to engrave, "He loved Shakespeare, Verdi and Chekhov".'

There is something of the Fifties atmosphere, something of that middle-class deadening after a period of struggle, in the emasculated world of *The Three Sisters*, where idle officers recite poems and spray themselves with scent, croon about the beauty of flowers, philosophize from morning to night, give small gifts to the ladies, eat sweets, chat, take tea and find that time drags. 'Of the absurd final duel,' Chekhov had advised, 'one should notice only noise coming from very far away, a muffled, vague noise, while on stage everyone is weary, almost asleep.'

They awaited the Messiah, they dreamed of a happier, more just society; the old world slowly dissolved into the snowy, sleepy background of the Russian plains, where occasionally were heard the bells of a distant troika. A new world was coming; as in *The Leopard*, it might be a world of jackals, of ignorant, hard-working parvenus – the world of the little ex-muzhik Lopakhin, who will take possession of the cherry orchard where his father and grandfather had been serfs. Lopakhin of the yellow vest and shoes is closely akin in his peasant foxiness to Don Calogero Sedara, the father of the beautiful Angelica in *The Leopard*, with his tail coat, white tie and patent-leather shoes.

The talk is all of progress and economic growth, but the country doctor in *Uncle Vanya* sees only ravaged forests around him, 'and always the same swamps, the mosquitoes, the lack of roads, the poverty, the typhus, the diphtheria . . .'. Poor relations looked the same in Chekhov's Russia as they did in Lampedusa's Sicily, crushed 'under the hail of fire that falls as on the accursed cities in the Bible'.

Five years after he staged *Uncle Vanya*, Visconti lambasted the other side of Italy's economic miracle. He deplored the optimistic official speeches 'picturing the Mezzogiorno and Sicily and Sardinia as miraculously transformed', whereas the people in the south 'have received only the crumbs from the great banquet of the so-called Italian economic miracle and are still waiting to escape the moral and spiritual isolation they are shut into'.

This was the period of *Rocco and His Brothers*, of *La Dolce Vita* and *La Notte*. On the one hand were the newly rich, the paparazzi, the starlets on the Via Veneto, and Milan's bored industrialists; on the other were the scorched earth of Sicily and the Basilicata of southern Italy, abandoned to women and old men while the young men – more than two million of them between the late 1950s and the early '60s – migrated to the cities of the north in search of work and prosperity. With his clumsily tied bundle, the southern emigrant became the Chaplinesque figure of the Italian tragi-comedy.

Visconti's disillusionment and pessimism spoke through Chekhov's muted, melancholy voice in those years when the Communist Party was unquestionably on the decline. But in Visconti that voice rang with the determination that, Togliatti said, 'invests our pessimism'. As it did in the 1952 staging of *The Three Sisters*, about which Visconti commented: 'Impotence, resignation, despair, that's true. But with the intellectual possibility of foreseeing a future, a change in humanity, without these things.' In the 1965 *Cherry Orchard*, Trofimov, the perpetual student and helpless prophet, played by Massimo Girotti decked out in Gramsci-style wire-rimmed spectacles, declares: 'As yet we have nothing, not even a point of view on the past. All we can do is talk interminably, complain of our vague yearnings and drink vodka. Yet it is luminously clear that to live in the present we must first expiate our past, must finish with it, and we can only expiate it through suffering and constant, incredible labour . . .'

First finish with the past. Visconti insisted that Chekhov was not the mawkish, twilit author he was often thought to be. 'His tragedies were vaudevilles,' the director maintained; 'it is in daily life that you find the tragedy. He was simply telling mankind: "Look how badly you are living and try to live better."' Visconti followed the playwright's advice to the letter, banning the sad faces from *The Three Sisters* and bustling along the finale of *The Cherry Orchard* hammer and tongs: the characters laugh and joke as they leave the house forever, while whips crack and horses snort. Such a swirl leaves no time for weeping and self-pity.

And thus the play takes on a wholly different meaning. It is no longer a tragedy of despair, but a story of liberation, the breaking of the delicious but deadly spell of childhood, of the past, of the family home awash in femininity, so maternal with its elderly nannies, its music, its pleasant food, its rituals. But this home closes up like a prison, like a tomb when the old servant who dies in it is forgotten and 'the mysterious sound of a rope breaking' is heard.

Visconti knew the enchantment of the past; those early years of the century, the homey, provincial atmosphere of the play recalled the Milan of his childhood. It was probably no mere coincidence that in his native city in the autumn of 1954 he staged a play by Puccini's Chekhovian librettist Giuseppe Giacosa, who had died there a month before Luchino was born; called *Come le Foglie* (*Like the Leaves*), it traces the fall of a wealthy family.

For *The Three Sisters*, the specific instructions the director gave the French costume designer Marcel Escoffier were aimed at recreating what he called 'a TONE, an AIR, an ATMOSPHERE that please me infinitely, and meet my desire for the "family thing", characters who are familiar, warm, alive, real'. Recommending strictness without rigidity, he saw the fashions as 'having an affectionate side'. They date from slightly before the year 1901, the year the play was first published; the designer could get an idea of the style from the pictures of Donna Carla that Visconti sent him.

He advised Zeffirelli, responsible for the sets, to begin with the key section, the last act. He maintained that the wet, neglected garden in autumn holds the deepest meaning in the play. The scenes inside the house are 'only a consequence of the garden, they are dominated by the garden, caught in the grip of the garden that is by turns wet, wintry, springlike, nocturnal, lit by the fire in Act III . . .'. An autumn garden . . . On the veranda, the glasses from which champagne has just been drunk. The play begins with a celebration, for Irina, on what is also the anniversary of their father's death. And it ends, amid happy preparations for a wedding, with tears of mourning.

Visconti was born in the autumn, on All Souls' Day. Almost all his celebrations have a funereal cast. The garden, 'like an old photo', Zeffirelli said, is the seat of memory. The house 'caught in the grip of the garden' is the birthplace. Chekhov guided Visconti to the house of childhood and its music – the music of time, of peacefully chiming clocks, of Andrei's violin, of the piano on which invisible hands play *The Maiden's Prayer*. This house has to be abandoned, has to be burned to allow for rebirth. While everyone laughs and Fedotik insists: 'I burned it! I burned it! Cleansed it . . . Everything burned, cleansed. The guitar has burned, and the photo has burned, and all my letters . . .'

'We must live,' insist the three sisters huddled together as they watch their past and their dreams disintegrate. For Visconti, to live meant to work, to devote his days and nights to that 'constant, incredible labour' that any production demanded of him, arousing the fanatical perfectionism that drove him, for example, to spend forty days rehearsing *The Three Sisters*. The theatre was his life, his 'island', which he knew he had created and, with a few other people, was still creating. The task was one 'of scouring rather than inventing', he specified, recalling in passing all that he owed Toscanini in his search for truth, his insistence on imposing order and discipline on actors, even on audiences.

'Re-educate the public, and fast!' he had decided at the start of his career. So he made latecomers wait outside until a play's first act was over. 'One of the first times we did this,' he said, 'was for *Oreste*.' But what made him truly proud was that he had followed his own way, against all odds, often 'ending up out of pocket', and had won over his audiences. 'In a way, too,' he added, 'I had the feeling of creating a school.' In five years he had succeeded in establishing a huge team of set and costume designers and technicians, rather like the Renaissance workshops where collections of artists and craftsmen worked under the direction of a 'master' of the trade who, in this case, was his own patron.

'People rightly spoke of Visconti as the "Master",' Rosi remarked. 'Exactly what did he teach, especially to those who worked with him? We know that an artist's personality is not transmissible, that it cannot be taught. On the other hand, work methods are the basic elements of training. Visconti's fundamental characteristic was to put his co-workers in the most difficult, but also the most exciting, predicament: that of learning. Visconti rarely dealt with established professionals. To his credit, he could spot the potential in those he would later chose to work with him, and could guide them, using a very personal form of discipline made up of rigour, order and careful definition of duties, so as to encourage everyone to assume maximum responsibility.'

Zeffirelli confirms this: 'Luchino called us, Franco [Rosi] and I, and immediately assigned us specific jobs, which considerably bolstered our self-assurance. He gave his co-workers a feeling of responsibility. He was a master in the literal sense, someone who taught, an educator who helped you to know yourself.'

Who were his creatures? Almost all those who worked for him, beginning with his first three disciples, whose names appear in the credits of *The Earth Trembles*.

First, Rosi, who had, it is true, acquired some theatrical experience working in Rome as assistant to director Ettore Giannini, but with no specific direction; like a good Neapolitan, he turned his hand to whatever he was asked to do. In the play Giannini staged, Salvatore di Giacomo's *The Vow*, he played and danced the role of a happy lunatic. He also did the voices of the merchants that came from the wings. He even wandered around Rome with signs he'd drawn himself to tout the show. As it happened, shortly before Giuseppe Patroni-Griffi introduced him to Visconti, he had submitted a plan for a stage version of the *Malavoglia* to Umberto Barbaro, still a teacher at the Experimental Film Centre. He had no other credentials. Visconti nevertheless took him on as an assistant for *The Earth Trembles*.

Second, Zeffirelli. Born in 1916, he was six years older than Rosi, but less experienced. There was some theatrical background: he had just directed and played in a staging of *Intimate Relations*; his sets were tasteful, a product of his Florentine childhood and his schooling as an architect. As far as movies went, he was still virginal.

Finally, there was Aldò, the magician of lights and shadows. For twenty-five years, Aldò Graziati, who was born in 1902, had worked in France as a stills photographer. One evening he climbed up on the stage during the production of *Crime and Punishment* and asked if he could photograph some of the scenes in the play. So enthusiastic was he, so fervent, that Visconti told him, 'Sure, do as you like.' The director recalled: 'I asked the members of the cast if they would pose for the French photographer, and they agreed. They were used to set photographers, and they thought the whole business would be over in fifteen or twenty minutes. But Aldò spent three-quarters of an hour taking his pictures. And the actors were flabbergasted. I wasn't at all flabbergasted, and I began to see how good Aldò Graziati was.'

By the time the terrible ordeal of filming had ended, the three men were fully fledged members of Visconti's 'stable'. They were to remain so for a long time. Rosi stayed, as assistant on *Bellissima* and on *Senso*, until 1954, when he struck out on his own. Many have said that Visconti tried hard to curb Zeffirelli's ambitions during their passionate and turbulent relationship. Franco did not leave until 1955.

Aldò, who died in an automobile accident on 14 November 1953, during the filming of *Senso*, showed himself to be more than a mere technician. 'He was a real artist,' movie-maker Augusto Genina called him, 'full of imagination, courage and – why not say it – a healthy dose of recklessness; he was an artist who "felt the light" and disconcerted everyone by his behaviour behind the camera, following no formulas, working with lights and shadows in a different way each time.' Only one thing mattered to him: finding the tone, the colours that expressed the director's intuition, his deep vision of a film. Aldò was constantly innovating, attempting the impossible, seeking special effects. One of these, as Zeffirelli has remarked, was the very special yellow tinting everything in the 'betrayal room' in *Senso*, where Livia gives her lover the revolutionaries' money. He was constantly searching for a colour that shone, so to speak, from within the characters themselves.

After Aldò died, Rosi and Zeffirelli suggested replacing him as cameraman with Giuseppe Rotunno, who had worked with Aldò on other films, especially in the previous year. But Visconti did not trust his work, and it was only because top photography director Robert Krasker quit that Rotunno was allowed to film the climactic execution and Countess Serpieri's coach trip. From Visconti he got no encouragement. 'Don't expect any help from me,' the director told him. 'Show me what you can do.'

Even (especially?) with beginners, Visconti was terribly demanding, and his rages were devastating. One of Zeffirelli's lifelong friends, Piero Tosi, was just twenty-five when Visconti asked him to design the costumes for *Bellissima*. The real crunch came, however, during the preparation of Goldoni's *La Locandiera* (*The Mistress of the Inn*) for the Fenice Theatre in Venice in October 1952. During the summer, crewmen and friends crowded the house in Ischia. In one room, Zeffirelli worked on the sets for *The Three Sisters*. Tosi was confined to another for weeks on end to design the costumes for Goldoni's insolent Mirandolina (Rina Morelli), the penniless Marquess of Forlimpopoli (Paolo Stoppa) and the newly rich and newly ennobled Count of Albafiorita (Marcello Mastroianni). Colour, line, style, accessories, every item of apparel had to express the characters' personalities.

'Visconti was very stern,' Tosi says. 'He explained how he saw a certain image, in full detail. I designed according to his indications and showed him what I'd done. Then we discussed the colour, and here, too, when he had a specific colour in mind, there was no way of putting anything past him. Like the red dress that Claudia Cardinale wears in *The Leopard*: only that red could express the sensuousness of the character and the scene.'

Finally, there was the research, everything pertaining to the period. If an almost imperceptible detail failed to give the desired effect, Visconti spotted it instantly. Tosi still remembers his explosion of anger when he arrived one morning at the Fenice where the first scene of *Senso* was being shot and saw that the men were wearing black top hats. '"Ignoramuses! Idiots!" he screamed at Escoffier and me, because at that period, in 1866, men wore grey top hats, not black, to the opera. That was a great lesson to me. From the start I learned from him to be meticulous about details. He knew the colour of a period exactly.'

To achieve what was then a novel tone for *La Locandiera*, of sober colours and restrained rhythm utterly unlike the naïve, rather gaudy Goldoni so familiar to Italians, Visconti rejected the sets *à la* Longhi and Tiepolo that were expected of him. Tosi was sent to Bologna, to the house where the painter Giorgio Morandi lived among the vases, the heavy glasses and the roses he painted in his tender, silent still lifes. Would he work on Visconti's *Locandiera*? Morandi refused: he was old, and he had never set foot in a theatre. But the sets designed jointly by Visconti and Tosi, of ochre earth and pink walls and a pale sky, were none the less infused with Morandi's vision.

Two long years were still to go by before the director felt he could fully trust the man who would soon be hailed as a magician of the Italian stage and screen, the man who had learned from Visconti that 'a costume is not an external decoration, it is life itself'. During the filming of *Senso*, the director at last praised him publicly, and that day remains engraved on Tosi's memory.

'We had to shoot a scene in the country, with peasants working in the sun. The heat was terrific. A peasant offered us some muscatel and we went up into a hayloft to drink it, me, Zeffirelli and some Garibaldian officers. I remember we were naked from the waist up because you could really melt that day. At one point, Aldò came and told us that Luchino was looking for us. We were five minutes late at the most. Even before we could stand up he burst in furiously. There was a frightful scene. He warned everybody to stay out of his sight for at least two or three days. "Pierino can stay, if he likes," he added, without looking at me. An extraordinary mark of favour!'

Such favour was rare indeed, and Visconti's Jovian rages remained legendary. While *The Earth Trembles* was being filmed, Zeffirelli reports, the two assistants literally trembled as well. 'He treated Rosi and me like animals. He never asked us to make coffee for him,' because making coffee, 'Luchino's awesome coffee', was an exceptional honour. But it was by acting the authoritarian father that Visconti trained 'his' disciples, stingily doling out compliments and rewards while lavishly distributing insults and criticism and decreeing exile and quarantine.

Gassman, a frequent target of the director's outbursts, got a bit of his own back by revealing that Visconti 'kicked the asses of the most illustrious actresses' and locked Zeffirelli in a wardrobe for daring to ask during the preparation of *A Streetcar Named Desire* if it was really essential to mess up the stockings and linen in a bureau drawer that 'no one was going to stick his nose into . . .'.

A whole anthology of stories about Visconti's tyranny is still going the rounds. Rosi shrewdly analysed the master's cyclonic temper tantrums: 'You got the feeling that Visconti dwelt coldly on the reasons for his irritation and then, still coldly, translated them into invective. I think this procedure was not only a mark of a domineering character, but, more important, was his method for getting what he wanted: he made your attitude towards your responsibilities as painful as possible to force you to think hard about them. It's like some parents with their children. I always noticed that his severity and authority were always mixed with delight at the panic he aroused in his victims. But I never saw them separated from his concern that in future we avoid mistakes, and improve.'

Arm outstretched, forefinger pointing, eyebrows knitted, eyes predatory and threatening: authority crackled in every Viscontian gesture, every expression; as an actors' director, he was a genius. 'He was unrecognizable when he directed,' says his niece Nicoletta, recalling his filming of *The Innocents*, even though by that time, in

1975, illness had seriously diminished both his peevishness and his strength. All the alumni of his terrifying school tell of his bitterly contemptuous remarks, his freezing glare, the ponderous coarseness of his insults. He made even seasoned performers quake. They lived in constant dread of his 'scenes', looking on in embarrassed silence when the directorial storm raged around someone else, some other providential but temporary lightning rod.

Visconti could spot an actor's faults at a glance: vanity, rebelliousness, overacting – everything he considered disorderly. He fostered, used and abused the jealousy that sprang up between actors. He destroyed old hierarchies and created new ones to suit himself, guided by his likes and dislikes, his passions and hatreds.

To needle the self-esteem of the young he was forever praising the old-timers, the actors 'born to the boards', the aristocrats of the stage, those who, like Miss Morelli, were born in harness, those with a name, a past, like Memo Benassi: 'What a marvellous instrument! I just wanted to rid him of his flaws, those ham mannerisms he had adopted on his own out of vague recollections of Max Reinhardt's direction . . . But you told him, "No, listen, let's start over from the beginning, get rid of that stuff, that's not the way you do it, that's not the way you say it, you say this clearly, and that calmly." He was an instrument, a wonderful cello. You simply had to know how to play a piece on an instrument like that. Do you find instruments like that among young people today? Precious few!'

Young people? They are all the students and products of his 'theatrical laboratory' – Giorgio de Lullo, Romolo Valli, Gassman, Mastroianni. He castigated them for lacking the fire, the total devotion to their art that transformed their elders into priests, celebrants of a sacred rite. They even lacked the determination, he said, that makes a boxer 'train seven or eight hours a day if he wants to become a champion'. 'Don't smoke, you dimwit!' he barked like the trainer in *Rocco and His Brothers*. 'Can't you see you're ruining your voice?'

He hated amateurism. 'Young people today just drift into acting, to show off a bit, to attract attention before moving on to something else,' Visconti said in 1953. 'They lack that sort of military training I found in Ruggeri, for example.' Hour after hour of rehearsal. Never mind if they're tired, they can sleep later. If they can't take it, if their nerves are too delicate, they ought to find another trade. Yet only these young protégés could fully satiate this Pygmalion's voracious ambition. Only they belonged to him, body and soul. If he happened to notice them, or they sought him out, he made them his creatures, he changed their lives. Sometimes their beauty alone sparked a brief flash of interest.

A case in point: Olga Villi, who made her début in Visconti's staging of Hemingway's *The Fifth Column*. 'I needed this extraordinarily handsome, blonde, indolent animal,' he said. 'I knew Olga, I'd seen her in a variety show and I thought she had what it took to move up into theatre. And I needed that figure then. What mattered in the play was the feminine presence of that superb "Cadillac" – that's what they called her – during the Spanish Civil War. I didn't hesitate to give Olga her start, and after that she played only in the theatre.' The actors to whom he grew attached for years on end, however, had something else, after all, something to give him.

What counted at the beginning was to find a 'bridge', a deeply anchored rapport between an actor and the character he was playing. There were no miracle formulas for doing that, Visconti said, but there were different ways, training techniques that varied with the performer's personality. 'With some of them you had to be a bit tougher, unbending, with others you could be more supple, you could even plead with them . . . One has to understand them . . . as one understands a horse. I've always said that actors are like horses. One horse may need to do a mile and a half every morning while another gets by with a trot. One has to understand them. If you make the trotter do a mile and a half, you ruin him.'

He was tough with Gassman, who was too reserved, especially in *Adam*. 'Then, one day,' Visconti said, 'I told him, shaking with rage, that he was nothing but putty in my hands and he had to do what I wanted him to do. After that he finally let himself go. He dropped his reserve, his defences, and created a character full of nuance and subtlety. He's not really a man for subtlety, he's a bit – how shall I put it? – all of a piece, right? So I arranged his ideas for him. I couldn't work with someone who resisted, I told him so clearly and he understood, because he's not a moron, after all, and after that everything went very well, he made a hit.'

Visconti was equally rigid with Mastroianni, but for other reasons, because of other flaws: his natural indolence, cohabiting with his acting talent. He always screamed at Mastroianni, Antonioni reports. But 'if he had a good actor he wasn't satisfied with, he knew how to handle him to get the best out of him'. Gassman would later attack him, discount him. But Mastroianni praised him whenever an occasion arose, for he owed him almost everything. 'He not only taught me the trade, he also taught me to love the trade,' the actor says. 'And he taught me not to be a ham, something so many excellent actors don't understand . . . Because of him I entered the theatre through the front door.'

At first this nonchalant actor seemed the least apt to figure in Visconti's troupe. The director had happened to see him act one day, and since he needed someone for *As You Like It*, he hired him. Mastroianni had begun acting more out of boredom than vocation. Before that he had worked as a producer's bookkeeper. The job was dull, and he spent his days reading and declaiming in his office, letting the others worry about the accounts. A fellow had to live . . . Finally fed up with this cramped, colourless existence, he enrolled in Rome's Academy of Dramatic Art, not really to appease an imperious itch, but because of 'the feminine component in my character, which goes with the acting trade and the touch of ham I have in me'.

Most of all, he says, 'I was lucky. Lucky that Visconti needed a raw young recruit like me, lucky that he ran the most important company [in Italy], with actors like Ruggeri, Stoppa, Morelli, Gassman. I was lucky that Gassman left and I could take his place. I was lucky to be in movies.' He, too, thought of Visconti as 'the master' par excellence, 'like the teachers you like best at school because they're intelligent, because they teach well, which is so rare. When I was asked the difference between him and Fellini, I always answered that Visconti was the teacher the pupils liked and Fellini was your neighbour in class.'

Visconti's empire expanded over the years. In both theatre and films he relied on 'human matériel' to provide a stable, solid foundation for his work. In preparing to film *Senso*, he was forced, for business reasons, to make do with Alida Valli and Farley Granger – he had wanted Bergman and Brando – but he knew he could count on a top-flight crew, people like Tosi, Marcel Escoffier, Aldò, the editor Mario Serandrei. All of them had become familiar with the romantic style and sweeping manner of this exceptional director 'who uses film the way a writer uses ink'. And he had the best scriptwriter of the period, Suso Cecchi d'Amico. *Senso*, after all, grew out of her suggestion, one of many, that he adapt a short story of that title by Camillo Boïto.

For some years, the producer Riccardo Gualino, who had financed Visconti's production of *Intimate Relations*, had wanted him to make a film, any film that was 'spectacular, but on a high artistic level'. Gualino, says Cecchi d'Amico, 'was a big Italian industrialist with a passion for the arts. He was from Turin, where he had built a magnificent theatre to which he had brought the Ballets Russes. He was really passionate, the sort of patron who had practically been run out by Fascism.' He also knew what he risked with Visconti, who was about as welcome as the plague at the Ministry of Culture.

Preparation of the movie stretched over a year. It involved painstaking historical research, carried out mainly by the writer Carlo Aianello, who had already worked with plots set in the period of the Risorgimento. Ms Cecchi d'Amico also loved this kind of scholarship. 'Historical research is an excuse, even if it isn't absolutely necessary,' she says. 'In fact, for *Senso* it was ridiculous. With Luchino we studied the battle of Custoza, where the Italian and Austrian soldiers were placed, how it all really happened. But I don't think the film really gives an idea of how the battle unfolded.'

The young woman who began working with Visconti in 1945, translating American plays for him, had been used to movies since childhood. 'I was born to movies, in a way,' Suso says. Her father, the writer and art historian Emilio Cecchi, helped introduce into Italy the American literature vilified by the Fascists. For a year he had been the artistic director of a major production company called CINES. In that heyday of the smart-set 'white telephone' film, it was Cecchi who pushed through the realistic films by Mario Camerini and Blasetti, including the latter's *1860*, about Garibaldi's Army of Sicily. Even after he quit to concentrate on his own work, he was regularly consulted and asked to read countless scripts. 'What happened to me then happened again a long time afterwards with my own children,' Suso Cecchi says. 'He gave me lots of scripts to read to get the reaction of someone younger than he.'

Visconti felt at home with these wealthy Catholic liberals. At first, during work on the *Coach of the Holy Sacrament*, his relationship with the scriptwriter was very formal, with fixed hours, daily work sessions, discussions followed by incessant revision of the script. But, over the years, a relaxed relationship grew up, based on mutual respect, in which attentive, maternally reassuring Suso functioned to some extent as a midwife for scripts.

'We worked quickly,' she says, 'because we enjoyed it, too, it wasn't a chore. It took the form of long, very long conversations. I made him talk on and on so I could get a clear understanding of what he had in mind, then I got it all down on paper and we went over it again, and so it went. Luchino was a perfectionist, and even for the most secondary scenes the transitions had to be flawless, absolutely precise, even if the scenes were later considered superfluous and had to be cut out. Beginning with the first scenarios I did with Luchino, we worked in great intellectual harmony.'

Later on, when he chose a subject, she knew in advance what would interest him, and the long run-up to actual filming gradually grew shorter. Her help was valuable, essential when Visconti was simultaneously directing so many theatrical and operatic works. Their collaboration, which went on until his death, should have been crowned by an adaptation of *Remembrance of Things Past*. 'We talked so often of the book and its characters over our thirty years together that once the beginning and end were chosen, writing the script wasn't difficult,' Suso says.

The first scenario for *Senso* – there were to be three – dates from April 1953. It was written in the Villa Bologna in Castiglioncello, where the d'Amico family spent its vacations. Emilio Cecchi was there, along with Suso's husband Fedele d'Amico, a highly influential member of the Catholic communist group; a musician and music critic, he was the son of the noted theatre critic Silvio d'Amico, who had founded the Academy of Dramatic Art (whose graduates included Paolo Stoppa) before the war. Between the director and the writer there developed a cloudless understanding based on a total communion of ideas and on matching cultures. Beginning with *Bellissima*, all of Visconti's films, except for the

'German' movies, with which Suso always felt ill at ease, were the product of this balance between the writer's serene Tuscan humour and the Milanese director's grave, tormented temperament.

Even today, this extremely conscientious writer regrets having 'miscalculated Viscontian time' in her work on *Senso*: 'Originally, the protagonist's journey through the battle area was of primary importance and should have occupied a lot of time in the movie. Unfortunately, Luchino had already shot too much film. So the most important passage in the movie was reduced to the coach sequence. That was my fault. I didn't know him well enough then, I didn't know that ordinary measurements always had to be converted to his scale.'

Filming of *Senso* was long, 'endless', according to Miss Valli, who even accused Visconti of deliberately slowing down some of the shooting only to make her pay for his annoyance at her idyll with one of his assistants, Giancarlo Zagni. The actress suggested that Visconti was in love with Zagni even though he was small and rather ugly. With Zeffirelli, Girotti and the seductive Farley Granger (whom the director tended to confuse with the character he was playing) all on the set together, the complexity of their relationships is easy to imagine. Be that as it may, the ordeal went on for nine months instead of the scheduled three.

At 9:15 on the morning of 29 April 1953, Visconti arrived from Verona at the first location for the film, Valeggio, in the Veneto. He reviewed the troops, checked the costumes and examined the horses lent by Aosta cavalry officials. The soldiers' equipment was incomplete: they lacked feedbags and mess tins.

On the very first day, the company was immersed in the atmosphere Visconti sought to give his film. It was not to be a faithful adaptation of Boïto's story, which focuses on the two characters of Livia Serpieri and her lover, the Austrian officer Remigio, both of them young, handsome and corrupt. Instead, this was to be an astonishing, sumptuous, melodramatic edifice in which the reciprocal degradation of the Venetian countess and the now much younger lieutenant, named Franz Mahler in the movie, reflects the decadence of the society to which they belong. Livia's passion leads her to betray the cause of Garibaldi that bound her to her cousin, Count Ussoni; Franz betrays the Habsburg Empire, whose defeat by Prussia at Sadova in July 1866, only a month after the Austrian victory over the Italians at Custoza, forecasts its inevitable decline. Visconti himself explained what he was driving at:

There is an exceptional tone in this story that reflects the great political and social movements that matured at the time of the battle of Custoza. And at the end of the love story there is an obvious reference to the twilight of a turbulent period in Italian history . . . In *Obsession*, the love affair of the two protagonists led directly to the murder, a fatal solution to a conflict of interests and to the clash of two personalities. Here it is the military defeat, the choral tragedy of a lost battle that triumphs over the sordid outcome of a love affair.

In Boïto's novella, the spotlight is on the characters. Visconti aimed to make history not just a vague background, but the protagonist of his film. The first title proposed, besides *The Defeated*, was *Custoza*. The film was not to end with Franz Mahler's execution after his mistress denounces him as a deserter. 'Nobody cared about Franz,' Visconti said. 'It didn't matter if he died or not.' Instead, it was to end with Livia fleeing through the streets of Verona, 'passing among the prostitutes and becoming a kind of prostitute herself, among the drunken soldiers. And the final scene showed a simple Austrian soldier, very young, around sixteen, dead drunk, leaning against a wall and singing a victory song. Then he stops and weeps, weeps, weeps, shouting "Long live Austria!" That's what *Senso* was supposed to be like.

'Old Gualino,' Visconti went on, 'my producer, a very amiable man, came to watch the filming and he murmured behind me, "It's dangerous, it's dangerous." Perhaps, but to me the ending was much more beautiful that way.' Those scenes, so similar to scenes in *The Damned* and *Ludwig*, were never shot. Others were cut, especially some of the battle scenes and those concerning the responsibility of Victor-Emmanuel's army in shunting aside Garibaldi's partisans and losing the battle, a defeat that lacked the heroic colour of some defeats suffered by the Risorgimento movement.

In the end there were so many cuts, Visconti said, that none of it made sense any more. The Venice audience did understand, however, that a Venetian woman gave the Garibaldian patriots' money to her lover to keep him out of the fighting, that the army's conduct was criticized, that the Risorgimento was shown as a great revolution betrayed, a great battle lost. The relevance of this to more current events, the inevitable comparison between the second world war's Resistance movement and Garibaldi's struggle for Italian liberation fed the blaze of protest that flared against Visconti. For he had dragged the previously untouchable Risorgimento through the mud.

'In *Senso*,' the director said, 'there is enough material to address both sides: those who want to understand and those who pretend not to understand. Even if people dressed differently in 1866, the problems and situations haven't changed.'

At the Venice film festival his film won no prize, the Golden Lion being awarded to Renato Castellani's very academic *Romeo and Juliet*. But the left was already praising the exemplary transition, achieved only by Visconti, from neo-realistic stories to true realism expanded to embrace history itself.

Despite the depredations of the censor, the movie remains a masterpiece, because of its realism, but also because of its depiction – so much more pitiless and pitiful than in the novella – of a love affair based on sex, squalid self-interest and unfettered romanticism. In this it resembled Strindberg's *Miss Julie*, which Visconti was to stage in Rome's Teatro degli Arti in 1957.

More important, neither Visconti nor anyone else had ever before achieved such perfect fusion between a historical romance and its background music. '*The Earth Trembles* followed my early experience in the theatre,' he said, 'and I can't say it was influenced by the theatre. *Senso* was, because that was how I wanted it. This is shown clearly at the beginning of the film. We see a stage performance of the melodrama and this performance passes over the footlights and into life. The story of *Senso* is a melodrama.'

By this is meant dramatic action accompanied by music, and not the 'melodrama in which Margot wept'*. In his operatic productions, as in *Senso*, Visconti restored life and nobility to an art which,

---

*A reference to the hyper-romantic nineteenth-century melodramas by Alfred de Musset (translator's note).

he said, 'had a bad reputation ever since its defenders abandoned it to formalized, conventional renditions. Italian audiences are naturally partial to melodrama, but it is equally suitable for [other] European audiences because of its very structure, so unified and direct. I like melodrama because it stands at the border between life and theatre. I tried to express my predilection for it in the opening sequences of the film *Senso*.'

By its melodic quality, its symphonic breadth and choral sweep, any Visconti production is musical. This is manifest in his choice of music from *La Traviata* in *Obsession*, from his use of dialect – and the musical quotation from Bellini's *La Sonnambula* – in *The Earth Trembles*, and in the ironic use of the charlatan's song from *L'Elisir d'Amore* in *Bellissima*. These features were never gratuitous or decorative; they served organic internal purposes.

'He was amazingly knowledgeable about music,' says the composer Franco Mannino. 'He had his preferences, of course, as everyone does. These ranged from Verdi to the great German romantics, with a particular fondness for Mozart, whose most obscure works he knew.'

Visconti's stroke of genius in *Senso* was the use of contrasting music by Verdi and Anton Bruckner. The Austrian's dirge-like *Seventh Symphony*, written under the impact of Wagner's death in Venice, accompanies the lovers' nocturnal wanderings through the narrow streets of Venice, Livia Serpieri's debasement, her trip over muddy roads to join Franz in Verona and her final disintegration in the city's streets where, maddened and damned, she shrieks at death.

Responding to this is the music of Verdi, to whom music was more an expression of civic than of romantic passion; Verdi's hymns, after all, were sung by the *carbonari* as they were led before firing squads. 'Talking about Verdi,' said the critic Massimo Mila in 1951, on the fiftieth anniversary of the composer's death, 'is like talking about a father, one who is younger and more enthusiastic than his sons. In Italians' consciousness, Verdi occupies the place Victor Hugo does for the French.'

For the opening of *Senso*, Visconti chose the passage from Act Three of *Il Trovatore* in which Manrico gives up Leonora to fly to the aid of his mother, the gypsy Azucena, who is to be put to death by Count de Luna. The stake is already awaiting her, and Manrico strides upstage singing:

'The dreadful flames of this pyre
'Are burning all the fibres of my being!
'. . . I was a son before I loved you.'*

When the opera was performed at the Fenice theatre in Venice in the 1850s, the chorus's call to arms was immediately echoed in the auditorium when a girl tossed the first bouquet of green, white and red flowers – the revolutionary tricolour – shouting 'Foreigners get out of Venice!' while a shower of tricoloured paper fell on the Austrian soldiers in the audience.

Such scenes, marking the birth and growth of the Risorgimento, occurred in the Fenice and, especially, in La Scala. This may be where *Senso* was really born. Zeffirelli recalls being with Visconti in a proscenium box at La Scala during a performance of *Il Trovatore*. 'At the beginning of Act Four, when the soprano stands at the front of the stage to sing . . . the song of a woman alone in the night, near the tower where her beloved is imprisoned, the feeling was truly extraordinary, shattering. This feeling probably suggested to Visconti the idea for what is now the movie called *Senso*.'

That was during the winter of 1952–3.

On that evening, 2 February 1953, Milan gazed at Leonora through Manrico's loving eyes, for the singer's name was nearly – within one letter – an anagram for La Scala: Maria Callas. But there is another name for that 'strange being who incarnates what is rare, extravagant, exceptional' of whom Visconti had dreamed since childhood: a diva.

*'Di quella pira l'orrendo foco
Tutte le fibre m'arse, avvampò
. . . Era gia figlio prima d'amarti.'

XVI

A Diva

*Nothing could touch those hard-hearted Romans
but a woman's blood.*

STENDHAL

*Only sadism gives the aesthetics of melodrama
a foundation in life.*

MARCEL PROUST

Callas: 'a total theatrical phenomenon. I think one can only find two
or three such cases in the whole history of the lyric theatre: Grisi, so
people said, and then Pasta and Malibran.' Visconti saw her first in
Rome, in the role of the priestess Norma, then in that of Kundry,
'the Rose of hell', in *Parsifal*, the accursed Eve and Redemptress. He
went to hear her every time she sang, fascinated by a soprano voice
that went from the most intense low notes to the most sparkling,
most incisive high ones. He was fascinated, too, by her presence,
the stage gestures that, he said, 'thrilled you. Where did she learn
them? On her own.'

   At the time, she was only twenty-four and fat. The writer Hector Bianciotti remarked that she had that 'naïvely joyous, commonplace [corpulence], bordering on vulgarity, resembling the image of
a soprano that so many sopranos had helped to establish, unattrac-
tive, grotesque'. But she was 'beautiful on the stage', Visconti said;
'I loved her fatness, which made her so commanding. She was
already distinctive then.'

   Not even the flaws in the staging of *Parsifal*, conducted by Tullio
Serafin in February and March 1949 at the Opera, could break the
spell: 'She was still enormous, she was half naked in the second act,

279

covered with yard on yard of transparent chiffon: a marvellous temptress, an odalisque . . . On her head was a little tambourine hat that flopped down on her forehead every time she hit a high note. She would bat it back in place . . .' So what? Visconti didn't miss a single one of her performances. 'Every night she sang, I secured a certain box, and shouted like a mad fanatic when she took her bows . . . I sent her flowers, and finally we met . . .'

Franco Mannino, already Visconti's friend and soon to become his brother-in-law by marrying Uberta, was a frequent visitor to the house on Via Salaria, along with many other artists, including Moravia and Elsa Morante. He introduced Maria Callas to Visconti, for he had worked in Venice with Serafin, the first Italian orchestra conductor to direct her. The meeting took place at Serafin's home, with Zeffirelli present as well. 'We began talking,' Mannino says, 'then Serafin suddenly told Maria to go to the piano with him, and she sang a passage from *La Traviata*. The way she sang that evening remained engraved in my memory and Visconti's.'

By no means everyone agreed that Miss Callas was a genius. Compared to the crystalline voice of Renata Tebaldi, who reigned at La Scala, Callas's voice was odd, lacking the clarity of Italian soprano voices. She surprised and disconcerted rather than charmed opera purists. The reaction to her audition at La Scala in September 1947 was merciless. 'There's nothing there,' her manager, Giovanni Battista Meneghini, was told. 'Send her back to America as fast as you can.'

Refusing to be discouraged, she tried harder, working without let-up. Even so, she had to wait four more years before being asked to take the place of her rival, Tebaldi, in the sanctum, La Scala. This she owed to her meeting in 1950 with the aged Toscanini, tutelary god and living icon of Milan's temple of opera. At eighty-four he had lost neither his fire nor his worship of Verdi. He wanted to celebrate the fiftieth anniversary of the composer's death by bor-rowing a production from La Scala and conducting it in Bussetto, his birthplace, and he was on the lookout for fresh talent.

Meneghini has told of the decisive interview on 28 September 1950, in Toscanini's home on Via Durini – of the maestro's piercing, questioning looks, his praise of her 'prodigious' interpretation of the role of Isolde, his enthusiasm when he heard her sing an aria from Verdi's *Macbeth* 'with impressive poise, power and tone'.

'You're the woman I've been looking so long for,' he exclaimed. 'I've been waiting for just your voice. I shall do *Macbeth* with you.' He had dreamed of staging the Verdi opera, and here at last was the ideal voice as defined by the composer, that of an 'ugly, wicked woman, with a harsh, muffled, sombre voice'.

His plan was never carried out, but Toscanini, who until then had lauded Tebaldi's 'angelic voice', opened the doors of La Scala to Callas, the soprano with a demon in her voice. On 7 December 1951, she opened the season at the Milan opera house singing Elena in *The Sicilian Vespers*, under the baton of Victor de Sabata. Visconti immediately sent her a telegram: 'Madly happy about your new triumph, I send you my most affectionate congratulations after hearing you on the radio last night. I hope I can see you again very soon and be able at last to work with you. Best wishes, best wishes. With my sincere friendship . . .'

Working with Callas – a long-standing wish that was not to be fulfilled until December 1954. In the autumn of 1950, Visconti had recommended that his friends in the Anti-parnaso Association, a group of opera lovers, choose Callas as the light soprano they wanted for a production of *Il Turco in Italia* at the Eliseo Theatre in Rome that October. And Visconti took advantage of his 'historic' revival of Rossini's opera, which had vanished from the repertory for a century, to attend all the rehearsals (two a day, each three to four hours long).

But this amusing role, this opera whose freshness and lightness had so charmed Stendhal, did not entirely satisfy Visconti. Like Toscanini, he loved melodrama and, anomalously in the 1950s, he preferred nineteenth-century melodrama for its grandeur, power and tragic aura. 'He wasn't afraid of ridicule,' notes Fedele d'Amico. 'And he didn't see it in opera. He felt no need at all to defend melodrama for what it isn't, he only wanted to stage it for what it is.'

Between 1948 and 1953 at least ten directorial projects fell through. In 1953 he was within an ace of mounting Verdi's *The Force of Destiny*, with Tebaldi singing Leonora, in Florence's May festival, but the Ministry of Culture stepped in to prevent this communist fellow-traveller from winning new artistic laurels. But political and private enmities alone do not explain his being shunted aside.

Visconti was eager to conquer the operatic stage, especially the Scala, queen of them all. But not at any price. He was asked to do Verdi's *Otello* at the San Carlo in Naples. He refused because only nine days were allowed for rehearsals. A modern opera was offered to him, then Leoncavallo's *Zaza*. Again he refused, openly display-ing his contempt for Leoncavallo's work as 'an opera and a musician with no imagination, no taste, no genius'.

Fate seemed to conspire to keep him out of La Scala: a ballet version of Mann's *Mario and the Magician*, with music by Mannino and book by Visconti, was finally programmed for the 1953–4 season. But shortly before it was to open, a scandal erupted at La Scala: in a work by Maria Peragallo, with a libretto by Moravia, a real automobile rolled out on the stage. Fearful of raising a similar storm when bicycles appeared on stage in Visconti's production, the management put off until some more propitious time – until 1956, in fact – the work that should have marked his admission into La Scala.

In May 1954 he expressed his disappointment and his growing irritation in a letter to Meneghini venting his spleen against 'this respectable management of muddled minds incapable of working out a serious programme'. But now he returned to his obsession: an opera with Maria Callas:

Obviously, if I finally do break into La Scala, I would like it to be with Maria. What do you know about their programmes? Has anyone talked to you about *A Masked Ball*? Should Maria sing it? And if it really is *A Masked Ball*, then *Norma* would be cancelled; in that case, would Maria sing *La Sonnambula*? And with whom? With Giulini? And would she like me as director of *La Sonnambula*? And when? And *La Traviata*? We might plan on slipping it in some time in March or April, or settling definitely on April, when I will be with my troupe in Milan.

At the moment I am busy organizing my work in the theatre and in films, and I am still thinking of working with Maria. Going to La Scala without her doesn't interest me, you understand?

The programme for the 1954–5 season was settled upon soon afterwards. Visconti was to open it with Gasparo Spontini's *La Vestale* before staging *La Sonnambula* and *La Traviata*. In the autumn he returned to Milan, paying frequent visits to Toscanini, who had no sooner recovered from a bout of pneumonia than he was talking about conducting his favourite opera, *Falstaff*, to open the following season at the Piccola Scala. 'Try to propose something new to me, you young people,' he told Visconti. 'All I can see are the old standard sets – always the same tavern, the same garden. Suggest something new, something pretty.'

Meanwhile, the director invited him to a rehearsal. A few days later, the maestro told Visconti what he thought: 'I like very much what you are doing, but don't forget that my eyesight is poor. I find this Callas woman very good, a wonderful voice and an interesting artist, but her diction is unintelligible . . . Opera is theatre, and the words are more important than the music.'

On 7 December the Scala auditorium was garlanded with the traditional red carnations for the opening of *La Vestale*. Toscanini watched the performance from manager Antonio Ghiringhelli's proscenium box. When it ended, the ovation became delirious as Mme Callas advanced to the front of the stage and presented Toscanini with a bouquet that had just been tossed to her.

After the performance, Visconti had supper with Giulini, Wally Toscanini and her father. The conductor, looking at Visconti, proposed a toast: 'To our *Falstaff*.' But his health would never permit them to realize his dream: Toscanini died eighteen months later.

In the book he dedicated to his wife, Maria Callas, Meneghini tries hard to minimize Toscanini's part in Visconti's La Scala début. He even headed a chapter, 'How We Brought Visconti Into La Scala'. According to his account, the director was out of favour with both Toscanini and Ghiringhelli. 'The only people who were really intent on his entering La Scala,' Meneghini wrote, 'were Maria and me. We kept bringing it up with Ghiringhelli; perhaps he got bored with hearing Visconti being recommended to him, and he decided to engage him.'

This was a wholly personal version of what happened, and it was refuted by the firm bonds uniting Wally's old playmate with the patriarch on Via Durini. But any trick was welcome if it tarnished the image of the charming director so publicly idolized by Meneghini's wife. 'Visconti,' he said, 'was vain, always talking about himself, showing off his culture; Zeffirelli, on the other hand, was modest, reserved, gentle, sweet. Maria liked talking to him because he was always moderate and spoke "correctly" . . .' He said that Maria, very reserved and even prudish, experienced great difficulty and disgust tolerating the 'filthy, obscene' language Visconti used – and 'especially at work, when he spoke to women', but never with her. 'You make me sick to my stomach when you talk like that,' she is said to have told Visconti. 'People are idiots,' he replied by way of apology, 'they don't understand anything, so you have to be clear.' Off stage, the soprano allegedly told her husband: 'If he dares talk to me like that I'll knock all his teeth out.' Comments Meneghini, perhaps 'Visconti guessed what was in Maria's mind, because with her he never allowed himself the slightest disrespect'.

The jealous husband reported with delight that one evening at the Hotel Quirinale in Rome, where he was staying with Maria and his mother, they saw Visconti come in with Miss Magnani. She 'wore a dress with a very deep décolletée that bared her breast'. 'How dreadful!' his mother couldn't help exclaiming, overcome by such indecency, and Meneghini assumed that his wife was equally repelled. And, he added, Maria was deeply shocked, 'devastated', to learn that Visconti was a homosexual. 'Visconti himself brought the subject up, making no secret of his preference, and from then on Maria couldn't stand him.'

· How then can we explain that Callas, supposedly so 'disgusted' by homosexuality, formed an affectionate and lasting friendship with Zeffirelli, long before her flaming relationship with Pier Paolo Pasolini? Zeffirelli was a delightful man, Meneghini declared, and Visconti did all he could to come between him and Maria: 'He was a superstar then, God the Father in the theatre and the movies. No one dared stand up to him. He was surrounded by a court of boot-lickers, blabbermouths, gossips, idlers and wastrels who spread all sorts of lies and slander in the salons of Milan society, making and breaking show-business reputations. If the word got out that Visconti was backing a young actor or actress, his or her career worries were over, but his disapproval was equivalent to a death sentence.'

'Visconti had a visceral, jealous relationship with his actresses,' says Suso Cecchi d'Amico. Perhaps he was annoyed by Maria's very public friendship with his 'protégé' Zeffirelli, who had just scored a triumph at La Scala with his splendid direction of *Il Turco in Italia*, starring Callas. The production was shown in April 1955, between Visconti's stagings of *La Sonnambula* and *La Traviata*. Zeffirelli, called the 'little zephyr' by people punning on his name, knew very well how to sail with the wind, to use his friendships – with Callas, with Magnani, with the actress Lilla Brignone, who headed the Olimpio Theatre Company in Milan – to further his ambition, his very high, very pressing ambition.

'A set designer, yes,' Visconti reportedly decreed, 'but never a director.' He wanted to try his own wings? Fine, but he would find out what that would cost him. Starting with strict quarantine, accompanied by veiled threats against anyone – like Ms Brignone – who might offer him a job directing.

There was great commotion and excitement among Visconti's courtiers at the proclamation of Zeffirelli's disgrace. Beware, all ye who, out of ignorance or friendship, continue to see or speak to the fallen favourite. A few weeks later, on a snowy night, the two enemy lovers met in front of the Piccolo Teatro of Milan; bitter, bruising remarks led to a fist fight.

But a year later, in March 1956, they went together to southern Italy and, in July, attended the baptism of Lucia Bosé's son in Spain. And they both sent streams of postcards to Callas. 'Yesterday and today,' Zeffirelli wrote to her, 'we visited Toledo and even watched a bullfight. Tomorrow we continue our trip via Andalusia, and I'm dying of impatience. The shadow of *Carmen* hovers over us. Luchino and I think of you often. And as we drive we always hope for a repeat of last year's wonderful stroke of luck, when, during a violent storm one night in northern France, we heard a rebroadcast of *Norma* on the radio.'

Even if Callas was 'devastated' to learn of Visconti's homosexuality, even if she did then see less of him or even avoid him, flee from him, nothing proves – despite her husband's rather determined insistence – that all she admired about him was his intelligence, his culture and his talent, and that she finally came to dislike him. Every actor and actress of the period succumbed to the tyrannical director's charm, at least for a while, that charm that waxed and bubbled through storms and joys on the job, through the endless rehearsals in which the players anxiously sought the 'master's' approval and admiration. Adriana Asti spoke of the 'magical effect' of Visconti's last-minute encouragement while she 'hung on his every word' before going on stage: 'Go on,' he'd say, 'go on, everything's going to be all right.'

Despite an occasional flare of rebellion, Callas's subjection to him was absolute. 'She did everything I asked so scrupulously, so meticulously, so wonderfully,' Visconti remarked in speaking of *La Vestale*. 'She gave me what I asked for without adding anything personal at all. Sometimes, in rehearsal, I'd say, "All right, Maria, do something you'd like to do." But she'd ask: "What should I do? How should I hold this hand? I don't know what to do with it." The fact is that because of her absurd passion for me, she wanted me to direct every step she took.'

During the production of *La Sonnambula*, she begged her director to accompany her through the wings to the very edge of the stage. To play the second act scene in which the young sleepwalker, Amina, crosses the bridge over the mill race, the singer – who, as we know, was so near-sighted that she really might have fallen – thought of a trick Visconti liked to describe: 'I always kept a hand-kerchief in my pocket with a drop of a particular English perfume on it, and Maria loved the scent. She told me always to put the handkerchief on the divan on which she had to lie during the inn scene. "That way I'll be able to walk directly to it with my eyes closed." And that's how we accomplished this effect. Luckily, no musician in the orchestra decided to wear the same perfume, or she might have walked right off the stage and into the pit.'

And the story is told that during an intermission in *La Traviata*, still wearing her third act costume, a red gown encrusted with glittering stones, she ran to join Visconti in the famous Biffi restaurant; he was leaving that evening for Rome, and she wanted to say a last goodbye. The effect, Visconti noted, 'could have been worse. Suppose she'd come into the Biffi in the nightgown Violetta wears in the last act!'

How much of a part did Visconti play in Callas's amazing physical transformation in the space of three years from buxom odalisque to the sublime Traviata, slender, eye-catching, marvellous, who appeared on the stage at La Scala in the spring of 1955? Her new shape was probably a product of his genius alone. This ideal figure was, wrote Hector Bianciotti, an 'intimate, hidden image', a creature of fiction, a vampire 'to which she would conform and sacrifice herself, and which was strong enough to force her body to bow to its demands'.

Long before he directed *La Traviata*, Visconti had spoken of a Violetta who would have not only the voice but also the body of *his* Traviata; she would not really be Dumas' Marguerite Gautier, but a dream woman, more majestic, more distinctive than a queen. Indeed, all his productions emphasize the diva's absolute monarchy, from *La Vestale* with its marble pavements and columns to *Anna Bolena* and *Iphigenia in Tauris*, in which the sets, costumes, trains, jewels never seemed sumptuous enough to him, or big enough 'to be adequate to the eyes, the face, the features, the stature' of Maria Callas.

At one point she objected to the improbable elegance of the villagers in *La Sonnambula*, the men in black with white gloves, the women in matching shades of pink, white and grey, herself dressed by Piero Tosi in a white silk gown and crowned with a garland of pink, mauve and lilac flowers. 'But Luchino,' she protested, 'I'm a village girl. Why do you want me to appear this way and wear one of my opal necklaces?' And he replied: 'No, you are not a village girl. You are Maria Callas playing a village girl, and don't you forget it.' To him she was more than Callas, she was the reincarnation of Giuditta Pasta, who first sang the leads in *Norma*, *La Sonnambula* and *Anna Bolena*, the first two roles written specially for her by Bellini and Donizetti, only months apart, in 1831.

She was also that unique instrument that would enable him to restore nineteenth-century melodrama in all its glory, to return to the era of Pasta and Malibran. So he could certainly 'pardon' her – the word is his – for the fits of jealousy she subjected him to when she thought he was too interested in Franco Corelli, the handsome tenor making his début as Licinio in *La Vestale*, and for spying anxiously on his conversations with the *Sonnambula* conductor, Leonard Bernstein. She alone, and he knew it, could help him to rejuvenate opera.

'How different,' he'd say, 'from contending with a singer of the old school, such as Ebe Stignani. As the High Priestess in *La Vestale* Stignani was hopeless, with her two stock gestures, worse than a charlady on stage. Unbearable! She was the antithesis of Maria, who learnt and grew from day to day. How, I don't know. By some uncanny theatrical instinct, if put on the right course, she always exceeded your hopes. What do I remember about her in rehearsals? Beauty. Something lovely. Intensity, expression, everything. She was a monstrous phenomenon. Almost a disease. A kind of actress that has passed for all time.'

For the first time, with Visconti and Callas, staging made the action of an opera credible. Not by breaking the rules: 'One should believe what one sees,' Visconti said, 'but the truth must be filtered through the sieve of art.' And that truth had to be reached through the conventions of opera.

When Visconti's début at La Scala was announced, the Milanese public expected that his staging would be colossal; there was talk of a record budget, of having to raise the level of the stage for the set. Spontini's *La Vestale*, written in 1807 at the height of the Napoleonic era, had marked the beginning of nineteenth-century opera, but it had been gone from the repertory for thirty-five years.

People expected a revolution. What they saw was a restoration, a double tribute – to the first of the nineteenth-century melodramatists, and to La Scala; the set, with its play of perspective and its neoclassical style, harmonized with the theatre's architecture. To emphasize this continuity, Visconti had planted columns along the apron like those flanking the boxes.

To end the evening, the director put on a divertissement, a light ballet of the kind opera-goers were used to seeing in the early nineteenth century. After the opera ended happily, with the goddess Vesta miraculously intervening to rescue Giulia, the lovelorn vestal virgin, for Licinio, the general, the curtain rose again on a gigantic set piece. From it emerged the Olympian deities while servants scurried in with tables, dishes, platters of food, even huge sugar peacocks. At the front of the stage, which was decorated with Napoleonic trophies and eagles, dancers performed a ballet. Opera ritual, conceived here as a magical baroque festival, was saved.

Spectators were taken back to the days when Stendhal attended 'the world's leading theatre'.

While Visconti sought to state clearly his faithfulness to the great operatic conventions, the opera itself was an example of understatement instead of the emphasis so natural to such pieces. The sets and costumes were notable for their simplicity and power of suggestion rather than for their profusion. The cast's performance and gestures, like the sets, were strictly guided to correspond to Spontini's music, with the accent on the drama's solemnity and funereal ritual; flame contrasted with cold colours that were to be 'like white marble, moon-struck marble'.

In the same vein, the gestures made by Callas and Corelli were inspired by those Visconti showed them in paintings by Ingres, David and Canova. Callas hated violence and flamboyant gestures. 'I don't like violence,' she said. 'I don't believe it is dramatically effective.' Although she easily achieved the 'sort of expanded feelings, gestures and attitudes that melodrama calls for', Visconti said, she always maintained 'astonishing control, finesse, taste'. A classicist in the grand manner, only she could reach these heights, this majestic nobility.

The atmosphere, like the protagonist, of the elegiac *Sonnambula* was something else again. Designer Tosi called the staging 'almost metaphysical'. The improbable story of young Amina rejected by her fiancé because she had sleepwalked into Count Rodolphe's bedroom one night is used to depict the struggle between the serene forces of daylight, reason and reality, and the uncontrollable forces of night and the subconscious mind. In *La Sonnambula*, Callas became what Tosi called 'a sylph moving through a moonbeam'; Visconti styled her a 'marvellous night-bird'. To heighten the character's evanescent lightness, he resurrected the famous romantic dancer Maria Taglioni and taught Callas to hold herself and move exactly as a dancer does.

The set, harmonizing with the melancholy tone of Bellini's music, was – already – a forecast of what the movie *Ludwig* would look like: the lake (Bellini had been thinking of Giuditta Pasta when he conceived the opera beside Visconti's beloved Lake Como), the castle towers rearing above the forest treetops, a background of blue mountains. 'Luchino and I tried to suggest a lost era, divine and melancholy,' Tosi said. And the bizarre Amina's voice had that coloration that is, so to speak, Callas's signature – all 'veil, moon, opal, with so much iridescence', as André Tubeuf put it. Visconti himself designed the sophisticated lighting to stress the gleaming moonlight and the sunbursts in Bellini's score. Nothing in the composer's stage directions suggested suddenly plunging the stage into darkness, as Visconti did for the mournful aria *Ah, non credea mirarti*, nor, equally suddenly, to turn on all the lights when the girl awakens. As Amina sang her final aria, he gradually raised the house lights, setting the closing measures against the glitter of La Scala's great chandelier.

Visconti's stagings never followed any formula. There was nothing realistic about the sets for *La Sonnambula*, taken from old postcards and engravings, but *La Traviata* had been the first melodrama to use contemporary characters and events. Visconti obeyed the directions in the libretto, making the bullfighters and gypsies mere guests in the dance interlude at the second act masked ball. And he seized the occasion to direct Callas exactly as he would have directed an actress. 'I staged *La Traviata* for her,' he said, 'not for myself . . . For one must serve a Callas. [The set designer] Lila de Nobili and I shifted the period of the story to the *fin de siècle*, about 1875. Why? Because she would look wonderful in costumes of that era. She was tall and slender, and in a gown with a tight bodice, a bustle and a long train, she would be a vision . . .'

By her acting as much as her singing, Callas became the ideal Traviata, a 'dream of the Belle Époque', the symbols Bernhardt and, even more, Duse were for *Camille*, or what Berma's crystallization of the tragedienne's art was for Proust. This was a technical feat, for Act One was designed for a coloratura soprano, with fearsome intervals, Act Two for a lyric soprano and Act Three for a dramatic soprano. It was also a purely theatrical feat, although music and theatre are hard to separate here for, as the conductor Giulini pointed out, 'the singer's every gesture was dictated uniquely by musical values'.

Visconti, Callas and Giulini spent hours analysing every nuance in the score, every subtlety in the character. 'In doing this we discovered a thousand delicate nuances,' Giulini said. 'Let me assure you, it was slow, fatiguing, meticulous work. Not done to win popular success, but for the theatre in its deepest expression.'

Truth and sublimity, theatre and music, art and life reconciled on an operatic stage for the first time – such was the miracle of the 1955 *Traviata*. On 28 May the opening-night curtain rose on a set of dark, heavy hangings, as overloaded with mirrors, exotic porcelains, opaline lamps and Japanese vases filled with pink chrysanthemums as Odette de Crécy's drawing-room in *Remembrance of Things Past*. This was not simply a set, it was reality. 'I was overwhelmed by the beauty before my eyes,' the conductor said. 'The set was the most thrilling, the most exquisite I had ever seen in my life. Every detail gave me the feeling that I was physically entering another world, an incredibly vital world. The illusion of art faded away. And I had the same feeling every time I directed that production, more than twenty times in two seasons.'

Tosi has described how artfully the set designer De Nobili used funereal blacks and golds and dark reds as a premonition of Violetta's death. He tells of how varied Callas's moods were, at times the modest girl frightened by love, at others as bold as Zola's Nana. At the end of the first ball, she strips off her jewels, tosses back her hair, throws her shoes in the air as she sings the famous *Madness! Madness!* When she did this during the third performance, the audience booed her.

In the peaceful country house in Act Two, sweetly nestled in green and blue foliage, the bright, serene garden became a setting for Violetta's tear-jerking interview with Alfredo's father. While writing her farewell letter, Callas adopted a particular way, carefully rehearsed with Visconti, of choking back her tears, holding her brow, dipping the pen in the inkwell and pressing her hand to her breast as she wrote.

Perhaps the most awesome sight was her brutal transformation in Act Three. 'It was frightening to see Callas get out of bed,' Tosi said. 'She looked like a cadaver, some decadent manikin from a wax museum, and no longer a human being but a living corpse. And she sang with a thread of voice, so weak, so ill, so touching; with great effort she reached the dressing-table, where she read Germont's letter and sang *Addio del passato*.'

The spectators had already acclaimed Margarita Wallmann's production of *Medea* in. which Callas, in a blood-red dress, sang lying across the high temple stairs with her long chestnut hair spread over the steps. Yet now some accused Visconti of making the diva sing 'in terrifying positions, through the long hair over her face, or slumped on the ground, or bent over a dressing-table'. Purists complained that 'She had to sing the *Addio del passato* much too broadly, a wail rather than a lament.' Yet this is just what Callas had striven for, a 'sickly quality' in the voice. 'After all, she is sick,' the singer pointed out. 'It's all a matter of breathing, and you need a very light voice to maintain that tired way of talking or singing. Her voice is tired. But that's exactly the feeling I was trying to generate. How, in her condition, could Violetta sing with a powerful, high, firm voice?'

In any event, passions rose at La Scala. Hadn't Visconti betrayed Verdi? 'More Visconti than Verdi, *La Traviata* at La Scala' headlined the *Corriere Lombardo*, and other reviewers publicly castigated Visconti and Callas for breeding this 'two-headed monster' of a *Traviata*.

Meneghini was still denying that the director and his singer were in perfect agreement. She had never obeyed him blindly, he insisted, not even in *La Traviata*. 'He wanted the dying Violetta to be dressed from head to foot by Annina, and that she even wear her little hat. Maria maintained that this was ridiculous; a dying woman doesn't think about putting on her hat. I had to step in and persuade Maria to give in to keep him from having a fit.

'On opening night, when the moment came, Maria let Annina put her hat on her head, as instructed. Then, while singing, she tossed it elegantly into a corner. Visconti, who was watching the opera with me in Ghiringhelli's box, cried, "My God, she's lost her ha!" I said, "She did it deliberately, didn't you notice?" He muttered: "The bitch! I'll make her pay for that!"

'After the performance, he went to protest to Maria, but he got nowhere. In all the performances of *La Traviata*, she refused to sing that scene with her hat on.'

His account is refuted by the shocked headline over one reviewer's story: 'Scala: Violetta Dies in Her Coat and Hat.' Be that as it may, one wonders why the director so oddly insisted on having Violetta die on her feet in this severe and seemly costume instead of leaving her in her nightgown with her hair awry, as tradition prescribed. To shroud her in last-minute respectability? Or, as Zola did in *Nana*, to denounce the conventions of that Third Republic society in which Umberto I, fuddled by pleasure, lost floods of money at the gambling tables and flattered his floozies and his hookers before tossing them aside in the sacrosanct name of bourgeois principle?

The characters portrayed by Callas are all outcasts, sacrificial victims bearing the burden of the tragic forces that crush them: religious authority in *La Vestale*, the conventions of marriage in *La Sonnambula*, middle-class codes of behaviour in *La Traviata*, the royal will in *Anna Bolena* and, in *Iphigenia in Tauris*, the laws of religion and the curse weighing on the family of the Atrides. In all these cases, love conflicts with reality, with society.

The dramatic high point in *La Traviata* is probably the scene in which Visconti sought to show Violetta as a creature whose love life exposes her to public scorn, making her a symbol of the gulf between desire and social conventions. Violetta is insulted by her lover before her chorus of guests, the money he hurls at her is like a slap in the face. 'At that moment,' Tosi said, 'Callas didn't move. She remained perfectly still, her arms outstretched as if she were being crucified.' Visconti would repeat the gesture at the climax of *Rocco and His Brothers*, for the 'crucifixion and killing of Nadia the prostitute'; just as Simone stabs her, she, too, slowly opens her arms.

This is opera presented as an apotheosis and sacrifice of the diva, an outcropping of a forbidden, subterranean world bursting with paroxysmal violence from under the weight of repression. The sets, too, evoked this counterplay: the marble of a temple versus the fire of passion; parades of luxury, rich clothes and jewels while hearts are stripped bare and bodies tortured; song becomes a heart-rending cry, a murmur, a smothered sob. It is savagery – Bianciotti called it 'the mysterious raw reality of love dramas' – and Callas the artist, instead of domesticating and smoothing it, expounds it in all its purity, 'in deep, shrill, murmured, harsh, joyous, painful sounds, as in love'.

Tragic love dramas, these, in which palaces shut like traps on the regal diva. In the 1957 *Anna Bolena* the trap was stifling Windsor Castle, its walls covered with dark portraits of princes and queens; no liberating wind will ever blow through here. Against monochromatic backgrounds of white, grey and black, a single colour splashes violently against Anne Boleyn's midnight blue robes: the scarlet worn by her rival, Jane Seymour.

Iphigenia in Tauris was a subject of tempestuous arguments: Callas, with her Greek background, expected Visconti to set it in ancient Greece, but the director chose an eighteenth-century décor. Gluck, he reminded her, wrote the opera in 1779. And to make the stage the scene of tragic error and sacrificial rite, Visconti needed the inspired architecture of the eighteenth century's greatest theatrical architects, the Bibienas: monumental, majestic sets dominated by marble columns and statues of armed deities silhouetted against a moving, storm-laden sky.

In no operatic production would Visconti ever try for 'reality' except in *La Traviata*, his 'birth opera', the one that took him back to the world he loved, of Proust, of D'Annunzio, his parents' world, perhaps the one through which he could again experience his mother's splendour, withdrawal, defeat and death. Michel Leiris has called opera 'a world apart, separated from reality, but where everything is raised to sublimity, moving in an area so much higher than daily reality that the tragedy twisting and untwisting in it must be seen as a kind of model or oracle'. This is life brought to a level on which passions must be overwrought, desires taboo, punishment bloody and death sublime.

Visconti's most successful production was not *La Traviata*, but *Anna Bolena*. In Donizetti's long-neglected work, Callas, her voice rising from suave nostalgia to the final cry of rebellion against the 'iniquitous pair' who sent her to the block, shattered the record for curtain calls at La Scala: twenty-four minutes of uninterrupted applause.

Visconti, however, said their finest achievement was the *Iphigenia*, in which he wanted to display the singer at the peak of her glory. Taking his cue from the Tiepolo frescoes in the Labia Palace in Venice, he adorned his priestess of Artemis like a queen, an idol. 'She wore a majestic, lavishly pleated robe of pale silk brocade,' he said, 'and an enormous train over which she had a large cloak of deep red.' Her hair was crowned with huge pearls, and a loop of pearls hung from her neck and down her breast.

'At a certain moment she ascended a high staircase, then raced

down the steep steps, her cloak flying wildly in the wind. Every
night she hit her high note on the eighth step, so extraordinarily
coordinated were her music movements. She was like a circus
horse, conditioned to pull off any theatrical stunt she was taught.
Whatever she may have thought of our *Iphigenia*, in my opinion it
was the most beautiful production we did together. After that I
staged many operas without her – in Spoleto, London, Rome,
Vienna. But what I did with Maria was something apart . . . created
for her alone.'

Who was she? What did she bring him? In the summer of 1956,
Visconti associated her with torrid Spain, which, he wrote to her,
'she would like enormously, for it is still vibrant with mystery and
an astonishing charm . . . Muslim and Arab blood runs in Spaniards'
veins like a precious enrichment that for centuries has altered and
embellished their race. It's a bit like the touch of orientalism in you,
which adds so much mystery and so much strength to your
temperament as an artist and as a woman.'

Until then, except for *La Traviata*, he had assigned her to roles as
vestal, as pure young girl, as a forsaken queen loved platonically by
a courtier, as a virgin destined for the chaste cult of Artemis. Now,
as if issuing a challenge, he offered her two roles that were wholly
new to her: Strauss's *Salome* and Bizet's *Carmen*. Both would enable
Callas to express the mystery, the sensuousness that she could only
unleash in song, on stage, where she could give free rein to the
temperament and unsatisfied desires whose power he had shown her
in life itself.

But Callas refused. She couldn't dance, she told him; despite her
past exercises with veils, she didn't want to show herself half-naked
on a stage. He knew that thanks to her he had reached a degree of
intensity, a depth that no other singer could ever offer him. 'La
Sonnambula, *La Traviata*, *Anna Bolena*, *Iphigenia* were Callas's
golden years,' he said, 'and I had some part in that too. With Maria,
I had the satisfaction of watching the birth of an extraordinary
actress. Her *Traviata* and her *Anna Bolena* remain two tremendous
examples of her acting, aside from her singing.' Even more than he
had with Magnani, 'more pagan than Christian, vigorously, noisily
primitive', he felt he had entered an inexhaustibly rich and complex
world that mirrored his torments, and that he was exploring

it, illuminating aspects of it he had never discovered before.

The harder they 'lived for art', the hotter their passions burned in real life. Callas was possessive and jealous of Visconti the man, and he was no less so of the woman he thought of as his creation. In those four years he thought of her constantly, writing to her or, since 'Maria never reads letters', expressing his love and respect for her through her husband. On 13 July 1956, he complained that 'the management at La Scala, as unpredictable as changes in the weather', was thinking of Herbert von Karajan rather than Giulini to conduct *La Traviata* in Vienna; he said how tired he was of working in Italy, and concluded on a teasing note that when he was fed up with everything, even movies, he would 'begin growing flowers. Tell Maria that if she wants to hire me as a gardener, I would happily accept. That way, at least, I'd hear her sing through an open window . . .'

She loved him, he worshipped her, not as a woman, but as the incarnation of his dream of woman, as a diva. The actress Adriana Asti remembers evenings at Via Salaria in the 1950s, with Zeffirelli there, and Callas, who sang and accompanied herself on the piano: 'Madly in love with him. And he with her, because he was always in love with the people who worshipped him. He was a great charmer, he loved to have around him the people who loved him, and he returned their love in his fashion . . . by torturing them, too, because he was very sensitive and fiendishly jealous. He was an incredible man. He punished people, too. "You'll never see so-and-so again . . ." "You'll never do such-and-such again . . ."

'Relationships with him were not like those with ordinary mortals. And there was no one who didn't fall in love with him: Morante, Callas, Marlene Dietrich . . . All those astonishing women covered with jewels, lying on sofas at Via Salaria. And Luchino was always in love. But with Callas it was something special. They went to the seaside together. She was thin and nibbled lettuce leaves, very beautiful, a bit Greek, with the kind of long hair he loved. Luchino transformed the people he loved, he manufactured them in addition to loving them.'

His *Traviata* – the glorification and humiliation of a body, the inexorable transformation of a magnificent creature sapped by illness – forecast the life and passion of his *Ludwig*. Of all the operas he staged 'for' Callas, *La Traviata* was the one most intimately bound up with Visconti's obsessions, with his private world. He had promised her that this would be his 'masterpiece', his 'Ninth Symphony'. He roared like a tiger when Meneghini announced to him with sadistic pleasure in 1954 that a television version was under discussion. 'Maria on TV, like in a goldfish bowl?' The news appalled him. And when Meneghini informed him that His Master's Voice was planning a recording of *La Traviata* sung by Giuseppe di Stefano with another soprano, not Callas, Visconti saw it as 'an insult, a personal insult to Maria and me'. He suspected 'a sly manoeuvre by Di Stefano', who had been so jealous of the favouritism shown to Callas during their *Traviata* curtain calls that he had rebelled after a few performances of *La Traviata* and quit in a rage. Visconti declared:

> Of course this new episode reeks of concerted hostility against Maria. And against the whole May *La Traviata*. Against a production that has on the whole terribly unnerved the incompetents, the idiots, the jealous, those who sensed the approaching end of a mean, routine, intellectually lazy world. Maria can tell them to go to hell. She can threaten not to sing at La Scala again. She can threaten, and she can do it, to sing elsewhere. And then we'll see them all . . . shit in their pants!

A year later, when asked to stage an *Aïda* at La Scala with Pariso Votto, Stella and Di Stefano, he informed Meneghini of his refusal. 'Put even a gramme of brain to work for that trio?' Certainly not. And he brought up the *Traviata* again:

> When an occasion of particular interest arises, if it does (such as the encounter with Maria, with an artist like Maria, for *La Traviata*), then I will again undertake (and, I think, honourably) to continue my work of *revising* our nineteenth-century opera, which badly needs it.
>
> But suppose Maria had sung *Aïda*, then my decision would have been very different, and so would my eagerness at work, my enthusiasm. Because *La Traviata* will endure (whatever the dimwits and the hopeless idiots may say), and it will endure because this 'revision' is now an artistic fact, established thanks

to the art of a great actress like Maria. And don't forget this, that all the *Traviatas* that follow it in the near future, not right away (because it takes time to eliminate the flaw of human presumption) will be a bit like Maria's. A bit, at first, then (when people think enough time has gone by to avoid direct comparisons) a great deal, and then, entirely.

Only a happy few saw the mythical *La Traviata*. Bianciotti, who was among the elect, notes with amusement that over the years the number of that happy few has steadily grown.

XVII

MIRACLE IN ITALY

Have you ever wondered why Italy,
throughout its history from Rome up to the
present, has never had a single real revolution?
The answer that opens all doors may hold the
history of Italy in a nutshell. The Italians are
not parricides, they are fratricides. The Italians
are the only people (I believe) that bases its
history (or its legend) on a fratricide. And
revolutions can only begin with parricide (the
death of the old).

UMBERTO SABA

Italy in the summer of 1956 seemed to Visconti a 'dead land as far as theatre and movies are concerned'. Bureaucracy and routine were stifling. How could he be satisfied with an environment that was so narrowly clerical and petit-bourgeois? This Don Juan of the boards soon considered extending his conquests to other stages, in Britain, in Germany, especially in France. His feverish activity from 1957 to 1959 – fifteen productions including one film, five operas, a ballet plus *Mario and the Magician* in 1956, no fewer than eight plays – bespeaks his insatiable craving for a new public and a new repertory.

From this mosaic of creations, aside from the two operas mounted for Callas at La Scala in the spring of 1957, a few – the most ambitious, the most titanic – stand out: Verdi's *Don Carlo* at Covent Garden in May 1958, followed a month later by *Macbeth* in Spoleto. To these add a series of lower-key productions that were not unanimously praised, but which kept on coming at a frantic pace: Strindberg's *Miss Julie*, a gloomy, exasperated, exaggerated reading at Rome's Teatro delle Arti in January 1957; *White Nights*, filmed almost on a dare in seven weeks and three days; a light, poetic version of *The Impresario from Smyrna*, by Goldini, in August at the Fenice, and, a month later, in Berlin, a ballet called *Dance Marathon*, to a musical pot-pourri by Hans Werner Henze.

The frenzy continued on into 1958, with a January production of Arthur Miller's *A View from the Bridge* in Rome. After an elaborate springtime of Verdi came an autumn seething with theatre: a tribute to Duse in October, an adaptation of Thomas Wolfe's *Look Homeward Angel* a week later, then Visconti's first Paris production, American playwright William Gibson's *Two for the Seesaw*, which Jean Marais had invited him to mount at the Théâtre des Ambassadeurs. The year ended with a Rome staging on 20 December of another American play, *Mrs Gibbons' Boys*, by Will Glickman and Joseph Stein.

That period, says his friend Francesco Maselli, a communist film-maker, was 'a turning point in his life, and because I was very close to him at the time, this was a source of violent arguments that finally separated us. He broke off his relationships with a certain type of people in favour of new kinds of friends. Not despicable people, of course, but less demanding: the theatre world and so on . . .' Many of these new disciples were merely young and handsome and courtiers at heart. Some surely resembled those 'male odalisques', 'petty characters and undistinguished minds' with which, Robert Merle★ tells us, Oscar Wilde liked to surround himself, the better to reign over a court 'that praised with a single voice when the Master praised, decried what he decried, exhaustively copied his vocabulary, his style'.

'If I learned anything,' Renato Salvatori was to say, 'I owe it to him. I was like a big dog, I followed him around everywhere with my ears pricked up, trying to learn. The reason I have those Gallé lamps on these tables is because I once went to Paris with him and he introduced me to them and taught me to love them.'

Thomas Milian, the actor in *The Job*, was more cynical about this. Although with a trace of remorse, he candidly explained why he 'paid court'. He told how, like Rameau's Nephew clowning at the table of the financier Bertin, he worked hard to amuse his host

★Merle, Robert, *Oscar Wilde*, Paris, Librairie Académique Perrin, 1984.

on Via Salaria. 'At table one day, they served a cheese he especially liked, with worms as long as tagliatelle that went in and out all over it. In my mind I revised the old Roman saying, "What a man has to do to eat," to "What a man has to eat to get a part." But at the same time, I was sure that "this time I won't make it." Luchino couldn't believe I was sophisticated enough [to eat] that, I was sure he was expecting me to say "That's disgusting." So I said "That's disgusting" and he burst out laughing while all the others, astonished at my boorishness, stared at me reprovingly, with worms still dangling out of their mouths.

'He befriended me, and to tell the truth I didn't deserve that friendship because all I thought about was myself and my career. Naturally Luchino wasn't interested in intellectual discussions with me about books. He saw me because I amused him – I'm Cuban, my accent is like a Genoese accent – and because I was cute. What's more I was two-faced, an opportunist. And naïve at the same time, and a little ridiculous. He laughed at what I did, for example, when I slipped the very flat, very long gold cigarette case he'd given me into the pocket of the only decent jacket I owned without realizing that it was a table case, and I paraded around proudly with that splendid thing sticking a good inch out of my pocket and falling out every time I bent over.'

Visconti's court, however, also contained people with brilliant minds and refined tastes, people of encyclopaedic knowledge, lively intelligence and insolence: the German composer Henze, the script-writer Enrico Medioli, the writer Alberto Arbasino, the playwright Giorgio Prosperi, and the new actors and actresses who were taking over from the departing old-timers: Corrado Pani, from Rome; the beautiful Florentine Ilaria Occhini; Adriana Asti, turbulent, facetious and very Milanese. To some extent, in those years of quest and crisis, the director leaned on them to push past the boundaries again – his own, and the barriers between categories – to reach an ideal of 'total spectacle in which speech, song, music, dancing and staging converge', and for which melodrama still seemed to him the most accomplished form.

This wasn't a new ambition. It probably crystallized in August 1951 when he signed a contract with Thomas Mann that authorized him to adapt *Mario and the Magician* as 'choreographic action'. He certainly did not take this lightly, given the intense admiration he had long felt for the novelist. The day they met, recalls Franco Mannino, he was extremely nervous, 'almost like a caged lion'. What a relief, what a delight to find that their ideas about the work coincided. 'You are a great man of the theatre,' the author of *The Magic Mountain* told him, 'and I am confident.' Then he read the whole score, including the orchestration. 'I am really pleased,' he said, 'because I was terrified by the idea that my story might be approached from an expressionistic angle. No expressionism in my work.'

So the direction would encompass both realism and the unreal atmosphere of an Italian spa during the fascist 1930s. We know that the character of Cipolla, the magician who exerts his dangerous magnetism on elegant holidaymakers and on Mario, the naïve, sentimental waiter in the Esquisito café – Mario the proud 'knight of the napkin' – was based partly on Mussolini, the clownish mountebank who magnetized the crowds. Visconti did not lean too hard on the anti-fascist implications in the text, however. He mainly tried, with the aid of Lila de Nobili's delicate, nostalgic sets, to re-create the special tone, at once charming and morbid, of his youthful years in Forte dei Marmi.

Long before *The Damned* and the retro fashion he launched, this was his first incursion into the atmosphere of the Thirties – very Italian, though, and magical, with a flying train, a cave full of Hindu deities, little girls with butterflies' wings suspended in mid-air, a bicycle race, a murder, a mixture of the grotesque and the poetic that recalled both Chagall and the Douanier Rousseau. 'We created a new, composite spectacle, chiefly choreographic, into which fit song, ballet and speech,' he said. The choreography was by Léonide Massine, a student at the Imperial School in Moscow who was discovered by Diaghilev; after the loss of Nijinsky and the departure of Mikhail Fokine, he became the star dancer and leading choreographer for the Ballets Russes.

It was a curious show, in which the dancers – with France's Jean Babilée in the role of Mario – were also required to sing, and a children's choir on stage performed along with the band at the Esquisito café and some bongo and clarinet players. The only purely dramatic function fell to the famous actor Salvo Randone as Cipolla the magician, the satanic illusionist, prestidigitator, *forzatore* whose whip makes people dance even when they don't want to. He also represented Visconti the tyrannical director.

After that came another composite show, *Dance Marathon*, taken partly from American Horace McCoy's novel *They Shoot Horses, Don't They?* In the Fifties, the dance contests that Pasolini would later depict were all the rage in the grim little towns on the outskirts of Rome. In *Dance Marathon* the sets and costumes were by a communist painter named Renzo Vespignani, 'a young Italian painter I admire and whom I had long held in reserve for the theatre,' Visconti said, 'ever since he showed me his first drawings condemning an alien world, that of the suburbs and their ghostly housing developments'. He said:

> The idea came to me at La Scala during rehearsals for another ballet – *Mario and the Magician* – that I had taken from a story by Thomas Mann. The idea was born with Jean Babilée in mind. Giving Jean Babilée a ballet idea is like dropping a Japanese flower into a bowl of water. The original vague, imprecise idea develops and blossoms into a big flower full of unexpected colours. So I thought of giving Jean a dance idea, and what could be more total and dramatic than a dance contest, one of those inhuman competitions that go on to exhaustion and hallucination?
>
> With Hans Henze. We'd known each other since the stormy Roman première of his [opera] *Boulevard Solitude*. In flashes of anguish his music revealed to me a musical personality full of genius and courage. I proposed the subject, and he accepted enthusiastically . . . Dick Sanders is another pawn in our game. He brings a fascinating freshness and a new, uncontaminated talent, interpreting life and human relations through dance with modern and imaginative sincerity and intuition, with the grace of a 'snake charmer'.

Berlin's tempestuous reception of this jumble of a show was predictable. Two orchestras were used, a symphony orchestra in the pit and a Cuban band on stage, and the music and dancing mixed pastiches and sophisticated quotations with the rawest street realism. 'I was interested in twelve-tone serial music then,' Henze says. 'Visconti kept asking me for changes, always towards greater musical realism. I even had to compose a pop tune that was played on a record. Luchino was very dictatorial, but in a very persuasive way; it wasn't easy to say no to him. He explained briefly what he wanted, but he left a lot of room for personal imagination.

'Like everyone who has worked for him, I too assumed the attitude of a pupil anxious to learn, to be taught. Because, obviously, Luchino had something that our generation [Henze was then thirty] had lost, this culture that a member of the governing class received before the bourgeoisie had started to turn decadent, a heritage of ideas that transcended fluctuations of taste. I think of myself a bit as his product; at the time, Luchino was interested in young people's work, he was a man who could communicate. His absolute nonconformism, his boldness greatly influenced me.'

White Nights is a typical example of this effort to fuse types and registers, the deliberate creation of a bastard product partaking of both films and theatre, of realism and artificiality, daily routine and 'magic'. A hybrid film, its prime purpose being to give Marcello Mastroianni a chance, without spending too much money, to break out of the taxi-driver parts he was always having to play. And Visconti wanted to get off the beaten track, 'to follow a different path from the one Italian movies were taking then'; the best of these were on the now condemned track of neo-realism.

For the first time, Visconti had his set built in Cinecittà – not the canals of Dostoyevsky's Saint Petersburg, but the Venezia district of old Leghorn, where he had decided to situate the action. The set by Mario Garbuglia and Maurizio Chiari, with its dark, narrow streets and snow-covered little bridges, was to remain a stage set. As in a theatre, tulle veils were used to simulate fog, the density of the mist changing with the lighting. Visconti considered the photography so important that he prepared it with Giuseppe Rotunno 'like a script'. He wanted 'everything to look artificial, false, but when you get the impression it's false, it should begin to look as if it were real'. Explains Rotunno: 'Uncertainty between reality and fiction, magical realism.'

Later on, while admitting that he had come down a bit too hard on the theatrical side, Visconti insisted that the specific techniques of stage and screen could co-exist very well. 'Avoiding theatricality in movies is not a rule. It's a matter of rethinking the origins [of movies], of Méliès, for example.' But what secret alloy, what impossible blend was he seeking when he melted down such a variety of ingredients in the cauldron of *White Nights*? It is a strange echo chamber ringing with quotations from and pastiches of Rossini's *Barber of Seville*, the love motif from *Tristan* and the rock'n'roll rhythm to which Sanders danced so frenetically.

The musician Nino Rota explains it this way: 'The theme of Natalia's love for the tenant is the dominant theme, the philtre music, doomed love . . . In spirit, it is a kind of German romantic music, between Schubert and Wagner. This is a love affair worthy of *Sturm und Drang*, a heroic, theatrical concept. To Visconti, love is Wotan's theme. He wanted trumpets.'

This heroic, archaic world jarred with the neo-realistic details showing the misery of Mario's life and the degradation of the prostitute, who was imported from a neo-realist film entitled *Obsession* – for she was the same woman, Clara Calamai. 'You remember Giovanna in *Obsession*?' Visconti asked the make-up man. 'Well, fifteen years have gone by, things have been tough, she has returned home after years in prison, and become a prostitute.'

All the stratifications of his life are in this: those of his past – the distant Rossinian pleasures, the embroiderers' workshop in Cernobbio – and of the present, with the young hoodlums in a crummy café. The *Obsession* period is in it, as are his years in Paris, with Jean Marais, the Cocteau influence in some of the scenes, and even the memory of Luchino's Austrian fiancée, whom Maria Schell would try, clumsily, to revive.

Then at the height of her fame after her appearance in René Clément's film *Gervaise*, Schell had asked a colossal fee to appear in *White Nights*. But Visconti had made it a point of honour to keep the budget low. He had formed a small production company with young Franco Cristaldi, Mastroianni and Ms Cecchi d'Amico, and had promised to complete the film in less than eight weeks because everyone said he was incapable of making a movie in under six months. While the timing was respected, the budget was stretched. Suso tells of 'spending months in adject terror' as she watched expenditure mounting by the day for this film that was supposed to be 'small, small', dreading that they would all end up with the law after them.

'All in all,' she says, 'it was a disaster because there wasn't a lira and we couldn't find a production firm that would help us. We other partners never made a penny on it. Luchino showed us every reel because, he said, "I don't want you to think I'm doing amateur work." "Don't worry, Luchino, no one thinks any such thing." But fog made with smoke wound up imitating reality, whereas it had to be stationary, and Luchino horrified us by ordering miles and miles of tulle. That was his idea of economy. He had no practical side. The money he spent! He was very rich, and didn't realize. And he was so generous. His gifts were legendary. But what can you do with someone who really functions on another scale? He had exquisite taste. Paper is made today that perfectly imitates fabrics and damask. But he wouldn't even look at it; he examined [fabric] samples and instinctively, invariably chose the one that cost twelve times more than the others.'

At the Venice film festival, Visconti was again denied the Golden Lion. And the film was a commercial flop. Mastroianni was already resigned to his fate: 'I'm a desperate case and I have to accept that. I'm condemned to playing taxi-drivers to the end of my days.'

Visconti nevertheless rebounded quickly from his extravagant, baroque theatricality in 1957 to more direct contact with reality. The American plays he staged then all seem in retrospect to be prologues to *Rocco and His Brothers* in their timeliness, their violence, their stories of family upheaval, their very use of motion-picture methods. For *A View from the Bridge*, which he mounted in Rome's Eliseo in January 1958, he used what is, in fact, a dollying technique: the gradual illumination of superimposed paintings brought the spectator through the streets of Brooklyn to the home of docker Eddie Carbone, finally framing the protagonist the way a tracking shot in a film ends in a close-up. He would repeat the stunt in his *Macbeth* in Spoleto five months later.

Miller's play is about Italian immigrants' difficulties in fitting into American life, and the internal rivalries dividing them; substitute Milan for America and you have the theme of *Rocco and His Brothers*, 'a tragedy of our flesh and blood', Visconti called it. This is banished realism revived after the search for an alternative in 1956–7,

The cult of the diva: with a transfigured Maria Callas as the princess-priestess of Artemis in Gluck's *Iphigenia in Tauris*, staged at La Scala in June 1957.

Passion and cruelty: Visconti controlled and directed Callas's ardour in the *Traviata* of the century (La Scala, May 1955).

Left: A pose Luchino would never forget: his mother offering herself up in his childhood for what sacrifice? Marked with what stigmata?
Below: Rehearsing the scene of Nadia'a 'crucifixion' in the 1960 movie *Rocco and His Brothers*: left, Renato Salvatori (holding the knife) and Visconti; right, Salvatori and Annie Girardot.

John Ford's *'Tis Pity She's a Whore* at the Théâtre de Paris in March 1961. With Visconti (centre) are two of the stars he made, Romy Schneider and Alain Delon – an incestuous father thrust between 'the fiancés of Europe'.

Romina coming to life under the hands of her Pygmalion: left, Visconti directing Romy in *'Tis Pity She's a Whore*; right, in *Le Travail* in 1962.

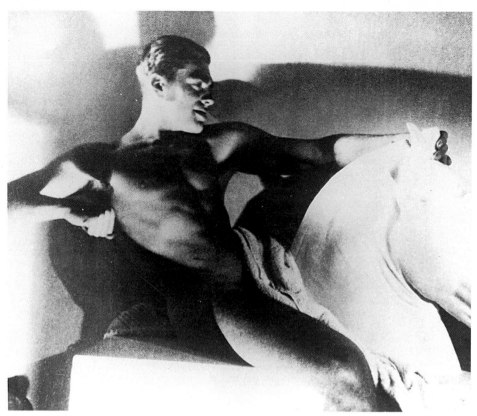

The German photographer Horst, seen by Georg Hoyningen-Huene in Paris in 1934 as a seductive centaur.

An obsessive landscape: the landing stage on the Erba estate at Cernobbio, on the shore of Lake Como.

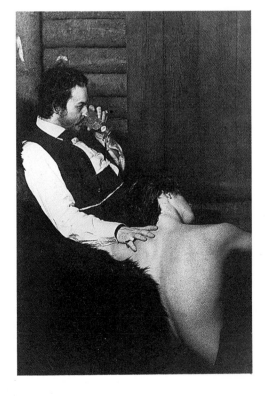

Above: The storm-troopers' orgy on Lake Attersee in the 1969 film *The Damned*.
Right: Ludwig (1972): the intoxication and damnation of the Moon King.

The piercing eye and pointing finger of the demiurge: with Claudia Cardinale and Alain Delon during the filming of *The Leopard* in the summer of 1962.

Making *Ludwig* with Helmut Berger and Romy Schneider in the winter of 1972.

Death in Venice (1971). Silvana Mangano and Bjørn Andresen as mother and son: harmony before the fall.

Grazzano, 1911: Donna Carla casts her spell.

Helmut Berger and Ingrid Thulin in the rape scene in *The Damned*: 'Naked came I out of my mother's womb, and naked shall I return thither.' (Job, I-21)

Visconti shortly before his death.

a period that represented, if not a break, at least a time of anxious questioning, of stock-taking for many leftist artists. Visconti's return to Verdi, to the political Verdi of *Don Carlo*, is part of the same reflux.

Visconti brought *Don Carlo* to London's Covent Garden Opera House on 9 May 1958, to mark the centenary of the Theatre Royal. The opera, composed for 'the big shop' (the Paris Opera) in 1867, had been in his mind for years; he had hoped to make his La Scala début with it. The few directors who risked staging it faced daunting problems: the opera, even with the customary amputation of Act One, was dismayingly long; it required the big treatment, including a cast of at least six top-flight singers who had to be watched to make sure that none of them tried to eclipse the others.

Disregarding the work's length, three and a half hours not counting intermissions, Visconti insisted on staging the uncut version, restoring the first act. He took particular care over his luminous, autumnal setting of Fontainebleau forest, near Paris, where, as in a dream, far from the austere Escorial, the Spanish prince first meets Princess Elisabeth de Valois, who is betrothed to his father, King Philip II.

For the other acts, Visconti deliberately turned his back on all the grim and gloomy sets used until then, especially in Germany, to evoke Philip's oppressive mausoleum-palace. 'Instead,' wrote Fedele d'Amico, 'he showed us a place in full celebration, with green and fire-red pennants floating in the wind, a bullfight atmosphere. And throughout the work he imposed the full weight of [Spanish court] etiquette on the characters – in the splendour of their costumes, the ceremonious dignity of the action. It was left to the music alone to show us the depths of their souls.'

Visconti and Giulini managed to keep an all-star cast working smoothly together: Boris Christoff as Philip II, Jon Vickers as Don Carlo, Tito Gobbi as Rodrigo, Marco Stefanoni as the Grand Inquisitor, Gré Brouwenstijn as Elisabeth and Fedora Barbieri as the Princess of Eboli. With that kind of a line-up, remarked a critic for the magazine *Opera*, 'you can only hope that the prima donna will not predominate, nor the orchestra conductor, nor the director, and that you will simply witness the opera's triumph as an art form – and this is what has happened.'

To celebrate this triumph, which was Visconti's as well, his friends gathered in London: Medioli and Filippo Sanjust, of course, both of whom had worked on the production. Sanjust was a mine of historical erudition and imagination and his name would soon appear in connection with other opera stagings. Medioli's career was to be inseparably linked with Visconti's. Then an assistant director, he would later write the scenarios for Visconti's German film trilogy and was to remain until his death the director's most devoted friend. Maria Laudomia Ercolani was there, too, glowing with youth and beauty; he had known her parents in Milan and he enjoyed her company, her elegance, her tactful, unfailing attentiveness. She went to all his premières, often travelled with him, accompanied him to museums and antique shops and confided in him as if he were a loving, indulgent father.

And they would all assemble again, when summer came, in the grand house on Ischia, in the Moorish tower of La Colombaia, hidden among pines and eucalyptus, where he never remained alone. There were always ten, twenty people around him, sharing his meals in the huge living-room furnished in Renaissance style but with early-twentieth-century Viennese paintings on the walls, the room always filled with the fragrance of roses and tuberoses. And the nightly charades, riddles and other parlour games revived the rites of childhood.

The friends were also sources of new ideas, of clusters of projects to work on together. Out of friendship, Visconti agreed to mount Verdi's *Macbeth* to inaugurate the Festival of Two Worlds introduced by composer Gian Carlo Menotti, and he would continue to participate in the festival in 1959 (with Donizetti's *Il Duca d'Alba*), in 1961 with Strauss's *Salome*, and in 1963 with a new rendering of *La Traviata*. The stage at Spoleto is small and its facilities limited. But the challenge appealed to him.

'Who's conducting?' he asked when Menotti asked him to participate.

'A young American named Thomas Schippers, twenty-eight years old, a child prodigy who became a conductor at eighteen.'

'Where can I stay?'

'With me,' Menotti told him.

'Luchino slept in a hole of a room alongside a terrace,' Medioli recalled. 'He said he felt as if he were in Regina Coeli [prison], but in fact he was having a wonderful time. He loved simple things, he took life like a sport, without making a drama of it.'

A few hours before the première of *Macbeth*, Menotti remembers, Visconti found a scorpion in his sink. 'For heaven's sake don't kill it,' he exclaimed. 'It's a lucky sign. I was born under the sign of the Scorpion. It's going to be a triumph!' It was indeed a great *Macbeth*, not only because of Schippers's conducting, but also because of the feelings of anxiety, sequestration and horror that Tosi and Visconti aroused with very simple means: a circular set like a skull that gradually bursts, with the lighting of painted tulle veils creating an autumn forest, a cathedral of dead branches, a well in the moonlight that looked, Tosi said, 'like a mouth full of rotten teeth'. Ruins and blood in a strange, magical light. In the middle of the performance, blond pages dressed in red velvet held up a big white sheet stained with Duncan's blood.

Why, in that period of cold war and disillusionment, did Visconti choose two of Verdi's gloomiest operas? Wasn't Verdi primarily the musician of heroism, fanfares, the fiery impetus of the Risorgimento, of Manrico's aria *Di quella pira* in *Il Trovatore*?

So he was, but he was also the musician of the sombre *Macbeth*, in which black-clad exiles rise up hopelessly, like the tragic mothers in *The Earth Trembles*. And of *Don Carlo*, finished just as the composer learned of the military defeats at Custoza and Lissa; this was a work of disenchantment, a broader, more realistic study than *Macbeth* of the tragedy of power, of sacrifice, of sons crushed under the combined weight of the Church and the Realm and their fathers' rule. At the heart of *Don Carlo* is the vain plea for independence for the subject people of the Low Countries, a theme that obsessed Visconti – he would take it up again in the 1959 *Duca d'Alba* and in *Egmont* in 1967. Between the two was to come a second production of *Don Carlo*, this one in Rome.

Don Carlo and, soon, *Simone Boccanegra* owed their revivals more to the shadowy government power plays that followed the end of Italy's dictatorship than to any renascence of old-style Verdi heroes whose 'romantic frenzies', said Alberto Moravia, 'anticipated the rhetoric of Fascism and the camomile of petit-bourgeois Christian Democracy'.

LUCHINO VISCONTI

Is there, in fact, a hero – aside from Rodrigo – in *Don Carlo*, a work of 'rare and tortured subtlety' in which the musicologist and conductor Gianandrea Gavazzeni (who directed the 1957 *Anna Bolena*) saw an imprint of 'decadence'? In contrast to many operas, the characters here are not one-dimensional. Philip II, although an absolute monarch, is drawn to the liberal Rodrigo, Marquess of Posa, who plots against him but admires his energy and strength of character. Don Carlo vows to assist his friend the marquess in helping the Netherlanders oppressed by his father, but his suicidal 'heroism' is veined with darker, more complex feelings: his rivalry with his father, his forbidden love for the woman he nevertheless calls his mother, and a homosexual impulse towards Posa. This is a family conflict that concentrates and reflects the towering confrontations of Throne and Altar, of Absolute Monarchy and its subjects, repression and revolutionary ferment.

Visconti's favourite mirrors were these family microcosms dramatizing both individual and social conflicts. Even in his preference for Verdi, 'the Prometheus of the Risorgimento', we see his passionate concern for and identification with oppressed sons. Except that in his works, as in those of Tennessee Williams, fathers remain perversely invisible. In *The Earth Trembles* the father is dying, in *Bellissima* he is withdrawn and powerless.

In *Rocco and His Brothers*, the film Visconti was already thinking about when he staged his first *Don Carlo*, the father is dead; in the family photo Nadia examines in the slum home of Mother Parondi and her sons, 'you hardly see the father,' Visconti notes, 'he's just a little fellow . . . The sons owe everything to their mother. She is their model, they the copies. All five sons, big, strong, handsome, as she sees them and dreams of them, take after her. Their father, obviously, was indispensable but insignificant. In fact, at one point this little man disappears, he dies, they have carried him off and thrown him into the sea.' The film should have begun with this sequence, to underline the continuity of the sea here with the tragic sea in *The Earth Trembles*.

The Earth Trembles has been conceived in an impoverished, 'purified' post-war Italy. Why go back to Verga, to the problem of southern Italy of which *Rocco* was the second chapter, in the Fifties, a euphoric period when a man like the industrialist Enrico Mattei

310

could in himself embody the victory of the new capitalism? Since 1950 roads had been built, and aqueducts, the Fund for the Mezzo-giorno had financed huge irrigation projects. Firms like Olivetti and Montecatini had opened plants in Naples and Sicily. And the big landowners had been obliged to grant nearly two million acres of fallow land to landless farmers.

To which Visconti retorted that Italy had never been so divided nor had the prejudices of northern Italians against southerners been more acute and tragic than in those years of the Italian economic miracle, 'when the press daily recorded the odyssey of southern workers going north in search of jobs and success'. These were the workers who provided the victims for the voracious serpent in the coats of arms of Milan and of Alfa Romeo – the serpent of rampant capitalism that also figured in the Viscontis' arms.

'I wanted to listen to the secret voice of reality in the south,' he said, meaning 'a civilization and a people kept by the north in a condition of inferiority, of moral and spiritual isolation based on privilege'. In this he joined Carlo Levi, the author of *Christ Stopped at Eboli*, who in 1960 described the misery of the south: 'Poverty, always, hunger, disease, promiscuity, the crowded houses, roads like sewers, debts, usury, unemployment, the flies, the insects . . . The age-old greyness of relentless poverty.'

Visconti was also emulating such writers as Danilo Dolci, who published studies on banditry and underdevelopment in the south, and Rocco Scotellaro, who died in 1953, aged thirty, in a poverty-stricken village in Lucania. The director entitled his film *Rocco and His Brothers* in honour of Scotellaro, 'one of those defenceless prophets in whom I believe', one of those who made people hear the 'secret voice' of the south, of those forgotten peasants in distant Lucania vainly protesting that their villages, too, were part of Italy.

Vainly indeed: southerners who went north were not considered 'brothers' but strangers, intruders, invaders who could be moulded and enslaved at will. To Visconti in 1958 – the year when argument raged over Lampedusa's book *The Leopard* and its restatement of the southern problem – it seemed urgent to talk about this fratricidal struggle, mainly between the southerners and the Milanese, between brothers 'as united as the fingers of your hand'. Not, the director said, to stir people's emotions, but to 'move them to reason'. And the story had to be told realistically, in keeping with 'that moral attitude towards events, towards life' that he called realism, 'an attitude, in short, that enables us to look clearly, critically, at society as it is today, and to recount the facts concerning that society'.

The idea that most interested Visconti, as it had Verga, was that of the defeated, the victims and martyrs whose degradation and suffering he chronicled and whose cause he espoused. There was no theme more modern, he declared than that of 'the failure and derision visited upon society's most generous individual impulses'. His adaptations of Miller's plays – *Death of a Salesman* and *A View from the Bridge* – and his production of *Dance Marathon* had already given him a chance to describe how individuals are crushed in a profit-seeking, competitive society.

But in *Rocco* Visconti was also depicting the crushing of a civilization. 'I don't mind at all conceding that a newspaper would run the story of *Rocco and His Brothers* as crime news,' he said, 'but I want to insist on its *exemplary* nature. Through the totally imaginary specifics of my characters and story I think I have posed a moral and idealistic problem typical of the historical moment in which we are living, and typical as well of the state of mind of people in the south: on the one hand, hope and a desire for renewal, on the other, because of the paucity of remedies, they take refuge in despair or in very incomplete solutions, like the individual assimilation of each southerner into a way of life imposed on him from outside. This is the framework for my story which, as we know, ends with murder, and which I focused on an aspect of the southern character that I think is extremely important: the sense, the law and the *taboo of honour*.'

Rocco is derived from a number of books, by Gramsci, Verga, Dostoyevsky, Mann, and the Milanese author Giovanni Testori. Mainly, however, it is based on the real lives of migrants in the great northern cities, on southern customs and on Milan, not the gilded Milan of Visconti's childhood with its palaces and patricians and La Scala, but the Milan of the Porta Ticinese, the sordid working-class quarters, the tawdry little bars and rows of slum tenements dimly lit by the street lamps.

One thread, slender but strong, guides his work: the story he discussed with Suso Cecchi d'Amico in the spring of 1958, about 'a family . . . a mother and her five sons. There absolutely had to be five of them. That was his idea. And everything started from there. Then he began saying, "I want to do this in a sports setting, boxing, a setting where there's violence."' Most Italian boxing champions were southerners.

A year of planning, of discussion, of hundreds and hundreds of surveys, of location scouting, research that soon grew to gigantic proportions. As with *Senso*, the writers fell away one by one, leaving the field to Suso Cecchi; with Medioli and Visconti, she wrote the final script. At first, each scriptwriter received a chip of a 'narrative bloc' centred around one of the five brothers. Pasqualino Festa Campanile and Massimo Franciosa, both southerners, worked on the funereal prelude that was finally dropped, and on two of the brothers, Vincenzo, the eldest, and Rocco. Medioli took on Ciro, the combative workman, while Ms Cecchi d'Amico concentrated on Simone, the boxer. Visconti himself did the angriest, most dramatic sequences, especially the murder scene, in a work designed as a descent into hell, a crescendo of violence.

Between each of the three treatments of the story, the writers referred back to the research reports, shuttling between their typewriters and reality. 'We spent countless hours in gymnasiums,' Ms Cecchi d'Amico reports. 'I spent a year in them, and I don't like boxing. Gradually the subject took shape. Luchino came to my place in Castiglioncello with Pratolini to talk and talk. When he talked he was a great actor. He began telling us what he'd seen in Milan, the southern emigration to Milan. Then we went to see those incredible houses where the southerners lived.' And each time, they added a detail, a scene, so that the first treatment was a staggering eight hundred pages long. Sometimes, too, a detail had to be changed. Contrary to what the writers had thought, for example, nostalgia did not count for much among the southerners; few of them wanted to go back home.

Two scheduled endings were also discarded. Visconti reported:

At a first stage of the scenario Ciro did not end up at Alfa Romeo. To unite southern and northern Italy ideally, he thought it necessary to find a job connecting Lucania with Lombardy. And we imagined that the brothers chipped in to buy a lorry. They paid for it in instalments . . . and used it to transport [goods] from Lucania . . . oil, for instance, or other products from there. So Ciro made those trips between Lucania and Milan and that way he was convinced that although he had settled in Milan, he hadn't deserted his village, he had bound it to the north. But that seemed so far-fetched to me that I killed it.

At another stage of the scenario, the film ended with Ciro returning to Milan after a visit home. He came back up with a load of Lucanian oil that his brothers then sold in Milan. But I thought that was vague, and I dropped it; Ciro was in Milan, and that's enough. Being in Milan, he goes to work in a big factory . . . and his ideals, which had started out a bit as petit-bourgeois ideals, changed, because he had been assimilated into his surroundings and his conscience was awakened.

Another possible ending was eliminated, too: Rocco going mad, and his mother deciding to go back home with one of her sons. Visconti also abandoned an even more didactic ending than 'the symbolic finale, emblematic of my pro-southern convictions', for which he finally opted. Ciro, the 'positive' character in the film, complains to his kid brother Luca during a strike that he's in a bind: at the plant he has to fight for the workers' rights while bearing the burden of the family's mistakes.

This was a long, wearying process of exhaustive research, endless corrections, continual pruning. To complicate matters during this slow preliminary process, Visconti broke his contract with producer Cristaldi, who tried to dictate shooting schedules, rules, even the cast; he suggested Brigitte Bardot and Pascale Petit. 'If the worst came to the worst,' Visconti told him, 'I could see hiring them as manicurists, but I want Annie Girardot.'

None of this was really important, Cristaldi says, but it was enough to make the director 'stop seeing me as an ideal producer and for him to appear to me as completely different from the one who for me had been not just a director, but a friend and associate. Our relationship ended after a series of telegrams that could never be published in a respectable book; I was even surprised the postal service agreed to send them.'

He was replaced as the film's financier by Goffredo Lombardo, of Titanus. Renato Salvatori said he had acted as the go-between in that arrangement. Tired of forever being stuck with supporting roles, he had brought up Visconti's name, hoping to profit if they got together, but not really believing they would. To his astonishment, the powerful Neapolitan producer and the famous Milanese director hit it off at once. Except that Lombardo didn't at all see an Italian actor doing *Rocco*. He wanted Paul Newman.

Everyone knew the importance Visconti gave to casting. To him, the actor was already the character. He had based Simone, the killer brother, on Salvatori, or so the actor says: a character deeply attached to his mother, sentimental, but subject to uncontrolled fits of violence. Visconti had seen him fight Umberto Orsini one evening over the beautiful Rossella Falk. 'That aroused his enthusiasm,' Salvatori says; 'we walked all night near his house and he kept saying: "But you could have killed him! That's not a bad backhand you've got, not bad."'

At Visconti's insistence, Lombardo accepted Salvatori. For the actor, this meant five months, four or five hours a day, of intensive training in a gym near Via Salaria. By the time filming began, that routine had put him completely in Simone's skin. He took the part so seriously that he even fell in love with Girardot and married her when the filming ended.

She was Nadia, the hooker. Visconti had already directed her in *Two for the Seesaw* with Jean Marais in Paris in 1958. The first time he saw her she amazed him; he had made her go through the entire play and she never once spoke to him familiarly. 'Out of respect,' Salvatori says, 'enormous respect. Alain,★ too. Luchino tried to put people at ease, but he just couldn't; he awed everyone.'

Always on the lookout for new talent, Visconti had quickly recognized Girardot's; she had a professional's flexibility, but she stuck to her own temperament, too, that sadness that Salvatori mentions, 'the anxiety that goes back to her childhood, her separation from her mother, her father a drug addict, the uncertainty she

★French actor Alain Delon.

carried deep inside her'. She, too, had recognized Visconti's astounding faculty for 'leading an actress until gradually she became, without realizing it, an extension of life itself, achieving, more by instinct than intelligence, a total fusion of the player with the character'.

Paolo Stoppa, making his motion-picture début in *Rocco and His Brothers*, sounded like the 'magician' Cipolla in *Mario and the Magician* when he spoke of Visconti's 'real clairvoyance'. Because the director, he said, 'has an undefinable inner strength, his direction is not instruction, but a kind of hold on an actor's subconscious mind. Only the great directors, the *real* ones, have this quality. Visconti is a genuine director, as Toscanini was when he conducted at La Scala.'

Katina Paxinou, who played Pilar in *For Whom the Bell Tolls* and who was accustomed to playing such roles as Electra, Jocasta and Hecuba, had no trouble slipping into the part of the mother, Rosaria, a 'Lucanian Hecuba, a southern Niobe', because southern Italy, she commented, 'is sort of Greek'. For Visconti she was a perfect model of a southern mother, not retiring and silent, like the Sicilian women in *The Earth Trembles*, but rather like Magnani in *Bellissima*. 'She's a woman who *believes*,' he said. 'And she is the source of all initiative. She wants to do everything, stick her nose in everywhere; she is a kind of maternal power who considers her children almost as objects, as forces to be exploited . . . She is everything, father and mother both. That's how I want her, I want her melodramatic, nervous, intrusive, domineering.'

And then there was Rocco. While staging *Don Carlo* in London, the actors' agent Olga Horstig, who worked for Visconti and for many of the top French stars of the period, introduced him to her new protége, Alain Delon. The moment the director saw him he *saw* Rocco. And he built the role around him. Delon, then twenty-three and unknown, was magnetically handsome. 'I needed his ingenuousness . . .' Visconti said. 'If I'd had to take another actor I would have refused to make the picture. Especially since he has that sadness of someone who has to force himself to hate when he fights because instinctively he's not like that.'

An angelic Delon. Even today, Giovanni Testori still sees him that way: 'He's unforgettable as a man, a person, a friend. There's a gulf in his life between his charm and success and his deepest wishes. He dreamed of being an ordinary fellow. That's impossible now. I'm sure that his most fervent wish today is to be forgotten.'

So, Delon as Rocco, not seeking glory in the ring, but trying to atone for his brother Simone's crime and to expiate his own transgression: as a good southerner, he feels guilty for breaking an age-old taboo by stealing Simone's woman. The two characters represent the two faces, one dark, the other sunny, of a single truth. Their confrontation, Visconti said, had to be 'terribly violent: each of the two brothers had to hit bottom . . .'. Simone is the fallen angel, knocked off his 'suburban superman' pedestal. Rocco is the glorious, martyred angel who renounces his love for Nadia. The scene, filmed on the upper level of Milan's Duomo, emphasizes the sacramental nature of that renunciation. In every prize-fight, taking punches, perhaps being booed at by the crowd, he is expunging and atoning for the blind violence he is horrified to recognize in himself.

'Rocco,' said Visconti, 'is the most sensitive, spiritually the most complex [of the brothers]; he wins success that, for him – since he feels responsible for Simone's misfortunes – is a form of self-punishment. He becomes famous through boxing, a trade he detests, because when he is facing an opponent in the ring he feels his hatred of everything and everybody explode inside him. A hatred that horrifies him.' This is a film about sacrifice, of Nadia the 'sinner', of Rocco the 'saint' – nowhere else would Visconti exalt sacrifice so highly. In the south, Rocco says in the movie, custom demands that a master mason, when he begins building a house, throw a stone at the shadow of the first person who passes by because a sacrifice is needed to make the house solid.

To show Delon what was expected of him, Visconti himself played the scene in French, amid a deathly silence. Was he personally aware of bearing a sort of ancient guilt, the 'burden' of errors by *his* family, of deep-rooted violence? And did he feel a need to atone for them through the struggle and self-purification of unrelenting work, to sublimate them through art? Didn't he see each of the characters in himself, each of the brothers, not to mention Morini (Roger Hanin), the homosexual trainer who bursts into a gym – it is lined with mirrors like a dance-hall – and runs a predatory eye over the young fighters' sweating bodies?

A prize ring: a theatre of truth under the implacable glare of overhead floodlights. It is no accident that Visconti installed his in Milan's old Principe Theatre. Here a boxing match becomes an eruption and a purification of violence, a ritual exhibition of pain, like Greek tragedies, or those wrestling matches that the critic Roland Barthes compared to bullfights, spectacles that bespeak both the Cross and the pillory. All through the film Visconti hinted that opera and theatre had that sort of relationship to prize-fighting. For the 'unnatural activity of boxing' is so close to show business with its rituals, its daily training, its days of glory and pitiless failures, its public displays of bodies triumphant or battered and defeated. Of course a boxer is first of all an athlete, a champion adulated or jeered. But he is also and equally an exhibitionist prima donna, a naked matador stripped of his suit of lights and subjected to inhuman physical torture. An illuminating reference to Bizet's *Carmen* is clear in the parallel filming of the end of the movie: Rocco-Escamillo fighting while Simone-Don José stabs Nadia-Carmen.

Rocco and His Brothers is all that at once. First, it is about the fall of a boxer, like so many falls from glory one reads about in the newspapers and which, Visconti remarked, often end in bloodshed, in 'compensatory murders'. It is also about the disintegration of a southern family engulfed by a modern city, one of those monstrously inhuman cities that, like the serpent swallowing the babe in Milan's coat of arms, devour all those they welcome – a family story in the Mann tradition, and a social tragedy about the fate of immigrants in Milan and elsewhere. Finally, it is a tragic ritual of the kind you might see on any stage in the world. It is a masterpiece because of the perfect realistic fusion of these various levels, individual and group, documentary and artistic, profane and sacred, and because it so successfully synchronizes melodrama and life.

From the first day of shooting, 22 February 1960, to the last, 2 June, the merciless progression of this realistic drama was caught by the dark eye of 'Carmen', one of Giuseppe Rotunno's three cameras which he adorned daily with a fresh red carnation. Most of the extras played themselves, prostitutes from the Naviglio, teenagers from the working-class suburbs, aristocrats in the luxury hotels in Bellagio, on Lake Como.

The sets were painstakingly spotted and reconstituted by Mario Garbuglia, who said he 'only slightly accentuated' the feeling of the hundreds of apartments he inspected, where he met a host of strange, pathetic people. 'Luchino wanted to feel a sort of virginity about the interiors I set up for him and which he refused to look at ahead of time,' Garbuglia said. 'He wanted to get a fresh, immediate impression. I remember how moved he was when shooting began and he walked into the interior set up for the Luca family celebration (of Vincenzo's engagement to Ginetta). I had even managed to have some typical Easter cakes sent up from Lucania.

'*Rocco* is a film that came entirely naturally to me; I didn't have to research it, I knew the atmosphere as well as Luchino knew the atmosphere of *The Leopard*. I had hunches. For example, no one knows that in the finale, the house giving on the backyard was not so much inspired by Milanese backyards as by the idea of having a chorus, as in Greek plays, for the tragedy occurring on the second floor. We raised this modern, contemporary story to the level of Greek tragedy.'

Similar fertility of imagination was required of Piero Tosi, who devised and designed the women's costumes, but who crisscrossed southern Italy in search of jackets, sweaters, undershirts that 'already had a long life behind them'. One day he saw a man working on a road and bought his coat and pants: just the thing for Simone. 'As he undressed he grumbled, things we couldn't hear. Then – he was no admirer of the party in power – he told us it was all the fault of the Christian Democrats. We asked him why and he replied that his "clothes are full of holes because the Christian Democrats are running things".'

Visconti's dark eye, more all-seeing even than the dark eye of Carmen the camera, let no false note get by him. From scene to scene he remembered every detail, every nuance, fold, colour, every lock of hair. A few jokes were allowed, a little kidding around by the favourites, especially Delon, but most of the time a religious silence shrouded the set. Shouting matches were frequent, especially with rebels like Salvatori. 'Luchino could blow out your nervous system,' he said. 'It's not that he was nasty, but he was a perfectionist.'

One day he told Salvatori to report for make-up at seven o'clock in the morning and then kept him waiting until eight that evening. Negligence? Personal revenge? It is true they were at daggers drawn at the time. Disorganization? Not at all. Visconti simply needed that exasperated, frantic face for a shot lasting only a few seconds. The result was even better than he had hoped for: when Salvatori was told he would have to do a retake because there had been a maverick bit of wire over the lens, he punched the wall in fury and broke his wrist – but the shot was perfect.

'Another time,' the actor reported, 'we went for two months without talking to each other. In a scene with Delon, the sound man came over to tell us we were talking too low and we couldn't be heard clearly. Luchino thought I was the one who was talking too low and he told me to talk louder. In fact it was Alain's fault, but [Visconti] got sore at me and screamed, "Where's your voice coming out of, your — —?" When he lost his temper he used pretty bad language. I answered him back just as obscenely and walked out of the theatre. Two months without talking to each other; it was a real ordeal, but I couldn't let him accuse me unjustly. It didn't matter, anyway. If only people like that, vile temper and all, could come back!'

As usual when Visconti filmed, work on *Rocco* was a series of battles, and not just with the actors. He fought with local officials who refused him access to some places, especially to the setting he had chosen for the murder, the Milan seaplane base, where a slain prostitute's body really was found a few weeks later. The ban was ordered because of 'the immorality and inappropriateness of a scene too closely related to reality'.

The dispute released a cascade of anti-Visconti vituperation in Milan's newspapers by Ambrosians furious at seeing their city being dragged through the mud, especially by a Milanese. Typical is the letter published by *Il Giorno*: 'Hasn't Luchino Visconti ever thought of making a movie about "his" native city, about its residents' generosity, passion for work and sincerity? You would almost think he'd be ashamed to say he was born in Milan! And now he's making a movie about the "passion" of southerners who come to Milan in search of work and food. For Mr Visconti's information, the "peasants" who really come here to work and live in peace with their northern brothers are welcomed as brothers . . .' Visconti had no choice but to forget about the seaplane base. The scene was finally shot on the shore of Lake Fogliano, near Latina.

This was just a foretaste of the commotion the film would foment. It was branded obscene not only because it dealt plainly with homosexuality, but also because the rape was considered intolerably realistic and brutal. In fact, the scene was darkened – literally – by the local censor in an access of modesty that recalled the days when fig leaves were clapped over the nudity of public statues. This was a lesser evil, producer Lombardo decided, than having the entire sequence cut out. 'People see it just as well,' he said. 'It's just a bit darker.'

At the Venice festival, Visconti expected to receive the Golden Lion. It went to France's André Cayatte for his *Passage du Rhin*. Hacked up, even banned in some districts of Italy, ensnarled in a lawsuit that dragged on for over ten years, *Rocco* was nevertheless director Visconti's first big money-maker. Nor had the censors' frenzies discouraged him: three months later in Rome's Eliseo Theatre he staged a play by Testori, *L'Arialda*, that showed the same thugs, the same migrants, the same homosexuals lost in the fog and neon of soulless suburbs. The *Rocco* scandal sprang to life again. When it was staged at the Teatro Nuovo in Milan, the play, by the Italian counterpart of France's Jean Genet, was immediately banned. On 25 February 1961, the newspaper *Corriere Lombardo* published the writ of embargo in full, listing all the morbid, erotic, porno-graphic and immoral situations in a work devoted exclusively, 'pathologically', to 'bottoms and penises'. The play was condemned as a 'symptomatic expression of homosexuality that is more a mat-ter of medicine than of art'.

The outcry quickly took on national proportions, prompting the Christian Democratic leader Andreotti to intervene; he publicly deplored the play's 'deleterious repercussions on the entire Italian theatre' and demanded that measures be taken 'to end a now grotesque situation'.

This was not the first time Visconti had provoked a scandal, and it would not be the last. But Italy as a scene of combat no longer interested him; for the time being, it was not worth the effort. He would do no more work in Italian theatres until his staging of *The Cherry Orchard* in the autumn of 1965.

On 24 October 1961, he published an open letter to the Minister of Culture decrying the campaign mounted against *Rocco and His Brothers*:

You have made a point of indicating that had it depended solely on your authority as a government minister, it would never have appeared on a screen, or would have appeared only insofar – I do not know how or to what extent – as it was clerically mutilated.

This confirms me in my already deeply rooted conviction that the few crumbs of freedom from which one can benefit in our country are not owed to government officials with your mentality (one frankly wonders by what miracle they hold such important posts), but to the vigilance, the resistance and the struggles of the opposition and of democratic public opinion. If there had not been so strong a protest at the time in favour of *Rocco and His Brothers*, not only on the part of Italian culture, but also from the parties, press and organizations of the left, we can be certain, after your statement today, that the film would have been stripped of its constitutional right to be shown to the great mass of spectators and thus enjoy the public support that everyone recognizes it has and which – this is worth noting – has turned it into the Italian motion picture industry's biggest box-office success of recent times, after *La Dolce Vita*.

Please allow me to recall these facts to you publicly, Minister, for they are closely related to the recovery of the cultural and industrial prestige of Italian cinema, for which you and your bureaucrats never fail to usurp the credit in your official reports and statements . . .

As regards me personally, Minister, you did not spare me the most insidious criticism when you referred to, no less, the negative opinion of a prominent Soviet representative on a visit to Italy.

I obviously cannot, on principle, exclude the possibility that old-fashioned and blameworthy ideas on art might still persist among the official representatives of a great socialist country like the USSR. If I understood correctly, however, the person to whom you alluded deplored the proliferation of pornography that has characterized Italian motion pictures in the shadow of administrative censorship by Christian Democratic governments. Have you ever wondered, Minister, if by any chance this person was referring to pictures signed by film-makers in your party, directors who, in any case, have never protested, neither in their work nor their words, against the clericalization of the State, and who are thriving like the proverbial worm in the apple?

To conclude this venomous tirade, Visconti again referred to his film's outstanding success, not only in Eastern Europe, but also in Britain and the United States, countries where 'partisanship and criticism are based on a love of truth and not on fear of the devil'.

XVIII

THE PRINCES

*Noblemen live in a private universe that was not
directly created by God. They created their own
universe over centuries and centuries with their
very particular sorrows and joys. You see, they
worry or rejoice about things to which you and I
attach no importance, but which are vital to them
. . . Prince Salina, for example. Why, for him it
would be a tragedy if he had to give up his
summer holiday in Donna Fugata . . . But if you
asked him what he thinks of the revolution, he'll
tell you that there is no revolution and that
everything will go on as before.*

FATHER PIRRONE in *The Leopard*

*I am neither Sicilian nor a prince. I do not weep
because an old-fashioned world is collapsing. I
would like the world to change faster.*

LUCHINO VISCONTI

Until the end, Visconti would cause scandal wherever he went,
would invite protest, controversy, official anathema. From the 1960
L'Arialda to Harold Pinter's *Old Times*, which he directed from a
wheelchair in 1973, he pursued his quest for truth, intent on tearing
off every mask, stripping every body brutally, ritually. At fifty-four
he was as unrelenting as ever. He was still being excoriated, still
being censored. That was a good sign: in the theatre, as in life, only
excess excited him; joy came from breaking rules and rousing the
torpid. He was not ready to lock up his passions, or to imprison and
chloroform Eros.

When [Antonioni's] film *L'Avventura* was released in 1960, he went to see it with Delon. It baffled him; this was a world that would always remain foreign to him. Intellectual puzzles, the new 'inability to communicate', the emotional frigidity besetting the new movies and novels in Italy and France – were they what modernism was all about? 'There is no old and new,' he replied. Elizabethan John Ford and 'decadent' Oscar Wilde were just as modern as the latest plays of Pinter or Miller or Testori. Visconti was interested in tortured bodies, not emotional crises. Love as he presented it did not decompose in the bleached, white light of Antonioni's movie *Eclipse*, like the light of a nuclear catastrophe; it was all dance, convulsion, animal rage in the violent light of *Rocco*, the blood-red skies of *L'Arialda* and the veiled and sickly moonlight of *Salome*.

In Visconti's work love is never tepid and garrulous. It is an explosive intrusion of fatal beauty: the first sight of Tadzio in *Death in Venice* and of Konrad in *Conversation Piece*, Angelica's first appearance in *The Leopard*, and Salome's arrival in his staging of the Strauss opera in the spring of 1961.

For that brief return to the Italian stage, Visconti personally designed the sets and costumes, basing himself on the series of lascivious Salomes painted by Gustave Moreau. The curtain opens slowly, ceremoniously, on Herod's palace, a building out of a desert fable, with a polished marble staircase flanked by boulders and guarded by a soldier. A half-risen moon casts a greenish light, half-naked slaves carry torches, the music is disturbed and sinuous. The black Salome, Margaret Tynes, appears at the top of the stairs and walks down, nude from the start except for an ample, pink-lined black cloak. Instead of the regulation striptease, the dance of the seven veils is turned into a frenetic pagan ritual during which, while the tetrarch looks on lustfully, the princess dons the veils the slaves bring her. The moon, too, becomes veiled, gradually taking on the blood-red cast it will have when Salome kisses the Baptist's icy lips.

Eroticism in Visconti's work is poised between the sacred and the profane, between exaltation and havoc; it is both a vibrant manifestation of life and a suggestion of the omnipresence of death. Most of all, it is cruelty and deadly danger. Beauty elicits idolatrous worship, but also provokes death-dealing profanation. This is true in *Salome*, of course, an early example of Wilde's dictum that 'each man kills the thing he loves'; here the lovelorn virgin demands the head of the man she desires, and is executed in turn by Herod, whose deadened senses she had briefly revived. Visconti was drawn to other works describing similar immolations, beginning with Herman Melville's *Billy Budd*: although Captain Vere, a latter-day Saul, thinks longingly of Billy, the handsome young foretopman, he nevertheless has him hanged.

Equally characteristic was the director's attitude towards beauty. He was often said to 'melt' when faced with a seductive creature. But the photographer Horst also remembers that at the house on Via Salaria Visconti kept a liveried servant who was very handsome, but whose head was shaved. 'He was too handsome,' his master explained. 'It's better this way.'

His approach to the performers whose charm most troubled him is revealing. An example: unlike the director Josef von Sternberg, who saw Marlene Dietrich as the 'blue angel', the 'scarlet empress', the pure glorification of a disembodied, ideal image forever immured in perfect, inaccessible beauty, Visconti subjected her entrancing body to outrages that made it seem, if only briefly, spoilt, soiled and punished.

Rocco marked the appearance of a sadistic attitude that fed on the raw violence in the plot; not even Delon could get through a prize-fight sequence without a scratch. In *The Leopard* the same actor shows a wound that, though heroically acquired, none the less leaves him temporarily one-eyed. The handsome, blue-eyed, catlike Arabs on the beach in *The Stranger* have bruised, swollen lips that recall Caravaggio paintings in which a spot on a velvety fruit foretells its spoilage. As vicious as the violence in *Rocco* is the beating that bloodies Helmut Berger in *Conversation Piece*, and in *Ludwig* his cruel transformation from unmarred beauty to puffy ugliness is extraordinarily suggestive.

Accounts of the director's personal relationships with his most intimate friends, such as Zeffirelli and Berger, all agree on one point: each affair was one of constant confrontation, an interplay of cruelty, jealousy, reciprocal humiliation, a war of nerves with occasional brief truces. Visconti was in fact attracted to those who could stand up to him, humiliate him, punish him as he humiliated and punished them.

'I first met him during the *Rocco* period,' Testori said, 'and I was his friend for years; I was so fond of him that our quarrel shattered me. Wonderful, the performances he got out of his actors; wonderful, the way he received you at home, as if the king himself had arrived. But he could also be pitiless. Maybe his secret passion was to dominate and destroy . . .'

Visconti could not contemplate pleasure or even beauty – as in *Death in Venice* – without pain and punishment, without a ritual death. Although he occasionally brought a frivolous, resolved atmosphere to life, it was always tinted with nostalgia, with the autumnal colours of eighteenth-century fantasy bathing a paradise lost forever. For him, as for Wilde and Proust, love was always guilty; no matter how lucid he was, no matter how free he fancied himself, he had to overcome obstacles and taboos to love, had to pay for the terrible pleasure of transgression in money and/or pain.

He only attached himself to men he could not possess: men who were married, like Massimo Girotti, or 'committed', as Delon was to Romy Schneider, or who were flighty, frivolous and capricious, like Berger. Love as Visconti depicted it was always forbidden love, even though all the talk in that period was of free love. Less a hedonist than a puritan, less pagan and Greek than Roman Catholic, he dwelt on the last remaining taboo, of incest, insistently staging it in *'Tis Pity She's a Whore* in 1961 and filming it in *Sandra* in 1965 and in *The Damned* in 1969.

John Ford's play, detailing with extravagant horror the love affair between Giovanni and his sister Annabella in elegant, depraved Renaissance Parma, opened at the Théâtre de Paris on 29 March 1961, to a tepid critical and public reception. Attacked in Italy for the violence and obscenity in *Rocco* and *L'Arialda*, Visconti was accused in France of portraying incest as a children's tale. Incredulous critics counted on their fingers and asked in chorus why he couldn't have displayed his mad magnificence at less cost: a cast of sixty, 600,000 francs' worth of painted backdrops, fabrics, jewels, furs, pounds and pounds of cloth for a performance that went on for three and a half hours. Parisians had praised the sobriety, the delicate, balanced aestheticism of Visconti's version of *La Locandiera*, done in the measured manner dear to the French. But they scorned '*Tis Pity*, as they later would *Ludwig*, for its opulence, for the director's wild prodigality.

An excuse to deal with a shocking and obsessive idea, the Elizabethan drama had been chosen mainly to introduce Delon to the stage. After hesitating briefly, Visconti decided that Annabella could only be played by the ravishing, twenty-three-year-old Austrian actress Romy Schneider, only recently emancipated from the candy-box-pink crinolines she wore in the movie *Sissi*. The newspapers were full of the Delon-Schneider idyll, which was said to have bloomed despite the opposition of Romy's mother, Magda, the celebrated star of Max Ophuls's film *Liebelei*. Called 'the fiancés of Europe', they were both young and charming, but neither had ever appeared on a stage before. And Romy still spoke German-accented French.

What's more, they were going to have to play opposite some of the period's most terrifying veterans: Valentine Tessier, Daniel Sorano, Sylvia Monfort, Lucien Baroux and others. 'We were two fledglings fallen out of the nest,' Delon says. 'The first day there was an Italian-style reading, at a big table on the stage, with the forty-five characters. Everybody who counted in French theatre was there, all the regulars . . . [Elvire] Popesco with her cane to see that "everything was *oll rrright*". And to top it all off, Romy and I couldn't find a cab and we arrived late. It was awful!

'We read – what hell! It was dreadful, total panic. But Luchino was extraordinary; he gradually put us at ease during rehearsals.' Visconti took the unusual step of starting Delon and Schneider off rehearsing for hours on end in their hotel, without the rest of the cast, who were 'monsters', he told the pair in the fond tone in which a lion-tamer might talk about his big cats, but very sweet, very nice. Then, one day, he threw them into the lions' den. 'I never rehearsed the death scene, the scene in which Giovanni kills his sister, with the rest of the company,' Visconti said. 'I always rehearsed it separately, so they would shed their reserve. For they'd had no stage experience.'

Finally he announced: '"Well, today you'll play the death scene."'

"In front of everybody?"

"Yes, in front of everybody."

'They played it so well that all the other people in the cast applauded them. From then on, Delon and Schneider felt at ease. And they were grateful to me for that. Because I had entirely "manufactured" them away from the others.'

Visconti did not mention Romy's hideous anxiety. True, hers was a family tradition of life behind the footlights. But would she be as good as her mother was? Or her grandmother, Rosa Rhetty, the Austrian Sarah Bernhardt, who had shared the public's heart with the equally famous Katharina Schratt, an intimate friend of Emperor Franz-Josef? At every rehearsal she felt Visconti's implacable, inquisitorial gaze upon her. Sitting in the darkened auditorium, he let slip an occasional 'Not bad, Romina, keep it up'. That was all. Then, one day when she was exhausted, stumbling over her lines, she felt she simply could not go on to finish the scene with a song in Italian, as he had ordered. Turning to him, trembling, she stammered that she just couldn't, not today . . . Tomorrow . . .

He blew up. 'Do what you please,' he said. 'But you might as well know that if you walk out that door, you can pack your bags and go home to your mother.' She sang the song – because, her director said, she really had the stuff that makes an actress.

The play was scheduled to open on 9 March. On 6 March, after the first of two dress rehearsals, Romy collapsed with acute peritonitis. But on 29 March, after a brief convalescence, she walked out on the stage gowned in silk brocade, as catty and snobbish as they come, to face the critics and audiences who were ridiculing Visconti as 'the scholar, the man of taste, the spoiled child'.

'Who cares?' he remarked in 1966. 'The most intelligent actors understood why I wanted to have real, precise, exact things on the stage. A legend has grown up about me, of the insatiable director, the terror of impresarios and theatre managers. There is a mountain of stories, amusing but false, about my care in staging a show. "That nut Visconti," they say, "wants real Cartier jewels, French perfumes in the bottles on the dressing-table, Belgian linen sheets on the beds . . ."

'I have always thought that theatre is first of all a spectacle, that is, the expression of a visual event. A staging should be judged uniquely on its relationship with the text and the way the text is played. If I am directing Miller's *Death of a Salesman*, the staging obviously need not be lavish. But if I am doing a seventeenth-century tragedy, John Ford's, say, I must necessarily consider its Elizabethan elements, which are extremely showy . . . The truth is that these accusations of waste and hedonistic self-indulgence have always come from people who still think it's a luxury to eat in a railway dining-car.'

The coolness of Paris audiences did not, of course, affect his Balzacian belief in the interplay of sets and characters. In *The Job*, the film sketch he made with Schneider that summer for *Boccaccio 70*, his characters – the Milanese Count Ottavio and his Austrian wife Pupe – perform against sets of breathtaking luxury.

The story, suggested by Suso Cecchi d'Amico, was based on Maupassant's novella *Au bord du lit* (*Beside the Bed*). A young wife makes her husband pay cash for her charms in revenge for his philandering with call-girls on whom he lavishes money. The scene is Milan, as it was for *Rocco*, but this time among the city's aristocrats and rich burghers, whom Visconti knew well and whom he analyses with a moralist's ironic detachment. Pupe the Austrian and Ottavio the Milanese count: the pair that Visconti and Irma Windisch-Graetz (Pupe to her friends) would probably have formed had he remained true to his class, immersed in gilded idleness. The wealthy heiress would have spent her life going to fashion shows and La Scala, lunching now and then with Wally – Wally Toscanini, of course. A lacquered existence, frivolous and empty, in which sophisticates read Alain Robbe-Grillet's *Les Gommes* (*The Erasers*) and Prince Tomasi's *The Leopard*.

Dressed and transformed by Coco Chanel, Romy was no longer the egregiously apple-cheeked young Austrian she had been. By offering her this new part, by exposing her body, Visconti was showing her a new image of herself in his libertine mirror: that of a real woman, sure of herself at last, elegant, sophisticated. The other two sketches in *Boccaccio 70* were dominated by two stars of the moment, Anita Ekberg and Sophia Loren. Against them Visconti ventured his latest discovery, his newest creature.

When the filming ended he took her to dinner and, at the end of the meal, slipped on her finger a bejewelled wooden ring that had belonged to his mother, an astonishing mark of favour. Antonio Pierfederici is one of the few other people to have been similarly honoured: while staging *Intimate Relations* in the Forties, Visconti had asked him to choose among several rings. When the choice was made, the director exclaimed: 'I knew it! You couldn't have chosen any other. It was my mother's.'

Now he was looking for a new sex symbol, which he thought he had found in Schneider, but which he also spotted in Girardot and Claudia Cardinale. From each he stole the natural power to shock that lurked in their gestures, eyes, voices. He dared to strip Romy naked, disgruntling the censor, who briskly did away with the tip of a breast he thought was not for display. In Miller's play *After the Fall* in 1965, Visconti had Girardot do a strip that shocked even the Parisians. And he intensified Cardinale's steamy sensuousness, her hoarse voice and laugh, to shake up the starchy formality at the prince's dinner table in *The Leopard*. As the actress noted in talking about Angelica, the character she played in the film: 'When she shows up at the Salinas' in Donna Fugata, her costume shows how aggressive and vulgar she is. The dress is a bit tight, not in the least elegant, but her eyes and body are ambitious. It's a kind of revenge on the land by the people.' With her earthy, incandescent, animal sensuality, Cardinale combined sexiness and innocence.

Life . . . Despite its pessimism, *The Leopard* is from beginning to end a vital reflection of a society and its members. Nothing in this movie is didactic or forced. 'The historical and political motifs do not overwhelm the others,' Visconti said, 'they run in the very veins of the characters, like essential elements in their life's blood.'

And what characters they are! There is Prince Fabrizio (Burt Lancaster), who sees his world collapsing, but who prefers irony and wit to lamentation even when courting death because, as Lampedusa put it, 'the nobility has the reserve that goes with its misfortunes'. And Tancredi (Delon), his nephew and favourite, like Stendhal's Fabrice del Dongo, makes for the hills where the Garibaldians' camp-fires flare in the darkness. There is the Jesuit priest Pirrone (Romolo Valli), trotting vainly behind Don Fabrizio and waiting for him to confess, meanwhile teaching the peasants of central Sicily a moving lesson in why aristocrats will always be different from other mortals. We meet Don Calogero Sedara (Stoppa), the newly rich Mafioso and the big winner in the struggles of the Risorgimento, who struts in evening dress at Prince Salina's and by turns applauds republican Garibaldi, the House of Savoy's accession to the throne, and the execution of Garibaldi's 'rebels'. And there is Angelica (Cardinale), now rich enough to restore Tancredi's fortunes. All of them are caught up in a twin flourish, of a ball, and of history; this is no longer simply the detailed reconstitution of a period, it is a true resurrection of a vanished society.

In 1958, Visconti's enthusiasm for Lampedusa's newly published novel contrasted with the suspicion, even the open hostility of many Communists who detected a whiff of reactionary ideology on every page. In the front ranks of its detractors was Alicata, who had been made even touchier about matters of orthodoxy by the upheavals in the Communist Party in 1956;* at the mere mention of *The Leopard* or of Prince Tomasi his temper flared. How could anyone defend a novel in which the Risorgimento was reduced to a 'noisy romantic comedy' with 'a few tiny specks of blood on its clownish dress'? And what was the moral of that line about everything having to change so that nothing changed?

Declared Visconti: 'I liked the novel by Giuseppe Tomasi de Lampedusa immensely. I developed an affection for that extraordinary character Prince Fabrizio di Salina. I was so excited by the critical controversy regarding the novel's contents that I had to step in and speak my piece. That may be what made me agree to make this film.' The proposition came in 1961 from Goffredo Lombardo, who had produced *Rocco and His Brothers*.

It has been widely stated and restated that Visconti was 'the Leopard' in his manners, his lifestyle and his sensitivity, in his ideas and critical appreciation of the Risorgimento. And in his view of Italy's progress since the end of the war-time Resistance, 'the leaden lid of "transformism" that has thus far prevented real change in our country'.

'I share Lampedusa's viewpoint,' he said, 'and, I may say, that of his character, Prince Fabrizio; I support them not only in their

---

*In 1956, Pietro Nenni broke away from the Communists to work with the Christian Democratic government on a reform programme as he gravitated towards the Socialists. At the same time, Soviet repression of the Hungarian uprising inspired communist leader Palmiro Togliatti's policy of 'national roads to Socialism' and what he called polycentrism in the world communist movement (translator's note).

analyses of the historical facts and the psychological situations [the facts] engendered, but even beyond this – meaning the places where the book is darkened by their pessimistic thoughts on contemporary events. Prince Salina's pessimism leads him to regret the end of an order which, however static it may have been, was nevertheless an order.' As a faithful follower of Togliatti, however, Visconti added that 'our pessimism vitalizes our determination, and instead of longing for a feudal, Bourbonian order, it aims at establishing a new order'.

In the film, the treachery of Tancredi, who swaps his Garibaldian red shirt for the uniform of a Savoyard cavalry regiment, grows directly out of the theme of a betrayed, deformed revolution. The ball is just what Togliatti saw in it: on the one hand, an 'apotheosis' of the old aristocracy facing its inevitable decline before the rising new class of parvenus represented by Angelica's father; on the other, the 'disaster' to revolutionary hopes indicated in Colonel Pallavicino's champagne toast to the failure of Garibaldi's march on Rome in 1862. The novel ends on the macabre, grotesque image of the stuffed dog Bendicò that, when thrown from a window, fleetingly takes on the fantastic form of the prince's heraldic leopard before crashing to the ground in 'a little heap of livid dust'. Visconti and Suso Cecchi d'Amico preferred to concentrate all the changes that had occurred in Italian society between 1860 and 1862 in a single climactic sequence, the famous final ball, so 'mercilessly critical' and yet so lyrically Proustian.

'It has been said,' Visconti noted in an interview with his friend Antonello Trombadori, 'that it was mainly "the memory" sequence and the premonition that fascinated me, the heartbreaking refuge in the past, and the obscure, unconfessed forebodings of a vague catastrophe, and that therefore I adopted a reading closer to Proust than to Verga . . .' In fact, he went on, he had merely continued the investigation he had begun with *The Earth Trembles*, in the shadow of Verga's *Malavoglia*, and had continued with *Rocco and His Brothers*, responding to an 'imperious need to trace the historical, economic and social bases' of the tragedy of southern Italy.

At the same time, he said, there was a 'love-hate' relationship towards 'a world fated to perish amid dazzling splendours'. This was Proust's world, too, casting its lights and shadows over the whole ball sequence. A perfect fusion occurs to illustrate the finale chosen for the film: in the small hours of the night, while Prince Fabrizio turns towards the morning star and dreams of the 'rendezvous' it will someday give him 'far from everything, in its realm of eternal certainties', shots crack out from across the city, where the last of the Garibaldians are being executed. In the carriage taking him home with Tancredi and Angelica from the Ponteleone palace, the dozing Don Calogero is awakened with a start by the gunshots. 'A fine army,' he says, 'they do things properly. That's what we needed. Now we'll have some peace.' Whereupon he yawns and goes back to sleep.

A new class has come to power, a new feudal order of hyenas and jackals, more rapacious than the 'leopards'. Its triumph shines out in the marriage of Tancredi the aristocrat to Angelica, the land-owner's daughter. Filmgoers saw more clearly than the book's readers what the emotional and sensual reasons for the marriage were, but the match is also recognized for what it is: a contract based on a coincidence of class interests that is opening the nobility to an alien caste. It is a marriage that, in fact, closely resembles the alliance of Carla Erba and Count Giuseppe Visconti di Modrone.

This new partnership in power will change nothing for Sicily, for the village of Donna Fugata with, as Visconti said, 'its peasants, obscure and lowly figures, almost faceless, but who nevertheless make their presence felt'. The Piedmontese, the northern Italians, merely replaced their predecessors, the traditional colonizers of enslaved Sicily. Tancredi's cynical prediction that 'if we want every-thing to be like before, everything has to change' comes to pass: Don Calogero can sleep peacefully.

In the 1960s, notwithstanding the formation of a centre-left government and some lightening of the Catholic Church's reaction-ary weight, Visconti expressed his disillusionment not only about *The Leopard*, but also about the rigidity of social relationships in contemporary Italy, where 'everything, despite a little moderniza-tion, remains what it was'. The country, he said, was still suffering from that 'disease in Italian history called transformism, which has succeeded after all the great turning points in this century in absorb-ing and deforming the yearning of the masses for freedom'.

While his critical conscience was close to Lampedusa's, Visconti distanced himself from the novelist on at least two scores. Surely the Milanese could never have said what the writer did in defining both his aristocracy and his identity as a Sicilian: 'The only sin we Sicilians never forgive ourselves for is simply action.' Seen through Fabrizio's eyes, Garibaldi's invasion and the fighting in Palermo and on the hills behind the Conca d'Oro came down to a few distant camp-fires, some 'bleating by the Bourbon police being tortured in the alleys' and a trickle of scarlet on Tancredi's cravat. Visconti, on the other hand, put all an old Resistance fighter's enthusiasm for the Risorgimento into his filming of street fighting, ruins, waving banners, summary executions, women screaming in fury at the mayor of Palermo, a child wandering in search of his dead mother, and other such scenes.

Two temperaments and two art forms are in contrast here. Prince Tomasi was essentially a believer in retreat, both political and personal. Besides, writers are almost inevitably solitary. Motion pictures, on the other hand, stress contrasts, make things and people immediately and physically real. Movies do not allow things to melt into muted, faded, lingering contemplation of the past. In Lampedusa's book everything about the ball is tinted with memory, 'a colour of burned and useless straw'. In the film the ball is all movement, music, incandescent glitter and Angelica's radiance. On film the fire is burning; in the book the flames have died to ashes.

For shooting the ball sequence in *The Leopard*, the old Gangi palace in Palermo was reopened to admit, along with the cast, the flower of Palermo's nobility, including Prince Tomasi's adopted son, Gioacchino Lanza. Plus, of course, twenty electricians, one hundred and twenty seamstresses, one hundred and fifty stage-hands, along with hairdressers and make-up men, all set up on the ground floor of the aristocratic residence. This being high summer, air-conditioning was installed, although it was not strong enough to allow for shooting before sunset. For forty-eight days, from seven in the evening until dawn, the Ponteleone palace described by Lampedusa resounded with the noise and music of high society dancing – the old and the new, Prince Salina and the Cinderella of the ball, Angelica Sedara.

The make-up staff was on the set by early afternoon. 'I remember that I began at one-thirty in the afternoon and finished at six in the morning,' one of them recalls. 'You didn't work any fixed hours. In fact, we all wound up with gastritis from eating sandwiches, smoking and drinking cup after cup of coffee. Before shooting began, Visconti inspected all the extras from head to foot – at least a hundred people.'

Says Cardinale: 'The set was an astonishing sight. Luchino was madly patient, he never missed a thing, and you'd better watch out if a minor detail wasn't perfect, authentic. My· costume was fabulous, but the corset was an antique, too, and so stiff I could hardly breathe. The smelling salts and scent I had in the little bag were also authentic, everything was, everything. He studied each detail almost obsessively, he attended fittings, supervised make-up, he was incredibly meticulous.

'After this film my hairdresser had a nervous breakdown because my hairdo was so complicated it took her over two hours everytime she had to set it. [Shooting] was exhausting, for everyone. The Sicilian nobles Luchino had playing themselves were dropping like flies. Between my make-up and my hair, I needed around four hours to get ready, but I was as strong as a horse, I had incredible vitality and none of these things bothered me. Whenever we took a break I watched people around me collapsing with fatigue, but I didn't even unlace my corset, not for a moment, to avoid breaking my concentration. I couldn't sit down all night because the whalebones were squeezing me too tightly. Luchino had a special chair made for me that I could lean my elbows on and take some of the weight off my feet.'

Oh yes, the stories about the ball sequence in *The Leopard* are true: the bushels of fresh flowers flown in daily from San Remo; real candles in the chandelier that had to be replaced once an hour; the kitchens set up near the ballroom so that the roasts and other dishes could arrive steaming hot; the ground-floor laundry for cleaning the men's white gloves, which after a few hours were sweat-stained. Dancing instructors were on hand to teach the waltz, the mazurka and the galop; gold and silver plate were lent by the old families of Palermo. In half an hour, the costumier Vera Marzot 'did' ten children to fill a hole at the end of the small square in Donna Fugata.

Extras assigned to the street-fighting scenes were painstakingly selected to make sure each was physically typical of the region he was supposed to have come from: Garibaldians from Piedmont, Liguria, the Veneto and Lombardy had to be tall and blond, the Bourbonians short, with very dark hair, eyes and moustaches; Visconti imported the blonds from Rome and hired short, dark Sicilians. He then subjected all of them to a course in basic military training under the stern eyes of Italian army colonels: not just marching and holding a rifle, but also, for the Bourbons' defenders, sitting stiff and straight in the saddle, as the custom was in the nineteenth century.

Count Visconti seemed more than ever like a Renaissance prince, in his ostentation and in the authority he exuded. 'On the set,' Cardinale says, 'he was the absolute master, the last prince of filmdom. Even the producer had trouble gaining admission to the set. Visconti was really a god there. Entering a place where he was filming was like entering a temple, you couldn't even hear a fly buzzing.'

While the cast got ready to film after the final rehearsals, technicians set up the cameras and checked the sets. Only then could shooting begin. For Delon and Cardinale, this was a *tour de force*, because they were working in three languages, speaking French to each other, English with Lancaster and Italian to everyone else. While the director was exquisitely nice to the actress he affectionately called, in French, Claudine, his dealings with Delon were tense, stormy and loving. 'He behaved badly towards me,' Visconti said. 'Instead of rehearsing a scene, as he should have, he simply vanished.'

Lncaster was a star at the peak of his fame then. Visconti received him suspiciously, quickly subjecting him to a reign of terror. Not only did he transform the American into a suave, elegant Leopard, but rendered him so docile that he became the director's admiring shadow. '[Visconti's] first meeting with Burt Lancaster was violent,' Cardinale reports. 'We had rehearsed with a ballet master the dance in which Luchino insisted on perfection. Burt had really just arrived on the set, this was his first scene. He had a very sore knee, and things went badly. When Luchino spotted this he started yelling. He told [Burt] he couldn't care less about this "star" business or about the strain he'd suffered because he still presumed to prance around like a young athlete. Then he turned on his heel with a monarch's disdain, took my hand and led me across the room without a word.

'In the palace where we were filming there was a sumptuous apartment for him, with servants, and that's where he took me, closing the door and still not saying anything. We remained there for maybe an hour, drinking champagne and talking, but not a word about the scene. Then I realized what was going on. Burt Lancaster was the star who'd arrived from Hollywood, and I think Luchino wanted Burt to understand that he, Visconti, was the sole boss on the set. Besides, Luchino didn't care about physical pain; you were supposed to forget all your problems when shooting began. After a while, an assistant came and told him that Burt wanted to talk to him. Luchino, when he left the room, had said only, "We'll come when you're ready". That had been very tough on Burt, Luchino had yelled it in front of hundreds of people. Then we picked up on the dance, and that was the start of a great friendship between Visconti and Lancaster.'

Would Marlon Brando, Visconti's first choice for the fascinating role of the Leopard, have let himself be led, scolded and transformed with the same docility and flexibility? Not only did Lancaster surrender unconditionally to the director, 'whose like I had never seen in Hollywood, although I've worked with John Sturges, Robert Aldrich and John Huston'; he read everything he could get his hands on about the period and the social set that he, the uncultured ex-acrobat and ex-cowboy, had to represent. Visconti called it a 'gradual development, hard to achieve, that benefited the film'. It also benefited the actor, who began modelling even his off-screen behaviour on the Sicilian aristocrat. By guiding Lancaster into his character, Visconti had also guided him towards the new creature he had discovered in himself.

The role of Tancredi probably did not so deeply mark the independent Delon, who had a history of rebelliousness. In 1961 an enraged Visconti had insulted and reviled him because the actor had asked him to shorten the run of *'Tis Pity She's a Whore* so that he could play in the film *Lawrence of Arabia*. And he forced Delon to sacrifice the movie part. Adriana Asti commented that Visconti 'changed Delon as an actor, not as a person'.

Cardinale says, however, that the 'character of Angelica will

mark me forever', and she adds: 'Visconti trained me to be beautiful
. . . I used to move my eyes vaguely but quickly; he made me look
at things precisely, to hold my eyes on them for a long time. He
always said I had to pull in my chin to make my eyes more brilliant
. . . He sculpted my eyes.'

The film was a hit in Europe, including Italy, but it flopped in
the United States. The enormous cost of *The Leopard*, coming on
top of the resounding box-office failure of *Sodom and Gomorrah*,
plunged Lombardo's production company into a financial hole billions of lire deep. Filming had taken seven months. During that
time, Visconti had been supervising the preparation of his next
show, a 'historical-pastoral' comedy in three acts and four tableaux
called *The Devil in the Garden*, written by Sanjust and Medioli with
music by Mannino. It was to open in Palermo's Teatro Massimo
only five months after the last retakes for *The Leopard* were done.

'He had almost too much energy,' says Ms Cecchi d'Amico.
Uberta speaks of his sturdiness, his astounding capacity for work.
'When he was working,' she says, 'he drank one coffee after
another, making his own coffee with infinite care. He made it so
strong that the first time Franco Mannino drank some with him he
didn't sleep for a week. Cigarettes, too, around eighty a day. And if
he was unlucky and got a sore throat, he'd swallow a whole bottle
of cough syrup. He was no man for half-measures. For example, he
loved to garden, and at Ischia we planted everything ourselves. But
no matter how I implored him not to, he always pruned rose bushes
down to the ground. When he used fertilizer he dumped it on by the
pound, and everything died.' He never spared himself, never
pampered himself; he was spendthrift in everything, a squanderer.

When he went out walking with friends in Ischia, he invariably
stopped to buy a book in one shop, a piece of jewellery in another.
Suso remembers that he had fat packages of socks, sweaters and
shirts sent to him from a select Milan haberdasher; he would open
them and tell his friends to take what they liked. He gave everyone
suitcases, handbags, the whole range of leather goods from Louis
Vuitton, a Paris shop he had discovered in the Thirties and had
made famous, so that all his friends carried the initials LV around
with them, which was also his own monogram. The end of every
stage show, the completion of every movie was an occasion for

lavish rewards to his most cherished actors and actresses: jewels, rare art objects lovingly unearthed in antique shops, as, for example, the eighteenth-century gold, ivory and tortoise-shell tobacco box, with a cupid shooting an arrow on the lid, that he gave to Pierfederici, who, clad in white silk, had been his Cherubino in *The Marriage of Figaro*.

At Christmas he outdid himself. As soon as he heard the first chords of the bagpipers in the streets of Rome announcing that the Abruzzi shepherds had come down from their mountains and Christmas was approaching, he began searching for offbeat gifts to delight his friends. He combed the fashionable boutiques, antique shops and jewellers in central Rome. 'We've forgotten this, of course,' says Tonino Cervi, 'but he was an immensely generous man.'

The party he gave at home on Christmas Eve was in itself a directorial masterpiece, with a tree he had personally decorated, and music, games, gifts. 'When I finished *The Leopard*,' Cardinale says, 'we dined together on Christmas Eve, and on New Year's Day he gave me a gold-embroidered Indian shawl; in the shawl, which lay on the table, was a period Cartier dance card, an exquisite thing. He was always doing sweet things like that, and when I played a bit part in *Conversation Piece*, he gave me a Bulgari gold purse.' And she repeats: 'He was one of the last of the princes. He was the Leopard.'

Visconti was princely in everything he did, in all his work, in his elegance, his love of games and parties, his exquisite manners, his love of everything that lightens and beautifies life. His was a spirit of another age, of the quicksilver, ironic, lucid and gay eighteenth century that he brought alive in at least two productions in 1963–4: *The Devil in the Garden* and *The Marriage of Figaro*.

The first, retelling the story of the queen's necklace, was a sort of festival for which Mannino wrote an iridescent, complex score full of crystalline echoes of Mozart, Verdi, Puccini and Offenbach. An aristocrat from Palermo, Mannino worked closely with his brother-in-law and, on 6 June 1962, while Visconti was busy filming *The Leopard* the composer received a letter from him asking for changes in the *Garden* music. 'Not that I think I'm a great music critic,' the director told him, 'heaven save me from such presumption, but since I am by nature a perfectionist, I think there is everything to gain from sweating a bit over the paper or the [camera] frame or the fabric.' To him, perfecting something meant sending it back to the drawing-board over and over; in this specific instance it involved checking to make sure a song like *Au clair de la lune* was historically appropriate and to eliminate anything from the book and score that might block the flow or confuse an already complicated plot.

Princely, too, was his insistence on perfection and his infallible knowledge of stagecraft. He proved this again by exploiting the relatively small stage of the Teatro Nuovo in Spoleto to reinforce a feeling of suffocation and confinement in a *Traviata* that was more orderly, more middle class, less uniquely centred on Violetta than it was in the golden years of the Callas era. Here the set was no longer a splendid, over-ornate projection of the diva, but a more rigid décor, hung in old gold, which Violetta seemed to feel was a prison. In the second act, Visconti even avoided the garden, heightening the intimacy of the action, its 'true confessions' feeling, by bringing it indoors. For the first act he had thought of putting a barrel-organ on the stage to play the ball music. The only section that remained unchanged from the 1955 production was the death of Violetta, with soprano Franca Fabbri wearing the same odd little hat. But she died sitting up, less nobly than Callas – or Donna Carla – could have done unsupported.

True, Visconti stuck to the same old music, to *La Traviata*. He even used it – out of fidelity to Lampedusa's book – in *The Leopard*, when the village band welcoming the prince and his family to Donna Fugata plays the second-act *Noi siamo le zingarelle*; when the members of the Salina family, dustier and more cadaverous than mummies in a museum, file into the church stalls, the organist, played by Serge Reggiani, grinds out the *Amami Alfredo*.

But, as Togliatti once noted, Visconti was a man for leitmotifs, obsessions, cyclical returns to the same works, the same themes – in short, for fidelity. Perhaps the barrel-organ in the 1963 *Traviata* was a persistent echo of long-ago days in the streets of Milan when little Luchino might, like Alberto Savinio, have heard the 'gravelly voice' of a hand-organ drawn by a mule 'in a street bounded by long factory buildings' near the Piazza Carlo Erba, grinding out arias from a 'poor, thin and plebeian *Traviata*'. Savinio wrote that 'to understand and savour *La Traviata*'s arias better, those frail butterflies of an evening with no tomorrow, we should not hear it in an opera house, but played on a barrel-organ. Because *La Traviata* comes across more emotionally in recollection than in the present, and a barrel-organ restores this music of urban sadness to its natural setting.'

Decorative overloading, the imperious, irrepressible invasion of art nouveau scrolls and arabesques, had not yet contaminated Visconti's stagings, as they would three years later in his third and last version of *La Traviata* in London. Indeed, in his 1964 staging of Mozart's *The Marriage of Figaro* in Rome he turned his back on what he called 'the baroquisms, the frippery of eighteenth-century Vienna, the affectation of the court theatre, the mannerisms of the Viennese court'. This new production, in collaboration with the conductor Carlo Maria Giulini, has been called a return to neo-realism, a new statement of loyalty to the Communist Party because of the director's care in stressing the haughtiness of Count Almaviva, the Spanish grandee, and the coarseness of Figaro, the man of the people.

Yet, to his audience's surprise, the whole last act is bathed in an atmosphere of fantasy: a garden sleeps under a starry sky, but it is a magical garden, like the fabulous wall of the palace at Palagonia, in Sicily, where people of stone disport among stone monsters with gaping jaws, rearing chimeras, threatening cyclops. In this Goyesque night when 'reason sleeps, breeding monsters', social hierarchies dissolve, identities are traded in a sombre and prophetic carnival.

The shadows grew deeper that autumn with the two versions of *Il Trovatore* produced two months apart, the first at the Bolshoi, the second at Covent Garden. Increasingly stylized staging, trading primarily on the effects of night, a play of blacks, greys and whites setting off the red glow of firelight.

A man of the night, Visconti. It dominates the film, in black and white, that he shot in the summer of 1964 in the lonely, mournful Etruscan city of Volterra, its towers, its convents, its grey stones thrusting upwards in the moonlight as the ghosts gathered. The movie, *Sandra*, finally won the director the highest award at the Venice festival, the Golden Lion that had been denied him until then.

Yet Visconti's star was already beginning to wane. The brilliant success of *The Leopard* would not be repeated in the five tormented years that open a new chapter in his life and work. Henceforth the arrows loosed at him would not come from the opponents he loved to enrage; increasingly, in that era of protest, one heard him accused of being academic, a pedant and a mystifier and, of course, decadent, even senile. *Sandra*, said the new generation of critics, at least showed the director for what he was. 'In Visconti,' one of them wrote, 'we saw a would-be great decadent and we realized that in him decadence is by no means a result of crisis and decomposition, but is in fact what leads him to D'Annunzian indulgence, to sumptuousness as an end in itself, to his folds and veils, to academically reconstituted atmospheres.'

Filming in Volterra, and especially in the Inghirami palace that provided the locale for D'Annunzio's novel *Forse Che Si, Forse Che No* (*Maybe Yes, Maybe No*), Visconti showed the D'Annunzian sources of his inspiration. This was visible in his treatment of incest and frenzied passion; over *Sandra*, a story of murder, madness and family revenge, hangs the black and fatal shadow of D'Annunzio's 'city of wind and stone suspended over its abyss between the walls of the fortress suffused with sin and the houses of San Girolamo suffused with madness'. Visible, too, was the director's attraction to this 'land without sweetness, this country of sterility and thirst, this blasted heath, this desert of ash'.

What did he see in that ominous mirror? Death, already being courted by Prince Fabrizio as he inspects a Greuze painting? An image of his own sterility, his condemnation? Or, rather, a possible new challenge?

XIX

SUNSET BOULEVARD

The family, my friends, the family!
Which of us can ever hope to unsnarl
The enigmatic knot of stone?

ALBERTO SAVINIO

The theatre should not deprive itself of any of
the theatre's bewitchments.

JEAN-PAUL SARTRE

In *The Leopard*, Visconti knew he had reached a peak. A private demon nevertheless drove him to seek new challenges, for himself and his public. He had a streak of gambler in him. Whatever he won had to be staked again immediately, at the heart-thrumming risk of losing everything. Rest on your laurels and die.

His new challenge was named *Vaghe Stelle dell'Orsa* [*Sandra*]. The opposite of *The Leopard*, this was an intimate, confidential movie 'in line with the *Kammerspiel* by Mayer and Lupu Pick'. It would be in black and white, with only a few characters, a tightly woven plot, a 'strongly coloured dramatic aura'. People whispered that he couldn't just make a film the way everyone else did, that he couldn't bring one in on time? He'd see about that. And between 26 August and 18 October 1964, the film was shot. The director never asked to see the rushes, never dithered, as if the picture were already written in his mind down to the last detail.

He was called Count *Rovinapopolo* – Count Ruin the People. Even Dino de Laurentiis finally decided against financing *The Bible*, a trilogy by Orson Welles, Robert Bresson and Visconti, with the Italian doing an episode based on Mann's *Joseph and His Brothers*.

344

Compared with his vision of the pharaonic court, all in real gold and lapis lazuli, Joseph Mankiewicz's *Cleopatra* would have looked strictly bargain-basement.

But for *Sandra* the budget was to be as tight as possible. This meant turning back to Cristaldi, the modest producer with whom he had already worked on a similar venture, *White Nights*. Cristaldi must have thought he was dreaming when the director of *The Leopard*, the darling of all the big production companies, came to him and casually asked, 'When are we going to make another movie together'?

Visconti had an ace-in-the-hole: Cristaldi's wife, in the fullness of her twenty-five years, with her cloud of dark hair, her man-eating laugh, stubborn brow and a frown the director had told her never to lose in *The Leopard*. Her name: Claudia Cardinale. He had to find a part for her, a part made to order for 'her type of slightly earthy, almost animal beauty'. And that shy sensuousness visible in every movement, the vital strength that gave her that jungle magnetism. 'Watch out for Claudine,' Visconti said while making *The Leopard*, 'she looks like a cat waiting to be caressed, but watch out, the cat will turn into a tigress.'

In Castiglioncello he discussed with Medioli and Ms Cecchi d'Amico what part to give her that would really exhibit her power and majesty. 'For days and days,' Suso says, 'we talked about a character for Cardinale. Until someone mentioned the name Electra, and we all stopped right there. We lost sight of Cardinale as anything but a symbol of filial piety, of order and loyalty demanding a murder as atrocious as the one that she was avenging.'

She was to be no frail Electra, but a hard, implacable Electra, relentless in her quest for truth, her thirst for justice, with 'the superiority complex of the Jewish race'. Said Suso, 'It seemed natural to us that this Electra be Jewish, and that Agamemnon had died in a concentration camp.'

Why this theme? First of all, because Visconti was simultaneously preparing to stage *After the Fall*, Miller's Auschwitz-shadowed play that makes the Holocaust a source of the guilt feelings, the tortured consciences of Europe and America, of the Old World and the New. Secondly, because no other approach could better plug the Electra of distant antiquity into the memories of a modern audience. 'Perhaps audiences in Sophocles' day left the theatre convinced that the real culprit was not Oedipus, but fate,' Visconti remarked. 'But this convenient explanation won't satisfy a modern spectator. He can only justify Oedipus insofar as he feels involved, as though he and [Oedipus] were rivals in sin . . .' And, also, a rival in sin with Oedipal, murderous, retributive Electra, who was both victim and criminal.

At first, everything in the film seems clear: after a long absence, Sandra comes home to Volterra, to the house where, years earlier, her parents had separated, and from where her Jewish father had been sent to a concentration camp, probably denounced by her mother, a new Clytemnestra, and her lover Gilardini, an attorney and latter-day Egisthus.

'But we don't say in *Sandra* who the real guilty parties and the real victims are,' Visconti specifies. 'In this sense, the reference I myself made to the *Oresteia* is merely a convenient indication. Sandra resembles Electra because of the motive that drives her, Gilardini resembles Egisthus because he is from outside the family circle, but these are only rough analogies. Sanda looks like a justiciary, Gilardini like a defendant, but in fact their positions could be reversed. What truly stamps all these characters, except for Sandra's husband, Andrew, is ambiguity.'

In maintaining that ambiguity, Visconti was observing the same conditions as Sartre in his play *The Condemned of Altona*. What mattered was to play on audiences' inchoate feeling of collective guilt, as he would in *After the Fall*, to implicate the spectator as both judge and defendant in the characters' trial, and prevent the public from becoming reconciled, as Sartre put it, 'with his queries, with his unresolved questions'.

In *Sandra*, Visconti said,

[. . .] the character closest to the spectator's conscience is Andrew, who wants a logical explanation for everything and instead collides with a world dominated by deep, contradictory, inexplicable passions. And because he cannot find a logical solution to events, he must in turn be directly involved, finally forced to wonder not so much if the mother and Gilardini are responsible for the teacher's death, or if Sandra is responsible for

Gianni's death, but whether a sin was committed, and which sin, and whether a Sandra, a Gianni, a Gilardini isn't hiding in all of us.

He thought this family tragedy should, by reflecting all our questions, all our uneasiness, 'help us to understand the reality of our historical time and where it is leading us'. As a backdrop to it, he chose a décor representing an enigma of Time and History, a parallel process of disintegration that makes the past as incomprehensible as the Etruscans. A woman leads us here, a sexually and emotionally dissatisfied woman intent on understanding the past. Around her is the city of Volterra, built over the 'antique Etruscan enigma' of its necropoles. There is a house, too, the shadowy childhood home remembered by the poet Giacomo Leopardi in his *Memories*, which gave the film its Italian title, *Vaghe Stelle dell'Orsa*:

> . . . this house where I lived as a child,
> and contemplate the end of all my joys.

Sandra's house was the famous Inghirami palace, a symbol of medieval Volterra that each day slips a little closer to the cliffs overhanging the abyss of the Balze. This was a grim chrysalis where Visconti was careful not to disturb the spider webs, not to dispel the air of dilapidation, so as to make it a proper theatre for a settling of family scores. Electra, then, is Etruscan, a messenger of life and death. She is linked to a world without mystery, with no depth, through her marriage with the American, Andrew, but she rediscovers her roots in Volterra, described by D'Annunzio as 'an underground city inhabited by the dead'. Like the characters in *Maybe Yes, Maybe No* she bore within herself 'an internal city inhabited by violent spirits'. By returning to her birthplace she returns to the bewitchments of childhood – the shared solitude of which her brother Gianni reminds her, the secrets, the walks along the cliff top, the sleepless nights, the music, the worries, the turbulent passions of childhood and the sinister enchantments of clandestine love affairs.

Cardinale's hairstyle – braids framing her brow like a crown – suggest both her perverse childish games and the funerary figures in the tomb frescoes in Tarquinia. Visconti patiently sculptured her face, her body, in which he sought to blend the mysteries of childhood with those of Etruria, a lost civilization and a lost paradise. 'Claudia sometimes gives you a static feeling,' Visconti said, 'but that's what lets me model her face, her skin, her eyes, her gaze, her smile. I immediately thought of her to play Sandra. In fact, the character was written around her, and not just because of the enigma hidden under her apparent simplicity, but also because of the somatic vestiges in her body (especially her face) of what has come to us from Etruscan womanhood.' There is in her Sandra a sort of sacerdotalism that gives a ritual quality to everything she does, even her haughty indifference to her mother's madness, and to her brother's death.

Visconti wanted the mother to be theatrical, unbearable and pathetic, all at once. First he thought of those divas with eyes 'as big as church windows' who haunted his childhood: Italia Almirante Manzini, Gianna Terribili Gonzales, Dianna Karenne . . . He went to see them, and found them all about as mad as Gloria Swanson in *Sunset Boulevard*, or dementedly, horribly avid to cash in on their past fame. He offered two million lire to Francesca Bertini, then seventy-six years old; she asked for a hundred million. On the first day of shooting, one of the many telegrams that arrived came from Geneva: 'Enormously sorry not working with you. Unbounded admiration. Francesca.'

It was finally Marie Bell, then sixty-four, who brought her long experience as a great tragedienne to the role of Corinna Wald Luzzatti. For her Visconti reserved the poignant scene – so rife with memories for him – in which the mother, a former pianist, begins playing César Franck's *Prelude* for her daughter and has to fumble vainly for the chords. She wears one of those long pearl necklaces Donna Carla favoured; in the film, white pearls alternate with black ones. As a child, Luchino used to lie in his room and hear his mother play the same Proustian music; here, with Bell laughing and crying at once, it becomes the sobbing of a failing memory.

For the part of Gianni, Sandra's brother, Luchino had his heart set on a French actor he had known for ages but had never worked with: Jean Sorel, whose handsome virility and huge grey eyes recalled Delon in many of the scenes in *Rocco*. It was a difficult role;

Gianni is a complex, roiled character, simultaneously satanic and angelic, cynical and childish, violent and vulnerable, eminently D'Annunzian. He is dangerously like Visconti, and the director instils in him his own love of literature, his gifts as an intimist writer, his attachment to and denigration of the past, his dissipation – Gianni gradually sells off all the furniture in the house and hastens his family's financial ruin. And his extravagant, feminine, morbid sensitivity.

Four cameras scrutinize the actor's every expression, gesture, step. But Visconti's glare was even more paralysing. How was Sorel to say Leopardi's poem after the director recited it to him 'with a mixture of bitterness and resentment'? How was he to move and walk by the director's strict instructions and still look natural? 'Why are you walking like that?' Visconti shouted at him. 'You look like a knight of the Grail.' The count was a fountain of stinging, petrifying remarks and ironies.

To put his cast at ease, but also to help immerse them in their characters, he sometimes chased everyone else off the set and remained alone with them in a sort of conclave, showing them exactly how each movement was to be made, demonstrating them himself – Gianni's movements with his sister, for example, his way of placing his head in her lap (Visconti carefully placed Sorel's face for a stationary shot calculated to within a fraction of an inch). At the end of the brawl scene – which was not to be faked – he dictated precisely how Gianni was to curl up in a foetal position in an armchair, making him repeat it over and over again.

Everything about Volterra was an invitation to a homecoming. Note that Visconti captured that home through the invisible welding – Mario Garbuglia called it a 'collage' – of two different buildings, the Inghirami palace and the Viti palace, as if to reconstitute for himself alone the two connected sides of his own ancestry in Milan: the maternal home on Via Marsala and his father's palace on Via Cerva. The places, the objects in them functioned as signs and symbols for him. At the Inghirami, the garden had not changed since D'Annunzio described it in his novel, with the same centenarian oak and the same magnolia tree.

'At the foot of the magnolia,' Rinaldo Ricci recorded in his filming log for *Sandra*, 'Visconti found a small [sculpture of a] woman's head, pre-Raphaelite in style, with a delightful art nouveau hairdo, but the nose gone forever. That is what happens to alabaster, which, like granite, is so important to the architecture and sculpture in Volterra and to its inevitable decadence. [A bit farther along] a small tower. And then a marvel, a cast-iron spiral stairway, almost hanging in space, vanishing into dimness to which the eye adjusts with difficulty. And we go down to find we are at the bottom of an old Roman cistern, now empty but still damp and cool. An aquarium light streams down from above. And the light is modulated by the indescribably tender green of maidenhair fern. Tall pillars of antique masonry recall Piranesi engravings and Egyptian tombs. We go back up, certain we have found something important.'

Here Sandra and Gianni arrange to meet by leaving notes, as they did in their childhood, in a vase – alabaster, of course, since that is the funerary stone found everywhere in Volterra. And they would descend to it via the same spiral staircase that snakes, like the Viscontis' heraldic serpent, into the damp, maternal womb of the earth, an archaic, accursed and infernal place where Gianni tries to win back his sister by removing her wedding ring, a theatrical gesture picked up from the incestuous *'Tis Pity She's a Whore*.

Incest, Visconti said, 'is contemporary society's last taboo'. And, he added, 'it's a theme that's in the air'. Sartre touched on it in 1959, with *The Condemned of Altona*. So, at the same time, did two new-wave movie directors. One was Bernardo Bertolucci, who made *Before the Revolution*, a modern version of *The Charterhouse of Parma*; the other was Marco Bellocchio, director of the most shocking, most violently anti-bourgeois movie of the period, *Fists in the Pocket*, which Pasolini saw as the triumph of revolutionary cinema, a 'cinema of poetry' that scuttled middle-class conventions and rationalism. For both Bertolucci and Bellocchio, incest was the supremely subversive act, the rebel's final gesture before he subsides into the tomb of family life and middle-class order.

Visconti probably took a different view of this fascinating sin, one that was firmly rationalistic and critical, stripped of romanticism and D'Annunzianism. 'Incest,' he said, 'is born uniquely from the environment in which the two young people grew up; it is an exaggerated, dramatic way to unite against the disintegration of the

family, against solitude. This disintegration is felt most keenly by
the brother, Gianni; it is he who, as a last resort, proposes to Sandra
that they live together in the old house. And Gianni's final gesture,
dying in his mother's bed as if he wanted to return to the womb, is
meant as a last effort to reunite the family nucleus.'

Visconti here is exorcizing the regressive tendency he had always
eluded, a death wish, by the sacrifice to Sandra – a strong character
played by Cardinale, that least D'Annunzian of actresses – of a
childish Orestes who 'no longer belongs in the world'; in his very
first appearance, disguised as a ghost beside his father's white-
shrouded gravestone, he seems already claimed for death.

Anyone seeing the film might imagine its maker grimly haunted
by death and, like a D'Annunzio character, 'full of ashes and
funereal time'. Not so. 'He was in great form,' Cardinale says, 'he
joked, fooled around, he was in an excellent mood, he drew slightly
smutty drawings that I found on my plate when I sat down to eat.
He had a lot of fun with the prudery of my sister, who had come to
see me and blushed when she saw the drawings.'

His family ties may never have been plainer than they were then.
Shortly before shooting began on *Sandra*, he bought a grand Renaissance villa, with private chapel and theatre, called La Suvera, the
Oak Grove, in which he was never to live. At the time, Suso Cecchi
d'Amico remembers that while he was looking for a house they
went together to see an abandoned house. On the second floor they
walked into a room that was infested with huge, black bats. Suso
panicked, and the next thing she knew she was at the foot of the
stairs. But Luchino stayed upstairs, she says, neither blanching nor
blinking nor hurrying, watching those hideous clusters hanging
from the beams. He chose La Suvera because it was near Querceto,
in the Val d'Elsa, where his brother Edoardo owned a farm amid
pines, olive trees, cypresses and vines. Members of his family came
frequently to visit while he was shooting *Sandra*, and there was a
picnic at Edoardo's.

In fact, Visconti saw the disintegration of family life as one of the
most obvious and serious evils of modern life. He deplored the
desertion of the family home, that vital hub, that 'hive' in which
each member 'lives and works in his cell' before going to the dining-
room, a place of reunions and of conflict, to join the Mother, 'the

queen bee'. Everyone in the family always returned there, not, as in *Sandra*, to find violence and rivalry, but for peace and warmth.

Visconti saw 'the most disastrous example' of this loss of home and family, which he blamed on industrial development, in America, where 'men are on one side, women on the other, divorce is too easy, couples are continually shifting, abandoned children are no longer anyone's children'. But 'in Italy, too, people are marching towards this chaos because they are more interested in foreign fashions than in the old customs'.

More than ever he returned to the notion of the mother as the conservator, the guarantor of order and social equilibrium. 'Women can also work,' he said, 'they can be artists, but they should put certain duties first: being a lover, a wife, probably a mother, and completely re-creating what was, until a century ago, a solid family group. To me this is very important for social progress. When the family disappears, everything disappears.'

For social unrest, an upsurge in mental illness, the disorientation of the young and the increased isolation of individuals in this ice age that beset a 'still evolving society', Visconti saw only one cause: the collapse of the family cell, with its resultant anxiety for young and old, 'the lack of love, of affection, of conversation by the fire, that even affects our culture. This is why the terror of old age is spreading so.'

Ms Cecchi d'Amico says he had 'a completely patriarchal sense' of family. 'The Viscontis are a family with a lot of brothers and sisters, each very different from the others, perhaps very distant from each other, too', she notes. 'That did not keep Luchino from loving them deeply and feeling unshakeably bound to them. His concept of the family was healthy, old-fashioned . . . Indeed, what were his favourite books? Mann's *Buddenbrooks* and *Joseph and His Brothers*. Family stories that no one experienced more deeply than he.'

Instead of rejoicing at each new fissure in Italian society, he viewed it with growing pessimism, always seeing in it the break-up of what he considered the fundamental family structure. He had no children, and adopted none. But he had a second family around him that paralleled his own. It was made up of his friends, especially his actors and actresses, and it saved him, as he said himself, from loneliness. And there were parasites and toadies, according to Mastroianni and Henze, people who amused him, but whom he mistrusted.

Then, in the autumn of 1964, the autumn of *Sandra*, a young man appeared to court the famous director. Visconti was thunderstruck. 'When confronted with beauty,' says Adriana Asti, 'he went almost blind . . . He saw himself in the mirror of those handsome faces and felt pleased with himself.'

It was evening when the boy of twenty, quivering with cold and emotion, showed up on the set with Salvador Dali's wife, Gala. He was blond, very handsome, Austrian. Having heard how Visconti worshipped Romy Schneider, he knew how bewitched the director was by a particular type of Austrian, with the right accent, the right kind of blondness.

Visconti saw him, made inquiries, asked him to lunch the following day in his house in Volterra, a house he'd had completely done over, and which was filled with the aroma of freshly roasted coffee and the scent of roses and tuberoses. This shy yet brazen young man, heaven-sent directly to the set of *Sandra*, was born in Salzburg, had theatrical ambitions and was named Helmut Berger.

He brought his youth at a time when Visconti increasingly felt a lack of understanding, even hostility towards him on the part of the young. Could his work still touch, charm, trouble young people? It was an important question for him. After three controversial stagings – his two *Trovatores* and, especially, *After the Fall* at the Théâtre du Gymnase in Paris in January 1965 – he had finally found his public: young people wildly applauding the actors in his troupe who were assembled one last time in *The Cherry Orchard* as if for a final Viscontian homecoming.

Before him, he said, no one had managed to free himself from the style imposed on *The Cherry Orchard* by Stanislavsky despite Chekhov's instructions. The play was given 'a dilated, feeble pace, with too much melancholy and a profusion of endless silences'. One evening, two and a half months after the play opened on 26 October 1965, he went to the Valle Theatre to greet his cast. 'There were a lot of young people,' he noted. 'You'd have thought you were in a jam-packed neighbourhood cinema instead of a theatre. On stage, the characters disappeared one by one until only old Firs remained, and the curtain fell; endless applause, like for a première, except maybe less condescending and certainly more spontaneous than first-night audiences usually give. I counted a good fifteen curtain calls.'

His meeting with Berger, while rejuvenating him, also opened new horizons to Visconti; this was a turning point that gave his life and work a new direction. Although he continued to work in Italy – with *Don Carlo* at the Rome Opera on 20 November 1965, and *La Traviata* in London beginning 19 April 1967 – and also finally realized his old plan to adapt *The Stranger* to the screen, he spent more and more time in Austria. He staged *Falstaff* there in the spring of 1966 and filmed an episode for the multi-sketch film *The Witches* in Kitzbühel the following year.

The Witch Burned Alive allowed him a return to a favourite theme: the diva, the witch of modern times. In the film she is embodied by Silvana Mangano, an archetype of the movie star consumed by love of money rather than art, and condemned, as Callas had been, to sterility, to the sacrifice of her maternity. More important, Visconti used the sketch to introduce his new protégé, in a secondary role.

He had to teach Berger everything, beginning with how to keep from trembling in front of a camera. 'Actors are like thorough-breds,' he said, 'each one is different. Lancaster is a great professional, Delon is Latin, European, more capricious, less marked by a method. Berger is a young hopeful, full of inspiration and talent, but he still needs conditioning. His moods are unpredictable.'

From the outset of their love affair, Visconti told him 'I'll write stories for you.' At the time, he was considering adapting *The Countess Tarnowska* for Romy Schneider to 'explain why the artificial and useless Belle Époque society disintegrated'. But for Helmut, so like the actress in his vulnerability, his sadness and moodiness, the unhappiness and instability that made them cousins in spirit long before they appeared together as cousins in *Ludwig*, Visconti nourished another idea: he would adapt Robert Musil's *Young Törless*, which he said 'contains the germ of the cruelty and sadism' that would inform Nazism later on. For him these two periods were historically close.

A third project was also firming up: he was slowly settling on the locale for his *Macbeth*, for which he and Ms Cecchi d'Amico wrote a script in 1967. At first he had thought of England, scene of the Profumo affair, then of booming Italy, with modern Milanese businessmen replacing Shakespeare's kings. Finally he fixed on the Krupp family in Germany during the Hitler era. There was a magnificent role for Berger, as Martin in *The Damned*.

Whenever Visconti went to Germany or Vienna he bought armfuls of knick-knacks, furniture, engravings by Gustav Klimt, Egon Schiele, Oskar Kokoschka. Gradually the decorating scheme changed at Via Salaria and at the Colombaia in Ischia to the art nouveau setting in which he would live from then on, reliving the long-ago years in the palace on Via Cerva. He could never live in a house where the décor was frozen, immutable. Being able to say that a house is 'furnished' robbed it of what he saw as a house's charm, its life. Wherever he went, he astonished his friends by buying masses of art objects and furniture. 'Oh, sure, you really needed that,' Suso would tell him ironically. And antique shops in Rome, as well as his friends' homes, were full of priceless pieces of furniture he discarded.

Each of the objects and paintings he owned was connected with a period, a sudden craze. It was all 'scattered around everywhere, any which way' in a disorder that nevertheless remained Viscontian disorder, a rich alchemy of colours, substances and styles. As soon as he took a liking to an object he began buying series, creating collections in which he eventually lost interest. So he had his clay-dog year, his wig-block year, his 'built-in' year and his bull year, years of marble balls, obelisks and alabaster.

Some even took over completely for a while. The early Sixties was the eighteenth-century Venetian period: in the entry hall of the house in Rome stood black-and-gold statues of turbanned blackamoors beside paintings by Crivellone (an early-eighteenth-century Milanese painter), Piazzetta and Pannini, console tables, busts of Louis XVI, crystal chandeliers. Later he collected Gallé lamps and vases, statuettes, mirrors, seals, Belle Époque engravings. Not only did he discover the paintings of Klimt then, but his friend Trombadori put him on to a Florentine painter, Galileo Chini, who was very visibly influenced by the Austrian; Chini had also done the sets for a number of Puccini operas.

Visconti's liking for Art Nouveau overflowed beyond the settings for his private life. The 1965 *Don Carlo* had been stark, with a simple palette of black and white and a few bloody splashes under a golden light out of an El Greco painting; in the spring of 1966, his *Falstaff* had been painstakingly realistic, so accurate as to be almost conventional. Then, a month later, came the delirious décor of *Der Rosenkavalier* mounted at Covent Garden. Could he have felt more at home in the Strauss opera than in Verdi's last masterpiece, that 'explosion of joy' in which the composer, then eighty and full of disillusioned wisdom, closed his cycle of the passions with a final *tutto è buffoneria* (all is buffoonery)? 'I mainly deal with Italian opera – Verdi, Donizetti, Bellini – because they are closer to my sensibility,' Visconti said. 'But I love Strauss and Wagner. I dream of staging *Tristan*.'

In *Der Rosenkavalier*, so 'full of love and eroticism', he related to the Marschallin, whose days of youth and love were fading. The soft, shimmering pastels, the light and graceful fantasy of the eighteenth-century sets and costumes were gradually invaded by a decorative overload of arabesques and ornaments and Jugendstil windows and Bosch-style monsters' heads. This transition to a 1900 style emphasized Strauss's, and Visconti's, sexual tension and anxiety. Audiences, however, seldom saw more than decadent self-indulgence and a gratuitous effort to shock the public.

The critic Peter Heyworth nevertheless noted that behind the tears of an ageing princess loomed the far more serious tragedy of a city weary of its Empire. And behind that, he said, is the tragedy of Strauss and Hofmannstal; when they wote this work in 1910 they were at the peak of their fame, but, like Vienna, they had difficult days ahead of them, so that the tragedy of the city reflected their own. Their work, Heyworth went on, is far more than a lament for the Marschallin's youth; it weeps for the culture that had bred and nourished their genius, but which was now collapsing before their eyes. And into their tapestry, he concluded, they lovingly wove the birth, maturity and decline of that culture – the worlds of Maria Theresa and Freud and, between the two, of Johann Strauss, and they called it *Der Rosenkavalier*.

One year later, almost to the day, having just completed filming *The Stranger*, Visconti presented a Beardsley-style *Traviata* in the same theatre. A few months earlier, he had asked the costumier Vera Marzot to go and see him at Via Salaria. 'The count is ill,' the butler told her when she got there: she was to go up to his room.

'Are you free around March–April?' Visconti asked as soon as she walked in. 'It'll be for a *Traviata*.' Then he explained what he had in mind: 'I want everything in black and white, except in the third act. But let's understand each other: use every possible nuance of black, which can veer towards purple or greenish, and the white can be lacquered or creamy or glossy.'

And the following day: 'Fine . . . We're going to shock the English a bit.'

While the sets and costumes were being readied, the company grumbled about Visconti's manias. He remained imperturbable, more amused than disturbed by the long faces he saw around him. He was dead set on meeting this new challenge, to have his black and white parlour with its fake Klimt, his frost-rimed garden and his Beardsley-style masked ball at which the gold, scarlet and fire-red of the Spanish dance would suddenly erupt. In the last act, Violetta dies in white amid snowy chrysanthemums. Her red shawl slips slowly from her shoulders, for she is too weak to hold it on.

Giulini was on the podium, Callas was in a box. Visconti had just murdered 'their' *Traviata*, the 1955 production. It was, wrote one critic, 'a glass of ice water hurled in the faces of opera fanatics who crave nothing but their standard fare'.

Perhaps, in those years of waning hopes and shifting values and paralysing reform movements, a wrenching conflict was growing in him to settle a constant wavering between what the biographer Gianni Rondolino called 'critical realism and decadentism, between two different concepts of life and art'. When he contemplated the mortal remains of Palmiro Togliatti, who died 21 August 1964, was he aware that an era of struggle and hope had ended? 'The world today is in crisis,' Visconti later said, 'a moral, social and spiritual crisis. But defeats are never total or final. They are only temporary. And each defeat breeds new strength, new vigour. I am not pessimistic.'

His 1965 *Don Carlo*, with its ghostly naves and frozen heaths, was a heroes' requiem. In 1966, the booming, buffoonish laughter of baritone Dietrich Fischer-Dieskau filled the stage for a *Falstaff*

357

deserted by tormented and defeated young idealists. In 1967, in the courtyard of the Pitti Palace in Florence, Visconti staged Goethe's tragedy *Egmont*, to Beethoven's incidental music, as the last, grandiose episode, after *Don Carlo* and *Il Duca d'Alba*, in a cycle commemorating the revolt in the Netherlands, the crushing of revolutionary fervour and, in the sacrifice of Egmont, an aristocratic hero of the Enlightenment, the failure of an ideal of life and human reason.

What is decadent about such a vision? Even if Visconti resorted to using a Belle Époque-Art Nouveau style, did he ever succumb to pure, solitary, ecstatic, morbid contemplation of decadentism and the disintegration it reflected? Do we call Fellini's *Satyricon* decadent, or Bertolucci's *Before the Revolution*, or Sartre's *The Condemned of Altona*? Gratuitous? Aestheticist? Visconti always contested these charges, more and more often levelled at his productions. He offered a one-word defence: realism. 'It must be clear,' he said in 1974 about the cutting attacks on *'Tis Pity* and *After the Fall*, 'that my work is realistic, even if it was and is inevitable that I resort to formalism . . .'

Art nouveau? Kitsch? He used them when he needed them, to further an inquiry into his own origins and into the deepest well-springs of European sensitivity. When a journalist referred in the Seventies to his 'continual harking back to the good old days, that prison of memory, the deliberately kitsch implications of his work', he replied: 'I was born and grew up in the Liberty [Art Nouveau] period, madam, and I obviously breathed that air, I had kitsch all around me . . .'

'But you are so aestheticist,' she insisted.

'You can use the word decadent, my dear, go ahead and say it. I'm used to it now, it's become a refrain. It's a pity that some people use the word to mean exactly the opposite of what it really means; to them it means depraved, morbid. Whereas, you know, it is only a way of looking at art, of evaluating it and creating it. Is Thomas Mann decadent? As a comparison, that suits me perfectly.'

Visconti was a humanist, not at all inclined to obliterate the past, and his great flashbacks were not returns to the lost paradise of childhood, to the family cocoon, to vague memories of pampering, they were not escapes into imaginary worlds. They were, in fact, interpretations of omens, and all the great works of the past that he reread were there as pointers to premonitory signs of historic changes that would not be visible until years later.

To him, the character of Tancredi in *The Leopard* foretold the future collusion between the Fascists and the new governing class of post-unification Italy. So did Tullio Hermil, the Nietzschean super-man of *The Innocents*. Memory is more than a landscape of nostalgia. It provides a perspective that connects the remotest past with the present moment, either because the present repeats the past or because the past contains the germs of the present, the first symptoms of the diseases from which the present still suffers, perhaps more grievously than ever.

This should also have characterized Visconti's 1967 film *The Stranger*, which he disavowed because he could not give it the mean-ing he read between the lines of Camus' 1946 novel. In the murder, for example, Visconti thought the 'terror of a *pied-noir*★, who grew up in this land, who feels unwelcome, who knows he is going to have to depart and leave it to those it belongs to', forecast the Algerian war, which ended not long before the movie was made.

'My interpretation of and my scenario for *The Stranger* still exist,' he later said. 'I wrote it with the help of Georges Conchon, and it is completely different from the film. It had echoes of *The Stranger*, echoes which . . . resound into today, into the OAS,† into the Algerian war. It was what Camus' novel really means; I would say it foretold what has happened, and I wanted to crystallize the novel's forecast cinematographically.' But Francine Camus, the author's widow, wouldn't hear of it.

To this was added De Laurentiis' refusal to pay the exorbitant price Delon was asking. But Visconti could see no one else in the role of Meursault. He was probably stimulated, too, by the chance to give Delon, as he gave all his favourite actors and actresses, a pivotal role that would mark his consecration as a star, as *Oreste* did for Gassman, *Sandra* did for Cardinale, and *Ludwig* would do for Helmut Berger. Instead of Delon, he got Mastroianni, who pro-

★The slightly pejorative nickname given to the French settlers in Algeria (trans-lator's note).
†The right-wing Secret Army Organization that plotted to maintain Algeria as a French possession (translator's note).

duced the film for De Laurentiis, to whom Visconti was bound by contract.

'People said, "Why Mastroianni?"' the actor recalls. 'They probably saw a protagonist like Gérard Philipe (I know there was some question of Delon before I got into it), and I must say they were wrong, because the character in *The Stranger* was not an intellectual, he was no mysterious, Philipe-style archangel. Meursault is a Mediterranean type, an optimist, a thoroughly normal man who likes girls and food and being with his friends. This is what makes the character so extraordinary, the fact that he was so healthy, very normal and very Mediterranean.'

This earthy view of the character suited the first part of the novel and the film, but not so much the second, in which the very Stendhalian Philipe would have done nicely, and in which Visconti would probably have brought out deeper and more delicate aspects of Delon's personality. 'Perhaps Mastroianni wasn't exactly the actor the part needed,' says Ms Cecchi d'Amico, 'because he never asked himself the existential questions and he's lazy . . . He didn't give the film enough dimension.'

For Visconti, Mastroianni was too 'Italian', and the director knew how much an actor's origins can add or detract from a character. Comparing Dirk Bogarde and Mastroianni, he saw in Bogarde 'a professional side, British, much deeper, much more disciplined over all. Bogarde never stopped being his character in *Death in Venice*. Even when he went home he was still Aschenbach, he was Aschenbach for two and a half months. Mastroianni is a fellow who sees tagliatelle or spaghetti and completely forgets he is doing Meursault. He eats, and then he picks up [his character] again. That's very different. It's the Italian side, a bit frivolous.'

There are magical moments reminiscent of Tennessee Williams at the start of the film, the story is told with stark clarity, and set designer Tosi faithfully re-created the Algiers of the Forties. There are marvellous sequences: the murder; the prison in which the camera slowly, sinuously moves up from the forms of sleeping Algerians to the figure of the flute-player; the damp heat of the courtroom that unavoidably recalls the 1945 trial of Pietro Koch in Rome. Yet the film as a whole is not uniformly lit by the personal 'participation' of the artist, who succeeded in his other movies in 'exalting the substance' on which they were based, always the same substance, which he defined as 'true stories, rooted in the earth, but which enable us to rise above the earth'.

'If the film had been shot as soon as the script was written,' says Ms Cecchi d'Amico, 'I think it would have been better, but it had to wait three years. I like parts of it, the murder, for example, and the conversation with the priest, but on the whole I don't think it's a very successful movie. We never saw it again with Luchino. While he was sick he wanted to see all his films again on videotapes, except for *Ludwig*, which he flatly refused to see because it was mutilated. *The Stranger* seemed simply forgotten.'

It lacked – as had its nocturnal counterpart *White Nights* – the violence that would have brought out the relevance Visconti had originally sought, since he saw the novel as a premonition, a prophecy of the tragedy of the *pieds-noirs*, of the 'extremism of the [French] paratroopers and the Algerian rebellion', the 'nightmarish explosion of violence among men who are no longer able to understand each other and live together'.

He was to express this much-needed violence frantically, paroxysmally, in the modern plays he staged in Rome between the end of 1967 and early 1969. One was Testori's *La Monaca di Monza* (*The Nun from Monza*). But Visconti's insistence on cutting the text touched off a public row between the two men, with critics chiming in to accuse the director of maiming the work.

A few years earlier, a historian had published documents he had found in the archives in the Milan archbishopric. The book, which enjoyed considerable popularity, exhumed a scandal that had set chroniclers twittering in the convent of Santa Margherita of Monza between 1598 and 1607, and had later given Manzoni the inspiration for a famous episode in *The Betrothed*. A young aristocrat, Marianna de Leyve – Sister Virginia – had been forcibly confined to the convent, and her lover, Gian Paolo Osio, had been convicted by the Curia's criminal court for their liaison and the murder of the children born of it. Testori had based his play on this 'Italian chronicle'.

For his staging, Visconti had cut the text heavily and had stressed the modern impact he saw in the characters' erotic tragedy. 'The action,' one critic said, 'should have taken place in the courtyard at Santa Margherita, as indicated on the first page of the play.

But Visconti presents us with a little curtain over a building site symbolizing Monza in 1966. And when the curtain rises, we find, with a slight shock, that the nun of Monza, her lovers' ghosts, along with the vicar, the priest and the others, have moved, who knows why, to a garage (with jerrycans, tyres, a tow-truck and even an old sink). And that's not enough. There are also neon signs, the latest pop tunes along with the mystic choirs, and the nefarious Osio is a zipper-jacketed delinquent who smokes his butts like a thug.'

As in Pasolini's work, there was a strange process here in which the past and present compete in violence and horror. The ugliness of the present shown by Visconti, however, outdoes Pasolini's; this is an irredeemable modern tragedy in a grim setting of rubble, vacant lots and stinking canals. Looming over it all is a huge steam shovel grubbing in the vitals of an earth crammed with skeletons.

A year later, on 21 February 1969, the curtain went up in a Milan theatre on bare walls as suffocating as the walls of a burial vault, where another process of destruction took place. Natalia Ginzburg's play *The Advertisement* was, like Sartre's *No Exit*, a modern couple's endless game of revenge, an absurd and brutal epilogue to an unsuccessful marriage. Rather than a dialogue between characters, it is a soliloquy for three voices in which Adriana Asti, for whom the play was written, cast a madwoman's image in this new mirror of this new era's aridity.

Between these two works of deep despair erupted the springtime upheavals of 1968: disorder in the universities, defiance of the political and social establishment. The spreading chaos could only have bolstered the feelings of hostility in old rebel Visconti.

In the world of movies, in cultural and political circles, the old unity was cracking as the generations faced off. Visconti, like Antonioni, was now consigned, at best, to a props closet. At worst he was considered an arch-symbol of reaction, of oppression by the intellectual élite. Unlike Pasolini, say, or Moravia, he felt no sympathy for the voices of protest in the Sixties. He could understand rebelling against the war in Vietnam, he'd done that himself. But what were the young people rebelling against? 'We often talked about it,' Ms Cecchi d'Amico says. 'He worried about it. But we agreed that all the changes, all the Marcuse-style slogans, had to have an aim; change that merely destroyed without building something else was useless. He didn't try, as Moravia and Pasolini did, to join the movement so as to appear young.'

As an echo of the student tumult, in the spring of 1969, Visconti staged Verdi's *Simone Boccanegra* in Vienna. Set in Genoa during the turbulent Renaissance, this is a political opera based on the fratricidal struggles among the great families and the conflict between commoners and the aristocracy in a divided Italy anxious for unity and reconciliation. Composed in 1856, *Simone Boccanegra* recounts the tragic story of Boccanegra, an ex-pirate who, despite his deepest wishes, becomes the doge of Genoa; he is the voice of Verdi's, and Visconti's, political ideal, of his dream of unity and justice.

Among the scenes in this first political opera is one, resonant with 1960s implications, of a Council meeting that is interrupted by the sound of an angry mob in the street below. In this opera – 'too sad, too depressing, but that's how it should be,' Verdi said – a skein of private rivalries, conflicting interests and the workings of history form an inescapable web of hatred and misunderstanding around the characters; its dream of a future reconciliation is blasted by the assassination of Boccanegra, a 'martyr to power'.

Seldom was a Visconti staging so unanimously criticized as this one. The modern sets, the warlike atmosphere, the geometrical lines of costumes that encased the singers in gleaming shells bordered on the grotesque, as did the singers' exaggeratedly theatrical diction. Fedele d'Amico notes that Visconti himself thought the production unconvincing. The fact remains that he had tackled one of the most difficult of all operas to stage because he was interested in its 'sad, depressing' echoes of a political and social situation he saw clamping down on Italy, on all of Europe, in those agitated years of protest when the older generation was disavowed.

'The young? I don't understand them,' he said. Their furies, enthusiasms, celebrations and demonstrations, their abstract perorations, their confused juggling of Mao and Marx and Che Guevara and Herbert Marcuse and Wilhelm Reich, the wave of intolerance and permissiveness that washed through the schools and universities and rolled on to engulf every institution – all this Visconti found alien and hostile to the point of nausea. New models of life and thought were springing up, borrowed from China's Cultural

Revolution, from Woodstock America and the student revolts in Berkeley. In Berlin and in the amphitheatres of the Sorbonne, slogans assailed the cornerstones of order and culture and challenged the Communist Party that a tormented, heart-sick Visconti continued to support despite the Soviet invasion of Czechoslovakia. In these phenomena he saw appalling confirmation of a process of decomposition that he had already denounced in his depictions of families sapped and torn by resentment and hatred.

There was no turning back now to traditions inherited from an agrarian society that had been dissected and destroyed by the irresistible advance of industrialization, whose sins he had already catalogued. Nor could there be any resorting to the 'illumination' of Marxist culture that had lighted his connection with his time, and in the feverish post-war period had turned Count Visconti into a leftist condottiere.

Neither Marx nor Gramsci had forseen this anarchic new type of protest decked out in the tawdry finery of the Revolution. The rise of criminal violence in December 1969 with the bombing of a Milan bank that left sixteen persons dead and signalled the advent of terrorism, both red and black, further stirred Visconti's deep fear of a return to Fascism. He was sixty-two years old, four years older than Mann had been at the time of the Reichstag fire in 1933.

For he now identified with the great humanistic novelist of Europe's decline. That he was quarantined, accused of arrogant senility, left him virtually unmoved. He would not howl with the wolves, would not blow the silly, sour trumpet of the new vanguard's new revolution. He would not compromise with disorder. He still hoped that the silent majority, at least, would not be fooled, and he took some bitter consolation in thinking of the empty movie theatres showing the films of young directors hungry for revolution.

'I certainly haven't forgotten that I was a young Italian moviemaker too,' he said. 'We were all young. We weren't born old. We all made films that, in a sense, were avant-garde. We adopted neo-realism. And moviegoers deserted our theatres, the public quarrelled with us. Does that mean it's starting all over again, that today is just like yesterday? No, they're not the same. Because, unfortunately, I'm one of those who doesn't go to see films by the new Italian directors. And that's serious. I should understand them. All they have to do is to say really new things, to communicate really new information and offer really new arguments and I'll be the first to go to see their films, to understand them and support them . . .

'They don't come to grips with the vital problems, the problems of their generation. When we were young we dealt with the problems of our generation. I would like young Italian film-makers to do the same. I don't think it is opportune for one of us to deal with their problems. I could try, but I'd feel uneasy, out of place, an interloper. Let everyone handle his own problems.'

Visconti made this statement in the Hôtel des Bains in the spring of 1970. He was looking at the beach, at the tents with their cool blue and white stripes, and at the figures in lace and voile of an epoch gone forever: Mann's time, Proust's, Mahler's, his own. 'The youngest revolutionary of them all,' he declared, 'is Luis Buñuel. And he's sixty-eight.' In looking back on the past, in tracing the roots of Europe's troubles, Visconti felt younger than a lot of directors who, at thirty, seemed to him to have dried up to become shrivelled little old men 'already resigned like men of eighty'.

He was less ready than ever to give up 'his' cinema. Decadent? Very well. Pessimistic? No, simply objective, Nostalgic? 'Living,' he said, 'is also remembering.' But for him the past was not a refuge or an escape. What good was the past? To explain the 'eternals'. Now the time had come for him to rediscover these eternals not only in Italy, but in Europe, to probe the century's roots and follow them back through those three periods that were as fateful as the witches' conclave in *Macbeth*: the Reichstag fire, the eve of the first world war, and the defeat of Austria-Hungary and Bavaria in 1866. This was a twilight journey, a remembrance of things past for today's use.

XX

GÖTTERDÄMMERUNG

*To the Germans, the idea of a catastrophe, I
mean a beauty, a real one, is as transportable
as that of the Revolution once was to the
French.*

PAUL CLAUDEL

*Civilization has other needs besides the stock
pot of health.*

FYODOR DOSTOYEVSKY

So Visconti turned to the Germany of yesterday and not to the
China or the United States of today or tomorrow. 'Today's world,'
he said, 'is so ugly, so grey, and the world to come is horrible, vile.'

Antonioni had been driven by his ardently open mind, his eagerness for novelty and his quest for adventure to embark on a treasure
hunt for current reality; what he brought back was *Zabriskie Point*,
an explosive, youthful, pseudo-documentary film with that dash of
lyricism and the casual touch that suited the new cinema style and
the new audiences. Faced by developing reality, he said, an artist has
only one task: 'to look around, to go down into the street, to get lost
in the crowd'. This had been the neo-realists' creed. Now, tanned
by the California sun and wearing blue jeans, the cinematographer
of alienation immersed himself in a pool of vitality and violence as if
it were a fountain of youth. To hell with the ideas and books and
narrative forms of old Europe.

' "Reading a film": those words don't make sense today,' he
said. 'What counts is feeling a film.' And if reality has become a
chaos of words and colours, then the work has every right to take

the forms of delirium. 'As an artist,' he proclaimed, 'I defend my right to delirium, if only because today's delirium may be tomorrow's truth.'

Visconti, however, insisted on the need for 'clear ideas when you undertake a movie', and on the importance to any serious, realistic analysis of the present of a knowledge of the past, of history and the great cultural movements that even a failing civilization maintains. 'I think the political, cultural and human crisis of the past few years,' he declared in 1969, 'is one that breaks all previous moulds and requires an awareness and attitude free of dogma. I did and do attach great importance to the role that the young have had, now have and seek to have in this situation. But I say very clearly and with keen concern that the eagerness of the young is often accompanied by new kinds of dogmatism and erraticism that confuse and defer the clarification humanity needs.'

He was the last man to trample on the culture that still nourished him. When asked in 1971 what part his work might play in 'salvaging Western civilization', Visconti replied quietly but firmly: 'Yes, it does come down to that a bit. Culture is increasingly becoming mass culture, and that's fatal. It can be a good thing if movies interest the general public in reading the great works of literature.'

Not only did he turn his back on experimentation, on devising new and chaotic forms, on everything he called gratuitious formalizing, but in defiance of fashions, conventions and box-office imperatives he chose stories that were more sweeping than ever, works that borrowed their grand symphonic formats from Balzac, Proust, Mann, Wagner. The notion that today's delirium might be tomorrow's truth shook him; he preferred to think that yesterday's delirium prefigured today's. He did not think Fascism was dead. In 1968, when he revived his old plans for *Macbeth*, he affirmed that the 'story of violence, of blood and the bestial craving for power that began on 2 February 1933', when the Nazis came to power in Germany, was still pertinent as 'a reminder and report on a still current reality'.

Only the uncontrolled criminal monstrosity of the German tragedy, he thought, compared with the confusion of the late Sixties, a clear sign that a society and civilization were decomposing, that humanistic values were being overturned and the forces of irrationality unleashed. He was intent on tracing the evil he called decadence back to its roots, on backtracking through all the phases of history that had led to this, from the Reichstag fire in *The Damned* to the hegemony of Bismarck's Germany in *Ludwig*. 'Decadentism,' he announced in 1973, 'is very valuable. It was an extremely important artistic movement. If we are now trying to immerse ourselves in such an atmosphere again it is because we want to show the evolution of society through the cataclysms that have rocked it and which led to the decadence of a great period. I think doing that is . . . a form of political commitment.'

Other, more personal, causes also moved him. Helmut Berger, of course, was one: Visconti wanted to give the young man his chance. But he was also anxious to peer into this pool of violence and see reflected in it the enormous tragedy looming for him both as an artist and as a man. 'In a way,' he said, 'we old movie-makers have said what we had to say. I did that from *Obsession* to *The Damned*, and when I gave myself a few brief respites, as in *White Nights*, they certainly were not disgraceful respites. Now we can deal with more particular, more private themes because we have behind us a history of struggle that, to some extent, justifies this belated and temporary return to a privacy we denied ourselves for years.'

He found his private themes in Proust and Mann. While completing *The Damned* and while shooting *Death in Venice*, he worked on what he thought of as his 'last film', his crowning work: an adaptation of *Remembrance of Things Past*. 'All his life, Luchino had thought of making a Proustian film, "his" film, as he called it,' says Ms Cecchi d'Amico, who wrote the script for what mysteriously remained an impossible dream. 'He was superstitious, and I'm sure the idea haunted him. It's a matter of repression, or exorcism. Proust was his author, he had known his books by heart since he was a child. He was Charlus.'

'Was he Ludwig, too?' we asked her.

She thought for a moment, her fingers clasping the gold-and-amethyst chain Visconti had given her, then replied firmly: 'No, he wasn't. He had a very strong character. Ludwig is a weakling.'

A strong man who was none the less interested in the failures of this world, the victims, those whose 'destinies are crushed by reality'. More like Mann than like Proust, he was drawn to tormented, pathetic people, the Promethean artists whose lives were a network of tumults, calamities, wars. The Germany that fascinated him was the one scarred by disaster, by the great catastrophes that wrecked its dreams of power and its apotheosis of pure romanticism. This was the Germany, Mann had remarked, where, in the heyday of Bismarck, the Iron Chancellor, Wagner expressed the nation's nostalgia, its insularity, its infatuation with the impossible and with death.

Visconti did not, of course, deny the importance to him of French culture, 'so formative,' he said, 'because, from my childhood, I have lived in France'. Like most of the great Italian humanist intellectuals, like the Settembrini in *The Magic Mountain*, he was saturated with Enlightenment philosophy. But, he said, 'although I came to it later, German culture prompted a sterner, more serious apprehension of the world . . .'.

In contrast with the luminous lightness of the eighteenth-century French spirit, there was a heaviness in the German spirit that slowed down works of art, studding them with moral rhetoric and reflections like those in *Death in Venice* and in *Ludwig*. And there was the pessimism, the atmosphere that Nietzsche, referring to Schopenhauer and Wagner, called ethical, 'a Faustian scent, the cross, death and the grave'. Visconti said that, like Mann, he was 'fascinated by the mystery of disease, of pain'. He declared that 'I always have *Buddenbrooks* in mind,' and '*The Magic Mountain* is a project I have always fondled.' While Verdi's place in his personal pantheon was assured, the music Visconti listened to came to be almost exclusively German: Mozart, of course, Strauss, Wagner, and also a composer he had long disdained, Mahler.

In Visconti's return to this new fatherland of the soul – he pointed out that Germany was his family's cradle – Mann played a major role. 'In his works,' the movie-maker said, 'he was all of us, good and bad. I managed to understand him even if he is a German from Lübeck and I'm a Milanese.' Not understanding him would have been more surprising, since the two were so close in their social origins, artistic tastes, musical sensibilities, their mixture of critical moralism and decadence and their explorations of the demoniac forces that composer Henze called 'the dangerous mystery of Germany'.

The Damned was inspired by *Buddenbrooks*, as is evident from the first scene of the Essenbecks dining *en famille*. But, like all Visconti's films, it is a complex alloy of literary influences: Shakespeare, Dostoyevsky, Sartre's *Altona*. It is dominated, however, by specifically German factors. 'I would have liked my portrayal to be even a bit more German than this,' the director said, 'but perhaps I don't know Germany well enough, unfortunately, even if I know Mann's works well. To understand some things better I should have lived with a . . . patriarchal German family.'

A vast collection of written sources was consulted on such families, on the Krupps, on the leading actors in the hideous guignol attending the birth of Hitler' Germany: fiction, biographies, memoirs, historical studies, anything and everything. To film the macabre scene of the climactic marriage of Sophie von Essenbeck, that stupefied Lady Macbeth, to her lover, Friederich Bruckman, every available account of the Hitler-Eva Braun suicides was acquired and carefully sifted. Visconti was never without William L. Shirer's book *The Rise and Fall of the Third Reich*, 'a genuine Bible'.

And, of course, period sets, settings and costumes were scrupulously, fanatically reproduced by Piero Tosi and Vera Marzot. Gossip has it that a Jewish motorist, seeing Nazi uniforms, banners and insignias materialize out of a nightmarish nowhere, suffered a heart attack. Again the director was derided because, for the Night of the Long Knives scene he was shooting in Austria, he supplied the Unterach am Attersee inn with pale veal sausages sent directly from Bavaria; the classic local *würstel*, it seemed, were coloured a distressingly Austrian pink.

The cast was also chosen to stress the specifically German nature of the story. With Helmut Griem playing the SS officer, Aschenbach, German actors took the leading parts, except for those of the liberal, Herbert Thalmann, played by Umberto Orsini, and the young cellist in Gunther von Essenbeck's family, assigned to a French actor, Renaud Verley. The film's two stars, Dirk Bogarde and Ingrid Thulin, fit nicely into the pattern: Bogarde – real name Dirk Van den Bogaerde – was of Dutch origin, and Thulin was married to a German.

The part of the degenerate son, grafted on to the first version of this modern *Macbeth*, was given, of course, to Berger, the newest colt in the Visconti stable, in his first major outing. He did not get through the four months of shooting without misery and public humiliation. Viscontian temper tantrums and threats – 'If you don't do it now, you little shit, you never will; you can go back to Austria' – were provoked by the young actor's blunders and fits of rebelliousness. Berger's parody of Marlene Dietrich brought on the worst of the directorial seizures: Visconti wasn't satisfied until he had repeated the scene more than twenty times and had screened *The Blue Angel* to get what he wanted through the young man's head.

Martin von Essenbeck was, with a slightly altered time factor, the Krupp heir, Arndt von Bohlen und Halbach, whose father, Gustav, had been a member of the SS and was the world's largest munitions maker. Krupp had also set up over one hundred factories in Auschwitz, staffed by camp inmates. The city of Essen, the industrial fief of the Krupp family – represented in the film as the Essenbecks – was turned into a vast labour camp where even six-year-old children were put to work. When the war ended, Krupp, a latter-day Macbeth, reportedly suffered from hallucinations; in the great dining-hall of his castle, he was said to rise from the table on occasion, point into the shadows and wonder aloud 'Who are all these people?'

Three years after the Nuremberg war-crimes tribunal sentenced him (to twelve years' imprisonment), he was released and his fortune was restored to him. Only then did he try to raise his son, who had been shunted off after his parents' divorce, when he was three. But the young man had no appetite for business, preferring to travel the world with his mother, or stay in an imitation Palace of Versailles south of Rio de Janeiro. On the firm's one hundred and fiftieth anniversary, his father introduced him for the first time to his faithful employees, the *Kruppianner*; they saw an amazingly hand-some playboy with mascaraed eyes and plucked eyebrows who was manifestly uninterested in the business that still fed old Gustav' rapacious passion. When his father died in 1967, Arndt gave up his shares in exchange for an income of around one million dollars a month and spent the remaining twenty years of his life in a whirl of rhinestones and spangles, reigning over a court of young men who adulated him and stole from him what they could, until he died of an AIDS-related disease in the spring of 1986. He and his mother were inseparable, although this did not prevent him from observing before he died that she had always had a pernicious influence on his life.

When *The Damned* premièred in Hamburg, 'little Krupp', as he was called, announced he would hold a grand reception to celebrate the event. 'I must confess,' Visconti said, 'that I liked that. I thought it showed wit.'

What happened to the Krupps symbolizes history's denial of Visconti's version of the facts: more big industrialists survived Nazism than were crushed by it. And Hitler' Germany promoted the rise of a whole new caste of sordid, lower-class third-raters who appear nowhere in this film about the tragic decline in the aristocracy. But Visconti had wanted to depict a twilight of the gods, those gods, said the director, borrowing from Karl Marx, 'through whom capitalism is expressed', who 'still excite and disturb humanity today as the pagan deities, Wagner's gods, used to do. Money is the instrument of their power and factories bristling with smoke-stacks are the temples of their cult.'

Visconti heard the same reproach that had been levelled at Sartre for *The Condemned of Altona*: his characters had been kings and princes of industry who 'find their sinister grandeur in crime, in a total adherence to evil'; in so doing he had shrouded Nazism in an infernal but romantic aura. Sartre's reply served as well for Visconti's Essenbecks as for his own Gerlachs: 'With such characters I could start right out with a fundamental contradiction, that between these people's industrial power, their aristocratic title, their past, their culture, and their collaboration with the Nazis they despised . . . Thus I could clearly pose the problem of collusion, which is essential if we want to understand mankind.'

Visconti obviously wanted to show the same sort of contamination, which neither his own family nor even the Savoys had escaped. And he laid painful stress on the contrast between the Essenbecks' aristocratic past, the patriarchal order that prevailed as long as old Joachim was alive, and the increasingly discordant present – the 'noble' Bach sonata played by Gunther versus the vulgar bawling of Martin in drag as Lola-Lola. A present marred by family rivalries, resentment and the revelation of flaws, perversions, death instincts.

'This very night, before the flames at the Reichstag have died,' predicts Aschenbach, the messenger of the dark forces that here replace *Macbeth*'s witches, 'the Old Germany will be burned to ashes.' And with it the Joachims, the Herberts, the Gunthers and their liberal, democratic, middle-class concept of politics. Victims, too, were Mann, Zweig, Gide, Erich Maria Remarque, Jack London, Zola, Proust and their like, whose books were burned on the public squares in gigantic *autos-da-fé* that recalled the days of the Inquisition.

It was like Visconti to have cut out the specifically historical sequences originally scheduled to begin and end the film, actual footage of the Reichstag fire and of Germany in 1935. 'I set my film in Germany,' he said, 'because I wanted a story about Nazism, which I think is important. But the film did not remain historical, it became something more. At some point the characters almost become symbols, meaning that this is no longer a film on the birth of Nazism, but a film set in the present to provoke arguments and, even more, to achieve a kind of catharsis through the characters. In any case, I never intended to make a historical film.'

The Damned is, of course, a fable about Nazism, but it can also be taken, like *Macbeth*, 'for a legend, a fiction of a dim and distant era'. It is also a Marxist fable that reiterates an anti-capitalist credo: 'I think that of all the interpretations of Fascism, the truest is the one that views it as the final phase of world capitalism, the final consequence of the class struggle taken to its final extreme, that of a monstrosity like Nazism and Fascism and that, naturally, can only precede a change to Socialism.'

Visconti's principal obsessions, however, can be glimpsed in this film's violently expressionistic and tormented style, which owes more to fantasy than to historical objectivity or any ideological rationale. The characters' ordeals of conscience, the quotations of a style Visconti had hitherto avoided but whose morbid rhetoric he now exploited, the use of grotesque and poignant parody – Martin's vulgar exhibition, the grim caricature of the marriage – all reflect the artist's anguish, here enormously magnified, over what he saw as the proliferating evidences of corruption, 'putrefaction' and death.

Visconti intended this film as a monstrous symphony, a nightmare in which he 'tried to mark out how far you can go before you reach Sodom and Gomorrah, buried under the ashes'; to do this he accumulated, *ad nauseam*, instances of violence, unpunished crime and the whole gamut of sexual perversion.

The film blossomed, then, as much in the shade of Dostoyevsky and Freud as in the light of Marx. It is the inverted mirror image of *The Leopard*: the family disintegrates, the young liquidate the old, 'personal morality is dead'; we are 'in a society of the elect who can do whatever they like': rape, murder, incest, parricide, matricide, infanticide, anything. Visconti, who so prized order and discipline, was hypnotized by Martin's brutal violation of all the taboos. And the most powerful scenes in *The Damned* are those that best express Visconti's mingled fascination and revulsion: the blue vertigo of incest, followed by the metamorphosis of Sofia, whose possession and debasement by her son suddenly awaken her maternity.

'A Freudian reversion,' the director explained. 'The child with the blond hair she compares to her own, Martin's sketchbook in which he has written *Martin tötet Mutti* (Martin kills Mummy) under a childish drawing showing himself as a little boy holding a knife, and a bleeding woman. This scene came to me during the shoot, because I felt a need to end on an image that already showed that the child was at least a danger, a kind of threat of what the child would become. So I asked people to find me a child who could draw, and right there at Cinecittà they found a little girl and told her to "draw a child killing a lady". She did the mother and child. I had to add the knife myself because she didn't want to draw it. It's really funny. Under the drawing I wrote what the boy would have written, *Martin tötet Mutti*, and under another one, *Mutti und Martin*.'

Equally inspired was the sequence of the Night of the Long Knives on the shores of the Attersee, in a mountain-lake setting that anticipates the locale of *Ludwig*, but also recalls Lake Como at Cernobbio. In the scenes of the storm-troopers bathing in the lake, the camera, more sinuous than ever, slowly caresses these beautifully feminized bodies, made languid by booze and somnolence, to an accompaninment of Nazi songs and nostalgic music from *Tristan*.

Then, at dawn, SS men burst in on the scene, turning the homosexual orgy into a riot of defiled bodies twisted like the forms in a

Francis Bacon painting. This bloody ritual of degradation is a sort of dramatic celebration of the artist's masochism, an image of the punishment feared and desired by many confirmed homosexuals, as Visconti was, as Proust was – a visualization of the curse dogging homosexuals.

Visconti wanted the film to be entitled *Götterdämmerung* (*The Twilight of the Gods*), but the American producers rejected that and insisted, despite his repeated objections, on *The Damned*; the title was better at the box-office, but less faithful to the spirit of the film, to those Wagnerian images of an inferno consuming the fortress of the masters of the world. Worse still, he was denied the use of Mahler's music, and had to settle for the ponderous thumpings of Maurice Jarre.

Sooner or later, a Visconti movie dominated by Mahler's music was inevitable, and the two finally joined forces in *Death in Venice*. 'Their personalities were in close affinity,' notes Franco Mannino, who directed excerpts from the Austrian's *Third* and *Fifth Symphonies* for the film. 'Extraordinary analogies existed between those two great dramatic artists: in the way they built their theatrical effects, in their refusal to make concessions to the weakness and erosion of routine, and their absolute fidelity to the literary works they nevertheless revivified for their audiences. Each had a profound knowledge of a variety of styles. And despite their knowledge, both tended towards decadence in their work because they lived with a total vision of the human and cultural decline that surrounded us in the nineteenth century.'

Death in Venice formed an ideal junction for Visconti and Mahler.

The music in the film, says Theodor Adorno, is 'critical music that breaks with a tradition for which it is still nostalgic'. Popping up in these 'gigantic symphonic potpourris' are popular songs, barrel-organs, old tunes and fashionable ditties, carnival and march music. Disdaining the good taste and serene harmonies that reassure the middle class, 'Mahler introduced popular music as it is, like yeast, into grand classical music.' For this 'vagabond of music', real polyphony is what we hear among fairground side-show stalls and shooting galleries, a commotion suddenly split by a blast of trumpets.

Organizing all this into a harmonious whole was a problem for a different, bygone age. What did it have to do with *Death in Venice*, with Mann? In his novella, the writer had given his protagonist not only Mahler's looks, but even the name of that 'truly great man', and he had certainly been influenced by the hourly medical bulletins he read in May 1911 recording the composer's death agony. In Mahler, Visconti reminded us, Mann saw 'the man who embodies the most stern and sacred artistic will of our time'. That alone justified his association with the movie.

Artistic creation, the artist's relationship with his public, his world, himself – that was the theme Visconti wished to 'come to grips with' in the era of short-term profit in which he now lived. He had needed years of work, the knowledge of failure and fiasco and challenge – in a word, maturity – to 'dare' face a theme he said had always interested him: 'the conflict that can arise between an artist, with his aesthetic aspirations, and life, between what seems to place him above the story and what makes him a part of the "historical" bourgeois condition'. He saw nothing obsolete about the problem at a time when politics was everywhere overruling aesthetics and people were concluding that 'art is dead'.

Like *The Damned*, Visconti's *Death in Venice* is the story of a conflict and a crisis in which disease, irrationality and self-destructiveness overwhelm the peaceful, reassuring but false order of middle-class life. As the film opens, the very substantial Gustav von Aschenbach, played by Dirk Bogarde, places photographs of his wife and daughter about his hotel room, thus ritually re-constituting the setting of his normal, secure life. Visconti piously re-created the charm of this intimate, upholstered orderliness by reviving his own childhood memories in his stays in luxury hotels in Venice and Paris, those grand turn-of-the-century hotels that were all a bit like the one in Balbec in Proust's *Remembrance*. In all his homes, Visconti worshipfully distributed pictures of his parents, especially of his mother, to exorcize his personal demons. The sovereign elegance of Tadzio's mother, played by Silvana Mangano, bespoke Donna Carla's distant majesty. More than any other art, movies can evoke the dead like spiritualist séances in which, Visconti said, 'people are no longer here [but] they can still tell us very interesting things'.

Aschenbach's fragile order and tranquillity, however, are those of a society at its zenith; barely three years later the horror of war would sweep it away, and with it, Visconti said, 'all the old solutions and the age-old illusions'. The sequence featuring a toothless, grinning accordeonist is premonitory: with three of his mates accompanying him on the guitar he plays beneath the terrace of the fashionable Hôtel des Bains. He climbs the stairs, approaches Aschenbach and Tadzio's mother for a handout and is shooed away by the manager. He and his companions then reappear singing the derisive Neapolitan song *La Risata*, ending with a traditional and taunting *mossa* (the obscene grinding of the hips in a tarantella) and sticking his tongue out at the hotel's dignified clientèle. The onlookers are amused at first, but they increasingly show their uneasiness and, finally, their pique.

Aschenbach himself is, like his kindred soul, Adrian Leverkühn in Mann's *Doctor Faustus*, a man of restraint, of decency, of *noli me tangere*. At fifty, crowned with fame and honour, he is driven by an ill-defined anxiety to escape to Venice as to an oriental city of sensuality and death. Like him, Venice shows the signs of ineluctable physical and moral decay. Old wounds of past failures open and fester there, of the scandals Aschenbach's music has caused, along with his fear of ageing, of the inexorable running of the sad sands.

The more austere, stern and unyielding the artist is in his puritanical, Protestant, middle-class morality, the more he is tempted by the mannered and 'dangerous sphere' of sexuality. Tadzio's angelic beauty binds Aschenbach as Leverkühn – and Nietzsche – were bound by the sensual, voluptuous and pollutant arts of Esmeralda, the syphilitic prostitute. She is, in fact, alluded to twice in the film: the boat in which the musician travels to Venice is called the Esmeralda, and later Tadzio is directly associated with the young whore. Through the troubled medium of music – the *Für Élise* played by Tadzio and the prostitute – Visconti connects purity and impurity, spiritual love and sensual love.

As a child identified with the whore, 'Tadzio represents a pole of attraction in Aschenbach's life,' Visconti said, 'the pole of real life – the alternative to and antithesis of the rigidly intellectual world, the "sublimated" life in which Aschenbach has sealed himself – that ends in death'.

377

The homosexual poet August von Platen-Hallermünde, who died in Sicily in 1835, wrote that 'He who has contemplated beauty with his own eyes is already dedicated to death', and the film's central theme is taken from that line. For the protagonist of *Death in Venice*, the illumination provided by beauty becomes the pathological luminescence of decay. This is shown in the physical deterioration of the sober musician who, made up like the homosexual clown in the first sequence, collapses at the foot of a polluted well and dies of cholera, 'completely made up, almost riduclous, like a clown, a broken marionette'.

The pathos is heightened by Aschenbach's growing awareness of his decomposition; when he collapses while wandering in search of Tadzio in the stinking alleys of Venice, he cannot restrain what Visconti says 'is a bitter and ironic laugh at himself. This laugh was not in the script, it was invented during the shoot. I realized that Aschenbach could not simply weep and thus show his pain, but that he had to feel sorry for himself here because he knew what his situation was.'

Nietzsche wrote that the degree and kind of a person's sexuality have repercussions on the very summits of his spirituality. Eros places an artist in conflict with the world, with what is average in life, he wrests him from the middle-class world and transports him to a sphere of tormented and ecstatic decay. At the same time he reveals to him the links between art and the hell of disintegration, gives him a clearer vision of the murky sources of sublimation. As both a break with and a link to the world, abjection in the quest for the sublime, the hope of redemption and the threat of perdition, art is by nature ambiguous and equivocal. This is especially true of music, the most mathematical yet irrational of the arts. Visconti tried to paint this ambiguity into his film. And, indeed, his work shines with so pure a light largely by contrast with the darkness that all artists mine.

The ambiguity, present in Mann's story, had to be preserved at all costs, what Mann called the novella's 'very decent' tone, wholly fitting and decorous, had to be respected. To remain true to this precept, Visconti spent months looking for his Tadzio, the beautiful boy with whom Aschenbach is smitten. In every city in central and northern Europe, from Budapest to Helsinki, he reviewed processions of the handsomest, blondest boys he could find as they undressed, walked, turned. Finally, in Stockholm, he found a fifteen-year-old with a fairy-tale name, Bjørn Andresen.

When Visconti the ogre first gazed upon his prey, the silence was slightly more intense than usual. Then: 'He is very handsome . . . Turn your head. Have you any photos here?' To his assistant he said, 'Tell him to take off his sweater and look at the camera . . . He's a bit too tall'. Not for a moment did the director lose sight of the ideal Tadzio described by Mann. Throughout the movie, Tadzio, the angel of the morning, angel of death, had to show the mute, tender, enigmatic smile we find on the faces of some of Leonardo da Vinci's angels.

The problem was to tell this story 'with detachment and delicacy that never slid towards sickliness, maintaining an ambiguous delicacy'. This is why Visconti decided not to film a sequence centring on Aschenbach's orgiastic nightmare. 'At first,' he said, 'I did think of shooting the nightmare *Blow Up* style, in a Munich nightclub like a kind of eighth circle of Dante's *Inferno*, with an orchestra from *The Damned*, into which I'd have propelled Aschenbach, skipping over half a century.

'Finally I gave it up because I realized that this would have broken the tone, [violated] the taste in the film . . . For the nightmare which, in the book, is the point of deepest depression and foretells [Aschenbach's] death, I substituted the concert fiasco, which fulfils the same function in the film and represents the despair that heralds the end.' The passage was inspired, Visconti admitted, by the jeering and whistling that had greeted *Rocco and His Brothers* ten years earlier.

The film teeters between irony and lyricism, the demoniac and the angelic, all the way to the ultimate mystery in the final scene inseparably paralleling the artist's face, a funeral mask caked with make-up, and the radiant visage of Tadzio pointing to the vast bluish horizon over the sea. This is the visual equivalent of Vinteuil's Septet in *Remembrance* and, like it, a 'call to extraterrestrial joy', a 'mystical expectation of the Scarlet Angel of the Morning'.

Proust, a contemporary of Mahler's, had his place in the film, too, in its elegiac contemplation of a vanished world, in its call to

Art to re-create a lost fatherland where death is 'less inglorious, perhaps less probable'. And he is there in the film's quest, described by Visconti as 'not decadent or aesthetic or hedonistic, but, more seriously and in a manner that is basically Greek, [for] perfection, for total harmony . . .'.

While their inner torments were similar, Aschenbach's way of struggling with his demon was not Visconti's. The musician withdrew from the world and abandoned himself to the forces of perdition, which carried him far from the public eye to where he could destroy himself with voluptuous anguish. Visconti's approach remained critical. It was no accident that the musician in *Death in Venice* and the SS officer in *The Damned* were both named Aschenbach. By establishing a genealogical link between the Nazi and the aesthete, Visconti was saying that the hideous degeneracy of Hitlerism in Germany had deep and distant sources in the culture that bred it and nourished it and to which it constantly referred. This was the culture of the Belle Époque, of *fin-de-siècle* art.

To follow it back to its roots, he shelved plans to adapt *Remembrance*, which was again being delayed by financial problems. Instead he returned to the subject of Germany's pessimism and its faltering values. Step by step, following Mann's analysis of the decline of humanistic culture, he backtracked to Wagner and the Wagnerian epidemic that seized Europe in the second half of the nineteenth century.

This 'intoxication with death conquering the world', Mann had commented, was a paradoxical and eternally enthralling phenomenon that turned its back on reality to wallow in irrationality and an atmosphere of dreams, magic and myth. The sensual, 'infernal' music of this Wagner, this 'Cagliostro' of modern times, doubtless broke with the dull, materialistic, bourgeois civilization that had grown up in the Second Reich of Bismarck and Kaiser Wilhelm II. But it also broke with a long-standing humanistic tradition.

Mann, though bewitched by *Tristan*, nevertheless concluded in his essay on 'The Suffering and Grandeur of Richard Wagner' that his troubled and troubling music was 'created and directed against civilization, against a whole culture and society that had been dominant since the Renaissance'; it stemmed, he said, from the era of bourgeois humanism in the same way that Hitlerism did.

How so? In that it flattered and exalted a Faustian arrogance of the mind, fostered a cult of darkness, death and destruction and unleashed irrational forces by contaminating a subjugated public – by questionable but infinitely seductive means – with a 'contraband religion' to supplant the French philosophy of the Enlightenment and Goethe's serene and measured ideals. Wagner's art was oddly contradictory, aspiring to 'total purity' yet using the 'impure' devices Mann listed: sensual ardour, intoxication, hypnotic caresses, lavish embroidery. Wasn't it this impurity, Mann asked, everything luxurious and luxuriant in Wagner's music, that won over the bourgeois masses?

Visconti's portrait of Wagner in *Ludwig* closely matches Mann's amused depiction of the 'Saxon gnome' with his snuffbox, his explosive talent and his meanness, all the things that made him so 'middle class', not in the noble sixteenth-century sense, Mann specified, but in a modern sense. He was none the less a powerful, enigmatic magician whose spells worked not only in the salon of Proust's Madame Verdurin, but also on so many novelists, poets and philsophers from Baudelaire to Nietzsche to Mann.

His most exemplary victim, however, was probably King Ludwig II of Bavaria, the one most withdrawn from the world, yet most symptomatic of the profound crisis then gripping European civilization. Ludwig's life engrossed Visconti enough to persuade him even to drop his plans – temporarily, he thought – for filming *Remembrance of Things Past*. For one thing, there was the king's relationship with Wagner, a direct link to Visconti's own love of German music. He said the idea for the film had occurred to him long before 1971, when he offered Romy Schneider 'the kind of role you're used to'.

'I see,' she replied. 'A whore?' And she burst out laughing.

Of course not. He was thinking of Empress Elizabeth of Austria, the legendary Sissi. Schneider, her young Austrian face shining with health, had played Sissi in the Fifties, and now the empress's destiny seemed to be pursuing her. While shooting *The Damned*, Visconti had checked locations in Bavaria, around Ludwig's pseudo-classical, pseudo-baroque, pseudo-gothic, absurdly kitsch castles. To astonished modern tourists, these pastiches of doubtful taste, hidden in forest fastnesses and shrouded in mountain mists, pose the enigma of Ludwig II and, in a larger sense, of a whole period of the nineteenth century when, Mann noted, platitude paired oddly with melancholy.

Visconti, then, had long been interested in the doomed House of Wittelsbach, allied with the Hohenzollerns and the Habsburgs, which reigned over Bavaria and its surrounding regions for over seven centuries until, in the nineteenth century, its peculiarities left it suspended between real sovereignty and a theatrical reverie of royalty, between sanity and madness. As far back as the Thirties, Visconti had considered making a film on the Mayerling tragedy involving Elizabeth's son.

In dropping preparations for *Remembrance*, for which the sets, costumes, cast and narrative line were already chosen, to devote himself to *Ludwig*, Visconti was not departing as decidedly from Proust's atmosphere as one might suppose. Many of the characters in *Remembrance* were as much at home in the pompous salons of the Munich Residenz as they were at Madame Verdurin's. Greta Garbo had been cast as Queen Marie-Sophie of Naples, sister of Elizabeth of Austria and a cousin of Ludwig II. The Princesse de Guermantes was allied with what the narrator, that busy bee among the flowers of heraldry, called 'one of History's noblest lineages, the richest in experience, scepticism and pride'. It was that bloodline that gave the Baron de Charlus his 'very special little laugh' in which, as in 'certain ancient instruments, now extremely rare', resonated the oldest of Europe's minor courts.

Ludwig, Visconti promised while shooting the film, 'is only an intermezzo' before Proust. He could not foresee that fate, and the work itself, would decide otherwise. For this ill-fated film was finally to take on the proportions of a masterpiece, a pathetic *Ivan the Terrible*, a tragic symphony of defeat that would end his 'German trilogy'.

From the start, the obstacles seemed insurmountable. The film's colossal budget had to be shared among four production companies, one Italian, two German and one French, and this was an endless source of financial complications. '*Ludwig* was particularly, exceptionally tiring for me,' Visconti said, 'in the preparation phase as well as in the filming, because of other people's uncertainties, because of all the difficulties I had to deal with before and during the shoot. One day we were making the movie, the next day it was off. These uncertainties of others rubbed my nerves raw . . . It wasn't easy to complete the film because it was too expensive. Not that I want to criticize the producer; on the contrary, I must say he did all he could to bring it through. It was a fine effort, but before making the film this effort did me a bit of damage. Six months of struggle. A step forward, a step back. We're doing it, we're not doing it. Then there was the search for locations and then the retakes, always at night, always in terribly cold climates. In fact, I didn't dislike the cold, but it may have affected my health.'

Months before 31 January 1972, when the traditional bottle of inaugural champagne was broken over one of the cameras, something happened that the director, pushing himself too hard, lightly dismissed. One summer evening in Ischia, his arm was suddenly paralysed. The incident only lasted around twenty seconds. 'I didn't go to bed,' he said, 'I didn't think, "I'm ill, something's wrong with me." No, I finished out the evening with my friends, went on smoking as usual.

'Maybe it was a warning and I should have paid more attention to it. But I thought, "I'm stronger than other people, so why bother?" The doctor gave me medication to take during the shooting of Ludwig, but I never took it because it annoyed me to carry that little bottle around in my pocket, where it was always leaking . . . One fine day I got sick of it and threw it away, saying "I'm fed up with always having my pockets soaked by this blasted medicine." I paid dearly for this bit of idiocy, very dearly.'

Filming finally began, a little over a mile from the small spa of Bad-Ischl, at night in the lighted horse-show tent where Elizabeth of Austria, 'Europe's leading amazon', met her cousin Ludwig II, 'Europe's handsomest king'. Visconti had long since worked out the lens sequence, camera movements and angles, the lighting. Re-creation of the period was as objective and detailed as it had been for The Leopard.

During the months of shooting in Bavaria, the crew's caravans migrated constantly from one castle to another. From Munich they went to Oberammergau, near which stood the rococo Linderhof palace, the only one Ludwig ever saw completed. Then to Herren-

chiemsee, another Versailles with a hall of mirrors 211 feet long and
36 feet wide that created complex problems of lighting and refrac-
tion for the cameraman Armando Nannuzzi. From there to the Isle
of Roses, to Lake Starnberg, to Hohenschwangau, to Nymphenburg, to Neuschwanstein, where the snow, the fog and the rain
were never dense enough for the director.

The furniture, trophies, engravings, paintings and silver lent by
the Habsburgs' descendants were the very pieces that had provided
the setting for Ludwig's life. Everything was authentic, even the
famous 'silent butler' at Linderhof, a table that rose from the floor
fully set with flowers and dishes so that the king need not be troubled by the presence of a servant. And everything was real, even the
bouquets of fresh violets Elizabeth wore pinned in the hair at her
temples.

The actors and actresses so closely resembled the originals that
they looked like a family album come to life. Basing himself on
photographs of King Ludwig, Visconti gradually altered Helmut
Berger's looks: the angelically handsome youth grew deformed, his
face became puffy, his body grew fat and age bent his back. The
director planned Berger's every line, every gesture, every intona-
tion. 'He's perfect,' Visconti said. 'And since his adolescence he has
had the same gentle hysteria, the same melancholy, growing deeper
as he grew older.'

Visconti read and saw everything he could concerning the Moon
King. 'This is his true story,' he said, 'reconstituted from old documents and exact descriptions. I learned nothing more about his
death than what is written in the history books. Nothing in the
family archives, no relative or descendant of the witnesses departed
from the official version.' He asked to see the Virgin King's tomb
and was ushered into the crypt of the Church of Saint Michael,
where the Jesuits, relentless foes of the renegade king, had stacked
the coffins of the Wittelsbachs for centuries. Ludwig's remains have
lain there ever since the day in June 1886 when, in loving farewell,
Empress Elizabeth placed a last bouquet of jasmine in his hands. 'An
old box covered with dust, among many others also covered with
dust. The crown can scarcely be seen any more.'

In Munich, not a single monument commemorates the king
who died barely a century ago after twenty-two years on the throne.

But a string of young people's 'Ludwig clubs' still celebrates his cult there. The clubs, Visconti said, 'are very much like the American clubs that commemorate James Dean and Marilyn Monroe'. Romanticism is not dead, and dreamy, nostalgic Ludwig, with his love of mountain tops and solitude, was its extreme example.

To Visconti, the king's lack of moderation, his worship of the grandiose, the castles he built and never lived in and his passion for Wagner, the 'adored friend' who saw in him 'a wonderfully handsome god come down from Olympus', a veritable Lohengrin, made him 'a complex, exceptional character, totally unorthodox, who lived life to its convulsive fullness, as in a long, exalted dream'. No wonder the Symbolist *poètes maudits* put him in the same tragic constellation as themselves, under the 'malign influence' of Saturn, where Verlaine had placed them.

Ludwig had turned his back on 'the deceptive clarity of daylight' to live, like Tristan, like Filippo Maria, the last Duke of Milan, in 'the wondrous kingdom of the night'. When he grew older, 'real life' began for him at sunset: he had his bath at six o'clock in the evening, then breakfasted; he lunched an hour or two past midnight, supped between six and seven in the morning and retired at eight. The film was accordingly shot entirely between twilight and dawn.

'Night is the haven and the kingdom of romanticism,' Mann said, 'it is its discovery. [Romanticism] has always considered it true, in opposition to the vain illusion of the day, the kingdom of sensitivity against reason. I will never forget the impression made on me by a visit to Linderhof, the castle of Ludwig II of Bavaria, the sick king in search of beauty, where the interior arrangement precisely affirms this preponderance of night.

'Inside this "folly" admirably situated in the silence of the mountains, the rooms designed to be lived in by day are small and, compared to the others, sober, mere closets. There is only one relatively huge and lavishly decorated room, full of gold and silk: the bedroom with its raised ceremonial bed surmounted by a tester and flanked by gilded candelabra – a true hall of state dedicated to the night. This insistence on the hegemony of night, the "most beautiful half of the day", is arch-romantic. It connects romanticism to the cult of the moon, a maternal myth that since the dawn of mankind has contested worship of the sun, the virile and paternal day; Tristan succumbed to the fascination of that world.'

And so, we might add, did Ludwig, whose last words in the movie echo Mann's: 'Prison makes me "hear" the silence, as night does,' he tells Dr von Gudden. 'Night . . . there is nothing more beautiful than night. They say the cult of the night, of the moon, is a maternal myth, while the cult of the day, of the sun, is a virile myth. Yet for me the mystery, the grandiose beauty of night have always been the limitless realm of heroes. And thus of reason as well. Poor Doctor Gudden. Obliged to study me from morning to night, night to morning. But I am an enigma. I want to remain an enigma forever, to others and even to myself.'

In that last line, Visconti, was quoting Ludwig directly. On 25 April 1876, at two o'clock in the morning, the king wrote to his cousin Elizabeth: 'Our souls, I think I can see, have quite a restricted part in the common hatred of all baseness and all injustice . . . Perhaps someday I, too, will make peace with this heavy earth. This will happen when all the essences of my ideal are utterly consumed and all the fervour with which I so devotedly kept alive the sacred fire is extinguished . . . But I do not wish this. I wish to remain, for myself and others, an eternal enigma. Dear and precious you are and will remain to me, for I know that you will never doubt me . . .'

Visconti took this passion for truth and justice as seriously as Zweig did the passion that raised Hölderlin, Kleist and Nietzsche 'high above the heavy earth', for these were 'three poets of that Promethean race that crack all bounds, break down the barriers of life and destroy themselves in passion and excess'.

Unusual, eccentric, unbalanced, abnormal – Ludwig was probably all of these; like so many poets, as the composer Adrian Leverkühn, the hero of *Doctor Faustus*, put it, he had 'spiders on the ceiling'. Mad he was not, despite the diagnosis of six government-appointed alienists. Nothing is more suspect, Mann remarked, than the reassuring notion of madness 'too eagerly fondled by petits-bourgeois on the basis of doubtful criteria'. Ludwig's biographers have dwelt at length on the Moon King's picturesque oddities, his love of disguise, the masks he made his guards and grooms wear, his cruelty towards his servants, his shifting moods and disorderly use of time, the strange protocol he decreed in his castles.

Visconti, on the other hand, played these aspects down considerably. True, he attributed the king's mental disturbance to a 'maternal complex' and to pathological 'delusions of grandeur'; he noted that 'his relationship with his mother was extremely conflictual', pointing out that 'when [Ludwig] decided, Catholic though he was, to reject the dogma of papal infallibility and expel the Jesuits from Bavaria, his mother instantly converted to Catholicism'.

But in his movie Visconti eliminated any sequences spotlighting Ludwig's hatred for the woman he contemptuously dismissed as 'my predecessor's widow' and, during the war of 1870, as 'the Prussian'. Although the director admitted this conflict was 'acute', his editing of the film reduced the imperious queen mother to the proportions of a hysterical puppet, a mechanical doll. No mention at all is made of the father, a niggling, obtuse, miserly bureaucrat whose corpse Ludwig dreamed he pummelled in the crypt of the Theatine church.

Witnesses parade through this film-investigation, the camera holds on pontificating psychiatrists, their faces half devoured by shadows that then swallow them up entirely. Mad or not mad? The enigma remains unsolved, as does the mystery of Ludwig's death, in which Mann saw proof of his dignity: 'This man had been degraded to the rank of meat for psychiatry, shut into a castle beside a lake with the doorknobs unscrewed and the windows barred. That he could not stand this, that he sought liberty or death, dragging his doctor-jailer with him into the grave, attested to his sense of dignity and in no way confirms the diagnosis of mental alienation.

'Neither was this confirmed by the attitude of his entourage, wholly devoted and ready to defend him, nor by the rural population's love of its king. When the peasants saw him crossing the mountain alone at night, by torchlight, wrapped in his furs, in a gilded sled escorted by outriders, they saw him not as a madman but as a king after their own rude but romantic hearts; and if Ludwig had succeeded in swimming across the lake, as he planned, they manifestly would have protected him with their pitchforks and their flails against medical science and politics.'

More attached to an abstract idea of power than to the real activity that power implies, Ludwig II was the last of the kings, 'the only real king in this century', Verlaine would write. He was not a bourgeois king like his father, nor, like Wilhelm I, a sovereign serving a bourgeois state and an iron chancellor. Ludwig was 'His Majesty the King', patterned on those absolute monarchs Louis XIV and Louis XV of France.

With this sense of majesty went a keen conviction that he had a high spiritual mission, 'to give humanity the possibility to mature spiritually', and to give his people a freedom and independence that went counter to the irresistible rise of a conquering middle class, and to the birth of the Second Reich which doomed the kingdom of Bavaria.

On 12 March 1864, at the age of eighteen, he staggered as he donned the regalia of royalty. Visconti's coronation scene uses jerky, staccato, pompous music, a profusion of mirrors and the actor's ill-disguised nervousness to accentuate the ceremony's ridiculously ponderous theatricality. 'Sceptre and crown no more protected Ludwig,' remarks the screenwriter Medioli, 'than power could save the Essenbecks in *The Damned*, or than Professor Aschenbach's stability as a famous artist could protect him in *Death in Venice*. Again the gods and their dreams were crushed by a fate stronger than the one they ordained.'

Ludwig denounced the futility of the wars he had to wage, and from which his brother returned with eyes glazed with horror. Taking refuge in his boyhood room in the Castle of Berg, he used a magic lantern to move the stars, since he could not change the way of the world. 'I deserted,' he tells the faithful Durkheim, 'from an idiotic war that I could not manage to stop. I am not a coward. I hate lies and I want to live with truth . . .' When his brother spoke of the filth of the battlefield, the screams of the wounded, of the dead, Ludwig responded by shouting 'War doesn't exist!'

A childish rejection of reality? True enough, but it was also a clear-sighted view of his powerlessness; he saw himself as the king in Victor Hugo's verse play *Marion de Lorme*, 'fallen, dethroned, helpless', and he, too, considered abdicating. This was in 1866, after the defeat at Sadowa, because, he said, 'If we must submit to Prussian hegemony, I would rather leave; I do not want to be a shadow king, stripped of power.' Visconti thought he aspired 'to be a sort of Renaissance sovereign, a modern Lorenzo de'Medici'. He wanted to reign, but, with an accuracy conceded even by Bismarck, that foxiest of politicians, he recognized how insurmountably reality resisted his dreams. Since he would not be a shadow king, he had no choice but to become a king of shadows.

Exasperated by his ministers' very real financial problems, he threatened to replace them with his hairdressers and grooms. He drained the state's treasury so that Wagner could realize his dreams and complete his work. Without Ludwig there would have been no *Die Meistersinger*, no *Ring*, no *Parsifal*, no Bayreuth. But his freedom and power were increasingly circumscribed and restrained. Even before a squadron of ministers came in rain-soaked cloaks to arrest him in his eagle's nest in Neuschwanstein, he had become a prisoner, a tragic figure, as divorced from reality as any character in a Racine play.

Ludwig was unquestionably guilty: no one banishes the day without suffering the day's revenge. No one can with impunity harness power to an abstract idea of royalty, however lofty the idea. No one can defy the narrow rules of man's duty, as the 'positive' Durkheim reminds him, without cutting himself off from humanity: 'For anyone who pursues sublime ideas that are not of this world, tolerating mediocrity takes a lot of courage. But it is his only hope of escaping from obscene loneliness.'

Throughout the movie, Visconti underscores his protagonist's pathetic struggle to recapture his sense of reality and exorcize his demons: Ludwig's ceaseless prayers and his appeals to God and to Elizabeth reveal it. So does his attempt to become 'normal': His engagement to Sophie, which, as his letters prove, he broke off with relief ('Sophie liquidated', he notes in his diary) rather than remorse. His long, painful and vain fight against his homosexuality, which he felt as a curse, a condemnation, is expressed in part in the film through the sterility of the dead tree in *Die Walküre* that provides a Wagnerian background for the orgy in the hut at Tegelberg; this is set against the tragic counterpoint of Christmas at the Wagners', with the tree stacked with gifts for the delighted children, and the luminous idyll the composer wrote for Cosima. The two extremes of Ludwig's world – and of Visconti's.

Ludwig's ordeal finally ends one night in the dark waters of Lake Starnberg, a place as obsessive as the Hôtel des Bains was in *Death in Venice*, and which so much resembles the landscape around Cernobbio. Here, before the naked body of his valet, Volk, Ludwig's irresistible desire and his resentment are manifest. His Catholicism, and Wagner's music, have doomed him to live torn beween rapture and asceticism, between a dream of impossible purity and the reality of his pleasures, with no hope of redemption or the happiness of a resolved spirit. 'What torments you?' Wagner asks him. Ludwig could have replied, like Isolde, that 'everything I know torments me, and everything I see; this sky torments me, and this sea, and my body, and my life'. Instead, he takes leave of the composer without answering him.

'Running into nothing that did not gash him', a commentator says of Marion de Lorme in Hugo's play. So too Ludwig, as he powerlessly watched his own fall and that of those he cherished. Everyone betrayed him, even Wagner, that ideal father who 'made him believe in heaven on earth', and whose human failings he suddenly discovered. Visconti blamed Wagner's departure from Munich chiefly on the public scandal over the *ménage à trois* in which he was involved with Cosima von Bülow and her husband, Hans; in fact, people were even more hostile towards the ex-revolutionary because of the fat subsidies he was receiving from the king. Visconti's insistence on this probably stems more from a sense of personal hurt because of his own parents' private lives than from Ludwig's puritanism.

The movie makes a point of contrasting the king's faithfulness with the betrayals by those around him. By Elizabeth, for example, who interposed her sister Sophie between them and who, more obedient to duty and reality than the king, wound up not understanding him at all. Whereas history tells us that the empress grew increasingly closer to her cousin, leaving poems for him in a pavilion on the Isle of Roses, poems that celebrated their closeness.

The actor Joseph Kainz, plied with gifts by Ludwig (as Visconti did his actors), finally wearied of the king's whims and demands and betrayed him by selling his letters – as Berger would sell Visconti's after the director's death. Holstein was another traitor, who furnished the authorities in Munich with evidence concerning the sovereign's mental instability, and who agreed to go and arrest him. And, finally, he was deceived by his servants, who formed a court within the court. 'You alone have remained faithful to me,' Ludwig says to Weber. 'Even Mayer betrayed me.'

'Ludwig is an eminently appealing character,' Visconti said, 'because, king though he was, he was a beaten man, a victim of reality. Heroes don't interest me. I seek men's essence.' Luchino was as much a victim of reality as Ludwig was. In love with his dreams, a prisoner of the magic grotto of childhood and its nocturnal glitter, a captive of his aspirations to perfection and purity, he was a Narcissus martyred, a stricken Icarus.

'What can any work be that deals with a fall and damnation but a religious work?' asks the narrator in *Doctor Faustus*. A political investigation and tragedy, *Ludwig* is also a liturgy; from the opening shot of the Angel in a fresco of the Nymphenburg Palace, to the image of Ludwig's dead body haloed in an El Greco light, it is a vast, moonlit window through which we watch humanity defeat a man and a civilization that dreamed Promethean dreams, and whose ashes still glow with a mysterious fire.

When the biographer Gaia Servadio asked Visconti why he was so drawn to Ludwig, and what their affinities might be, the director stressed the defeat 'of a sovereign who believed in absolute monarchy, but who was also an unhappy man, a victim. What interested me was his weak side, his inability to live the reality of daily life. He excites compassion even when he thinks he has won. But he lost with Wagner, with Elizabeth, with the actor, Kainz, his last favourite.

'What interests me about him is that he lived at the outer limit of the exceptional, beyond the rules. The same can even be said of Wagner and Elizabeth. I am fascinated by this story of sacred cows, of people outside daily reality. But I see no affinities between my characters and me. I don't think I'm weak, a loser. I came unharmed out of all the betrayals and struggles I've had to endure, whereas Ludwig was shattered. The feeling I want to arouse in this film is pity.'

The fates, the forces of reality were nevertheless unleashed against this film so obviously made in disregard of the rules, a sort of challenge to standard productions and standard movie realities. Visconti was becoming the stricken Icarus whose headlong fall he could contemplate in the Galileo Chini painting he had acquired a

few years earlier. The powerful lord, symbolized by his heraldic
serpent, was not altogether to escape the fate of Lohengrin,
Wagner's vulnerable Knight of the Swan.

XXI

THE FINAL DUELS

Life is a battlefield.

LUCHINO VISCONTI

The idea of death settled permanently in me, as love does.

MARCEL PROUST

27 July 1972: three months had gone by since Bavaria, three months absorbed in completing *Ludwig*, shooting murderously difficult scenes, like the coronation, in overheated Cinecittà studios. Only snatches of rest: a few days at Ischia, a few more in Tunisia in numbing heat and glaring light.

Rome was stifling, too, even among the great trees on Via Salaria. For Visconti that day was 'absolutely normal', meaning a day of work: innumerable cups of coffee, countless cigarettes and the prospect of dinner with a pair of producers named Ianni and Perugia to discuss future projects. Suso went by to pick him up. He was unusually pale that evening. But in the garden bar on the terrace of the Hotel Eden, the air was deliciously cool and all Rome stretched at his feet. Visconti had never been there before. He ordered champagne, raised the glass to his lips. 'I don't think it's cold enough,' he said. Just as he put down his glass, he was struck 'as if by lightning'.

It all remained clearly etched in his memory. 'I remember everything, very precisely,' he told Costanzo Constantini. 'There wasn't a moment when I wasn't perfectly lucid.'

Suso saw him not so much fall as lean on the arms of his chair and 'double over', paler than ever. He remembered her saying: 'Luchino, Luchino, what's the matter? Don't you feel well?' Then someone else said 'Maybe we'd better get him out of here.'

They took him to a room and undressed him while waiting for a doctor to arrive. The screenwriter Medioli came at once, and when he removed Visconti's shoes to reveal electric blue socks, the director remembered obsessively saying 'How could I do such a thing? So garish.' He kept apologizing, over and over, to Suso. 'One of his legs moved by itself, in an utterly uncontrolled way,' she recalls. 'I'd never seen anything like it. You'd think the leg had gone mad. And Luchino went on apologizing, so that I finally left the room to keep from worrying him any more.'

Visconti heard the name of the Mater Dei clinic mentioned and, he said, 'I thought everything was all right. But I was taken to another clinic, a bad clinic at that, because that was where my doctor worked then. It was terribly hot. The room was too small. People kept coming in, so many people. They gathered to talk in the corridor or at the bar. I remember everyone who came into the room, one by one. I even chatted with them. Almost all my friends came. I was lying down, I was given injections, they tried to assure me that I hadn't lost consciousness; no, of course I hadn't lost consciousness. I remember a Dr Lopez who had come expressly from Madrid, he leaned over me, he wore a black tie, had grey hair and wore glasses.'

Two weeks of absolute immobility, half paralysed, his mind grasping at every sign that, while his body had taken 'a slap', a 'low blow', a hideously violent shock, his brain remained intact, that he could still think, reason, listen to music, lots of music, on a cassette player at 'full blast' – Wagner, Mozart, *The Magic Flute* . . . 'Luckily I was struck on the right side. If I'd been struck on the left I'd have had it, because the seat of language and intelligence, assuming I have any, is on the left.'

He blamed himself more than anyone, raging helplessly at his heedlessness and lack of restraint. 'The way someone who stumbles and breaks a leg might say, "What an idiot I am, why didn't I watch where I was going?" I immediately realized that this was all my fault because I had not followed the treatments I should have followed, because I went on smoking, because I never rested . . . I understand that my stroke was caused by cigarettes. It's true, I smoked a lot, seventy or eighty cigarettes a day, some days as many as a hundred and twenty. I smoked like a locomotive. It had become a reflex. I no longer even noticed. When you're working you don't even notice you're smoking so much.'

As soon as his condition allowed, on 14 August, he was transferred to the care of a noted Swiss neurologist, Dr Hugo Krayenbühl, in the Zurich district hospital. To beat 'this blasted sickness' that nailed him to his bed he had to undergo interminable exercises, hours and hours of callisthenics. He would never recover the full use of his limbs, but this was his only hope of being able at least to move about again.

And all this was endlessly humiliating. Like a child, he had to be helped to get up, to put on his shoes. He couldn't even sit in an armchair without toppling forward like a rag doll. 'It's terrible,' he said, 'it's boring, terribly boring,' and he hated this illness that had suddenly snatched away his youth and freedom.

'Before, I was free,' he said. 'Before, I mistreated my body as if that were the most natural thing in the world . . . Then, abruptly, the slap, with everything changing. The sudden discoveries that there were things I could no longer do . . . That my freedom had absconded forever. That's why I hate my illness: because it has deprived me of freedom. Because it humiliated me and was still humiliating me. Because I have to learn all over again to walk, to move my hands, to use them again . . . And then there's having to be helped, needing someone here all the time, to dress you, put on your shoes, shave you, comb your hair. It's so degrading. It hits you so horribly. And then you rebel.'

Patience, went the doctors' litany, prudence. 'But both those words sent him up the wall,' Medioli notes. He had never before known the humiliation of pain and infirmity. Around him, of course, he saw other patients. 'The hospital was full of Italians,' he said, 'Calabrian workmen whose daughters came to see them, and they all wanted to meet me . . . Such moving shows of affection.' Day after day Medioli read him the letters, a mountain of letters, from his actors, Lancaster, Delon, Bogarde, Callas, along with writers and directors he scarcely knew, like Joseph Losey. A photograph came that he would keep at his bedside from then on, of

Marlene Dietrich, inscribed in French, *'Je pense à toi toujours'* – 'I'm always thinking of you.'

In the two months he spent in Zurich, his friends, the real ones, all came to see him, some for a day, others for a month. His sister Uberta moved to Zurich, and so did Medioli, 'who helped me like a nurse', Visconti said, 'to the point where I sometimes hated him. I told him, "Listen, Enrico, go away, you're a pain in the ass."'

'It's not selfishness,' he told Lina Coletti two years later. 'It's not egocentrism. It's that, when someone is going through the most fundamental moment of his life, if you really love him, that comes before anything else: distance, obligations, obstacles. It's so obvious ... If you are human, that is. If you are sensitive. If you have suffered, too, and if you have allowed life to claw you instead of doing everything you could to let it slide past without grazing you. I'll tell you frankly, I much prefer a sensitive idiot to a cynical, cold intellectual giant. Guys like that have always made me uneasy and they always will. My friends aren't like that, the people I love are different. . . Helmut Berger, seemingly so touchy and difficult, and down deep so sweet, generous, sincere . . . And Delon, too, a man who would go to any extreme to help you and get you out of trouble. In other words, I can do without those simpering hypocrites who come visiting with their bouquets of carnations. I've always detested a certain kind of insincere, worldly, stupid relationship.'

Vulnerable and sentimental, he insisted with ferocious determination on defending the most ungrateful of his 'sons', Helmut Berger, who in public usually showed himself as arrogant and contemptuous even of Visconti. Yet Berger was not one of those who came to stay in Zurich.

What enabled Visconti to hold up his head proudly and defy the terrible blow fate had dealt him was the thought of the abandoned *Ludwig*, still not completely edited and without a finished soundtrack. Never had he felt 'the will to work, even stronger than the will to live', so imperiously, so vitally as he did in that interminable hospital ordeal. 'The film. The film. The fear of not managing to finish *Ludwig*, the fear of never seeing it come out. My first and principal concern was *Ludwig*. Not for a moment, not for a second did I stop worrying about *Ludwig*. In fact, that worry gave me the strength to fight my illness, gave me the strength to do those exhausting physical exercises every day to get my joints moving again. This is why *Ludwig* is the film I love best.'

In November 1974, he declared that 'If I were forced to stay in bed and wait for the time to run out . . . there is no doubt I would die faster. Professor Krayenbühl grasped that at once. And indeed he told me: "Visconti, you mustn't stay here. Go away, leave the hospital and start over." I left as soon as I could.'

At the end of September he went to his beloved Cernobbio. An editing studio was set up for him in one of the old stables at the Villa Vecchia. *Ludwig* would finally be completed. And not just *Ludwig*. There were many more projects in the works. After his 'torturous experience of hospital life', he was more intent than ever on adapting Mann's novel *The Magic Mountain*.

Was it a sign that, a few days before he left, an elderly professor of literature, a friend of Mann's, had visited Visconti? 'He spent two hours with me, talking the whole time about Thomas Mann. I asked him, "Did Thomas Mann die in this hospital?" He replied: "You're the one who said it. Here it's never talked about. But since you said it, yes, I admit it: he died here."

'I never understood why they didn't want to tell me that. Perhaps because he died in the very room I occupied? Who knows?'

Returning to Cernobbio, in that luminous autumn filled with the golden dust of childhood memories, meant returning to life so that he could devote his life to his king of the shadows, *Ludwig*, that fruit plucked from hell and ripened in darkness. Here, between sunlight and darkness, between the grinding of age and a return to childhood, Visconti completed a film in which darkness struggles with light. To evoke his lost paradise, the director opened and closed the movie with Schumann's *Children's Games* (*Kinderszenen*). At Cernobbio nothing had changed, not even 'the light peculiar to some rooms, depending on the time of day', or the sun that 'gives life and joy as never before'.

'What is growing increasingly strong in me,' he'd said while shooting *Ludwig*, 'is everything that came to me from the maternal side.' His mother had been ill in Cernobbio, but until the end she had fought it and given her children the heartening image of a strong, dignified woman. The same determination motivated her

son, who went back to work two months after his 'fall'. His technicians and writers had followed him to Lake Como and with them he
finished editing the film.

Wholesale cuts had already been made: a performance of *Tristan*
attended by Ludwig was out, and so was Wagner's funeral. Gone
was Elizabeth's enraged cry of 'They killed him! Traitors!
Murderers!' when she learned of her cousin's death. With it went the
testimony of an elderly servant that he had seen a hole over the heart
in the king's coat. Although a full half-dozen sequences were
excised, the film still ran for four hours and ten minutes. Visconti
thought of doing what Bertolucci would later do with *Novecento*
(*1900*), show it in two instalments.

Finally, however, says the editor Ruggero Mastroianni, 'the film
was cut back to three hours. That was very long for a single showing, and it had all become incomprehensible. *Ludwig* depended on
the dialogue and its relationship with the images; all that was lost in
the cutting.' Also lost was the lovely rhythm of *Ludwig*, what Suso
Cecchi called 'a slow waltz rhythm'. They settled for a structure that
this filmer of memory had always disliked: a series of flashbacks that
broke the story's smooth flow, hindered the march of destiny,
syncopated the uninterrupted beating of a heart. He nevertheless
had to go along, helplessly watching while his work was hacked to
pieces.

Despite these compromises with marketability, the movie was
not even a box-office success, at times being somewhat gingerly
received. The producer went bankrupt. Much later on, this enabled
Visconti's close relatives and most devoted friends – Suso Cecchi
d'Amico, Mario Garbuglia, the cameraman Armando Nannuzzi,
Piero Tosi and Ruggero Mastroianni – to buy the rights to the
disfigured masterpiece and piously restore it.

Visconti the old fighter may have been floored by his illness, but
he did not consider himself beaten. 'The incident is closed,' he said
on his return to Rome in late November. Now he was living in a
small, two-room flat facing Uberta's on Via Fleming. 'My attic,' he
called it.

The house on Via Salaria had been put up for sale; he felt too
desperately alone in that huge mansion. Besides, there were all those
stairs he could no longer climb. 'I don't like that house any more,'

he explained. 'Who knows why . . . But I'm through with it. I'm fine here, it's cheerful, everything is so bright.'

His view over Rome, the huge trees, the terrace, the pink orchids blooming on the white drapes designed by Valentino, the profusion of vases bursting with scented flowers, roses and snapdragons, the few objects and paintings he had asked to be brought from Via Salaria, his books, of course, his photographs, his dearest mementoes – this, he thought, was the setting in which he would rebuild his life and strength. He considered it temporary: 'I've decided to move to a villa in Castelgandolfo. There I can recover faster and work more. I must carry out all my plans. I cannot give them up. I must do this.'

The noise and excitement of Rome, the hippies clustered on the Spanish Steps of the Trinità dei Monti church made him want to run away. In Castelgandolfo he would find peace in a house that, says Uberta, 'had a very handsome winter garden and a view over the lake that reminded him of Lake Como. Whole lorryloads of furniture and objects were shipped there. But, inevitably, the house was "visited": it's impossible to say how many times it was burgled. All the missing things were found once, then they were lost again. Did he value his things greatly? No, he didn't make a fuss over them. Yet he who all his life had thrown away millions without a backward glance now had to count his pennies.'

Despite his 'interminable' daily workouts, Visconti had only attenuated control over his body. His left arm and leg were still hard to move; he walked with difficulty, leaning on a cane. His face became deeply lined. He seemed shorter. 'But he held himself straight, he was tanned, his expression was lively,' says Costanzo Constantini. 'He was as mordant as ever. He spoke freely, as if nothing had happened to him, with the same old acuteness, the same caustic wit, sometimes insolently. He was quick, attentive, lucid, tremendously lucid, and, most striking, he showed surprising determination. He was set not only on living with his illness, but on overcoming it.'

He could no longer go to art shows and movies, but he kept up with everything that appeared. He read Jacques Laurent's *les Bêtises*, more reminiscent of Céline than of Stendhal; he reread Proust, as usual, this time starting at the end and working backwards. And, in a schoolboy's notebook, he kept a diary of his illness. He'd had to drop so many plans. *The Ring* at La Scala? Impossible, the doctors decreed. That would keep him in Milan, and he couldn't take the climate. *The Magic Mountain*? He'd have to film in Davos, in the Swiss Alps: much too cold. Mann's story *The Holy Sinner*? Reproduce medieval Rome, direct hundreds of actors? Unthinkable. But he persisted, churning out new proposals, 'watching for people's reactions in a murderous mood', Medioli says, 'accusations at the ready the instant he sensed a hint of hesitation creep into the expected assent'.

He never felt so compelling a need to work. 'If I don't work,' he said, 'I'll throw myself off the terrace in boredom. A person like me, who has worked without let-up for thirty or forty years, can't remain inert. That would be like depriving a drug addict of his morphine.' The prospect of mounting Harold Pinter's *Old Times* at Rome's Teatro Argentina, and then Puccini's *Manon Lescaut* for the Spoleto festival excited him enough to let him turn the page less bitterly on *Ludwig*, the abridged version of which was shown in Italy in January 1973.

But he was like a surgeon who has lost the ability to operate. No longer could he show his actors the movements he wanted from them, or physically enter their roles with them. For a month, rehearsals of *Old Times* were held in Via Fleming. After that he went to the theatre daily and, from a box seat, issued his instructions to the three members of the cast, Umberto Orsini, Valentina Cortese and Adriana Asti, on the stage. Some of the orchestra seats were removed to create a circular central stage around which playgoers would sit as in a theatre in the round.

Against all expectations, then, the man who had sworn never to work in a theatre again was once more breathing the stage dust he couldn't live without. On opening night, 3 May, Roman society thronged to see the Pinter play, an intimate massacre in which the characters torture each other like prize-fighters sparring in a pastel set taken from a Balthus painting.

'Few words are needed,' wrote Giorgio Prosperi in *Il Tempo*, 'to say that he is still theatre incarnate: there is Visconti, plus a few others. Or is it him alone? True, Roman high society was at the Argentina last night, including those who came not to see or hear, but to be seen. But that's theatre, too, and the old lion, his mastery intact, wasn't bothered by it. He watched them from his box, where he has been temporarily confined by his illness, observing all these leading lights of stage and screen, the ones he terrified, drilling them like conscripts quaking with fear. Many came to applaud him, but also to see how illness had diminished him. Well, I hope they realized that he is still top man.'

On the same day, however, a translator, aggrieved that the staging had been based on a translation of the play by Gerardo Guerrieri rather than on hers, won an order suspending further performances. Pinter had flown down from London unexpectedly to attend the show; the next day he called a press conference to denounce the indignities Visconti had inflicted on his play by show-ing a pair of lesbians tirelessly caressing each other, a man mastur-bating his wife and, with a girlfriend's help, sprinkling talcum powder on her bare breasts. The director was forced to agree to his demands for changes in the production.

Visconti took his revenge, and in spades, at Spoleto on 21 June. *Manon* had never been unreservedly popular, partly because of its slow third act, and to mount it he called in his regulars, Lila de Nobili and Piero Tosi. Their painstaking realism, a sensuality that swung between exaggeration and delicacy, the melancholy poetry of their sets and costumes beautifully expressed the wild, doomed passion of Puccini's lovers.

The composer had once written to his librettist Marco Praga that he did not want his opera, which he called 'the soul of his passionate youth', staged with 'powdered wigs and minuets' but with 'despair-ing passion'. Aided by the conductor Thomas Schippers, Visconti elicited this realistic emotional intensity not only from his singers – none of them first-rank – but from every last walk-on in the cast.

Who knew how much effort that youthful grace had cost its enfeebled director? Knowing he had to climb steps to reach the stage at Spoleto, he had a similar flight built at home and practised going up and down it daily. 'Before rehearsals,' says Suso Cecchi, 'he practised walking from his car to his seat facing the stage, leaning on his cane without seeming to.' He had been told it would take at least a year to recover. 'But I think it will take a lot more,' he remarked. 'It will take patience and it will take determination. I've never been very patient, but I am very determined.'

A year had gone by. Lacking a more ambitious project, he prepared a film called *Conversation Piece* (*Gruppo di Famiglia in un Interno*). He still lacked full control over his legs when shooting began in April 1974. But he stood to direct most of the film, while Suso, afraid he might fall, watched anxiously.

For years, before he had done *Ludwig* and *Death in Venice*, he had thought of telling a contemporary story, something simple, with no splashy effects. In Zurich, Medioli recalls, someone had asked Visconti what film he would like to make if he had billions of dollars to spend on it. 'A story with two characters,' he had replied ironically, 'simple and brief, taking place entirely in one room.' For he knew that the days when he could film a ball scene, as in *The Leopard*, a Night of the Long Knives, as in *The Damned*, or a *Ludwig*-style coronation scene were over for him. Yet the idea Medioli had suggested – a modern film about the rightist terrorism then rife in Italy – interested him. 'Luchino kept after me,' the writer says. 'He'd push his glasses down to the tip of his nose and scrutinize me impatiently: "Have you thought of anything? Have you begun writing?" There was no time to lose.'

In the winter of 1973 the scriptwriter suggested a story line. All the action would take place in two rooms located on different floors in a single building and contrastingly decorated, one old-fashioned, the other modern. The protagonist would be a teacher living alone with an elderly maid amid his books, art objects and old paintings – his collection of *conversation pieces* or 'family groups'. Married and divorced, he has no children, no family but those cracked, softly glowing groups he so carefully studies in his precious paintings. As Medioli saw him he was 'an elderly man, at the threshold of old age, an exceptionally cultivated man'. But, he suggested, he is guilty because he has withdrawn into his ivory tower, 'into prosperous and protected solitude as into a mother's bosom, where he stagnates unperturbed, attached to his habits and his works of art'.

Into this sealed, padded theatre of a room erupt four young intruders who involve him, against his will, in a maelstrom of passions that finally shakes him out of the 'deep dream' in which, like the protagonist of *Death in Venice*, and with the same result, he had been comfortably ensconced.

'I like the story,' Visconti had said. Although he insisted there was nothing autobiographical about it, Lancaster would copy his director's gestures and attitudes to play the part. Visconti and his protagonist were the same age, had the same tastes and experiences ('He collects portraits and I have mine,' Visconti said, 'from *Rocco and His Brothers* to *Ludwig* via *The Damned* and *The Leopard*'). Both were disappointed in their search for 'a balance between politics and morality', an issue in the film, the director conceded, 'that I can certainly share'. And both were lonely men: Visconti had no children either, and never considered adopting any.

Even so, he protested, the teacher was no portrait of him, for one basic reason: 'This character is egocentric, a man shut in on himself who, instead of forming relationships with people, collects pictures of them. He is thing-crazy. But it's people and their problems that matter, not the things they produce. People and their problems are far more important than their works or their things. I'm not that egotistical. I have helped so many young people, both with advice and, when I could, materially. I have so many friends . . .'

Closer to the teacher's model was the art critic and collector Mario Praz, whose life and work, particularly an erudite essay entitled *Conversation Pieces*, obviously inspired Visconti and his writers. He too lived in a sort of egotistical museum, with an elderly maid, in an apartment in Rome's Palazzo Ricci that he called his 'house of life'. Far more than Visconti he preferred mirrors to life because mirrors reflect images that are already 'a bit removed from life, already changed into pictures'.

Praz was not at all put out to recognize himself in the Lancaster character. 'Luchino Visconti must have had a prophetic inspiration when he imagined that a band of dissolute drug addicts might come and live in the same building,' he said. 'This more or less happened in the palace where I live, but only after the film appeared. As I saw, the film is respectful towards my double, but it may have been unfair to the tenants. All I can say of them is that, when one of them asked me to dedicate one of my books to him, I wrote: "To (his name), my fellow tenant, a stranger to ideas".'

Praz was known throughout Italy as 'the man whose name is never uttered' because he reputedly had the evil eye and brought bad luck. In this case, however, Visconti's power of evil had rivalled the elderly warlock's. Years later, the collector, 'grown even older, if that's possible', pondered his empty life and the 'emblematic message' of his statues of Cupid with their upended quivers and broken bows. And he felt the same qualms that grip the teacher when, in the movie, he examines his own life, deliberately, moralistically removed from the joys and stings of love.

Lancaster was certain his character was Luchino Visconti himself. 'I knew the old man I was playing was him,' the actor says. 'In fact, he told me so: "It's my life, I'm a very lonely man, I was never capable of love, I never had a family." He meant he had never fathered a family. He thought about this, searching for reasons, but there were other areas of his life he could never bring himself to examine, and I think the film would have done him a lot of good if he could have made it.' In other words, Lancaster saw *Conversation Piece* as a requiem, a timid confession, a halting analysis of the relationship Visconti had experienced with Helmut Berger. Now all that was past, for in the flat on Via Fleming, Visconti lived alone.

That he had loved Berger is clear in the film, loved him with a tormented tenderness he had never before mustered. He loved even the worst of Berger: the young man's disorderliness, his insolent audacity, his spoiled-brat whims and ingratitude, and the fragility that brought on floods of tears when he had to face a camera and led him into taking drugs. Lancaster's way of approaching and treating the young man who seeks refuge with him is maternal rather than paternal, summed up in the final image, like a Pietà, of the old man carrying Konrad's body in his arms.

Lancaster is manifestly wrong in saying that Visconti was afraid to bear down on homosexual relationships and explore these complex feelings. He constantly did precisely that in all his work. But never had Visconti dealt with a homosexual relationship more gently, never was it more religiously purified of any desire for possession, than at this period when fate forced him to live alone in an ivory tower from which he tried desperately to escape.

His return to a topical subject clearly proves that, unlike his character, he still needed to open himself to life, to call on youth to react to events, to 'bar the road to Fascism', and not to 'become Napoleon's army after Waterloo'.

The background to *Conversation Piece* was a politically stagnant

Italy, a grotesque round of revolving-door governments led by political hacks engrossed in their Byzantine quarrels and petty intrigues in a country with 800,000 unemployed where terrorism, of both the right and the left, was assuming alarming proportions.

To finance the movie, Visconti resigned himself to the inevitable attacks from his friends on the left and turned to Edilio Rusconi, a rightist publisher with a recent interest in movies. He could have justified his choice by pointing out that no producer in the chaotic summer of 1973 would have risked a billion lire on a film made by an invalid. But rather than publicly plead his state of health, he chose defiance, and this duly aroused a spate of venomous criticism. 'I couldn't care less about these accusations,' he retorted. 'I made my own film, not Edilio Rusconi's. Where are other directors getting their money? From labour unions, maybe? I don't know any leftist industrialists. I have never known any, never seen any. What matters is the film, and the film is not rightist . . . Which other directors have come out against the putsch attempts in our country?'

And he added: 'Movies are made with money; this money is supplied by producers, and producers are not ascetics tormented by the problem of social injustice. They are businessmen, even the best of them. Sometimes they are sordid, and scared stiff, too, because they are tied hand and foot to foreign capital . . . Only dollars are carrying the nation's cinema forward. American dollars, of course. And the United States will not allow the advent of a leftist government. They make no compromises in the field of cinema, either.'

Although no exteriors were used in *Conversation Piece*, it consumed a huge budget despite the producer's petty scrounging. Again Visconti recruited a crowd of skilled artisans, sculptors, painters, scenographers, 'the last survivors of those demanding workmen, the best in the world, who are now growing older and rarer', commented Mario Garbuglia. 'We've never been able to maintain a school to teach all this.'

Financed by a conservative producer it may have been, but this 'vivisection of the Italian situation' fulfilled its maker's aesthetic and moral requirements. Visconti tackled the revival of Fascism in Italy head-on through his characters, Marchioness Bianca Brumonti (Silvana Mangano), the wife of a fascist businessman; her lover, Konrad (played by Berger), a veteran of the 1968 demonstrations who had gone over to the Fascists, and the marchesa's future son-in-law, a young neo-Fascist.

The story was based on an extreme-rightist plot organized in the spring of 1971 by the 'black prince', Valerio Borghese, but also grew out of a wave of terrorist attacks that rolled over Italy following the bombing of the Farm Credit Bank that left fourteen people dead on Milan's Piazza Fontana on 12 December 1969. Neo-fascist groups mushroomed after 1968, complete with dagger-and-death's-head emblems; after 1971 their attacks alternated with those by commando groups styling themselves the Sinistra Proletaria (Proleterian Left) or the Nuova Resistenza (New Resistance). A 'black' (rightist) attack was always answered by a 'red' one, although the public could never clearly distinguish between the rightists' random bombings and the more surgically precise terrorism carried out by the Red Brigades in the hope of detonating a revolution.

Filming of *Conversation Piece* began on 8 April 1974, and ended on 15 July. The first few days were just like the start of any other movie: baskets of red roses and best wishes from friends, especially Federico Fellini, who insisted on hailing his friend's return behind the camera 'one fine April day'. There was a steady stream of journalists, photographers and old 'accomplices' – Suso Cecchi d'Amico and her children, Masolino and Silvia; Peppino Patroni Griffi; Medioli. The actresses Ursula Andress and Valentina Cortese came, and so did Luchino's old friends, Trombadori and Francesco Rosi. Every afternoon between 12:30 and 1:30 Visconti arrived at the studio and went to work. On 18 April four scenes were shot despite some difficulty in persuading Berger to 'recite from his heart and not from his head' the scene in which, on the telephone, he calls his mistress the Marchioness of Shit.

The next morning, the front pages of all the newspapers carried news and commentary – outraged – on the kidnapping of Judge Mario Sossi in Genoa the previous evening. It was the eve of a referendum on legalizing divorce, and most people assumed this was an attempt by the extreme right to swing the vote to the conservatives led by Amintore Fanfani. In fact, as a Red Brigade communiqué announced, it was a public protest both against the magistrate's zeal in pursuing militant leftists and against the nomination, on that 18 April, of [Fiat chairman] Gianni Agnelli as president of Confindustria, the National Confederation of Industrialists.

This 'revolutionary' message went unappreciated by the public and the men of the left. It touched off the great manhunt for members of the Red Brigade, with first blood, the murder of a policeman, shed the following October. 'Armed propaganda,' said the journalist Giorgio Bocca, 'has ended, and we are heading now towards an increasingly bitter and bloody guerrilla war.' Sossi was finally released after thirty-five days' detention in a 'people's prison'. A wave of arrests followed which, by the following spring, seemed finally to have dismantled the Red Brigade.

Not so black terrorism which, on 28 May, killed eight more people and injured one hundred and two on Brescia's Piazza della Loggia. On that day, Visconti filmed the scene in which Konrad, implicated in a rightist plot, is beaten nearly to death and is rescued, hidden and treated by the teacher in a secret room where, he said, his mother had hidden Resistance fighters and Jews during the war. The violence in the film can as easily be blamed on outright criminals as on fascist terrorists; Konrad may very well have been 'disciplined' because of a few packets of narcotics; even his death can be explained non-politically. Visconti nevertheless believed in the danger of a 'neo-fascist cataclysm'. On 4 August 1974, while he was editing his film, his fears were reinforced when a train named Italicus was blown up in San Benedetto Val di Sambro, twenty-five miles from the left-wing city of Bologna; twelve people died and forty-eight were wounded.

Visconti maintained this conspiratorial atmosphere throughout the film without ever resorting to an exterior scene. Five characters, moulded by events into a sort of family in a tragic, closed-off environment, were all he needed to show 'the phenomena of degeneration', the breakdown of social balance. Here the serenely delightful art of the eighteenth century is walled off from the violence of life today, the noble crusades of the Forties have decayed into the murky cruelties of the Sixties, yesterday's family peace has become today's 'tribal warfare'; the generations fight a fierce war of attrition in which brother confronts brother.

Everything here is devastated, beginning with the family home that is invaded by young people living in the fast lane, high on drugs and mouthing obscenities as they destroy themselves. Morality is dead: the unhappy Konrad is a loser, a bit of 1968's flotsam, an intruder who pays with his life for insisting on truth and refusing his allotted role as lapdog.

In *Conversation Piece*, all the big Viscontian themes are set out and rearranged to form a jagged line as raw as an open wound. The movie is a crucible in which the director shrewdly combines the materials, raw and processed, that make up his world. And it all has a mysteriously religious flavour lent by Mozart's music – excerpts from *Vorrei spiegarvi, oh dio* and the *Sinfonia Concertante in E Flat Major*, K.364 – as well as by highlighting icons and by the final allusion to Mantegna's painting *The Dead Christ*.

Proust is here, too. First, in the teacher's reference to a book he continually rereads and that evokes 'the terrible knowledge' that illness brings, 'less by the suffering it causes than by the strange novelty of permanent restrictions it imposes on life. One sees oneself dead, in such a case, not at the moment of death, but months, sometimes years earlier, from the time it came hideously to abide in us.'

And the author of *Remembrance* is present like a nostalgic recall in the film's recurrent flashes of memory, a film Visconti never wanted to call anything but *Gruppo di Famiglia in un Interno*. The last image he shot was the fleeting and affectionate appearance of the mother. Dominique Sanda, her hair dressed like Donna Carla's in Antonio Arquani's portrait of her, her mauve and gold gown inspired by one of Duse's costumes, wearing a long string of pearls and a snake bracelet, makes us believe for a moment that time has been recaptured. To her, this forever lost Eurydice, Visconti would turn again for his last film, his last earthly journey towards the kingdom of darkness.

Autumn 1974. The editing of *Conversation Piece* was still unfinished, but Visconti, more energetic than ever even though he still had to walk with a cane, was seething with movie and stage projects. One was a life of Puccini centred on his last love affair, with the British Sybil Seligman, and based on *Puccini's Letters to Sybil*; Mastroianni could have played the lead because he resembled the composer.

Another was a film on Zelda Fitzgerald based on her novel *Save*

Me the Waltz. A movie about the Fitzgeralds, Suso Cecchi says, 'would have given him a chance to bring back pre-1929 Paris, the Paris he knew . . . I'd like to have done this film with and for Luchino. We knew and felt close to that world, I because I'd read about it and he because he'd lived in it.' But Zelda's daughter demanded an exorbitant amount of money and insisted on approval rights over the script. 'She was afraid her mother would be mistreated,' Visconti said. 'What could I have said to abuse an alcoholic woman who died in a lunatic asylum?'

He got a more understanding reception from Mann's second son, Golo, to whom he spoke about adapting *The Magic Mountain.* 'That one would really be an autobiographical film,' the moviemaker said, 'because it's a story about an invalid, and I, from now on . . .' There was to be only one set, and a small cast: Charlotte Rampling as Claudia Chauchat, Berger as Hans Castorp, in 'one of the last love stories in western literature, perhaps the last'. The project started Visconti dreaming of returning to the mountains. 'But no producer would hear of it,' Suso says. 'A story about sickness, told by a sick man . . .'

And so, finally, it came down to *L'Innocente* (*The Intruder*), the novel that D'Annunzio, who wrote it when he was thirty, was sure would make him famous. Visconti would have preferred *Il Piacere* (*The Child of Pleasure*), but the prospect of filming in a Rome disfigured by automobile traffic and overrun by rancid hippies appalled him. *The Intruder* may not have been a masterpiece, but masterpieces do not always make the best movie scripts. And the novel was based on a specific event, which had always recommended it to Visconti: the murder of a child. Count Tullio Hermil and his wife Giuliana represented not only the breakdown of family life, but also, Visconti said, 'a particular society, and a particular Italy, for they belong to the upper middle class responsible for the advent of Fascism'.

In 1897, drawing partly on his own marital troubles with Maria di Gallese, D'Annunzio had set out to tell the story of a dissolute aristocrat who punishes his wife's infidelity by murdering the child she has by a young writer. Through Tullio, D'Annunzio was expressing his admiration for the Nietzschean superman. The count, after committing his crime, tells his mistress, Teresa Raffo, that human justice cannot touch him, that he alone can determine his fate. To Visconti, such 'provincial' fatuousness was ridiculous; 'today a character like that would be unreal, he'd make people laugh'. So he altered the epilogue, adding Tullio's suicide to 'point up the character's failure'.

So the director approached his subject with some detachment, his critical antennae bristling. It amused him to discuss the details of D'Annunzio's life. He 'could not understand why he was so successful with women. Because of the way he talked? But his voice was shrill and unpleasant. He had gone completely bald after a duel with the Neapolitan journalist Scarfoglio, who wrote that he'd been cuckolded. Scarfoglio had wounded him in the head and the doctors had put some overly strong mixture on his skull. Bald as he was, though, he managed to seduce a great many women, Duse, Rudini, Mancini. Maybe he was prodigious in bed, maybe he was unusually well endowed, I don't know . . .'

Although Visconti despised D'Annunzio as a man, disliking his histrionics, his flights of rhetoric, his cult of Nietzsche and the superman, he nevertheless admitted that he admired 'the poet and writer; we must admit it, we're all his children. We've all come via him, even those of us born half a century later. No one, even today, can avoid his influence. Who can think of music without Wagner? Despicable things have been written about him, especially by Moravia, Pasolini and those people. If only they could write the things D'Annunzio wrote.' The fact remains, however, that Visconti chose the least 'D'Annunzian', the least mannerist and bombastic of the master's works.

He found a producer, a publisher named Rizzoli, but casting proved more difficult. Romy Schneider? She was pregnant. Delon? On another film. Besides, 'he'd give us a handsome enough, seductive enough Tullio, loutish enough, too. But satanic, as Tullio is – frankly, no.'

Instead he approached two Italian actors. First, Giancarlo Giannini; the public thought of him as a comic actor, but Visconti always liked this kind of switch. Then, Laura Antonelli; everyone was aware of her shapely figure, but fewer appreciated her acting talent. 'Maybe they hate her because she's too beautiful,' Visconti said in reply to some malicious critics. 'But who said a beautiful woman

can't be a talented actress? What's more, she is absolutely D'Annunzian. D'Annunzio would have gone mad for her at first sight.
She is sensual, haughty, exactly like Barbara Leoni, D'Annunzio's
great love at the time. There's nothing fake about her, and I really
like that: the mouth is her mouth, without lipstick; the eyes are her
eyes, without mascara. And you should see her naked! From the
back she is stunning; the line of her hips and pelvis is the line of a
cello.'

He pinned photos of her on the walls of his small apartment.
'Look how much she resembles the Duchess of Gallese, D'Annunzio's wife,' he told a newspaperman. 'Duse, too, but especially
Gallese.' He needed this marvellous animal, this body that D'Annunzio would have gone mad for, to express what he thought was
most modern about the writer, his eroticism. 'D'Annunzio's concept of life is modern,' he said. 'We live in a brutal and very
externalized era. D'Annunzio went to the bottom of eroticism, and
what is more erotic than the time we're living in?'

Would the film's eroticism have been more incandescent if the
maker had not been cut off from the wild, voluptuous pleasures of
sex? With the script taking shape in that spring of 1975 and shooting
only weeks away, Visconti had almost recovered all his old vigour.
But he insisted on working on his feet, without a cane. Every day he
turned everyone out of his room and, alone, practised walking
unaided. On 3 April he fell and broke his right leg.

The hospital again. Immobilized again. He raged helplessly
against this life that until then 'had been a friend and now had
become the cruellest of enemies', the life that 'I had always dominated and which now dominates me'.

'When they had to operate,' says Suso Cecchi d'Amico, 'he
realized that his other leg was gone, too. Then he let himself go. He
wouldn't speak, wouldn't eat. He grew so small . . . One day
Medioli and I went to see him and I told him: "When you break a
leg, why can't you get around in a wheelchair? Or even on a
stretcher?" We were ready to start shooting, the producers had lost
money, the actors were beginning to drop out. "You've got to
make up your mind now," I said, "either the film gets made or it
doesn't."'

He made his movie, now entitled *The Innocents*, from a wheelchair. But in the evening he continued his exercises, not because he thought he could improve his condition, but because his painful body martyred him.

This film will destroy him, his doctors had predicted when they let him leave the hospital after those long, despairing weeks in the glare of a summer heat wave, but they agreed that he had to do it. On 27 September he installed the whole crew in an eighteenth-century villa, the Principessa, that had been turned into a hotel a few miles outside Lucca. Solid as a rock he was – or so it seemed. 'Wheelchair and all, here I am ready to make another film,' Visconti told reporters. 'Next time I might be on a stretcher, but I'll never give up.'

Every day he prepared for the next day's shoot, never getting to bed before two in the morning. He was smoking again. For the movie he had recruited not only his usual cast and crew – including the gravely ailing Rina Morelli, who was to survive the director by only three months – but his family as well. His nieces and nephews appeared in scenes in the Villa Mirafiori in Rome, built on Via Nomentana by King Victor-Emmanuel II for his lover, the beauteous Rosina. When one of them pushed him in his wheelchair, their uncle commented sarcastically, 'Let's move the corpse.'

He lived with the thought of death now. The music of his childhood, Chopin's *Berceuse et Valse*, Mozart's *Turkish March*, Liszt's *Jeux d'eau à la Villa d'Este*, blended now with the music of death, like the poignant *Che farò senza Euridice*, from Gluck's *Orfeo ed Euridice*. Like Orpheus, Visconti was making his final journey to the head-waters of time past, a forlorn journey to where parents quarrelled around a child, where 'order, luxury and beauty' lock people into sterile loneliness, where sexual frenzy is intoxication with death; the characters come forward, some masked, some not, from the black-and-white fencing mask in the movie's opening scene to the black, funereal figure of Teresa Raffo at the end, walking away down a foggy lane, abandoning Tullio Hermil's body to its 'monstrous' secret.

Giuliana herself, despite her simplicity and transparence, is also a victim of Visconti's cruel use of masks. He recommended to Tosi a certain type of hat that he had seen his mother and Duse wear. 'It had so many veils it deformed the face a bit,' the designer notes. 'I made four of them and Luchino chose the one that suited Laura Antonelli the least, but which had the heaviest veil. "My mother wore them exactly like that," he told me. "She was swathed in veils when she went to La Scala in 1910, followed by a footman, and when she travelled, too: long veils around her neck and over her hat."'

The Innocents is the last of his own masks, the final ritual before Visconti's descent into death and his origins. This was an ultimate family tragedy, in which a mother and father momentarily join in their desire to rid themselves of a bastard child, an intruder. And, in voluptuously mournful red and black lighting, the film is a final scrutiny of a life in which the dominance of women is affirmed as it is in no other Visconti film – the reign of the three Fates presiding over birth, sex and death.

Again, this turning back was no mere refuge or consolation, no mere elegiac self-indulgence. Visconti knew those salons of the past where, before the petits-fours, one assumed a worshipful air and suffered through one Mozart, two Schuberts and four Liszts; where lowered eyes and evasive looks told more than words about the fluttering of a heart, and people looked like moths trapped in lacquer and velvet boxes. The couple in the film, united by their mutual jealousy until they are tragically sundered, were Visconti's parents. And his portrait of Giuliana Hermil, one of the loveliest portraits of wife and mother ever drawn in film, was his last declaration of love to Donna Carla.

'Why,' Teresa Raffo asks her vain lover Tullio, 'must men sometimes raise women up to the stars and at other times drag them through the mud?'

Visconti's Giuliana has the eternally fresh charm held in the memory of a child absorbed by everything a mother ever touched, wore, loved, by the smallest and most intimate of her clothes, all the troubling equipment of veils, laces, ribbons, lace, pins and hooks that we see in the movie. In his mind her femininity is carnal, her motherliness anguished, almost animal.

'Mother really had eight children,' Uberta notes. 'Between the birth of Edoardo and that of Ida Pace, there was one pregnancy she couldn't bring to term.' And the secret spring of this final film, this act of retrospection, is Carla Erba, that Madonna of the seven children, the sum of all the pain and anxiety, the physical and mental suffering of absolute maternity. Here memory is indeed that 'sort of pharmacy or chemist's laboratory in which', Proust said, 'one's hand lights at random, here on a sedative drug, there on a dangerous poison'.

In this last mirror, Visconti watched death at work: the horses drawing the hearse, the shuttered houses, soon sold, filled with the mortuary whiteness of furniture covers, the child's death, the theatrically absurd death of Tullio Hermil. Visconti knew that *The Innocents* was an announcement of his own death. This was his last family portrait, in which figure the children of Uberta and of Ida as well as Wanda Toscanini's daughter, Margherita Horowitz, with Mannino's piano playing all the musical memories. In the movie's titles, against a background of garnet velvet, Visconti's hand slowly turns the yellowed pages of an early edition of *The Intruder*, lingering over each leaf as if to stroke the soft, thick paper.

His life now hung by a single film, a last, hopeless confession. At least the shoot had magically injected him with all his old vigour and authority. Visconti had never sought salvation in art, had never thought of art as an absolute promise of beauty and joy. He knew as well as the next man that we all return to dust some day, that men's lives and struggles matter more than the works of art that reflect them. But he had vowed to make this movie and that was enough to keep him alive. 'The day I can't work any more I'll blow my brains out,' he once said.

Magnani was dead now; De Sica, who had worried so much about Visconti's health, had preceded him into the grave. On 2 November, his birthday, Pasolini's body was found on the beach at Ostia. The films of all three were being shown in tribute to them. 'It'll be my turn soon,' he said. 'Before it or after it they'll show my films, too. It's logical, but it's the sign that you're finished.'

'Visconti knew very well that death was near,' Mannino says. 'So much so that when the executive producer, Lucio Trentini, showed him a title layout for *The Innocents* before printing it, [Visconti] erased the first words, "This is a film by Luchino Visconti", and wrote in "This was a film by . . ."'

He talked a lot about death, his own death. 'I'll die among my gardenias,' he announced. He asked his sister to promise she would scatter his ashes over the sea at Ischia. At times he enjoyed torturing his friends with sick jokes. If someone remarked that his name had appeared in the newspapers, he'd say, 'Ah, yes, of course: "Luchino Visconti, born 2 November 1906 . . ."' Not long after *The Innocents* was completed, Garbuglia came to see him and was startled to see how much he smoked.

'How many cigarettes do you smoke a day?'

'Around three thousand,' Visconti told him. 'Think that's enough?'

Uberta tells of the evening when she and his faithful Abruzzese maid Fidalma put him to bed and he said, 'Tie a handkerchief around under my chin. As a sort of dress rehearsal.'

On 17 March 1976, he stayed in bed; for several days he had been fighting feverish influenza. His two dogs wandered in and out of the flower-filled room; one of them, the big white Pyrenean sheepdog, had been named Konrad, after the character in *Conversation Piece*. The afternoon light was dimming; in their carved silver frames, the photographs, of a sober-looking Berger and the one of Dietrich inscribed 'I am always thinking of you', slowly faded. Uberta was sitting beside him. They were listening to Brahms's *Second Symphony*.

'When it ended,' Uberta says, 'he looked at me and said, in Milanese, "That's enough. I'm tired." Then he died.'

On the days that followed, the walls of Rome were covered with big posters on which the name of the last of the great Viscontis stood out black against a white background: 'A man of high culture whose immense body of work, covering more than thirty years, illustrated the history of art, cinema and theatre in our country, in Europe and the world.' It also specified that he was a 'militant anti-fascist of the Resistance who always displayed deep and sincere solidarity with those who work and struggle'.

'He was buried like a king,' says the painter Fabrizio Clerici. The religious ceremony on Friday 19 March was held in the Jesuit church of San Ignazio, the church in which, during the Easter services, young aristocrats go to the altar dressed as sixteenth-century pages. At eleven in the morning, Rosi and Trombadori delivered funeral orations on the square in front of the church. Inside, at noon, mass was heard by a capacity crowd that included Communist Party Secretary Enrico Berlinguer and Italian President Giovanni Leone. When the coffin, after lying in state throughout the afternoon, was carried outside, the throng massed in the small, amphitheatre-shaped, eighteenth-century plaza applauded, as it had three years earlier for the coffin of that daughter of the working class, their beloved Anna Magnani.

He had wanted his body to disappear entirely, so that nothing remained of him but a memory of the man and the splendour of his work. His body did not join his father's at Grazzano or his mother's in Milan's Monumental Cemetery. His body was claimed by fire, that fire that had governed his life, as he had suggested in November 1974: 'The day after tomorrow I'll be sixty-eight. But I swear that neither age nor illness have blunted my determination to live and do things . . . Film, theatre, music . . . I want to tackle everything, absolutely everything. With passion. Because you must always burn with passion when you tackle something. That, in fact, is why we're here: to burn until death, the last act of life, comes to finish the job by turning us to ashes.'

And his ashes? Their whereabouts is still heavily cloaked in mystery. In some Viscontian residence, no doubt, where neither death nor oblivion – 'oblivion as total and peaceful as a cemetery's', Proust mused – can enter. What place could be more piously, more jealously devoted to his memory than the villa on Ischia that he willed to Donna Uberta.

'We have no secrets,' she told us without batting an eyelid.

A Visconti always says 'we'.

Luchino's bloodlines made him a Visconti forever, custodian, like the prince in The Leopard, of 'those rare memories that no other family can have'. But this Visconti, out of an almost religious conviction, allied himself with the communist 'family'. And out of passion, and through his daily labour, he created a theatrical family in which his favourites were his lovers and his children, sometimes docile and loyal, sometimes rebellious and ungrateful, always beloved, frequently tortured.

Luchino loved the communist leader Palmiro Togliatti, 'whose true grandeur came in his identification with his people'; Mann, who 'in his works was all of us, for better or for worse', and Verdi, who 'wept and loved for us all'.

In Visconti's work, his heartbeat is inextricably synchronized with the convulsions of history. He experienced and remembered for us all.

APPENDIX: THE GUIVRE

> *Don't you think that a living creature entered
> in a coat of arms is implicitly associated with
> the idea of sacrifice? Generally speaking, if we
> go back to its origins, the totemic animal is an
> animal that is possessed, killed, eaten, which in
> fact is how it transmits its valour to the bearer
> of the emblem. Now what, I ask you, is the
> best known, the holiest human emblem? Christ
> on the cross, the pre-eminent symbol of the
> supreme holocaust. Hence evoking in one's
> armorial shield the ritual sacrifice of an eagle or
> a dragon or the minotaur, or yet the domination
> of a black slave or a savage is in the same line.
> But especially of a warrior, a woman, a child.*
>
> MICHEL TOURNIER, *The Ogre*

The Visconti arms: 'argent a guivre wavy azure vorant a child gules'
(an undulant serpent on a silver ground swallowing a red child).
This fabulous creature of Luchino's past was everywhere. Even
before he learned to read, the child continually ran into its ominous
puzzle – on stone tablets in the Cerva palace, in family portraits, in
books, on familiar objects and furniture. He found it in Milan, its
cathedral and its Sforza castle, in Grazzano, in old churches with
dark red wall hangings. The totem was in all the places ever controlled by the Viscontis and their condottieri, in the castles they built
to prepare their wars, weave their plots and plan their murders, and
in all the abbeys where they went to offer vows and implore pardon
from a God they had so frequently offended.

Many other coats of arms show fantastic animals; some, like that of the Colberts, harbour rampant snakes. But in the Visconti-Milan arms the serpent is a monster with gaping jaws whose sharp teeth grip a naked child, his arms outstretched in despair, who is already half swallowed. Victor Hugo, in a volume of poems entitled *Les Orientales*, recalled that

> Rome has its keys, Milan the child who howls still
> In the teeth of the guivre . . .

A relatively recent tradition assigns the emblem of 'the viper that in battle is raised in Milan', as Dante contemptuously refers to it in Canto VII of the *Purgatory*, to the Viscontis alone; in fact, it had been the badge of Milan before the Viscontis took over the city and appropriated its emblem. In the eleventh century the white standard flying over the town bore the blue serpent that was then thought to have, like Christ regenerating humanity with whom it was sometimes identified, a beneficial, vital power:

'And the Lord said unto Moses, Make thee a fiery serpent, and set it upon a pole: and . . . every one that is bitten, when he looketh upon it, shall live.

'And Moses made a serpent of brass, and put it upon a pole, and it came to pass that if a serpent had bitten any man, when he beheld the serpent of brass, he lived.' (*Numbers* 21. 6, 9)

Archbishop Arnolfo of Milan, who granted hereditary status to the title of 'vice comites' from which the name and fortune of the Viscontis are derived, was said to have brought Moses' brass serpent back from Byzantium along with a talking machine that foretold the future. The talisman can still be seen atop a porphyry column in the church of San Ambrogio; devout Milanese believe it has the miraculous power to cure certain children's diseases.

Not until after the First Crusade was the emblem modified to include a human figure that seems at first glance to be a child, but which is in fact a defeated Saracen. According to the Augustinian monk Pietro da Castelleto, who delivered the funeral oration for Gian Galeazzo Visconti in 1402, archbishop Ottone, the first of the great Viscontis, killed a Saracen king in single combat and incorporated the victim's arms into his own: 'a dragon carrying in his maw a flayed man with outstretched arms'.

To soften the image's expression of murderous violence, Petrarch, who was a long-time guest of the Viscontis, offered a poem that mainly highlighted the skill and courage of another of their ancestors, Azzone, the Holy Roman Emperor's vicar for Lombardy in the fourteenth century. While warring against the Florentines, he fell asleep under a tree with his helmet beside him. A viper slithered onto the helmet; when the warrior awoke, he put on the helmet and, as his terrified soldiers looked on, the snake reared, ready to strike. But Azzone calmly removed his helmet and let the creature go without even killing it.

The descendants of the early Visconti men of war, anxious to assert their spiritual power, added more traditional, more peaceful emblems to their arms: a dog lying on a log and crested with the serpent; firebrands from which hang two buckets held up by a lion wearing a serpent-adorned helmet; the guivre emerging from the sun; a leopard; palms and greyhounds, and, most important, a turtle dove emerging from a sunburst to accompany the motto devised by Petrarch, *à bon droit* – with good reason (or, more to the point, legitimately). None of these symbols could replace the serpent devouring its prey or obliterate its infernal connotation, a meaning corroborated by most of the Viscontis, who earned *à bon droit* their places in the deepest circles of Dante's hell, most appropriately in the seventh circle, filled with 'a mass of serpents . . . diverse and daunting' that beset naked men whose 'hands were held behind their backs and tied with snakes, whose head and tail transfixed the loin, writhing in knots convolved on the other side'.

Visconti, while playing down his nobility, nevertheless clung to his coat of arms. Jean Marais remembers his notepaper struck with the seal of the guivre. Tonino Cervi, co-producer of *Boccaccio 70*, says that Luchino once offered him a gift. 'At home I heard him talked about as Luchino, the count, so refined. I observed him closely and I will always remember that when he sat down he took out of his pocket a gold cigarette case marked with a child in a serpent's mouth, the family emblem. I asked him for that, but he wouldn't give it to me because it was a gift from his mother.'

In this attachment to the old family emblem can probably be seen Visconti's visceral link to his mother, not to mention his father and the rest of his family. So striking an image must, however, have aroused a host of questions in his mind as a boy that surely influenced his work as an adult. How did the boy, and later the artist, see the fierce symbol of the crowned serpent before which, remarked the French philosopher Gaston Bachelard, 'a whole line of ancestors is struck with fright in our troubled hearts'.

To interpreters of heraldry like Gérard de Sorval, 'the symbolism of the guivre – also written as "vivre"* – the bisse† or great serpent swallowing a man or a child [also represents] the universal life force that holds man and into which he must descend to re-emerge as a crowned child. The vivre symbolizes the cosmic Mother who engenders the Child-Verb.' Before becoming associated with evil and Satan, in antiquity snakes were attributes of goddess mothers, Isis, Cybele, Demeter, and were connected with the symbolism of birth and the creation of life.

Bachelard recalled the Aztec fertility symbol of the plumed serpent sleeping at the very heart of the planet in the earth's 'vital fire'. He described as 'energy-giving' the dreams stimulated by the primordial snake that 'combines contradictory attributes: it has feathers and scales, it is airy and metallic; it incorporates all the powers of living things, of human strength and the indolence of plants, the power of creating while asleep'. He who undergoes a perilous initiation and learns to master and use the serpent's powers will know the secrets of life and death and will acquire the power, among others, to heal.

In the light of this reading, the two snakes that presided over the birth of those the Milanese call the *biscioni*, the progeny of the bisse, the serpent in the Erba caduceus and the Visconti guivre combine into a single energy-giving and vital power. Now, it is true that Milan's blue snake swallowing the Saracen symbolized the victory of Good over Evil, of Christ over the Devil. Yet how could a child brought up to strict Roman Catholicism fail to be troubled by the conflict between this animal-human figure and the Church's traditional images of the struggle between divinity and the forces of Evil – the Madonna trampling the serpent underfoot, Saint George slaying the dragon? In the Church versions, the human figure triumphs and the base serpent is justly conquered, but in the heraldic universe

*The French verb meaning 'to live' (translator's note).
†In heraldry, an erect and sometimes knotted serpent (translator's note).

the animal figure is crowned and victorious, and the child or man is sacrificed, martyred, screaming with pain and terror.

Instinctively, the child, and the adult, can only feel a secret tremor of fear at the myths and fairy tales telling of men being devoured by monsters – Jonah swallowed by the whale – or by their own fathers, like Saturn consuming his children. Other 'mouths' can revive these fears: the mouths of caves, for example, black holes that both attract and repel. The novelist Michel Leiris, talking about excursions to caves that 'imitate the concavity of a mouth in the earth', remarks on the feeling of fright, 'very possibly connected with our childhood fear of being eaten', swallowed by 'death, a dark, unseeing thing', that we feel in wells, caves and other images of the maternal womb. This, he says, is 'a memory of a true incursion into the bowels of death (as if I had been devoured alive by the monster, as the adepts of many archaic cults supposedly were), a memory of contact with the abyss, or a descent into hell'.*

An armorial shield is a talisman, a fantasy trap, an oracle. Its mysterious language mirrors the origins and career of a family or an individual. And the child in the maw of the beast is both life and death, birth – emerging from the jaws – and extinction, the descent into 'the bowels of death'. This was the twin sign of Luchino Visconti's birth on All Souls' Day, the Day of the Dead. 'Dying and being born,' he said in 1971, 'are the same thing.'

What fascinates and terrifies in the Visconti emblem is not the notion of a Saracen sacrificed, but that of a child martyred. Reason cannot dispel it, nor can Christianity with its clear separation between good and evil, darkness and light, body and soul. This nest of conflicts represented by the child and the serpent, innocence and the diabolic forces, overlay the birth of Luchino Visconti, 'expected' on All Saints' Day but born under the shocking sign of the infernal powers. That this unresolvable conflict exuded fantasies in his mind is shown by the outline he wrote as a boy for a story, directly linked to the problem of illegitimate birth, called *The Three, or Experience:*

A scientist, a great expert in biology, has lived for a long time in a dark castle remote from the everyday world, lost in a moun-

*In *La Règle du jeu*, II Fourbis, Paris (Gallimard), 1955.

tain gorge. He has built a laboratory for his experiments and he lives in isolation, entirely devoted to his study of nature, oblivious to a world he chooses to ignore. The scholar has erected his own arid and austere philosophy based on the materialistic laws of nature. His wife lives with him; she is much younger than he and he married her before shutting himself up with his dreams of science in the old house at the end of the earth. She is a purely carnal creature, beautiful, hollow, fragile, with no will of her own, subjected to the stern tyranny of her husband and his autocratic habits of scholarship. Their life is monotonous and uneventful, the old man remaining shut up in his laboratory and the young wife moving between her apartments and the virgin forest.

The arrival of a young assistant to the scientist troubles the couple's specious harmony. Seeing that the man and his wife are in love, the old man undertakes an experiment to prove that love is nothing more than a physical instinct and cannot resist the ordeal to which he will subject the two lovers: he locks them in the castle dungeon and observes them with scientifically diabolical attentiveness.

Months and months go by. By all sorts of stratagems, the old madman succeeds in dispelling the suspicions aroused by the two lovers' disappearance . . . But his theoretical edifice begins to rock. His science is no longer as convincing as it was. Madness creeps into his brain. One night, for the first time, he hears piercing screams coming from the dungeon. He gets up in terror. Those animal screams freeze his soul even though they bring proof at last of his beliefs. He is gripped by an unexplainable anxiety. He goes down with a torch to the tomb of the two people he immured alive and, peering through his peephole in the door, he is struck with horror. The woman is lying lifeless, sprawled in a lake of blood as if she had been torn apart. The young man is beside the staring corpse. In his arms, as living proof of the falsity, the error, the criminality of [the scientist's] theories, the collapse of a whole world of study, of science, of belief, is a bright, luminous new-born babe whose wailing lights the whole dark dungeon. The old man kills himself.

In this Poe-style narrative, Visconti expressed the anxiety of birth following months of gestation in an infernal subterranean place. Conception, stemming from the weakness of the flesh, is linked to blood and death. To free himself from this he concocts a murky spiritualist theory to counter that of the tyrannical, jealous scientist, a theory he outlines in explanatory notes preceding the narrative:

> Thesis: the extreme etiolation of matter leads to redemption of the matter itself and transubstantiation of the flesh into spirit.
> The scientist's theory: man is essentially an animal. His nature cannot detach itself from and escape biological laws. All manifestations of his personality are naturalistic, materialistic manifestations. Only science can shed light on obscure matter, and that is knowledge. Spirit exists only on an intellectual level.

Birth, linked to 'obscure' matter and to Evil, nevertheless is presented as a manifestation of a 'luminous' and supernatural life force. Influenced by Christian belief in the redemption of matter through suffering, Visconti exhibits the same tormented faith in the existence of laws overriding reason and science that Ludwig II expressed to his valet, Weber, before he died: 'I have read a great deal about materialism. It will never satisfy a man if he does not want to be reduced to the status of a beast.'

More important, Visconti's narrative reveals an obsession that runs subliminally throughout his work, lurking behind certain cultural preferences and bursting into the open in his last film, *The Innocents*. Here we come again upon the Oedipal triad of father, mother and son. And, like Visconti's boyhood narrative, D'Annunzio ended his story by casting an equivocal light on the burial of Giuliana Hermil's illegitimate child by Filipo d'Aborio: through the crystal coffin 'that livid little face, those tiny hands joined, and that gown and those chrysanthemums and all those white things seem indefinably distant, intangible, as if through the coffin's transparent lid we could glimpse a fragment of a sweet and frightening supernatural mystery'.

Was bastardy merely a Viscontian literary theme or the haunting consciousness of a difference between himself and his better-loved brothers, and of the constant dissension between himself and his father? One thing is sure: except in *The Leopard*, the father figure is missing from all his movies. It reappears in *The Innocents* only to take cold and ferocious revenge against 'the intruder', the tiny bastard exposed to the cold and snow of a Christmas Eve. And when the grandmother takes this convulsive infant in her arms she is illustrating the primordial sacrifice symbolized by the guivre on the Visconti shield.

Is this a metaphor for the infanticide an enemy father can commit, as long as he is alive, against an illegitimate son? Or of paternal revenge for the son's monstrous temptation to reform, through incest, the elementary Mother–Child couple, even though this would imply an equally monstrous change of the mother, sweet as a Madonna, into a witch, a hellish snake?

This phallic mother, possessed of all the dead father's virile strength, appears in *The Damned*. Indeed, her son Martin, who is wholly under her thumb, refers to her in a letter as a 'viper'. It is interesting to see two twin themes join without totally blending in this film: incest and rape and Martin's guilt for the death of the Jewish child. Visconti borrowed the rape theme from one of his favourite authors, Dostoyevsky, who was also haunted by the idea of bastardy; it is also woven into the fabric of *Macbeth*. In the film he reverses the standard arrangement (the child threatened, exposed, killed at birth) in a chain of sadistic and murderous impulses: the son, presented at first as victim of a mother who will not let him grow up, frees himself by appropriating her body (through incest) and her venomous power (through murder, by poison symbolizing the lethal filial sperm).

Whenever Visconti touched on the theme of incest, he hid behind works he admired. In *Sandra*, for example, the love between brother and sister derives from Sartre's *Condemned of Altona* as well as from D'Annunzio and Mann. Here again, the ancient connotation of the theme is accentuated by the setting chosen: Volterra, an eminently infernal place that Suarès, in his *Voyage du condottière*, describes as the realm of obscure, subterranean forces:

'This is the slope down to hell, a magnificent place for killing, for swallowing up the guilty and losing oneself. Everything here can be done in the name of hatred. Nowhere does medieval Italy

speak more loudly than here . . . Volterra is the capital of funereal
Etruria . . . the torch of this funerary country, haunted by death,
obsessed by visions of darkness, and of the life – or is it a dream? –
that men deprived of the light live underground . . . I would not be
surprised to run into some sad, cruel ghost. Like the Medusas with
snakes coiling in their gaping mouths, like the diabolical figures
imagined by the Etruscans, this landscape reminds me of brilliant,
mournful Mexico. I expect to encounter the baleful Inca gods, those
clowns of horror who terrify without making you laugh. Who
knows if these strange, so far mysterious Etruscans aren't the Incas
of the West?'

Sandra and Gianni, the two bastards, meet, then, in an archaic,
spectral setting, an ancient cistern reached via a spiral staircase that
resembles the descent into Dante's circles, or a snake's coils. But this
descent into hell is also a return to childhood. While Gianni removes
his sister's wedding ring, a planned but later dropped flashback
showed the mother saying, 'Two monsters, my children . . . I want
to know if my children are monsters.'

While his incest fantasies are probably the earliest, they nevertheless mask an equally fundamental element of Visconti's obsessiveness: homosexuality, the chosen alternative to the temptation of
incest. Once more the troubling image of the guivre arises as symbolic of a doomed relationship in which milk is sperm and poison,
orgasm is pain and horror, self-indulgence is torture and ecstasy.
This is Swinburne's serpent, teeth and claws convulsed by a terrible
orgasm of pain, breathing visible venom at the divine human soul.
Homosexuality, as irresistibly compelling and fascinating, as
undulant, serpentine and pestilential as the Venetian canals that
breathe cholera. In *Death in Venice*, the composer Gustav von
Aschenbach surrenders to them to contemplate Tadzio's unearthly,
golden beauty. And although this film is a return to the hell visited
in *The Damned*, the maternal figure is here restored to its incorruptible, ideal beauty as nowhere else in Visconti's work.

The auspices of doom surrounding his birth condemned the
artist to a hellish world, as they did Dr Faustus. But in recompense
for his pact with the Devil he acceded to the world of beauty,
making good the sterility of the flesh by the fecundity of his art. The
creator, in Oedipal rebellion against his father, 'uses his characters to

invent for himself an illegitimate birth that entitles him to interfere in his parents' intimate relationship', wrote Marthe Robert.* He thus 'strips the father-god of the pre-eminent phallic power that alone equips him to equal his model'. His works are his sons; for Visconti, his works are his 'family portraits'.

Does our analysis exaggerate the influence of the family guivre? Look at the titles in Visconti's penultimate film, *Conversation Piece*: thirty seconds of silence, an entirely dark screen; then, to a cello's lament, an electrocardiogram unrolls. The same roll, like a reel of film, or a snake uncoiling, is used at the end: life, like the film, is over. The serpent still reigns secretly over the life of an old man who is going to die, and over that most nocturnal of arts, the cinema.

*Roman des origines et origines du roman, Paris (Grasset), 1972.

Chronology

1906 (2 November): Luchino Visconti is born in Milan, the fourth child of Duke Giuseppe Visconti di Modrone and Carla Erba, heiress in one of the city's richest industrial families.

1910–15: Luchino is subjected in childhood to a very strict upbringing, which includes musical training. He frequently attends La Scala. While still a boy, he mounts his own shows in the family's small private theatre, Shakespeare plays, or operas he composes and performs with his brothers, sisters and friends.

1915–18: The first world war moderates the Viscontis' lavish lifestyle. Duke Giuseppe enlists in the army and is away from home for long periods.

1919–22: Organization and expansion of the Fascist Party in Milan. During the year of Benito Mussolini's march on Rome, Luchino discovers the writings of Marcel Proust. With his mother, he attends the final performance of Eleonora Duse.

1924: Assassination of the socialist deputy Arnaldo Matteotti. Dissension in the Visconti family. Final separation of Don Giuseppe and Donna Carla. Luchino repeatedly runs away from home.

1926–8: He attends the Pinerolo Cavalry School, then serves as a sergeant in the Savoy regiment.

1929: Visconti makes a two-month trip into the Libyan desert. He buys his first racehorses, building a model stable for them near Milan.

1930–6: He races his horses, breeds thoroughbreds, travels in France, Germany and England. Composes but does not finish literary works. Directs a 35-mm film. Late in 1934, he meets Princess Irma Windisch-Graetz, to whom he proposes marriage. Parental opposition annuls the engagement.

1936: He meets the German photographer H. Horst. With the aid of the fashion designer Coco Chanel, Visconti becomes an assistant director and costume designer for director Jean Renoir's film *A Day in the Country*, participating in the filming throughout the summer. He spends more and more time in Paris.

1936–9: He takes a hand in directing three productions financed by his father. Travels in Greece (summer of 1937) and the United States (winter of 1937–8). Donna Carla dies 16 January 1939. Luchino leaves Milan and settles in Rome.

1939–41: Renoir asks him to join his crew for his film version of *Tosca*, but the second world war interrupts the filming. Carl Koch, aided by Visconti, completes the film. Visconti meets the actor Massimo Girotti and the group of young anti-fascist intellectuals gravitating around the Experimental Film Centre and the magazine *Cinema*: Giuseppe De Santis, Dario and Gianni Puccini, Mario Alicata, Pietro Ingrao, the painter Renato Guttuso. He conceives a number of movie projects, including adaptations of Alain-Fournier's novel *Le Grand Meaulnes* (*The Lost Domain*) and Giovanni Verga's *Malavoglia* (*The House by the Medlar Tree*). Duke Giuseppe dies in December 1941. Luchino inherits his house on Via Salaria, in Rome.

1942: *Ossessione* (*Obsession*) is filmed from 15 June to 10 November. On 28 October Luchino's older brother, Guido, is killed at El Alamein. In December, Alicata and the Puccini brothers are arrested as Communists.

1943–4: On 16 May 1943, *Obsession* creates a scandal and is seized by the authorities. Resistance activity, support for the victims of Fascism, aid to escaped British and American prisoners. The house on Via Salaria is used as an asylum for Resistance fighters pursued by the Gestapo. Visconti is arrested on 15 April 1944, and taken to the Pension Jaccarino, the notorious 'sad villa', then to San Gregorio Prison. He leaves there on 3 June, eve of the arrival of American forces.

1945: 30 January: success of Jean Cocteau's *Les Parents terribles* (*Intimate Relations*), staged by Visconti at the Teatro Eliseo in Rome.

23 March: adaptation of Ernest Hemingway's *The Fifth Column*, translated by Suso Cecchi d'Amico and with sets by Guttuso. Beginning of Visconti's friendship with the communist leader Antonello Trombadori.

4 June: He is called as a witness in the trial of Pietro Koch, former boss at the Pension Jaccarino. His testimony is damning. He films

part of the trial as well as the executions of Koch and Pietro Caruso, Rome's chief of police during the German occupation. The footage is used in the group film *Giorni di Gloria*, financed by the Italian Communist Party and shown in October.

October–December: he stages Cocteau's *The Typewriter* (with Vittorio Gassman), Jean Anouilh's *Antigone*, Jean-Paul Sartre's *No Exit*, *Adam*, by Marcel Achard, and the play based on Erskine Caldwell's novel *Tobacco Road*. Roman audiences are scandalized.

1946–7: 19 January: *The Marriage of Figaro*, with Vittorio De Sica.

12 May: constitutional referendum in Italy: in an article in the Communist newspaper *L'Unità*, Visconti comes out for the republic and the Communist Party.

He meets Franco Zeffirelli, with whom he forms a passionate and, despite numerous interruptions, durable relationship. In September he founds the Compagnia Italiana di Prosa with Rina Morelli and Paolo Stoppa. He stages an adaptation of Dostoyevsky's *Crime and Punishment* (12 November), Tennessee Williams's *The Glass Menagerie* (13 December) and, in February 1947, Anouilh's *Eurydice*.

1947–8: After abandoning several projects, including a film about the trial of Maria Tarnowska, on which he works with Michelangelo Antonioni, he films *La Terra Trema* (*The Earth Trembles*) with the aid of Zeffirelli and Francesco Rosi. This drama of the sea was to be the first episode in a Sicilian trilogy. Shot from November 1947 to May 1948 in the village of Aci Trezza, the film is presented at the Venice film festival on 1 September 1948. Two months later he mounts his first Shakespearean production, *As You Like It*, with remarkable sets by Salvador Dali. The play also marks Marcello Mastroianni's stage début.

1949–51: Visconti attends all the performances by Maria Callas in Rome. In his current direction and his plans, his love of opera and of elaborate staging becomes increasingly clear, from the Tennessee Williams play *A Streetcar Named Desire* (January 1949) to Vittorio Alfieri's *Oreste* (April) and, most notably, in Shakespeare's *Troilus and Cressida* (June) in the Boboli Gardens in Florence.

June 1950: Visconti joins the Peace Partisans Movement.

In February 1951 he mounts Arthur Miller's *Death of a Salesman*, followed in April by a new version of *Streetcar*, with sets by Zeffirelli, and with Mastroianni replacing Gassman. He films *Bellis-*

sima with Anna Magnani. In August he meets Thomas Mann, who authorizes him to create a ballet based on his story, *Mario and the Magician*. In October, Visconti protests against the banning of an Italian tour by Bertolt Brecht and the Berliner Ensemble.

He directs a short film called *Appunti su un Fatto di Cronaca* (*Notes on a News Item*), based on the rape and murder of a little girl in a Roman suburb.

1952–5: Endless obstructionism by Christian Democratic censors forces Visconti to abandon a number of projects, including a script called *Marzia Nuptiale* (*Wedding March*) written with Suso Cecchi d'Amico. After staging Goldoni's *La Locandiera* in Venice in October 1952 and his first Chekhov play, *The Three Sisters*, in December, in the spring of 1953 he begins filming *Senso*; shooting lasts until the end of the year. The film receives a hostile reception at the Venice festival in September 1954. A month later, in Milan, Visconti mounts Giuseppe Giacosa's play *Come le Foglie* while preparing his entry into La Scala, where, on 7 December, he opens the season with Gaspare Spontini's opera *La Vestale*, with Maria Callas singing the lead and Antonio Votto conducting. On 3 March 1955, again with Callas, Visconti mounts Vincenzo Bellini's *La Sonnambula*, conducted by Leonard Bernstein. This is followed on 28 May by the *Traviata* of the century, on which Visconti works closely with Callas and the conductor Carlo Maria Giulini. The production brings him as many brickbats as kudos. At the end of the year he returns to the theatre with Miller's *The Crucible* and Chekhov's *Uncle Vanya*.

1956–7: February 1956: Visconti at last brings off a project he had been planning since the summer of 1951: a ballet based on *Mario and the Magician*, with music by his brother-in-law Franco Mannino.

On 29 October he is among the 101 signatories of a protest against Soviet repression of the Hungarian uprising. The same autumn, with Suso Cecchi d'Amico, Marcello Mastroianni and the young producer Franco Cristaldi, he organizes a movie cooperative to finance his next film, *Le Notti Bianche* (*White Nights*), which he shoots in seven weeks after directing Massimo Girotti and Lilla Brignone in Strindberg's *Miss Julie* in January 1957.

In the spring he mounts two more operas with Callas: Donizetti's *Anna Bolena*, directed by Gianandrea Gavazzeni (14 April), and

Gluck's *Iphigenia in Tauris*, with Nino Sanzogno conducting (1 June).

On 1 August he is in Venice to present Goldoni's *The Impresario from Smyrna* at the Fenice theatre; he is there again on 6 September to show *White Nights* at the film festival. On 24 September at the Berlin Städtische Oper, Jean Babilée performs *Dance Marathon*, composed by Hans Werner Henze, choreographed by Dick Sanders and written by Visconti.

1958–60: On 18 January 1958, Visconti returns to Arthur Miller and to neo-realism with a highly 'cinematographic' production of *A View from the Bridge*. On 9 May his version of *Don Carlo* triumphs in London's Covent Garden Opera House, confirming Visconti's international standing as an opera director. At this time he is introduced to an unknown French actor named Alain Delon, who will inspire his next film, *Rocco e i Suoi Fratelli* (*Rocco and His Brothers*). In June he inaugurates the Festival of Two Worlds in Spoleto with a production of Verdi's *Macbeth*. That autumn he returns to the theatre with a meditation on an actor's lot in *Impressions and Times of Eleonora Duse* on 3 October 1958, and, on 1 March 1959, a staging of Diego Fabbri's *Figli d'Arte* (*Children of Art*). In Rome he also mounts an adaptation of Thomas Wolfe's novel *Look Homeward, Angel*; then to Paris, with Jean Marais and Annie Girardot in William Gibson's *Two for the Seesaw*. At Spoleto he presents Donizetti's *Il Duca d'Alba*, assisted by Enrico Medioli (11 June 1959).

1959–60: Publication of Prince Giuseppe Tomasi di Lampedusa's novel *Il Gattopardo* (*The Leopard*) the previous year had stirred fierce debate among Italian leftists. The book excites Visconti. In 1959, after extensively researching the plight of southern Italian immigrants to the northern industrial cities, he completes the screenplay of *Rocco*, filmed from February to June 1960. In Venice in September, the film is badly received and the censors insist on cuts, but in the theatres it wins its maker a wide audience. Three months later the row blows up again over Visconti's staging of Giovanni Testori's play *L'Arialda*, which a Milan tribunal bans as obscene (25 February 1961). Visconti decides to work abroad, at least in the theatre.

1961–4: Only one play, which opens 29 March 1961, at the Théâtre de Paris: John Ford's *'Tis Pity She's a Whore*, with Romy Schneider and Alain Delon making their stage débuts in the leading roles. On

30 June at Spoleto, Visconti presents Richard Strauss's *Salome*, with his own sets and costumes. During the summer he shoots *Il Lavoro* (*The Job*), one of three episodes in the film *Boccaccio 70*, with Miss Schneider. The year 1962 is mainly devoted to preparing and filming *The Leopard* (first shown on 27 March 1963), but he also supervises work on a 'pastoral comedy' written by himself, Medioli and Filippo Sanjust and set to music by Mannino. It has its première on 28 February 1963, at the Teatro Massimo in Palermo. In June he does a second version of *La Traviata* at Spoleto. A year later, on 21 May 1964, he directs Mozart's *The Marriage of Figaro*, conducted by Giulini.

Filming of *Vaghe Stelle dell'Orsa* (*Sandra*), a film built around Claudia Cardinale, is postponed because of the death of the Communist Party leader Palmiro Togliatti on 21 August 1964. Visconti keeps vigil by the coffin. After work is resumed that autumn, he meets Helmut Berger. Ideas for film scripts burgeon around Berger and Miss Schneider (*Young Törless*) or are revived (*Countess Tarnowska*). Meanwhile, Visconti directs *Il Trovatore* (for the Bolshoi in September 1964, for Covent Garden in November).

1965–7: On 19 January 1965, Visconti mounts Miller's *After the Fall* at the Gymnase in Paris, starring Girardot and Michel Auclair. In September, *Sandra* wins the Golden Lion at the Venice festival, but is a box-office flop. On 26 October Visconti inaugurates his last and most difficult Chekhov production, *The Cherry Orchard*, which triumphs at the Teatro Valle in Rome.

In November, he declares his support of pacifist demonstrations against the war in Vietnam.

He again focuses on opera: *Don Carlo* in Rome on 20 November 1965, with Giulini; *Falstaff* on 14 March 1966, with Dietrich Fischer-Dieskau singing the lead and Bernstein conducting, at the Vienna Staatsoper; Strauss's *Der Rosenkavalier* 21 April 1966, with Sena Jurinac (Georg Solti conducting) at Covent Garden. After directing an episode about a diva, *La Strega Bruciata Viva* (*The Witch Burned Alive*) for the film *Le Streghe* (*The Witches*), Visconti mounts his last *Traviata* on 19 April 1967, at Covent Garden. In June of that year he stages Goethe's tragedy *Egmont* to incidental music by Beethoven at the Pitti Palace in Florence.

Between these lavish stagings Visconti films *The Stranger*, an adaptation of Albert Camus's novel *L'Étranger*, completing it early in

1967 and presenting it at the Venice festival that September. Because too many constraints disfigured his original plans for it, *The Stranger* is the only one of his movies he would disown, at least in part.

On 28 October his adaptation of Testori's play *La Monaca di Monza* (*The Nun from Monza*) arouses a storm of censure. He turns progressively away from the theatre.

1968–72: Aside from staging Natalia Ginzburg's *La Petite Annonce* (*The Advertisement*), starring Adriana Asti, in 1969, and a highly criticized (even by Visconti himself) *Simone Boccanegra* at the Vienna Staatsoper, he concentrates entirely on motion pictures. His old plan for a modern *Macbeth* set among the Milanese upper middle class gives rise to *La Caduta degli Dei* (*The Damned*), first shown on 16 October 1969. In 1970 Visconti roams northern and eastern Europe in search of an ideal Tadzio, whom he finally locates in Sweden. While making *Death in Venice* he works on a scenario of Proust's *Remembrance of Things Past*. When shooting ends on *Death in Venice* early in 1971, he even spends time scouting for locations in Paris and Normandy. But the project is sidetracked by a disagreement with producer Nicole Stéphane.

He decides to begin filming *Ludwig* at once. The work is exhausting, dragging on from 31 July 1971 to 5 June 1972. On 27 July Visconti suffers a cerebral haemorrhage that leaves his left side paralysed. After two months in a Zurich hospital and a month convalescing at Cernobbio, on Lake Como, he returns to work editing *Ludwig*. The producers insist, however, that the film be drastically cut; badly mutilated, it is released at the start of 1973. Not until 1978, after his co-workers, friends and family buy the rights to the film, is it shown in the uncut version.

1973–6: Visconti moves to a small apartment in Rome, where he amasses projects: staging Wagner's *Ring* cycle at La Scala, filming *The Magic Mountain* or *The Holy Sinner*, both by Thomas Mann. 3 May 1973 marks his return to the theatre with Harold Pinter's *Old Times* at the Teatro Argentina in Rome. A quarrel erupts with the playwright.

Visconti successfully stages Puccini's *Manon Lescaut* on 21 June at Spoleto. At the same time, he works with Medioli and Suso Cecchi d'Amico on the script of *Gruppo di Famiglia in un Interno* (*Conversation Piece*), a story of a peaceful life shattered by terrorism.

The movie is shot from 8 April to 15 July 1974, and premièred in December. Public debate over the financing of the film by rightist publisher Edilio Rusconi. Although saddened by the death of his friends Anna Magnani and Vittorio De Sica (in 1973 and 1974), Visconti continues to devise new projects. A fall on 3 April 1975 hospitalizes him again and he is obliged to direct his last film, *L'Innocente* (*The Innocents*) from a wheelchair. Shot from 27 September 1975 until the beginning of 1976, the movie is in the process of sound synchronization when, at 5:30 on the afternoon of 17 March 1976, Luchino Visconti dies in his apartment at 101 Via Fleming, in Rome.

Selected Bibliography

Historical and Cultural Setting

HISTORY OF MILAN

Francesco Cognasso, *I Visconti*, ed. dall'Oglio, 1966.

Fondazione Treccani degli Alfieri per la storia di Milano, 1955.

Borghesi e imprenditori a Milano dall'Unità alla Prima Guerra mondiale, edited by Giorgio Fiocca, Biblioteca di Cultura Moderna, Laterza, 1984.

Carlo Gatti, *Il teatro alla Scala nella storia di Milano*, Ricordi, Milan, 1964.

Carlo Gatti, *Verdi*, Mondadori, 1950.

Guglielmo Barblan, *Toscanini e la Scala*, La Scala, 1972.

Massimo Mila, *L'Arte di Verdi*, Einaudi, 1980.

Mosco Carner, *Giacomo Puccini*, Lattès, 1984.

Alberto Savinio, *Ville, j'écoute ton coeur*, Gallimard, 1982.

André Suarès, *Voyage du condottière*, Granit, 1984.

Guido Piovene, *Voyage en Italie*, Grasset, 1958.

Harvey Sachs, *Toscanini*, F. Van de Velde, 1980.

GENERAL BACKGROUND

Denis Mack Smith, *Il Risorgimento italiano*, Rizzoli, 1976.

Denis Mack Smith, *Storia d'Italia 1861–1969*, Laterza, 1972.

Adrian Lyttelton, *La conquista del potere: il fascismo dal 1919 al 1929*, Laterza, 1974.

Angelo Tasca, *Naissance du fascisme*, Gallimard, 1967.

Antonio Gramsci, *Letteratura e vita nazionale*, editori riuniti, 1975.

Giuseppe Antonio Borgese, *Golia Marcia del Fascismo*, Mondadori, 1983.

André Brissaud, *Mussolini*, Librairie Académique Perrin, 1983.

437

Nello Ajello, *Intellettuali e PCI (1944–1958)*, Laterza, 1979.

Giorgio Bocca, *Palmiro Togliatti*, Laterza, 1973.

Giorgio Bocca, *Il terrorismo italiano*, Rizzoli, 1978.

Fulco di Verdura, *Estati felici. Un infanzia in Sicilia*, Feltrinelli, 1977.

Camilla Cederna, *Il mondo di Camilla*, Feltrinelli, 1980.

Camilla Cederna, *Nostra Italia del miracolo*, Longanesi, 1980.

Horst and Hoyningen-Huene, *Salute to the Thirties*, Viking Press, New York, 1971.

Valentine Lawford, *Horst by Horst*, Viking Press, New York, 1984.

Arthur Gold and Robert Fizdale, *Misia. La vie de Misia Sert*, Gallimard, 1981.

Edmonde Charles-Roux, *L'Irrégulière ou mon itinéraire Chanel*, Grasset, 1974.

Claude Delay, *Chanel solitaire*, Gallimard, 1983.

Francis Steegmuller, *Cocteau*, Macmillan, 1970.

Irene Brin, *Usi e costumi 1920–1940*, Sellerio, Palermo, 1981.

G. A. Borgese, *Gabriele D'Annunzio*, R. Ricciardi, Naples, 1909.

G. A. Borgese, *Risurrezioni*, Società anomina editrice, F. Perrella, Florence, 1922.

M. A. Macciocchi, *Deux mille ans de bonheur*, Grasset, 1983.

John Ardoin and Gerald Fitzgerald, *Callas*, Holt, Rinehart and Winston, New York, 1974.

Pierre-Jean Rémy, *Callas, une vie*, Ramsay, 1978.

Serge Segalini, *Callas, les images d'une voix*, F. Van de Velde, 1979.

G. B. Meneghini, *Maria Callas, ma femme*, Flammarion, 1983.

Arianna Stassinopoulos, *Maria: Beyond the Callas Legend*, Weidenfield and Nicolson, London, 1980.

WORKS ON THE THEATRE AND THE CINEMA

Silvio d'Amico, *Palcoscenico del dopoguerra*, ERI, Turin, 1953.

Fedele d'Amico, *I casi della musica*, Il saggiatore, 1962.

Silvio d'Amico, *Cronache del teatro*, edited by E. F. Palmieri and Sandro d'Amico, Laterza, 1964.

Il lungo viaggio del cinema italiano, anthology of *Cinema* 1936–1943, edited by O. Caldiron, Marsilio, 1965.

Dai telefoni bianchi al neorealismo, edited by M. Mida and L. Quaglietti, Laterza, 1980.

Il cinema italiano dal fascismo all'antifascismo, edited by G. Tinazzi, Marsilio, 1966.

Cinema italiano tra le due guerre, Mursia, 1975.

G. Vento and M. Mida, *Cinema e Resistenza*, Landi, 1959.

G. De Santis, *Verso il neorealismo*, edited by Callisto Cosulich, Bulzoni, 1982.

Il neorealismo cinematografico italiano, edited by L. Micciché, Marsilio, 1975.

Antologia di 'Cinema Nuovo', edited by Guido Aristarco, Guaraldi, 1975.

L. Micciché, *Il cinema italiano degli anni 60*, Marsilio, 1975.

L'avventurosa storia del cinema italiano raccontata dai suoi protagonisti, edited by F. Faldini and G. Fofi (1939–1959 and 1960–1969), and Feltrinelli, 1979–1981.

STUDIES ON THE LIFE AND WORKS OF LUCHINO VISCONTI

G. Ferrara, *L. Visconti*, Seghers, 1963.

Yves Guillaume, *L. Visconti*, éd. Universitaires, Paris, 1966.

Geoffrey Nowell-Smith, *Visconti*, Secker and Warburg, London, 1973.

Pio Baldelli, *Luchino Visconti*, G. Mazzotta, 1973.

Monica Stirling, *A Screen of Time. A Study of Luchino Visconti*, Harcourt Brace Jovanovich, New York–London, 1979.

Gaia Servadio, *Luchino Visconti*, Mondadori, 1980.

Gianni Rondolino, *Visconti*, UTET, Turin, 1981.

Album Visconti, edited by Caterina d'Amico de Carvalho, Sonzogno, 1978.

Visconti: il teatro: Catalogo della mostra, edited by Caterina d'Amico de Carvalho, Teatro Municipale di Reggio Emilia, 1977.

Visconti: il cinema: Catalogo critico, edited by Adelio Ferrero, Comune di Modena, 1977.

Luchino Visconti, *Il mio teatro*, edited by Caterina d'Amico de Carvalho and Renzo Renzi, Cappelli, 1979.

Visconti e il suo lavoro: Catalogo della mostra, edited by Caterina d'Amico de Carvalho, Electa, Milan, 1981.

Costanzo Constantini, *L'ultimo Visconti*, Sugarco, Milan, 1976.

A. Bencivenni, *Visconti*, La Nuova Italia/il castoro cinema, 1983.

Alain Sanzio and Paul-Louis Thirard, *Luchino Visconti cinéaste*, Persona, 1984.

Naoki Tachikawa and Toshiichi Nakajima, *Le Visage inconnu de Luchino Visconti*, Shôgaku-Kan, Tokyo, 1981.

SCENARIOS

With the exception of *The Stranger* and *The Innocents*, all of the screenplays for Visconti's films have been published in Italian by Edizione Cappelli, Bologna.

Ossessione, edited by E. Ungari and G. B. Cavallaro, Bologna, 1977.

La Terra Trema, edited by E. Ungari, C. Battistini and G. B. Cavallaro, Bologna, 1977.

Bellissima, edited by E. Ungari, Bologna, 1978.

Senso, edited by G. B. Cavallaro, Bologna, 1955.

Le Notti Bianche, edited by R. Renzi, Bologna, 1957.

Rocco e i Suoi Fratelli, edited by G. Aristarco and G. Cavancini, Bologna, 1960.

Il gattopardo, edited by Suso Cecchi d'Amico, Bologna, 1963.

Vaghe stelle dell'Orsa, edited by P. Bianchi, 1965.

La caduta degli dei, edited by S. Roncoroni, 1969.

Morte a Venezia, edited by L. Micciché, 1971.

Ludwig, edited by G. Ferrara, 1973.

Gruppo di famiglia in un interno, edited by G. Treves, 1975.

The screenplay for the episode *Il lavoro* (*The Job*) appears in the volume devoted to *Boccaccio 70*, edited by C. di Carlo, Cappelli, Bologna, 1962.

The scenario of *A la recherche du temps perdu*, by Suso Cecchi d'Amico and Luchino Visconti, was published by éditions Persona in 1984.

The libretto of *Diavolo in giardino*, by Luchino Visconti, Filippo Sanjust and Enrico Medioli, was published by Curci, Milan, 1963.

SHORT FILMS ABOUT LUCHINO VISCONTI

Luchino Visconti, *Alla ricerca di Tadzio*, RAI TV 1970.

Giorgio Ferrara, Luca de Mata: *Luchino Visconti*, RAI TV 1975.

Michel Random, *Luchino Visconti ou la puissance d'être*, RTF, 1977.

Walter Licastro, *Luchino Visconti: ricordo in musica*, RAI TV 1977.

Index

445